Programming for Musicians
and Digital Artists

Programming for Musicians and Digital Artists

CREATING MUSIC WITH CHUCK

AJAY KAPUR
PERRY COOK
SPENCER SALAZAR
GE WANG

MANNING
SHELTER ISLAND

Manning Publications Co.
20 Baldwin Road
Shelter Island, NY 11964

Development editor:	Susanna Kline
Technical development editor:	Bunny Blake
Copyeditor:	Linda Recktenwald
Proofreader:	Elizabeth Martin
Technical proofreader:	Doug Sparling
Typesetter:	Dottie Marsico
Cover designer:	Leslie Haimes

ISBN 9781617291708
Printed in the United States of America
1 2 3 4 5 6 7 8 9 10 – EBM – 20 19 18 17 16 15 14

To Max V. Mathews (1926-2011)
who started it all

brief contents

0 ▪ Introduction: ChucK programming for artists   1

PART 1 INTRODUCTION TO PROGRAMMING IN CHUCK 11

1 ▪ Basics: sound, waves, and ChucK programming   13

2 ▪ Libraries: ChucK's built-in tools   47

3 ▪ Arrays: arranging and accessing your compositional data   61

4 ▪ Sound files and sound manipulation   70

5 ▪ Functions: making your own tools   92

PART 2 NOW IT GETS REALLY INTERESTING! 115

6 ▪ Unit generators: ChucK objects for sound synthesis and processing   117

7 ▪ Synthesis ToolKit instruments   139

8 ▪ Multithreading and concurrency: running many programs at once   160

9 ▪ Objects and classes: making your own ChucK power tools   177

10 ▪ Events: signaling between shreds and syncing to the outside world   203

11 ▪ Integrating with other systems via MIDI, OSC, serial, and more   217

contents

foreword xv
preface xvii
acknowledgments xxii
about this book xxiv
about the authors xxviii

0 Introduction: ChucK programming for artists   1

0.1   Why do musicians and artists need to program?   2

0.2   What is ChucK? How is it different?   3

0.3   Why program in ChucK?   4

0.4   ChucK-powered and pre-ChucK computer-mediated art   5

0.5   Summary   8

PART 1   INTRODUCTION TO PROGRAMMING IN CHUCK....11

1 Basics: sound, waves, and ChucK programming   13

1.1   Sound waves and waveforms   14

1.2   Your first ChucK programs   17

Your first program: "Hello World"   18 • Your first sound program: "Hello Sine!"   18 • Now let's make music   20 • Trying new waveforms   22

1.3   Data types and variables   24

ix

1.4 Time in ChucK: It's about now 30

Variables of type dur 30 • The importance of time 31
Variables of type time 32 • Working with now 33

1.5 Logic and control structures for your compositions 35

Programming power through logic statements: the if statement 37
Logical operators and conditions 40 • The for loop control
structure 40 • The while loop control structure 42

1.6 Using multiple oscillators in your music 43

1.7 A final example: "Twinkle" with oscillators, variables, logic,
and control structures 43

1.8 Summary 46

2 Libraries: ChucK's built-in tools 47

2.1 The Standard library: tools for pitch, loudness,
and more 48

Deriving musical frequencies from MIDI note numbers 48
Converting between data types: float to int 51 • Obtaining
an int from a number expressed as text 52

2.2 The ChucK Math library 53

Math library random functions 53 • Rounding numbers:
being more fair about float-to-int conversion 55

2.3 Stereo and panning 56

2.4 Example: random music with two voices and panning 58

2.5 Summary 60

3 Arrays: arranging and accessing your
compositional data 61

3.1 Declaring and storing data in arrays 62

3.2 Reading and modifying array data 63

3.3 Using array data to play a melody 64

3.4 Storing other types of data in arrays 65

Using an array to store durations 65 • Arrays of strings: text can
be musical too 67

3.5 Example: a song with melody, harmony, and lyrics! 68

3.6 Summary 69

4 Sound files and sound manipulation 70

4.1 Sampling: turning sound into numbers 71

4.2   SndBuf: loading and playing sound files in ChucK   72

*Organizing your sound files   73 ▪ Looping (automatically
repeating) your samples   75 ▪ Playing your samples backward   77
Managing multiple samples at a time   78*

4.3   Stereo sound files and playback   80

4.4   Example: making a drum machine   83

*Adding logic for different drums on different beats   83
Controlling when drums play using logic arrays   85*

4.5   A new math/music tool: the modulo operator   86

4.6   Tying it all together: your coolest drum machine yet   88

4.7   Summary   90

4.8   For further reading   91

5   *Functions: making your own tools*   92

5.1   Creating and using functions in your programs   93

*Declaring functions   93 ▪ Your first musical function   94
Local vs. global variables   96*

5.2   Some functions to compute gain and frequency   97

*Making real music with functions   98 ▪ Using a function to
gradually change sonic parameters   100 ▪ Granularize: an audio
blender function for SndBuf   101*

5.3   Functions to make compositional forms   102

*Playing a scale with functions and global variables   102
Changing scale pitches by using a function on an array   104
Building a drum machine with functions and arrays   107*

5.4   Recursion (functions that call themselves)   108

*Computing factorial by recursion   109 ▪ Sonifying the recursive
factorial function   110 ▪ Using recursion to make rhythmic
structures   111*

5.5   Example: making chords using functions   112

5.6   Summary   113

PART 2   NOW IT GETS REALLY INTERESTING! 115

6   *Unit generators: ChucK objects for sound synthesis and
processing*   117

6.1   ChucK's special UGens: adc, dac, and blackhole   118

6.2   The pulse width oscillator: an electronic music
classic   120

6.3   Envelope (smooth slow function) unit generators   121

Making a clarinet sound using SqrOsc and Envelope   122
Making a violin sound with SawOsc and the ADSR Envelope
UG   123

6.4   Frequency modulation synthesis   125

6.5   Plucked string synthesis by physical modeling   126

The simplest plucked string   127 ▪ Exciting the plucked string with
noise   128 ▪ Modeling frequency-dependent decay with a
filter   129 ▪ Modeling fractional (tuning) delay and adding an
ADSR for plucking   129

6.6   Intro to filter UGens: frequency-dependent gain   130

6.7   More on delays: room acoustics and reverberation   132

6.8   Delay-based audio effects   135

6.9   Example: fun with Filter and Delay UGens   136

6.10 Summary   137

7   **Synthesis ToolKit instruments   139**

7.1   STK wind instruments   140

The STK brass instrument physical model UGen   141
The STK Flute physical model UGen   142

7.2   Better stringed instruments   143

The STK Sitar physical model UGen   144 ▪ The STK Mandolin
physical model UGen   145 ▪ The STK bowed string instrument
UGen   145

7.3   Bars and other rigid things   147

7.4   Particle models   150

7.5   Synth soundz   151

7.6   Voices   153

7.7   Example: Indian music   156

7.8   Summary   158

7.9   For further reading   159

8   **Multithreading and concurrency: running many**
     programs at once   160

8.1   Programming with concurrency   161

8.2   Shreds and sporking   163

8.3   A parallel, multithreaded, concurrent drum machine   165

8.4   Using concurrency to control aspects of common
      objects   167

8.5 Machine commands: adding ChucK files as new
shreds   168

ChucK Machine commands for adding and running files   169
Using Machine functions for composition   169

8.6 Example: building a multithreaded jazz band   170

A file organization structure for your jazz band   171
Programming the individual players   171 ▪ *An architecture for*
running your concurrent code   175

8.7 Summary   176

9   **Objects and classes: making your own ChucK power tools   177**

9.1 Object-oriented programming: objects and classes   178

Objects in general   178 ▪ *Classes   179*

9.2 Writing your own classes   181

9.3 Overloading: different functions can share the same
name   183

9.4 Public vs. private classes   185

Useful applications for public classes   186 ▪ *The Clear VM*
button   187 ▪ *Static variables   187*

9.5 Initialize.ck: an architecture for organizing your
code   188

9.6 Conducting a drum pattern using a time-varying BPM   190

9.7 Making new classes from existing classes   195

Inheritance: modeling and modifying parents   195
Polymorphism: managing many children   197

9.8 Example: building a smart mandolin player   199

9.9 Summary   202

10   **Events: signaling between shreds and syncing to the outside**
world   203

10.1 What are events?   204

10.2 Programming with events: keyboard input   205

10.3 Inter-shred communication using events   208

Using event.signal() to synchronize one shred to another   209
Using signal to synchronize multiple shreds   210 ▪ *Triggering*
multiple shreds at the same time using events   212

10.4 Customized events example: a multi-instrument
gamelan   213

10.5 Summary   216

11 **Integrating with other systems via MIDI, OSC, serial, and more 217**

    11.1   Using MIDI: history, basics, and advanced applications 218

        MIDI messages 220 ▪ External MIDI controllers for ChucK 223 ▪ ChucK to ChucK using a virtual MIDI port 225 ▪ Controlling robots via MIDI 226

    11.2   Open Sound Control: networking music 227

    11.3   Serial input/output to the outside world 230

    11.4   Summary: looking outward and forward 231

appendix A   *Installing ChucK and miniAudicle 233*
appendix B   *Library functions: Std, Math, other 241*
appendix C   *Unit generators 249*
appendix D   *Network communication with Open Sound Control 271*
appendix E   *File I/O 276*
appendix F   *Serial I/O 282*
appendix G   *ChucK on the command line 287*
appendix H   *Extending ChucK 298*
            index 303

foreword

"Happy ChucKing!"

What could this short phrase, uttered by Ge Wang, one of the authors of this excellent book, mean? My interpretation is "Happy ChucKing!" means exploring and composing sound in a playful way with ChucK, the programming language that is the basis of this book. But, "ChucKing" is more than that—it's an approach to learning to code with a focus on the arts; it is both lively and profound.

Like many, I care about the visual arts and music more than anything else. I am interested in computers too, but primarily as tools to make images and noise. However, through the many times I failed to learn how to program computers from the ages of 10 to 25, I was forced to learn to code by making text—by printing "Hello World" to a screen or writing code to calculate numbers. To clarify, I like to write and I find math invaluable for what I love to do, but words and numbers are never the focus. They are always a means to an end.

What if I could have learned to program through what I cared about the most? To learn to program by making images and noise? Before computers became the extraordinary media machines they are today, most people used computers to work with only text. Students who were most interested in images and sound weren't able to learn to program by pursuing their passions. Fortunately, this has changed and now computers (from mobile phones to supercomputers) can generate images, synthesize sound, and do much more. Unfortunately, most learn-to-program classes remain the same way they were 40 years ago—learning to program forces everyone, visual artists and musicians alike, into the rigid constraints of inputting and outputting alphanumeric characters.

I struggled through learning to code in the traditional way. For the last decade, I have taught people how to program through a new programming platform that I co-invented with Ben Fry. At MIT in 2001, we started to develop a programming language and environment called Processing. Processing was created for people to learn how to program for the first time and to encourage "sketching" with code. The most important thing about Processing is that people learn all of the basics of coding, but they learn through working with dynamic visual media—for instance, drawing, color, and animation. At the time we were starting Processing, we didn't know that Ge Wang, then a graduate student at Princeton, was doing the same thing for the domain of music. Through his "on-the-fly" programming language, ChucK, people learn to program through creating sound.

One of the first programs you'll see in this book cuts to the core:

```
SinOsc s => dac;
440 => s.freq;
1:: second => now;
```

This program creates a pure tone for one second; it's the software equivalent of hitting a piano key for the first time. This is an extraordinary way to learn to program; it invites exciting questions. What is this strange => symbol? To what does 440 refer? The answers to these questions open a new world; a new way to think about making sound and music while simultaneously learning the basics of coding. From this program, a new world of possibilities opens.

I was thrilled to read *Programming for Musicians and Digital Artists*. With a plethora of well-explained examples in the fascinating ChucK language, readers learn in an engaged, hands-on way. I can't imagine a more knowledgeable and clever group to write about learning to program through creating music. Ajay Kapur, Perry Cook, Spencer Salazar, and Ge created ChucK and developed the way it is taught. After over a decade of experience with ChucK in the classroom and deep experience prior to that, this book sets the bar impossibly high. I hope you enjoy learning to code the "ChucKian" way and "Happy ChucKing!"

CASEY REAS
ASSOCIATE PROFESSOR
DEPARTMENT OF DESIGN MEDIA ARTS AT UCLA
COCREATOR OF THE PROCESSING PROGRAMMING LANGUAGE

preface

Welcome to ChucK!!

We tend to do our best work when we follow our true interests. ChucK was created because we genuinely love both music and programming—and *for* anyone who wants to make music with computers (or learn to do so). As the creator and chief designer of ChucK, I earnestly believe that programming is (or should be) a creative endeavor in and of itself. It should be fun, expressive, rewarding. And to create music through programming, well, that is doubly awesome.

I started working on ChucK in 2002, having started in the Computer Science PhD. program at Princeton University a year earlier. If rock music was my gateway-drug into music-making (and my undergrad alma mater Duke University my passage to programming) then Princeton was where I started putting these elements together. Although I couldn't quite articulate it at the time, I was drawn to the elegance of certain features in programming languages, and aspired to create things, *programmable software things*, that empower people to make music, but in a way that was aesthetically nuanced and fun. I wanted to *rock*, and help others rock—with the computer.

Perry R. Cook was my adviser (one of the best things professionally and personally to happen to me); his work on physical interaction design and his Synthesis ToolKit (STK) were great inspiration. Also, Perry's fun, whimsical, and imaginative personality helped set the tone and encouraged freedom in exploration. I still remember showing Perry the initial ideas for "a new programming language for music" glued together by the *ChucK operator* (which looks like =>, something you will see a lot in this book), and Perry saying, "Well that's pretty insane. Go for it!"

FACT   Portions of my initial scribbling remained on Perry's office whiteboard for the next five years, though I later discovered that it was due to a malfunction with the board that made it nearly impossible to erase.

Soon thereafter, and somewhat serendipitously, I designed the time and concurrency mechanisms (both intrinsic to how ChucK works) into the fledgling language. I say *serendipitously* because both components began as casual mind-wandering, but once I worked out how these mechanisms might function together, it resonated so deeply with my warped mind that I had to see it through. And thus began a journey to make ChucK that, surprisingly to me, remains stronger-than-ever over a decade later, and that has involved some of the craziest and most wonderful collaborators I have ever known.

Ajay Kapur was a crazy and most industrious undergrad in Perry's lab, building the eTabla, eSitar, eDholak (a two-person Indian drum), who would go on to create entire orchestras of robotic machines. Wonderfully supportive of ChucK since the very beginning, Ajay pioneered new ways to teach computer music and interaction design with ChucK. Currently he teaches at CalArts and is the (and still crazy) associate dean of music technology there.

One day in 2004, a Princeton undergraduate student by the name of Spencer Salazar emailed me, confessed that he enjoys programming and building things, and asked if he could help with the ChucK project. Answering "yup" changed ChucK forever, for Spencer turned out to be a monster coder and a most thoughtful innovator. In addition to adding support for joysticks, mice, keyboards, WiiMotes (via the HID interfaces, covered in chapter 10), Spencer authored the *miniAudicle*, the ChucK development environment used in this book. And all that was in the first year! Serial support, ChuGins, Chugens, and Chubgraphs are among his recent additions (covered in appendix H). Spencer is now pursuing a PhD. at Stanford University's CCRMA.

FACT   Spencer and I are avid StarCraft fans, and semi-regularly get owned online by players who possess actual skill. Ajay once played StarCraft for 8 hours straight on a road trip to Montreal, and has never played since (that I know of). Perry, to my knowledge, has never touched the game.

By this point, you are probably getting a sense of the type of crazy (and actually pretty laid-back) folks who labored to make ChucK happen. The list doesn't stop there. Philip Davidson and Ari Lazier both contributed large chunks of ChucK; Phil and I even built a prototype for a real-time animated development environment called the *Audicle* (a rough predecessor to the miniAudicle). Ananya Misra and Matt Hoffman pitched in generously and threw down large servings of new functionality, while elsewhere Adam Tindale wrote a ChucK manual. Meanwhile, sage individuals like Paul Lansky, Roger Dannenberg, Andrew Appel, and Brian Kernighan (all programming language creators themselves) generously dispensed wisdom on the direction of ChucK.

The online ChucK community formed between 2003 and 2004, and we started to rapidly release bug fixes and new features (and new bugs). It was magical how folks we have never met stepped up to generously contribute to an open source project and community such as this. One particularly notable individual is Kassen Oud, who has shepherded countless new users, answered endless questions, and generally distributed peace and good will to all ChucK users for more than 10 years. (Kassen is credited on the ChucK website as Sporksperson, Forum Moderator, and ChucKian Sherpa.) I have never met Kassen face-to-face, though I sense a kindred spirit out there!

There is a rule of software development from *The Mythical Man-Month* (a great treatise on how humans create software) that says: *plan to throw one away.* The idea is that when building something new, the first implementation is often not architected suitably. One *should not fear starting over*, armed with the knowledge gained from the initial endeavor (this is actually a pretty good rule for many things in life). In 2005, I completely overhauled ChucK's core to support arrays and objects, and made it easier to add a bazillion other features. This turned out to be a good move, for the (totally insane) Princeton Laptop Orchestra (PLOrk) started that fall, led by the magnificent Dan Trueman and Perry, with Scott Smallwood and myself as teaching assistants. ChucK was to be used as a primary programming and teaching tool.

This was another transformative moment, for it was the first time we taught ChucK in a formal classroom setting, for a full semester, to 15 college freshmen with no previous programming experience. It also happened to be the first time anybody has ever taught a laptop orchestra, so we literally had to make it up as we went along. It was delightfully harrowing and exhilarating because we were neither guided nor bounded by established rules. The course turned out to be a resounding success, ChucK was battle-tested like never before, and we knew we could teach ChucK to pretty much anyone who has the heart and interest to learn.

Awesome things continued to happen, for Rebecca Fiebrink arrived in 2006 to begin her PhD. and I found a most dear and amazing collaborator. During the one year we overlapped at Princeton (before I left to teach at Stanford University), Rebecca and I accomplished a rather insane amount of new ChucK-related things, including the Small Musically Expressive Laptop Toolkit (ChucK SMELT), as well as the architecture for Unit Analyzers in ChucK. Through all of this, I can say that cool things happen because (and really only because) of great people involved, and ChucK definitely embodies the personalities of the folks who make it.

In 2007 (and while still working on my PhD. dissertation on ChucK) I joined the faculty at Stanford University's Center for Computer Research in Music and Acoustics (CCRMA, pronounced "karma"). CCRMA Director Chris Chafe (another kindred spirit) was already teaching ChucK in his courses, and I started to do the same in the all-new Stanford Laptop Orchestra (SLOrk), complete with speakers arrays fashioned out of IKEA salad bowls. (Presently, with Spencer and me both at CCRMA, it is the central hub of ChucK research and development.)

As if things weren't crazy enough already, I cofounded a startup in 2008 called Smule, aimed to bring computer-mediated music-making to a wide audience on mobile devices, and in synergy with academic computer music research. Spencer was a founding developer and Perry a founding adviser. ChucK became our rapid prototyping platform and part of the core audio engine. I designed Ocarina, an app that transformed the iPhone into an expressive flute-like instrument, and even allowed users to listen in on each other around the world, and used ChucK as the audio and interaction engine. To date, ChucK is on more than 10 million iPhones via the Ocarina and Ocarina 2 apps for iPhone.

Meanwhile, more and more people in and beyond academic institutions are programming with ChucK. For example, Ajay has fashioned an entire curriculum at CalArts to teach music technology with ChucK (audio programming), processing (visual programming), and Arduino (microcontroller). Through a NSF-funded initiative, Ajay and Perry set out to create a ChucK-based curriculum aimed at digital art students. They got the proverbial band back together to write this book.

WHY WE USE CHUCK

As devoted users of ChucK, we each have own reasons for using it. Perry loves ChucK because he needs to program often to keep his sanity, and ChucK is "the only language that lets me drop in for a few seconds, or as long as I like, and get something gratifying done. If I have an idea, I can try it out immediately in ChucK."

Spencer likes ChucK because it allows him to clearly and concisely express complex and nuanced aesthetic ideas in code. "Moreso than any other tool, ChucK gives me both the ability to control computational processes and the means to synthesize them satisfyingly."

As a robotic artist, Ajay works with MIDI from custom-built controllers and for custom built robotic instruments. "The power of ChucK has been the multithreading and how I can have multiple processes running sensor data, actuator control and composition processes all at different rates! This is why I use the language in teaching computer science to artists... showing them a language paradigm of the future..."

We asked a few other people why they use ChucK, and here is what they had to say:

[ChucK] suggests a mindset in approaching music, and the design of music, the experimentation with music, and the learning of coding. [...] I like the way that ChucK makes me think, and I was really depressed about music programming before I found ChucK.
—Rebecca Fiebrink
Lecturer in Graphics and Interaction
Department of Computing
Goldsmiths, University of London

With ChucK, I can easily think about the flow of time and how I might combine multiple musical layers simultaneously. It is the only language I know that is inherently contrapuntal, and it is by nature extraordinarily musical (and fun) to code with.
—Dan Trueman
Professor of Music, Princeton University

[...] when everything worked the way it was supposed to, when my spontaneous arrangement of computer lingo transformed into a musical composition, it was a truly amazing experience. The ability to control duration and pitch with loops, integers, and frequency notation sent me on a serious power trip. (On learning to program with ChucK)
—Anna Wittstruck
Princeton University, class of 2008

And so now here we are—and here *you* are—with a book on ChucK. But really it's a book about learning to get the computer to *help you express yourself,* sonically, interactively, and musically. To this end, I will leave you with a bit of advice on learning ChucK.

- *Don't panic.* When things don't work as you expect, don't be discouraged. ChucK is a language for *experimenting* with sounds, music, and interactions, and even the most seasoned programmer will make mistakes and introduce bugs in their code. Don't think too much about the fact you are programming, and let your logic, curiosity, and creative vision drive you.
- *Stick with it.* It doesn't matter what your experience with programming is (even if it's zero; even if you think it's less than zero)—as long as you have interest, then you can learn to ChucK. Also, coding to make sound is one of the best and fastest ways to learn programming; for one, you can immediately hear the results of your actions.
- *Do the suggested exercises and examples found throughout the book and don't be afraid to experiment.* You might start by tweaking the numbers in related sample programs and listening to the result, and as you start to grok how the code works, incorporate your own logic and imagination into the code, or incorporate it into your own creations.
- *Listen.* It's all about making sound, so use your ear and use it often!

In closing, I feel a combination of happiness (that people are using ChucK to be creative, expressive, and making music) and perpetual dread/consternation (I know where all the "potholes" are in the implementation). That adds up to a great deal of gratitude to everyone who has bravely programmed a line of ChucK, who has created a new sound, interaction, or a new piece of music, and to anyone who wants to learn.

So as we like to say in ChucK land (where you now find yourself): the time is now. There is no better time than the present. Have fun and make whimsical, wonderful music!

On behalf of my coauthors,

GE WANG
ASSISTANT PROFESSOR
CENTER FOR COMPUTER RESEARCH IN MUSIC AND ACOUSTICS (CCRMA)
STANFORD UNIVERSITY
CREATOR OF CHUCK, COFOUNDER OF SMULE

acknowledgments

The authors thank the editors at Manning who worked closely with us to make this book better for introducing all kinds of people to ChucK, especially Susanna Kline, Bert Bates, and Jeff Bleiel, and the many others who worked with us on the production of the book.

We also thank the following outside reviewers for all of their helpful comments and suggestions: Edward Borasky, Brent Boylan, Matthew Dickinson, Boyan Dzhorgov, Pierre Jolivet, Hector Lee, James Matlock, Ari Pappas, Patrick Regan, Gabriel Rey-Goodlatte, Alvin Scudder, Sergiy Seletskyy, Nathan Smutz, David Sumberg, Danny Vinson, Dan Warren, and Stephen Wolff. Special thanks to Doug Sparling, who did a thorough technical review of the manuscript shortly before it went into production.

As Ge mentioned in his preface, the people who went into creating, developing, and maturing ChucK are many, but we must thank particularly Ari Lazier, Philip Davidson, Dan Trueman, Scott Smallwood, Rebecca Fiebrink, Ananya Misra, Kassen Oud, and Chris Chafe.

We also thank the now generations of LOrk (Laptop Orchestra) students, teaching assistants, and composers who used ChucK with us and made it a better language. These include the members of the Princeton Laptop Orchestra (PLOrk), Stanford Laptop Orchestra (SLOrk), Stanford CCRMA, and the ChucK user community.

We also thank the CalArts students and TAs who helped us in debugging our ChucK curriculum, the code examples, this book, and our Massive Online ChucK course as well. These include Jordan Hochenbaum, Owen Vallis, Dimitri Diakopoulos, Ness Morris, Bruce Lott, and Rodrigo Sena.

Special thanks to Casey Reas of UCLA, cocreator of the Processing programming language, for contributing the foreword to our book.

This book was developed in part with support from the National Science Foundation under Grant No. 1140336. Any opinions, findings, and conclusions or recommendations expressed in this material are those of the author(s) and do not necessarily reflect the views of the National Science Foundation.

Finally, we thank all of the ChucK users over the years, all around the world, for hanging out on the ChucK developer and user forums, for joining our merry band of artist programmers, or programmer artists, suggesting, complaining, and praising the language, and for helping us to make it even better in the process.

about this book

We wrote this book to teach novice programmers how to code in ChucK. Thus, we start at the very beginning, so don't be afraid. We will teach programming through musical examples. We believe that being able to "hear" what your code is doing will aid you in learning the key concepts, as well as make the process enjoyable. If you are an experienced programmer, you may be able to skip a couple of the beginning chapters depending on your level, but note that ChucK is quite different from other languages. We promise that there is something to learn here for everyone.

If you're an advanced programmer who is already familiar with another language, "What's different about ChucK?," later in this front matter, gives a strategy for approaching ChucK from your vantage point.

How the book is organized

Throughout the chapters there are suggested composition exercises to expand what you have learned. In a way, you can view each chapter as "unlocking" new parts of the language you can use in your compositions.

In chapter 0 (computer scientists almost always number from zero), we tell you why ChucK is different from other languages, and how we, and many others have used it in myriad music and art projects.

The next two chapters are for the beginning programmer, introducing key concepts needed to be able to begin coding. Chapter 1 begins with the basics of computer science, languages, and ChucK, including variables, types, conditional statements, and looping structures. Of course, we also make sound and music using ChucK. Chapter 2 introduces the libraries (tools) built into ChucK, and shows how random numbers and mathematical calculations can be used to make more expressive programs and songs.

In chapter 3 we introduce arrays, and show how to more easily make, store, and play melodies, and control other parameters in ChucK.

In chapter 4 we introduce how to use sound files in ChucK and how you can use them to create soundscapes and even a cool electronic dance piece.

Chapter 5 introduces the concept of functions and how they can be used in modularizing and organizing your code, which can result in even more expressive compositions and more orderly programs.

Chapter 6 dives deeper into Unit Generators (UGens), ChucK's built-in audio processing and synthesis objects. Here you will learn about more oscillators, envelope generators, FM synthesis, physical modeling synthesis, and audio effects. Chapter 7 continues this, introducing many physical, modal (resonant), and particle synthesis UGens.

Chapter 8 introduces multithreading and concurrency and you will learn how to make your programs "juggle" multiple things at the same time, all in perfect synchrony.

Chapter 9 introduces object-oriented programming (OOP) and how you can create your own *Objects* and *Classes* to use in your code.

Chapter 10 covers Events, which allow ChucK programs to signal each other. Events also allow ChucK to respond to signals and data from the "outside world." This lets us begin to think of ChucK as a live performance tool, by introducing how you can use your keyboard and mouse for real-time control over your compositions.

Chapter 11 goes into ways that ChucK can communicate with other programs, computers, and control devices. We briefly cover how MIDI can be used with ChucK, both using an external MIDI device (such as a keyboard) to play ChucK as a synthesizer, and how ChucK can control other synthesizers, both software and external hardware synths. We also introduce Open Sound Control (OSC), which is another standard way for music programs and devices to communicate. We then look at Serial Input/Output, which allows us to talk to even more devices.

The appendixes cover lots of details and include more examples of ChucK's features and capabilities. Appendix A covers installing and running the miniAudicle Integrated Development Environment (IDE), and Appendix G covers how to use ChucK in the command line (text-only interface).

Appendix B documents all of the library functions built into ChucK. Appendix C documents all of the built-in UGens. Appendix G covers ChucK on the command line. Appendix D covers OSC. Appendix E covers File I/O, and Appendix F covers Serial I/O. Appendix H discusses ways to extend the ChucK language itself with new UGens.

FOR THOSE INTERESTED IN INSTANT GRATIFICATION

If you're impatient and want to see the power of what ChucK can do (even without understanding exactly how), once you've installed the miniAudicle (appendix A) and run your first two programs ("Hello World" and "Hello Sine", section 1.2), you could type in and run the end-of-chapter example of listing 6.15. Inspired by this powerful ChucK flourish, you can then go back and systematically work through the book.

FOR PROGRAMMERS FAMILIAR WITH OTHER LANGUAGES,

Appendix A talks about how to install and run the miniAudicle IDE (Integrated Development Environment), and how to install and run ChucK for the command line (Terminal, Command, etc.). If you haven't already installed ChucK and/or miniAudicle on your machine, you should begin at appendix A.

Section 1.2 ("Your first ChucK programs") shows the miniAudicle, and introduces you to the ChucK operator and ChucK's way of dealing with time. If you're a command-line type, consult appendix G ("ChucK on the command line") for instructions.

WHAT'S DIFFERENT ABOUT CHUCK?

On the surface, ChucK looks like a lot of other languages such as Java and Objective C, with a few main differences. First and most important, the ChucK operator (=>) is used for assignment, connecting audio Unit Generators (UGens) together, and other things. Designed to look like an arrow indicating direction, the ChucK operator encourages left to right flow of audio connections, assignment and time, among others. There is no use of the single equals (=) sign in ChucK, so if you're familiar with languages that use a syntax like:

float temp = 0.0;   in ChucK you'll need to get used to   `0.0 => float temp;`

Another thing about ChucK that will likely be new to you is how ChucK deals with time. You as the programmer have to explicitly control time in your code, so we'd recommend you look over section 1.4 ("Time in ChucK: It's about now") carefully. The `time` and `dur` datatypes are fundamental to, and what's so different about, ChucK, and you won't be able to program successfully (or hear any sound) unless you learn about them.

From there, you could motivate yourself with a couple of examples of the power of ChucK by typing in and running examples, such as listing 3.8 and/or listing 6.15.

You should then go back and work through chapter 4 to learn about how ChucK deals with sound files. You'll finish that chapter with the drum machines of listing 4.11.

If you're satisfied you have a grasp of the examples so far, you're probably ready to jump directly into part 2 (beginning with chapter 6), learning about all of the powerful UGens available in ChucK. From there on it's all new, so keep reading and running the examples. The next fundamentally new ChucK thing you'll encounter will be covered in chapter 8 where you'll learn about sporking (like forking) shreds (like threads, but ChucK-ian). Objects and classes (chapter 9) might look pretty familiar to you, as might events (chapter 10), but ChucK is unique in that events can be generated by lots of external devices (Joysticks, MIDI, Open Sound Control), so that should look quite different to you. Chapter 11 finishes up with MIDI, OSC, and Serial, for advanced users/programmers.

There are quite comprehensive appendixes at the end with references to pretty much everything in ChucK, so remember that you can look some things up there as well as in the index.

About the code

All source code in the book is in a `typeface like this`, which sets it off from the surrounding text. In many listings, the code is annotated to point out the key concepts, and numbered bullets are sometimes used in the text to provide additional information about the code.

In the ebook, certain terms in text and code appear in color, just as they would as you type into the miniAudicle editor window. This is the miniAudicle recognizing those reserved words and coloring them by type.

Just about all of the code shown in the book can be found in various forms in the sample source code that accompanies this book. The sample code can be downloaded free of charge from the Manning website at www.manning.com/ProgrammingforMusicians andDigitalArtists.

The accompanying sample code (including related audio files) is installed automatically when you install ChucK. On a Mac it can be found in /Library/ChucK/ examples/book/digital-artists/, while on Windows it is located at C:\Program Files\ChucK\examples\book\digital-artists\. On Linux, if you follow the installation procedure described in appendix A, the sample code can be found in /usr/local/ share/doc/chuck/examples/book/digital-artists/.

All of the sample code from this book can be accessed directly in miniAudicle by navigating to File > Open Example and locating book/digital-artists in the Example Browser.

NOTE ChucK works on Mac OS X 10.5+ or later, Windows XP or later, or a suitable Linux system.

Author Online

Purchase of *Programming for Musicians and Digital Artists* includes free access to a private web forum run by Manning Publications where you can make comments about the book, ask technical questions, and receive help from the authors and from other users. To access the forum and subscribe to it, point your web browser to www.manning.com/ProgrammingforMusiciansandDigitalArtists. This page provides information on how to get on the forum once you're registered, what kind of help is available, and the rules of conduct on the forum.

Manning's commitment to our readers is to provide a venue where a meaningful dialog between individual readers and between readers and the authors can take place. It's not a commitment to any specific amount of participation on the part of the authors, whose contributions to the AO remain voluntary (and unpaid). We suggest you ask the authors challenging questions lest their interest stray!

about the authors

AJAY KAPUR is currently the Director of the Music Technology program (MTIID) at the California Institute of the Arts, as well as the Associate Dean for Research and Development in Digital Arts. He is also a Senior Lecturer of Sonic Arts at the New Zealand School of Music at Victoria University of Wellington. Ajay is also co-founder (with Perry and others) of Kadenze, an online arts/technology education startup company. He received an Interdisciplinary PhD in 2007 from University of Victoria combining computer science, electrical engineering, mechanical engineering, music, and psychology with a focus on intelligent music systems and media technology. Ajay graduated with a Bachelor of Science in Engineering and Computer Science from Princeton University in 2002.

PERRY R. COOK received a BA in music in 1985 and a BS in Electrical Engineering in 1986 from the University of Missouri, Kansas City, graduating Magna Cum Laude. He received a Masters and PhD in Electrical Engineering from Stanford in 1990. Along with working for companies such as NeXT Inc., Media Vision, Xenon/Chromatic, and Interval Research, he continued at Stanford as Technical/Acting Director of the Center for Computer Research in Music and Acoustics, until joining the faculty of Princeton Univer-

sity in 1996 as a Professor of Computer Science, with a joint appointment in Music. Cook is also the author of the Synthesis Toolkit in C++ (STK), which he comaintains with Gary Scavone. Perry is also coauthor (with Ge Wang) of the ChucK audio programming language. He is now Emeritus Professor at Princeton, and holds faculty/arts fellowships at the California Institute of the Arts, Arizona State University, and other institutions. Perry is also a founding adviser/consultant to the mobile music startup Smule, and cofounder (with Ajay and others) of Kadenze, an online arts/technology education startup.

SPENCER SALAZAR is a doctoral student at the Stanford Center for Computer Research in Music and Acoustics (CCRMA), researching computer-based forms of music performance and experience. Previously he created new software and hardware interfaces for the ChucK audio programming language, developed prototype consumer electronics for top technology companies, architected large-scale social music interactions for mobile application company Smule, composed for laptop and mobile phone ensembles, and taught numerous workshops on computer music topics. He received a BSE in Computer Science from Princeton University in 2006.

GE WANG is an Assistant Professor at Stanford University's Center for Computer Research in Music and Acoustics (CCRMA). He received his BS in Computer Science in 2000 from Duke University, and his PhD in Computer Science in 2008 from Princeton University (adviser Perry Cook). Ge is the creator (with Perry) and chief architect of the ChucK audio programming language. He is the founding director of the Stanford Laptop Orchestra (SLOrk) and Stanford Mobile Phone Orchestra (MoPhO). Ge is the cofounder of the mobile music startup Smule, and the designer of the iPhone's Ocarina and Magic Piano, reaching more than 80 million users.

Introduction: ChucK programming for artists

For many years, the words *musician* and *artist* have been changing meaning, rapidly, almost daily, largely due to the introduction of computer technology. Artists perform live with computer technology all the time. The ones who interact directly with computers as part of their performances might call themselves *DJs, laptop artists, controllerists, live coders,* and a host of other names. Many of these musicians don't program or write software, but an increasing number want more direct control over their process and the results. Learning to program is one way to get that extra level of control.

Other artists want to make new instruments or controllers or to configure existing controllers such as drum pads, DJ control decks, and the like to use in new ways for their live performances. Still others want to produce songs and albums (.wav and/or .mp3 files) as the final result but would like more control in the process than off-the-shelf music software provides. Some others like (or want) to program as the basis of their creative process and workflow.

Nonmusical artists also use computers in their art making, such as graphic designers, animators, film editors, set designers, sculptors, and others who use computer graphics and design software. Many of these software tool users also want more control over their creations than their commercial software packages provide.

Increasingly, many multimedia artists create installation art, public art, sound sculptures, or soundscapes. These new works involve using combinations of sound, sensors, graphics, video, and displays to create interactive environments. These pieces can make the audience part of the performance or experience. In some cases, members of the public witnessing these pieces don't know exactly what the artists/performers are doing or controlling, but the discovery, learning, and interacting are much of the point and of the reward. Although this book doesn't specifically teach you to make all kinds of artworks, many forms of new media involve computerized sound and music, and learning specific tools to create and manipulate sound in the computer is precisely what this book is about.

Many people call these new types of art and performance opportunities computer-mediated art systems. In all cases, the musician or artist either needed to know how to program or collaborated with someone who could. You'll learn to program through the chapters, examples, and exercises in this book.

This increasingly popular movement of computers as a new medium for creativity motivated our team to write this book to make it easier and more fun for everyone to learn to write their own programs. Specifically, we want to teach you how to program through making code that translates into music and sound, and we accomplish this via a programming language called ChucK, which is specially designed for sound and music.

We begin with a discussion on why we think musicians and artists need to learn how to program. We explain why we believe ChucK is a great first language to learn. We conclude by describing how programming has allowed the authors and others to create new works using ChucK and its predecessor languages.

0.1   *Why do musicians and artists need to program?*

As we mentioned earlier, many artists are happy with over-the-counter software systems and controllers for real-time performance work. And there are many who only want to use computers to produce static final products in the form of .wav/.mp3 files, CDs or collections of songs, sound tracks for videos, and more. A large number of those artists are happy to learn and use the packages and tools from commercial or free sources.

But there are many, and we're betting you're one, who want more. Maybe you're coming to this book with a big idea (or many big ideas) and want the tools to help you realize it/them. Maybe you're looking to shift directions in your art making. Or perhaps you already know how to program in a language such as Java, but you find it doesn't do what you want.

Others think that learning programming will help them get a job. Although we can't promise immediate outplacement after you finish this book, we can say that we have nice jobs, and our students have nice jobs (those who want them ☺), due in no small part to their ability to program and solve problems with computers.

We, in our individual projects, art works, and teaching, have used ChucK and other computer music/art languages for years. Some of us have programmed, and still do, in multiple languages. Whether or not you're already a programmer, you'll think differently after working through the examples and exercises presented here. Few painters ever suffered because they knew more about the chemistry and physics of their paints, canvases, brushes, and solvents. Even self-taught artists have developed and used natural knowledge of the processes underlying their art making. Knowing programming is similar for the digital artist. Any artist who knows one or more computer languages, even one who doesn't write computer code daily, still has a better sense of what's going on when they drag down a menu, select an item, and watch the progress bar move.

We're certain that by the end of this book you'll be able to do lots of what you want and likely much more than you might have thought possible. The power available in ChucK will suggest new things to do, and you'll know how to do them—or how to figure out how. And, even if you use commercial software a lot, we're going to show you new ways to control and interact with it using ChucK. It's like being able to put a new engine in your car.

0.2 What is ChucK? How is it different?

If you're used to working with popular sound tools on computers, you might be used to connecting sound synthesis and processing boxes, managing tracks and instruments, cut/copy/paste sound editing, moving virtual dials and sliders on digital audio workstation (DAW) programs, and so on. In this book, you'll be learning an actual programming language, ChucK, which will let you do essentially anything, but you'll need to type in some lines of computer code (text) in order to accomplish your goals. The first few examples might make it seem like it's harder than the tools you're used to for making sound and music, but soon you'll be doing things that you'd have never thought of or known possible. In this sense you can consider ChucK a power tool. There's a little to learn up front, but soon your results will make you wonder how you lived without it.

ChucK is a programming language designed specifically for real-time sound synthesis and music creation. *Real time* means that ChucK synthesizes the sound as you're hearing it (rather than playing back a sound file), often in response to signals and gestures from the outside world. Gestures to control sound might include your typing on the keyboard, moving the computer mouse, manipulating a joystick or other game controller, or playing the keys on a musical keyboard connected to your computer.

ChucK is also good for controlling and/or interacting with almost any type of real-time computer media and art, such as graphics, robots, or whatever can communicate with your computer.

ChucK was designed specifically to allow and encourage on-the-fly programming, which means you can add, remove, modify, edit, and layer segments of code at any and all times, hearing the results instantly, without interrupting other sounds being synthesized and heard. This is one of the primary ways ChucK differs from all other languages, which makes it extremely fun to learn and use, because you can try things and immediately hear the results. Most other languages require you to compile, run, and debug code in a way that doesn't let you hear immediately what you're doing. Most computer languages, such as C, C++, or Java, weren't designed specifically from the ground up for sound, music, and other real-time tasks. ChucK makes immediate, real-time sound a priority.

If you know other computer languages such as Java or C++, or even other music/sound languages and systems such as Csound, SuperCollider, JSyn, Max/MSP, or PD (Pure Data), you'll soon see that ChucK is really different. It's more expressive and powerful at manipulating time and sound than the graphical interfaces of Max/MSP and PD, giving you greater under-the-hood access than these other languages and systems. Compared to other text-based music/sound languages such as SuperCollider or Csound, ChucK is generally more succinct, requiring much less code (lines of typed text) than these other languages in order to accomplish any particular task.

If you don't know any computer languages, when you've finished this book, it will be easier for you to learn Java, C, C++, and any other language you desire to learn. ChucK is different from other languages for sure, but it shares many things that will be similar and recognizable to programmers of nearly any language.

Another great feature of ChucK is that it's open source (not secret or protected by licenses, passwords, keys, and so on), and it's freely available on all major computer platforms, including Mac OS X, Windows, and Linux. Open source means that the community of ChucK users can have direct input into the process of making ChucK better in the future. It also means that ChucK doesn't cost anything to get and use.

0.3   *Why program in ChucK?*

A tool, which is one way to look at a programming language, can't help but shape its user's mindset, and it naturally suggests ways of achieving various tasks. And like any tool, a programming language *should* change the way you think and go about doing things. ChucK definitely presents a different way to program sound and music. Although there are tradeoffs that make certain things straightforward and other things more difficult, our sincere hope is that for the programmer, the language design choices help more than they hinder a particular task.

ChucK was created by Ge Wang, formerly coauthor Perry Cook's graduate student at Princeton University (and now an assistant professor at Stanford University and coauthor of this book), to provide a different way to think about programming sound using a rapid prototyping (trying out lots of ideas quickly) mindset. More than a decade later, ChucK research and development have only intensified. Ge's detailed chronicle of the history, motivation, and people behind ChucK can be found in this book's preface. As for more detail on *why* you might learn and use ChucK, here are a few more reasons:

- *It's all about time.* Time is at the core of how ChucK works and how you work with ChucK to make sound. As a programmer, you specify how to move through time and assert control at specific points, and sound essentially *just happens*—conveniently, for precisely the amount of time you've moved through. Why such emphasis on time? Sound is a time-based phenomenon; without the passage of time, there would be no sound. By controlling how and when you do things through time, you have a different and powerful way to work with sound at every level—every *molecule* of it.

- *It's text, plain and simple.* Although programming with text may initially seem more abstract or complex than, say, with graphical representations, it's arguably much easier once you start adding a lot of expressive nuance and logic into your code (which you'll invariably need to do). Little is hidden or inferred. The important parts are in plain sight; for example, how time flows in a program. At the same time, many mundane aspects are taken care of under the hood: scheduling, real-time sound input/output, bookkeeping for all the sound generators, and so on. Readability is a central design goal of the language, and that makes it a good learning tool as well.

- *It's fun and immediate.* ChucK was designed to be a fun language and environment to work in, to experiment in. You can synthesize sounds, make fantastical automations, map physical gestures (for example, with controllers) to sound, network computers together, and even use signal analysis to (computationally) make sense of sound.

0.4 *ChucK-powered and pre-ChucK computer-mediated art*

The goal of this section is to present examples of computer-mediated artworks that we've created using computer programming—creating musical instruments, controllers, ensembles, and systems. One time-honored way of making a new instrument is to look at existing instruments and find ways to augment or improve them. Many of our experiences lie in this area. From the Cook/Morrill MIDI Trumpet in 1988 (this didn't use ChucK, because it didn't yet exist, but it used the predecessor of ChucK, STK, which is now included in ChucK) and Kapur's ESitar of 2004, through the Laptop Orchestras of 2005 to present, to mobile musical instruments and beyond, we, along with our crazy friends, have created a variety of computer-mediated systems based on and inspired by traditional musical instruments and groups. In some cases we put sensors on the instrument, leaving the inherent sound-producing capabilities in place. In other cases, we gutted the acoustical parts of the instrument and filled it with processors, sensors, and speakers, leaving only the shell and form to suggest the interaction

Figure 0.1   Top row: Cook-Morrill Trumpet, DigitalDoo (Cook), SqueezeVox Maggie (Cook), SBass (Bahn); bottom row: BoSSA (Trueman), ESitar (Kapur), Smule's Ocarina (Wang)

(experience). These include the DigitalDoo, SqueezeVox (accordions, Perry Cook and Colby Leider), the ETabla and EDholak (Ajay Kapur), BoSSA (the Bowed Sensor, Speaker Array, Dan Trueman and Perry Cook), and the SBass (Sensor Bass, Curtis Bahn). Figure 0.1 shows some of these computer-augmented instruments. In all of these cases, we needed to write custom code to have a microchip or a cell phone transform gesture into musical experience.

The proliferation of powerful mobile devices such as the iPhone and iPad gave rise to a re-envisioning for the mobile era of traditional musical instruments, such as the Ocarina for iPhone (Ge Wang/Smule), as well as entirely new mobile musical interactions. With millions of worldwide users, Ocarina and a number of other mobile apps have used ChucK for synthesis.

Another way to make entirely new musical performance systems is to put sensors on dancers or other artists who do not traditionally perform music. Figure 0.2 shows PikaPika, an Anime-inspired dancer character created by Tomie Hahn. PikaPika is fully loaded with sensors, wireless transceivers, amplifiers, and speakers. Pika's SSPeaPer (Sensor-Speaker Performer) dancer hardware was created and programmed by Curtis Bahn. Figure 0.2 also shows Raakhi Kapur, an Indian dancer, wearing sensors on her wrists that control musical robots in a KarmetiK Machine Orchestra production featuring musical robots and human musicians (more on that soon). A lot of computer programming was needed to successfully map these dancers' gestures to sonic responses. Pika uses STK (as included in Max/MSP), and Raakhi's dance system uses ChucK for synthesis and robot control.

Another means to make amusing art and music works is to put sensors on other objects that are not traditionally associated with musical performance. Figure 0.3 shows musical kitchenware; Perry Cook's jazz JavaMug and the Fillup Glass atop the musical table of P-Ray's Café. Also shown is an early prototype of a computer-mediated

Figure 0.2   Cyber-Anime PikaPika (dancer Tomie Hahn). Raakhi Kapur (right) controls musical robots.

musical TapShoe. Turning these everyday objects into musical instruments obviously requires programming and, once again, mapping, to make them sonically interesting. These devices all put out signals that the computer must use to make sound or control other objects/processes, and ChucK is the easiest place to do that type of mapping. In one of our favorite ChucK programs, Perry turned the JavaMug (computerized coffee mug shown in figure 0.3) into a digital trumpet.

The possibilities of entire ensembles of laptops and/or other large-scale computer-mediated musical groups brought about the Princeton Laptop Orchestra (PLOrk), followed by the Stanford Laptop Orchestra (SLOrk), and the human + robot–populated KarmetiK Machine Orchestra. All of these ensembles rely heavily on augmenting human performers with sensors, networking, and ChucK. Further, each orchestra instrument features player-local sound via individual hemispherical speakers. This means that there's no routing of laptops to a mixer and house sound, but rather each laptop connects to an individual multichannel (six speakers arranged evenly on the face of a hemisphere) speaker located next to each player. Thus the sound of the

Figure 0.3   P-Ray's Café musical table with JavaMug and Fillup Glass; (right) musical TapShoe

Figure 0.4   Top row: Princeton Laptop Orchestra and KarmetiK Machine Orchestra mobile music performance; bottom row: Stanford Mobile Phone Orchestra (MoPhO), Stanford Laptop Orchestra. At right: coauthor Spencer Salazar, a MoPhO-ist sporting wearable speakers.

ensemble is the acoustic mixture, in the room or concert hall, of the individual sounds from each player, just as it would be with a traditional orchestra. Figure 0.4 shows the original (freshman class of) PLOrk, the first mobile phone orchestra at Stanford, SLOrk, and the KarmetiK Machine Orchestra.

These examples only scratch the surface of possible artistic things when you know how to hack. Here we use *hack* in the best sense of the word, combining the inventor's dream with the ability to modify, build, experiment, and, possibly most important, program.

0.5   *Summary*

In this chapter, we hope we've convinced you that learning to program is important for digital artists and that ChucK is a really good way to learn programming. We spent quite a bit of time talking about what ChucK is, a little on how it was designed, and why we and many others think it's the best programming language for doing digital art. For now, the things to remember are these:

- Artists, especially digital artists, can benefit from knowing how to program. You can make your own tools and wholly new creations, and programming gives you ideas you wouldn't have had without being skilled at a computer language.
- ChucK, as a language, is different from other languages and music programs. It was designed from the ground up to support powerful control over time and sound, and input devices from the outside world (joysticks, trackpads, and the like), and networking.

- For those who already know a programming language, we think you'll find that ChucK allows you to do many things that you might find hard or impossible in other languages, and do them very quickly.

We have showed you some of the types of projects we've created using computers and programming, but those only scratch the surface of what can be done with a powerful tool like ChucK.

We hope you're convinced, inspired, and ready to begin to learn to program in ChucK!

Part 1

Introduction to programming in ChucK

In chapter 0 we told you why we wrote ChucK, why we love programming in it so much, and some of the things we've done in our own art making.

Now, in these first five chapters we will teach you the basics of programming in ChucK. Chapter 1 begins with the basics of ChucK, including variables, types, conditional statements, and looping structures. With these features of ChucK, you will quickly be putting together a program to synthesize the first few notes and bars of a song. Chapter 2 introduces the libraries (tools) built into ChucK. Using those functions, you'll be able to set and modify pitches, volumes, and durations of the notes in your songs. You'll also learn how random numbers and mathematical calculations can be used to make much more interesting music automatically, letting the computer do most of the work.

In chapter 3 we introduce arrays, and show how to make, store, and play melodies more easily. We also show how to control other parameters in ChucK. In chapter 4 we show you how to use sound files in ChucK and how you can use them to create soundscapes and even a cool electronic dance piece. Chapter 5 introduces the concept of functions and how they can be used in modularizing and organizing your code.

Basics: sound, waves, and ChucK programming

This chapter covers

- Introduction to acoustics, sound, and waveforms
- Sine waves and other oscillators
- Variables
- Control structures and logic

So far we've talked about why we think ChucK is the best and most powerful language to make all kinds of art and artistic systems. Now it's time to begin learning how to program in ChucK to make sound and music. We'll first talk about sound in general, looking at a graphed sound waveform or two. We'll talk about properties of sounds in terms of loudness, pitch, and noise. You'll learn that things that oscillate are fundamental to physics, sound, and music, and you'll make music with ChucK's built-in oscillators. You'll learn:

- How data is managed and manipulated in ChucK by the use of variables.
- About the timing mechanisms built into ChucK. The way it handles timing is one of the things that makes it different from all other programming languages, and which makes it so great for programming music, sound, and time-based art.

13

- About controlling the flow of your programs by using logical variables and tests, and looping.

By the end of the chapter, you'll have written your first composition in ChucK!

1.1 Sound waves and waveforms

We'll begin by talking about the physics and nature of sound. Sound consists of high and low pressure fluctuations (waves) of air caused by one or more vibrating objects. Sound waves then propagate through the air, maybe bouncing off walls and other surfaces, finally reaching your ears or a microphone. People who work with sound often graph waveforms (amplitude of air pressure, or voltage from a microphone, as a function of time). Figure 1.1 shows a plot of wave values as a function of time of a man saying the word "see."

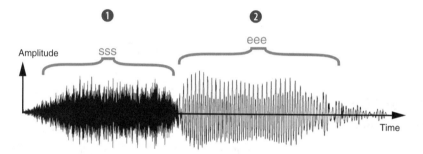

Figure 1.1   Waveform (sound amplitude versus time) of the spoken word "see"

Some things are obvious from this plot. The noisy consonant "sss" ❶ in the first half of the sound changes quickly to a different structure for the "eee" vowel in the second half ❷. If you zoom into the transition area, more things become obvious, as shown in figure 1.2.

The "sss" ❸ looks about the same, still noisy with lots of wiggles in the waveform, but the "eee" sound quickly enters into what's called *periodic oscillation*, with a basic shape repeating over and over ❹. There might be small deviations due to noise, quavers in

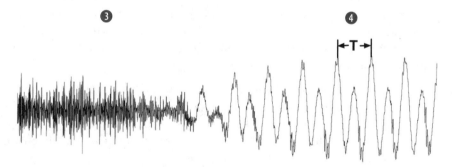

Figure 1.2   Waveform zoomed in to the transition between "sss" and "eee"

the voice itself, or other factors, but the oscillation generally repeats over and over again. This is characteristic of sounds that have pitch. *Pitch* is your perception of frequency from low to high. It's what you sing or whistle of a song melody, and it's what musicians notate and talk about in terms of note names and numbers. The keys of the piano keyboard are oriented from low (left) to high (right) pitches.

Most anything that gives you a sense of pitch exhibits periodic oscillation, and anything that oscillates periodically will sound pitchy (within certain frequency ranges). The region marked as T in figure 1.2 is the period of oscillation (usually given in seconds), and $1/T$ is the frequency of the oscillation in cycles per second. So in the case of the "eee" sound, if the period T is measured as 6.6 milliseconds (a millisecond is one 1000th of a second), then the frequency of oscillation will be $1/0.0066 = 150$ cycles per second, or 150 Hz (the unit of frequency named after physicist Heinrich Hertz, pronounced "hurts").

If you repeat that single period of "eee" over and over, looping at a convenient point like at the main peaks, you could synthesize an "eee" sound of any length you like. If you play that loop slightly faster, the pitch will go up. Play it slower and you get a lower pitch. That synthetic sound would be pretty dull and boring, because by selecting one period and looping that exactly over and over, you'll have removed all the noise, slight deviations of pitch, and other things that made the original sound natural. This is one reason that synthetic speech sounds so, uh, synthetic.

Much of electronic music history, and of music history in general, and actually much of physics, centers on the notion of oscillation. We'll use ChucK's many flavors of built-in oscillators in coming sections, but for now we'll look at one of the most fundamental forms of oscillation in nature and sound: the sine wave. You'll use ChucK's sine wave oscillator soon to write your first program that plays a musical note. So what's a sine wave? A sine wave rises and falls smoothly and periodically, as shown (a few "periods" worth) in figure 1.3.

The circle on the left shows one way that sine waves can be pictured, explained, and generated. If you rotate the circle counterclockwise at a constant rate, say N rotations per second, then the height of the dot that begins on the right side of the circle (the left side of the graph) traces out a sine curve shown to the right, as time progresses from left to right. One way to picture this is to imagine the dot on the circle edge as a pencil, and if you pull a piece of paper from right to left as the circle turns,

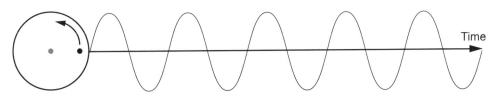

Figure 1.3 A sine wave (right) can be generated by rotating the circle (left) counterclockwise and tracing the height of the dot as it changes in time.

it will draw a sine wave. If N were five cycles per second, then the circle and sine wave would complete five cycles in one second.

You might have heard of sine functions if you've studied trigonometry, but as we noted before, sine waves can be found all over in nature and mathematics. Things that rotate can be described in terms of sine waves. The electricity coming out of AC wall sockets alternates in a sine wave pattern, because the generators in electrical power plants rotate in circles. But not just rotating things generate sine waves. A pendulum sweeps out a sine wave pattern in displacement as it oscillates back and forth. A simple mechanical system of a mass and spring oscillates in a sine wave pattern. An electrical circuit containing an inductor and a capacitor oscillates in a sine wave pattern. Acoustically, the single resonance of the air inside a pop bottle oscillates in a sine wave pattern. So, as you can see, sine waves are pervasive and important characters in the real world.

Other simple waveforms that are common in nature and in electronic music include triangle, sawtooth, and square waves. Figure 1.4 shows two cycles each of sine, triangle, sawtooth, and square waves.

Figure 1.4   Two cycles each of sine wave, triangle wave, sawtooth wave, and square wave

Sine waves are at the heart of the analysis of sound as well as synthesis. More complex periodic waves can be built of sine waves. You can make any sound possible by adding together sine waves of different frequencies, phases (delays), and amplitudes (loudness). Sine waves are the fundamental building blocks of what's called the spectral view of sound, where instead of looking at the individual wiggles of the waveform, you look at the sine components that make up that waveform. Figure 1.5 shows that a sawtooth wave can be built by adding sine waves at integer multiples (1, 2, 3, ...) of some fundamental frequency. Such components are called *harmonic*. Triangle and square waves can be made up of odd sine harmonic (1, 3, 5, ...) frequencies at differing amplitudes.

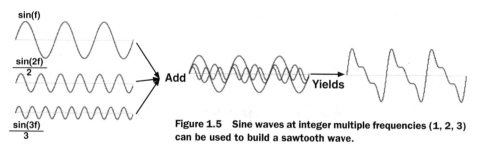

Figure 1.5   Sine waves at integer multiple frequencies (1, 2, 3) can be used to build a sawtooth wave.

The sawtooth also has a nice physical analogy in the musical instrument world, because when a bowed string oscillates, the bow alternately sticks to the string, dragging it along, and then slips, allowing the string to snap back. This creates a sawtooth motion, as observed long ago by Herman von Helmholtz (1821–1894). Helmholtz gave us some of the earliest acoustic theory and experiments with the spectral descriptions of instruments and sounds. A sawtooth wave can be a good start on a violin synthesis, and we'll do that shortly.

Physically, a clarinet playing its lowest note oscillates very much like a square wave, so you could build a very simple clarinet-sounding synthesis by using a square wave and an envelope generator (more on those soon). But first, let's program!

1.2 Your first ChucK programs

It's time to get started learning how to program. At this point, you should have read the instructions in appendix A on how to install miniAudicle and the basic functionality of the programming environment. Once it's installed, open miniAudicle and we'll guide you in writing your first programs. Figure 1.6 shows the miniAudicle ready to run ChucK code.

There are three main windows in the miniAudicle. The main window that you see at the top of figure 1.6 is initially called Untitled, and it's the window in which you write your programs. You can change the name of this window, which you'll do shortly when you write and save your first program. The lower-right window is the Virtual Machine (VM) monitor, which shows the status of the VM server while your ChucK code runs. Once started, the VM is always there and running, waiting for things to do.

When you click Start Virtual Machine, it creates a window called the Console Monitor (lower left of figure 1.6). This is where you'll receive messages from the computer to help you with your program. If there are errors in your code, this is

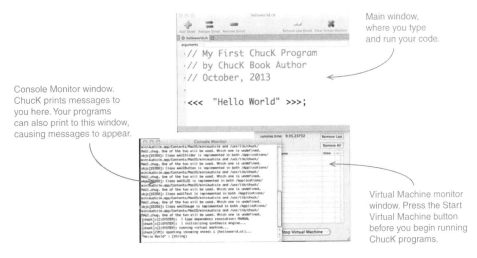

Figure 1.6   Main windows of the miniAudicle ChucK Integrated Development Environment (IDE)

where the computer will tell you that there are problems and specifically where (in which lines) they occur. You can also print messages to yourself from your running code in the Console Monitor to help you debug your program or to keep you informed of what's going on.

1.2.1   *Your first program: "Hello World"*

In almost all languages, the first program you learn to write is "Hello World", so we'll begin by showing you how to do this in ChucK. Go to the Untitled window, save it as helloworld.ck using the File menu, and then type in this line.

```
<<< "Hello World" >>>;
```

Don't forget the semicolon, which is important for ending every line of code in ChucK.

Next, make sure that your VM is running (you'll see the running time: value increasing constantly), and then click Add Shred on the main window, which is now labeled helloworld.ck. You'll instantly see that "Hello World" appears in the Console Monitor. Congratulations, you successfully executed your first ChucK program! Clicking the Add Shred button told ChucK to run the "Hello World" code that you typed into the main window. You'll click this button each time you want to run a ChucK program.

Even though you'll always be typing and running code from the main window, from now on we'll show code as text, with labels and comments. We won't show you the whole main window with control buttons, but we'll show parts of figure 1.6 in the future to point out some of those controls. All of the windows can be moved around on your desktop as you like, as with many of the programs you're used to working with on your computer.

As discussed previously, it's useful to you as a programmer to print to the Console Monitor for debugging purposes and as a composer to tell you what section of your song you're currently running. From this first example you know that putting items between <<< >>> allows you to print. Putting anything in quotes between the triple <<< >>> print characters prints that directly. We'll give you more advanced techniques on printing other things as you continue through this chapter.

1.2.2   *Your first sound program: "Hello Sine!"*

Because ChucK is a language focused on sound, and our goal is to teach you to program through writing compositions, you need to go a lot further in our programs than printing text to your Console Monitor window. You need to learn how to make sound. Thus, you'll name your second program "Hello Sine!" Because a sine wave is periodic, it produces a sound that you hear as a pitch. So think of this first sine wave sound that you make as the beginning note of your first song, "Twinkle, Twinkle, Little Star."

When you enter the code of listing 1.1, make sure you save it as a new file called HelloSine.ck. You should get used to the idea of saving your programs with meaningful names. When you change your programs in major ways, it's often good to save them as a new file, giving them a related name such as HelloSine2.ck.

Also note that as you type the program of listing 1.1 into the miniAudicle editor window, some of the words magically change colors. This is the miniAudicle recognizing those reserved words and coloring them by type. You'll learn more about that later.

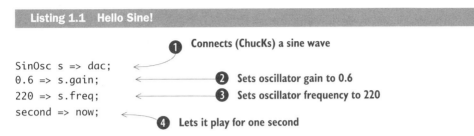

Listing 1.1   Hello Sine!

① Connects (ChucKs) a sine wave

```
SinOsc s => dac;
0.6 => s.gain;
220 => s.freq;
second => now;
```

② Sets oscillator gain to 0.6
③ Sets oscillator frequency to 220
④ Lets it play for one second

Let's dissect this program line by line. In line ①, you make your first sound signal chain, also called a patch, which we'll talk about shortly. SinOsc is called a unit generator (UGen), an object that will generate the sound of a sine wave. The name you give your oscillator is s, which is called a variable name in programming because its value can change. It's also a variable in that you could have chosen any name such as t or mywave. You as the programmer pick how you name the things you make. For simplicity, we've chosen s.

The next important thing is the => symbol. Notice that it looks like an arrow. This is the ChucK operator, and ChucK is the name for the entire language. It's designed to look like a signal flowing from one side of the arrow to the next. When you use it, you say you're ChucKing whatever is on the left side of the arrow to whatever is on the right side. So right now, you have a SinOsc that you've named s and you want to send that sound out to your speakers or headphones. For that you use a special object called a digital-to-analog converter (DAC), which is connected inside your computer to the output of your sound card (speakers, headphones, and the like).

So, by ChucKing a SinOsc named s to the dac, you've made a sine wave that you'll be able to hear from your speakers. Another term for connecting your sine oscillator unit generator to the dac is *making a patch*, which comes from the old days of analog synthesizers where sound-making and -processing components were connected using patch cords, or physical wires with plugs that made the connections.

Now that you've created a sound-making signal chain, you should know that there are three main aspects of this program in creating a sound: how loud, which frequency (or pitch), and how long. In line ②, you work with how loud. All sound-generating and -processing objects in ChucK have a .gain method, which you can use to control the volume level of sound. Gain can be set to any number, but it usually ranges between 0.0 and 1.0. Note in this code that you set the volume to .6 by ChucKing it to s.gain.

In line ③, you work with frequency. This is how you're able to compose and determine which pitch (specific frequency) you want your SinOsc to make. The .freq method of your SinOsc accepts a number in Hertz from 0 to 20,000, which covers, and goes well below, the range of frequencies of human hearing. Note that in this example you set the frequency by ChucKing 220 to s.freq. This is the pitch of the first note of your "Twinkle" song. We'll talk more in the next chapter about how to determine frequencies for particular musical pitches.

In line ❹, you determine how long your synthesis will run, or the duration of your first note. For now you want your sound to play for 1 second, which you accomplish by ChucKing a duration of 1 second to an object called now. ChucKing second to now tells ChucK that you want to wait 1 second while sound is synthesized. If you didn't have this line that manipulates time, you'd hear no sound, because the program would end right there.

Units of time and duration in ChucK

You could have played your sine wave for any amount of time by ChucKing a different duration to now. For example, if you change line ❹ in listing 1.1 to

```
2.0::second => now;
```

then the sound will play for 2 seconds. The double colon tells ChucK that you want to talk about units of time (duration in seconds), so 2::second is 2 seconds, 0.1::second is 1/10 of a second, and so on. Also note that there can be spaces (or not) around the double colon. We'll talk about other units of ChucK time/duration shortly.

One of the most powerful aspects of ChucK is that as the programmer you have absolute control of time. But you're also obligated to control time to make sounds. We'll discuss time and the now object in more detail in section 1.4.

1.2.3   *Now let's make music*

Playing a single sine wave is a big deal, but now let's expand your program to play four notes. The next step in building your song is creating a score of pitches and durations that you'd like your SinOsc to make. First, add a comment at the beginning of the program, to help document it ❶. Then, extend your previous program as follows.

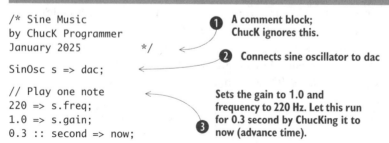

Listing 1.2 Sine wave music

```
/* Sine Music
by ChucK Programmer
January 2025        */

SinOsc s => dac;

// Play one note
220 => s.freq;
1.0 => s.gain;
0.3 :: second => now;
```

❶ A comment block; ChucK ignores this.

❷ Connects sine oscillator to dac

❸ Sets the gain to 1.0 and frequency to 220 Hz. Let this run for 0.3 second by ChucKing it to now (advance time).

```
0.0 => s.gain;
0.3 :: second => now;

// Play another note, same pitch
1.0 => s.gain;
0.3 :: second => now;

0.0 => s.gain;
0.3 :: second => now;

// Play two more notes, higher, less loud
330 => s.freq;
0.3 => s.gain;
0.3 :: second => now;

0.0 => s.gain;
0.3 :: second => now;

0.3 => s.gain;
0.3 :: second => now;

0.0 => s.gain;
0.3 :: second => now;
```

4 Makes your sine oscillator silent for 0.3 seconds to separate it from the next note.

5 Repeats the process of blocks **1** and **3**.

6 Repeats the same two-note pattern of blocks **1**, **3**, and **4** but with a different frequency (pitch) and gain (loudness).

Note that you're creating the first individual note by setting the gain of the dac-connected sine oscillator **2** to 1.0 **3** and then zero **4**, letting your sound patch run for a little while each time by ChucKing a duration of .3 seconds to now. You repeat the same note in **5**. You have to make that silence between the notes (by setting .gain to 0.0) or else those first two repeated notes would sound like one long note. In **6**, you repeat the whole two-note sequence but with a higher pitch (the second "twinkle" in your song) and at a quieter volume (the gain of an oscillator correlates to volume; larger gain equals higher volume). You can probably imagine creating an entire composition, stringing commands like this together. But that's a lot of work, and by the end of this chapter we'll show you many techniques to create notes like this in a much more concise and powerful way.

ChucK is a real programming language

To those of you who have worked with music software, like GarageBand for Mac or FruityLoops for PC or many other such programs, this might seem like quite a bit of typing to make only a few sine tones. Remember when we mentioned in the introduction ("What is ChucK? How is it different?") that because ChucK is text-based, typing is part of the bargain? But copy-paste is possible and encouraged, and in actuality the amount of typing required in ChucK is much less than in almost any other text-based language, even ones that were designed for music.

For now, to give you a glimpse of the power of ChucK, you can type in (or copy/paste) and run this short program. Don't worry if there are things that you don't understand; just be careful to type it in exactly as you see it here:

(continued)

```
Impulse imp => ResonZ filt => NRev rev => dac;
0.04 => rev.mix;
100.0 => filt.Q => filt.gain;

while (1) {
    Std.mtof(Math.random2(60,84)) => filt.freq;
    1.0 => imp.next;
    100::ms => now;
}
```

Once you've typed in the code, save it as WowExample.ck (or whatever name you like), and click the Add Shred button (figure 1.6, top left). You'll hear a steady stream of tuned pops with random pitches. Lots of sound can come from very little code, once you know the powerful features of the language. You can click Add Shred again and hear even more notes. In fact, you can click Add Shred lots of times and hear even more.

When you're through and want to stop the sound, click the Clear Virtual Machine button at the top right of the miniAudicle window (figure 1.6).

Over the next examples and couple of chapters, you'll be building up your basic knowledge of ChucK, enabling you to make more and more powerful programs. If it sometimes feels like you're not getting much for your lines of typed code, bear with us, because by the end of this chapter you'll learn new things in ChucK that will allow you to make much more, even hours of music, for comparatively little typing.

1.2.4   *Trying new waveforms*

Because you're now ready to start composing using an oscillator, we want to enable you to use more than only the SinOsc object to make music. As discussed in section 1.1, it's possible to make sound using many different types of waveforms. Try out the three waveforms shown in figure 1.7 in the program in listing 1.2 by changing the SinOsc in code block ❷ to one of the following: a square wave (SqrOsc), a triangle wave (TriOsc), or a sawtooth wave (SawOsc).

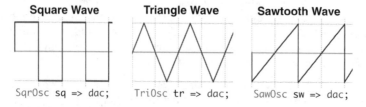

Square Wave	Triangle Wave	Sawtooth Wave
SqrOsc sq => dac;	TriOsc tr => dac;	SawOsc sw => dac;

Figure 1.7   ChucK has built-in oscillator types for square, triangle, and sawtooth waveforms.

Some of the most important elements in programming are the comments the author makes while creating the code. As shown in the first few lines of listing 1.2 and shown again here, comments are made in two ways: ❶ a set of slashes and asterisks, /* and */, or ❷ two forward slashes, //. In method 2, anything on the line past the // isn't registered by ChucK as computer code. Method 1 is for multiple lines where all lines in between the two sets of characters are to be ignored by the compiler.

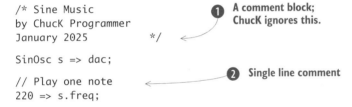

```
/* Sine Music
by ChucK Programmer
January 2025              */        ❶  A comment block;
                                        ChucK ignores this.
SinOsc s => dac;

// Play one note                   ❷  Single line comment
220 => s.freq;
```

The example of listing 1.3 brings together all the concepts discussed in section 1.2. The code is well documented (commented), and you print something to the Console output ❶ at the beginning and then play two notes of music.

In the last block ❷, we show how you can use the multiline /*...*/ form of comments to cause some code to not be executed, because ChucK assumes that this text is a comment and not code. This can be extremely helpful for debugging your code or skipping across some of your composition so you can work with later parts.

Listing 1.3   Using comments to document code and control execution

```
// Author: ChucK Team                    Initial comment, documents who
// Date: Today's date                    wrote the program and when.

// make a sound chain ("patch")
SinOsc s => dac;                         Sets up sound signal chain.

// prints out program name
<<< "Hello Sine!" >>>;                 ❶ Prints a greeting message.

// set volume to 0.6
.6 => s.gain;                            Sets up parameters to play a note.
// set frequency to 220.0
220.0 => s.freq;
// play for 1 second
second => now;

0.5 => s.gain; // set volume to 0.5
440 => s.freq; // set frequency to 440     Plays another note.
2::second => now; // play for two seconds

// comment out this third note for now
/*                                       ❷ Don't play this last note
0.3 => s.gain;                             right now, because we've
330  => s.freq;                            commented it out.
3::second => now;
*/
```

You now know how to make sound with oscillators, how to change pitch using `.freq` and volume using `.gain`, and how to control the durations of your notes using `now`. But there are other things you need to know to make better music.

1.3   Data types and variables

The programs you've seen so far make sound, but it would be really hard to think about making a whole song using this type of literal coding of each gain, frequency, and time. The next concept to learn is how to make your program easy to change, given decisions you might make as a composer or even decisions the program itself might make.

One key to doing this is to use variables. In ChucK and many other programming languages, each variable has to have a particular data type, meaning that it can hold only one specific type of value or collection of values. Just like our examples in listing 1.2, where a variable s contained our SinOsc, you can declare variables to hold a number, a time, or even words. But each one can hold only one type of data.

A very important ChucK data type is designed to hold integer (`int`) numbers. An integer is a special type of number that doesn't have a fractional part; thus it needs no decimal point. In ChucK, an integer variable can store any number in the range of $-2,147,483,648$ to $+2,147,483,647$. You can declare and initialize (give a value to) an integer variable as shown in listing 1.4. Declaring a new variable creates space in the computer to store that variable and registers the newly declared name and type for that variable, so you can refer to it by name later. Initializing a variable gives it a value. In listing 1.4, right after you declare the new `myPitch` variable, you store the value of 220 into it by ChucKing.

Good coding practices: variable names

Because you're the programmer, you can pick any name you like for your variables, but it's almost always better to pick names that are meaningful. Names like `myPitch`, `myVolume`, and `fastTempo` are much more meaningful than x, j, and z. People reading your code can see those names and have an idea of their purpose. Later you'll see that some variables are temporary, used quickly in code just after they're created, and never used again. For these types of variables, `i`, `temp`, `x`, and the like are fine. But for most variables, a good name (not too long but definitely not too short) is important.

Listing 1.4   Defining and using an integer variable

```
// declare an integer
int myPitch;

// store a value in it
220 => myPitch;

// print it out
<<< myPitch >>>;
```

You can also initialize integers at the time they're declared. For example, you can simultaneously declare an `int` named `myPitch` and set its value to 220, as shown in the following listing.

Listing 1.5   Initializing an integer as it's declared

```
// another way to initialize integers
// store 220 in newly declared myPitch, all at once

220 => int myPitch;
   <<< myPitch >>>;
```

Many times you want to change the value of a variable—that's one reason they're called *variables*. And there are times when you want to use the value of a variable to initialize a new variable. You might set the value of one variable as related to another to use them as frequencies for a musical chord or scale. Also, deriving new variables from others can make your programs more readable and easier to modify. You'll first learn how to use math to change variable values and derive new variables from others in listings 1.6 and 1.7; then you'll use those tools to play music in listing 1.8. Because integers are numbers, you can do all sorts of arithmetic with them, as shown in the following listing. This will become more important later on when you want to play more and more notes.

Listing 1.6 Doing math with integers

```
// arithmetic with integers
220 => int myPitch;

// add or subtract
myPitch + myPitch - 110 => int anotherPitch;

// multiply
2 * myPitch => int higherPitch;

// divide
myPitch / 2 => int lowerPitch;

// print them all out
<<< myPitch, anotherPitch, higherPitch, lowerPitch >>>;
```

The code prints the following in the Console Monitor window:

```
220  330  440  110
```

Exercise

Walk through the variable math operations of listing 1.6 using pencil and paper. See if you come up with the same numbers. Type this code into ChucK to check your answers. Which was easier? You can use ChucK as a calculator!

The next listing shows a few shorthand methods to do arithmetic on variables to change their values in place. By adding a math operator to the beginning of the ChucK => operator, that math is performed on the variable and stored back into the variable.

Listing 1.7 Shorthand math: multiply, subtract, and ChucK in one step!

```
// longhand math with integers        // shorthand math with integers

int myPitch;                          220 => int myPitch;
220 => myPitch;

// multiply by 2                      // multiply by 2, in-place
2 * myPitch => myPitch;               2 *=> myPitch;   //  "times ChucK"

// subtraction                        // in-place subtraction
myPitch - 110 => myPitch;             110 -=> myPitch;   // "minus ChucK"

<<< myPitch >>>;                      <<< myPitch >>>;
```

Both of these print the following in the Console Monitor window:

```
330  :(int)
```

Let's use your newfound knowledge about integer variables to play a couple of notes, as shown in the next listing. Here you store your pitch in an integer variable, and you create two integers called `onGain` and `offGain` to store the values of 1 and 0 so you can turn the sound of your oscillator on and off.

Listing 1.8 Playing notes with integer variables

```
/* Sine Music with integer variables
by ChucK Programmer
January 2025            */

SinOsc s => dac;                          ❶ Declares and initializes
                                             an integer variable
220 => int myPitch;                          called myPitch       ❷ Declares and initializes
                                                                     two integers for
1 => int onGain;                                                     controlling gain
0 => int offGain;
                                          ❸ Plays a note using your
// Play one note                             new integer variables
myPitch => s.freq;
onGain => s.gain;
0.3 :: second => now;                     ❹ Turns off the sound of
                                             your oscillator to
offGain => s.gain;                           separate the notes
0.3 :: second => now;
                                          ❺ Multiplies your pitch
1 *=> myPitch;                               by 2, in place

// Play another note, with a higher pitch  ❻ Sets frequency and turns on
myPitch => s.freq;                            oscillator, to start your 2nd note
onGain => s.gain;
0.3 :: second => now;                     ❹ Turns off the sound of
                                             your oscillator again to
offGain => s.gain;                           end the 2nd note
0.3 :: second => now;
```

By creating integer variables in ❶ and ❷, you can use those instead of numbers to set your sine wave parameters ❸, ❹, ❻. Because they're variables, you can change their value at any time, so the beauty lies in ❺, where you multiply your pitch by 2. Setting the sine wave frequency to this new value makes the pitch higher.

This amount of frequency change (doubling) is called a musical interval of one octave up, for somewhat obscure reasons. An *octave* is a doubling (upward) or halving (downward) of frequency. For those familiar with keyboard instruments, an octave is the space between any two C notes (middle C to the octave above, for instance), A notes, G notes, and the like. If you play an open string on a guitar or other stringed instrument and then put your finger on the 12th fret and play that same string, you'll hear a difference of an octave (doubling of frequency, and not coincidentally you're cutting the string length in half).

You can play some notes using integer variables, but what if you wanted to play a different interval, as is the case in the "Twinkle" song, where you want to play two notes at 220 Hz and then two notes at 330 Hz? You might note that you could multiply 220 by 1.5 to yield 330.0, but ChucK won't allow you to do that because you can't use fractions or decimal points when dealing with integers. And what about the next two notes ("little") in the song? These notes need to have a frequency of 369.994 (which you could maybe round to 370), but what if you wanted to get creative and fiddle with the melody even more? You might want to play the word "little" on F# and G#, with frequencies of 369.994 and 415.305 Hz. We'll talk more about pitch and frequency in the next chapter, but you know that integer variables can store only numbers with no fractional part (no decimal points allowed).

Fortunately, there's another ChucK data type called float. Floating-point numbers are numbers that have a decimal point (fractional part) and can thus be more precise. But as you can imagine, these numbers are stored and operated upon differently inside the computer; thus there's a separate data type for these. You can declare and initialize float variables just as you've done with integers. All of the arithmetic and shorthand operators also apply to floats. Listing 1.9 shows how you can declare and initialize a float to hold your first "twinkle" frequency. You can use math on that, multiplying it by 1.5 to store it in a newly declared variable called twinkle2. Similarly, you can derive your pitches for "little" by multiplying twinkle or twinkle2 by the correct floating-point numbers.

Listing 1.9   Using and manipulating float variables

1 Declares and initializes a float to hold your twinkle pitch.

```
220 => float twinkle;
```

Uses math to derive your 2nd twinkle pitch from the first one.

```
1.5 * twinkle => float twinkle2;
```

Uses more math to derive lit pitch from your base twinkle.

```
1.6818 * twinkle => float lit;
```

Uses more math to derive tle pitch from twinkle2.

```
1.2585 * twinkle2 => float tle;
```

```
2 * twinkle => float octave;
```

Makes a new pitch an octave above twinkle.

```
<<< twinkle, twinkle2, lit, tle, octave >>>;
```

The code produces the following console output:

```
220.000000      330.000000      369.996000      415.305000      440.000000
```

The beauty of this code is that just by changing the initialization of your first twinkle, all of the other pitches change as well. Because variables are used to set pitches, if you changed **1** to

```
110 => float twinkle;
```

then all of the pitches would go down by an octave. Setting the initial twinkle to 261.616 Hz would play "Twinkle" in the key of C. Changing a whole melody or song into a different key is called *transposition*. You could initialize that initial twinkle variable to any reasonable number, and all others would change proportionally. So the "Twinkle" song would still be intact but in a different musical key. The power of programming!

Note that you already used floats when you set the gain of your SinOsc UGen in listing 1.2 (first to 1.0 and then to 0.3 to make it quieter). We'll look at one more example in the following listing to reinforce the use of floats. The ability to turn volume and frequency into variables will become an important element in making expressive compositions, as you'll soon see.

Listing 1.10 **Twinkle with floats**

```
/* Sine Twinkle Music with float variables
by ChucK Programmer
January 2025           */

SinOsc s => dac;

220.0 => float twinkle;
1.6818 * twinkle => float little;

1 => int onGain;
0 => int offGain;

// Play one note
twinkle => s.freq;
onGain => s.gain;
0.3 :: second => now;
offGain => s.gain;
0.3 :: second => now;

1.5 *=> twinkle;

// Play other note of 2nd "twinkle"
twinkle => s.freq;
onGain => s.gain;
0.3 :: second => now;
offGain => s.gain;
0.3 :: second => now;

// Play one note of "little"
little => s.freq;
onGain => s.gain;
0.3 :: second => now;
offGain => s.gain;
0.3 :: second => now;
```

You can make a float variable for your twinkle pitch and use math to compute the value of another variable to use later for little.

Turns twinkle note on (sets gain using onGain variable and advances time).

Turns off note (sets gain to offGain and advances time).

Modifies twinkle pitch using math, so you can do the 2nd, higher twinkle.

You've now used variables (both int and float) to make your code more flexible and readable. But can you do something about all of those lines with numbers controlling time? You could make a float variable and initialize it to 0.3 and then use it something like this:

```
0.3 => float myDur;
myDur :: second => now;
```

But there's a better way! You'll now learn about two more data types that are built into ChucK, specifically to control times and durations.

1.4   *Time in ChucK: It's about now*

So far you've been making sound by hooking a sine or other oscillator to the dac, setting its frequency and gain, and ChucKing some duration, such as 0.3::second, to a magical keyword called now. Now we're going to dig into the timing mechanisms of ChucK, introducing two new data types (like float and int) to deal with time and durations.

> **WHAT'S A KEYWORD?**   *Keywords* are special reserved words in computer languages and systems. We've used lots of keywords already, such as dac, SinOsc, and second. You can tell a keyword when you type or see it in the mini-Audicle, because it changes color automatically. The one thing you must remember as a programmer is that you can't choose those keywords for your variable names. ChucK won't allow that, because those words already have been defined (by the authors of ChucK) for special uses. Rule of thumb: if the miniAudicle colorizes a word, you can't use it as a variable name (except for comments which are automatically colored green).

1.4.1   *Variables of type dur*

You've already ChucKed durations of time to the ChucK keyword now to control time in all of the previous examples, but you can improve the "Twinkle" song further by using variables of a new data type called dur, for duration.

> **Listing 1.11   Twinkle with dur variables**

```
/* Sine Music using dur variables
by ChucK Programmer
January 2025          */

SinOsc s => dac;

220.0 => float twinkle;                    ❶ Defines note durations
0.55 :: second => dur onDur;                 as variables
0.05 :: second => dur offDur;

1 => int onGain;
0 => int offGain;

// Play one note
twinkle => s.freq;
onGain => s.gain;                          ❷ Waits while note
onDur => now;                                sounds...

offGain => s.gain;                         ❸ ...then waits for space
offDur => now;                               between notes

1.5 *=> twinkle;                           ❹ Next note frequency

// Play other note of 2nd "twinkle"
twinkle => s.freq;                         ❺ Sets it and plays another note
onGain => s.gain;
onDur => now;
```

```
offGain => s.gain;
offDur => now;
```

In ❶, you make two variables of type dur, which you initialize to different values. One controls the amount of time the sine wave is making sound ❷, and the other controls the sound off time ❸; this silent time is often called a *rest* by musicians. In ❹, you use in-place variable arithmetic to change the frequency of twinkle so you can use it for the second pair of twinkle2 notes; for musicians and physicists, this musical interval of 3/2 is called a *perfect fifth*. In ❺ you turn the oscillator on and off again, advancing time using your dur variables, to play the next note.

Understanding time and duration (and floats and ints) is essential for ChucK programmers. By default, ChucK provides the special duration keywords shown in table 1.1. You likely know second, minute, hour, day, and week, but the values in the table that you might not be familiar with are ms and samp. One 1000th of a second is called a millisecond, abbreviated ms. So 1000 :: ms is equal to 1 :: second.

The samp duration depends on the sample rate at which your sound hardware is running, but it's always the fundamental unit of time in any digital audio system. A samp is usually 1/44100 of a second (because there are 44100 audio samples used to capture a second of audio). For reasons that are both technical (syncing audio to the most common video formats) and perceptual (a sample rate that's high enough to capture the audible range of human hearing), 44100 is the sample rate most commonly used in CDs, MP3s, and other storage devices.

Table 1.1 Special ChucK duration keywords and their corresponding durations

Keyword	Duration
samp	1 digital sample in ChucK time (usually 1/44100 of a second)
ms	1 millisecond
second	1 second
minute	1 minute
hour	1 hour
day	1 day
week	1 week

> **THOUGHT PROBLEM** Why didn't the ChucK designers define a "year" or "month" keyword? Answer: month and year don't have a specific duration. Months can range from 28 to 31 days, and years can be either 365 or 366 days long. ChucK is very precise about time, so month and year were not included.

1.4.2 The importance of time

Now that you've used time and dur a little, let's talk a bit more deeply about why time is so important in ChucK and why it's so important for you as a programmer to understand how time is dealt with in ChucK. Sound is a time-based medium. Sound, and by extension, music, happens over time. Without the *passage* of time, there'd be no sound. This fundamental relationship between time and sound is at the core of the ChucK language, and it allows you to govern how time flows in order to make sound happen—and to control sound precisely over time.

There are a few things in ChucK that work together to make this possible:

- time and dur are native data types, just like int and float.
- The now keyword holds the current ChucK time, which starts at zero when you click the Start Virtual Machine button in the miniAudicle.
- By manipulating now (ChucKing a duration to it), and only by manipulating now, you can cause the passage of time in a ChucK program to generate sound.

In ChucK, time (time) and duration (dur) are basic data types that you can work with much like integers and floating-point numbers. They represent values of a particular type. You can declare variables of those types and set their values and perform arithmetic on them.

1.4.3   *Variables of type time*

The time type holds a point in time (referenced from zero when the ChucK VM is started). The dur type holds a *duration*, which is a *length* of time, the space between two times. Just as you might arrange to meet someone at a particular time—"I'll meet you at 1:00 p.m."—or specify something as a duration—"I'll be back in an hour"—this is the nature of time and dur in ChucK. A time specifies a point in time (the duration since ChucK was started), and dur specifies a length of time. For example, 2::second in ChucK is a value of type dur. You can add durations together to form new durations, (for example, 2::second + 1::minute) and store durations into newly declared variables, for example,

```
0.8::second => dur quarter;  // quarter note duration
```

The duration of a quarter note in music depends on the tempo, often expressed in how many quarter-note durations happen per second, also called BPM (beats per minute). Here we've defined a quarter note to be 0.8 seconds, meaning that our tempo is 75 BPM (60 seconds per minute / 0.8 seconds per beat = 75 beats per minute).

Variables can be reused to create new variables, for example,

```
4::quarter => dur whole;
```

Once you've set your quarter note duration (thus tempo), you can define a whole note from that, made up of four quarter notes. You could similarly define eighth notes (quarter / 2) and half notes (2 * quarter or whole / 2), like this:

```
4::quarter => dur whole;

4 * quarter => dur whole;

whole / 2 => dur half;

quarter / 2 => dur eighth;
```

The special keyword now is at the heart of working with time in ChucK, and it is of type time. The word now has two special functions. First, when read, now holds the current logical ChucK time. Essentially now is ChucK's master clock. Second, even though now is a variable, you can't change its value directly, at least not in the normal way. When you try to change the value of now, for example, by ChucKing a particular duration to now, it has the important side effect of letting time pass (and letting sound generate) for precisely that duration. In effect, ChucK is advancing time until now becomes the value you want it to be!

Figure 1.8 shows this for the two-note "Twinkle" example of listing 1.11, illustrating how time advances between blocks of code being executed.

Another way to look at time in ChucK is that your code stops executing for any duration you ChucK to now, but all the synthesis stuff you've connected (SinOsc => dac, for example) keeps running and making sound. When that particular duration that you ChucKed to now has passed, the next line of code executes.

1.4.4   Working with now

Working with now is simple and fun and yet is absolutely essential to programming in ChucK—you must use it to make sound, period. Because the way that ChucK deals with time is so important and is what makes it so different from every other language, we need to reinforce points about time, dur, and dealing with now. Here are some important things to keep in mind when working with now.

- ChucKing a duration to now advances ChucK time precisely by that amount: while time is advancing, your code is automatically and temporarily suspended (the next line is not executed) *and sound is generated by the system.* How it does this depends on how you've set up the sound synthesis.
- now will never move forward unless or until you manipulate it. So until you explicitly advance time, you're actually working within a *single instant in time.*
- Another way to think about all this is that ChucK code execution waits until now becomes the time you want to reach. For this reason, you should never ChucK a negative duration to now, for example, –1::second => now. ChucK can't (yet) go backward in time, so trying to do this will halt your program.
- There are no restrictions on how much time is advanced, as long as it's by a non-negative amount! So it's possible to advance time, say, by a microsecond, a samp, 2 hours, or 51 weeks with the same mechanism—it's all up to you; the system will behave accordingly and predictably.

There are other ways to advance time; for example, by chucking an Event to now (such as clicking the computer mouse, pressing the fire button on a joystick, or playing a note on a musical MIDI keyboard connected to your computer) for when you don't know beforehand how much time to advance. We'll leave that for a later discussion. For now, you've just learned one of the most important aspects of ChucK: controlling time using durations.

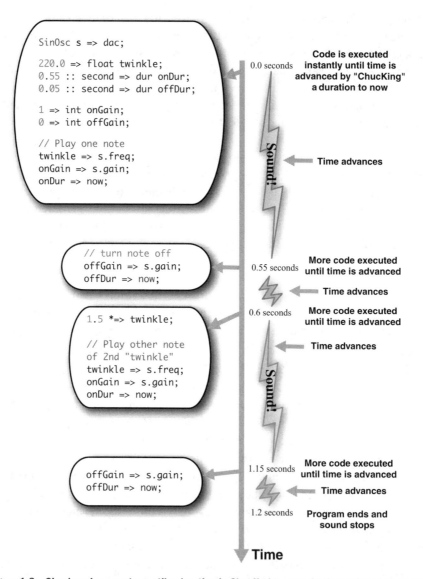

Figure 1.8 Chuck code executes until a duration is ChucKed to now. At that point, time keeps advancing and sound is synthesized until the duration has passed. The cycle continues, with code being executed until now is advanced by some duration and sound is synthesized for that duration. When all code has run and time has advanced as far as the last point, the program stops and sound stops as well.

Now that you know about the int, float, time, and dur data types, we should mention that ChucK has a couple of other built-in (called primitive) data types, including string (a string of text characters like "hello world") and void (a type with no type, in case you need a variable but don't need a type). We know this notion of a void data-type might be confusing, but you'll need this later in the book. Table 1.2 summarizes all of ChucK's built-in data types.

Table 1.2 ChucK data types

Data Type	Description	Example	Comment
int	Integer	3, 3541	No decimal point
float	Floating point	2.23, 3.14159, 22.0	Decimal point
string	Description	"hello", "data/a.wav"	Comment or text
dur	Distance between times	1:: second, ms, 3*day	Duration
time	ChucKianTime	22050.0	Time in samples
void	No type		

You've learned a lot about variables and data and using those to control your sound parameters and advancing through time. But you're still typing many lines of ChucK code to make each note. There must be a better way, and there is. Read on.

1.5 *Logic and control structures for your compositions*

To motivate the ideas of this next section, let's look at a different, non-"Twinkle" example that plays around with modifying pitch and duration (by advancing time) in a new and flexible way. The very few lines of code in the next listing can make really interesting sounds, forever, by repeatedly moving through time with now. Type in this program and run it. The magic that you're hearing is ChucK playing a constant stream of notes, randomly changing the frequency and duration of each.

Listing 1.12 Random triangle wave music

```
/* Random Triangle Wave Music
   by ChucK Programmer */

  TriOsc t => dac;

// infinite loop runs forever
while (true)
{
    // randomly choose frequency from 30 to 1000
    Math.random2(30,1000) => t.freq;

    // random choose duration from 30 to 1000 ms
    Math.random2f(30,1000) :: ms => now;
}
```

Uses a triangle wave for variety.

❶ Infinite loop runs forever (more on this shortly).

❷ Generates a random number between 30 and 1000 and use that for your pitch.

❸ Advances time by ChucKing a random number between 30 ms and 1 second to now.

Now play with the numbers (30, 1000) ❷. Each time you make a change, click the Replace Shred button on the miniAudicle, and the code that was running will be magically replaced with the new code. If you made significant changes, you'll instantly hear the difference! This is another extremely powerful aspect of ChucK—the ability to modify your code on the fly while sound is still being synthesized.

Try this

Don't click Replace Shred each time you make a change to the code of listing 1.12. Instead, click Add Shred. Now you hear more magic of ChucK, which is that it can run multiple programs, called shreds, at the same time! You can add more running random sine programs, almost as many as you like, and hear that ChucK is happily generating many sounds at the same time. You'll use this power of ChucK and learn a lot more about it later, but for now, isn't it amazing how much sound/music you can make with just a little bit of code? We promised that your ratio of sound to typing would increase.

Once you're tired of hearing this and ready to move on, click the Clear Virtual Machine button (marked with a big X in the upper-right corner of your main window, as shown in figure 1.9), and that will stop the sound.

Wow! With only the four lines of actual ChucK code of listing 1.12 you've made more notes than you ever could by typing them in one at a time. You're going to learn some of how that's possible next, and you'll learn the rest in chapter 2.

The program of listing 1.12 randomly changes the frequency of a triangle wave ❷. Each new frequency is random, and the time it lasts until the next one is played is also random. The while (true) line ❶ begins what programmers call an infinite loop, essentially meaning "do everything within the curly braces forever." We'll talk about more ways to loop shortly. In the last line ❸ of the while loop's body, you're advancing now by a random amount, at which point ChucK knows to automatically suspend the code, let time pass for that time, and meanwhile generate sound. Precisely after that time has passed, ChucK resumes executing your code. Clicking the Clear Virtual Machine button ends the infinite while loop and stops sound.

You've now written your first loop using the while keyword. The while keyword, combined with the brackets, is called a control structure. So next let's look at exactly how that loop and other loops work. You'll learn about logic and control structures, which are essential to making expressive and interesting compositions from your ChucK code.

Figure 1.9   **Clear Virtual Machine button in the miniAudicle main editor window**

1.5.1 *Programming power through logic statements: the if statement*

Logic statements are either true or false, as in "seven is not equal to two" or "-3 is a negative number, *and* negative numbers are less than zero, therefore -3 is less than zero." Control structures use logic to determine how your computer code runs and what the effects of it will be. ChucK employs many standard control structures found in programming languages, including if, else, for, and while.

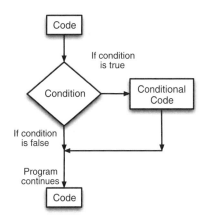

Figure 1.10   Flow chart of an if conditional. If the condition is true, then some ChucK code is executed. If the condition is false, then the code is skipped, and the next code in the program executes.

We'll start by looking closely at the if statement. We all use if statements in everyday life, such as "If I get hungry enough, I'll stop and get food." if statements in ChucK can be used to make decisions in code, based on the conditions of variables or other things that hold values. Figure 1.10 shows a diagram of what happens with an if condition, walking procedurally (line by line) through the code (shown in listing 1.13).

Listing 1.13   If statement example

```
// sound chain
SinOsc s => dac;                          The usual sound patch.

// set frequency                          Sets frequency and gain.
220.0 => s.freq;
// set volume                         ❶ Defines an integer named chance
0.6 => s.gain;                           to use as a logical variable (will
                                         have a value of either 1 or 0).
// chance logical variable
1 => int chance;                      ❷ if statement. If the value in the
                                         parentheses is equal to 1, then do
if (chance == 1)                         what's in the { }; otherwise skip that
{
    // sound will play only if chance == 1   ❸ Advances time and lets
    1 :: second => now;                         sound happen if true.

}
// set new frequency                      Sets new frequency for a different note...
330.0 => s.freq;
1 :: second => now;                   ❹ ...then plays this new note.
```

Translating the diagram in figure 1.10 into code, you see in the listing a simple program that uses a new integer variable chance ❶ that's initialized to 1. If chance is equal to 1 (chance == 1) ❷, then something will happen.

With the control structures you're learning in this section, you're using the characters { and }. You can consider these to be like paragraphs, but programmers call them blocks. In this case, if the condition is `true`, then you enter and execute the code ❸ in the block. If the condition is not `true`, then you move on. Also notice that two equal signs are used to express the conditional test. That's the convention in ChucK and many other programming languages, to use the == symbol to indicate you're doing a logical test for equality, in this case "is the variable named `chance` equal to 1?"

There are logical conditions in addition to equals, such as less than, greater than, and not equal to. For that, ChucK provides other symbols (called relational operators) to test values, as summarized in table 1.3.

Table 1.3   Logical conditionals

Symbol	Meaning in words	Example use
==	is equal to	if (x == 0)
!=	is not equal to	if (x != 0)
<	is less than	if (x < y)
>	is greater than	if (x > y)
>=	is greater than or equal to	if (x >= y)
<=	is less than or equal to	if (x <= y)

In the random triangle frequency program from listing 1.12, you use a ChucK reserved word, `true`, which always has the value of 1. In ChucK, the value 1 is used to represent `true`, and the value 0 represents `false`. If you type and run this line of ChucK code

```
<<< true, false >>>;
```

you'll see that ChucK prints

```
1   0
```

Note that you can print two items by placing a comma between them in your <<< >>> print statement. Similarly, you can type and run this

```
<<< -3 < 0, true==1, true==false, 1 > 10 >>>;
```

yielding

```
1   1   0   0
```

meaning that -3 is less than 0, and `true` does equal 1, but `true` does not equal `false`, and 1 is not greater than 10. Cool, huh?

Continuing the example from listing 1.13, because `chance==1`, the test is true, so the program continues into the block and executes line ❸, advances time by 1 second, and plays sound for 1 second.

Now, go and change line ❶, setting `chance` to 0, and rerun the newly edited code. This in essence changes line ❷ to be `false` and thus line ❸ will never be executed, so no time will pass and no sound will be made in that conditional code. The program goes on to play the second note ❹, which is why you hear only that higher note. So when chance==1, you hear two notes, and when chance != 1 you hear only one note.

The else statement goes hand and hand with the if statement. As you can see from figure 1.11, the if/else structure forms a fork in the road: if the condition is true, then go right; if the condition is false, then go left. As you can see from listing 1.14, the else statement ❹ has its own block of code, following the if statement's block ❸. In this case the test ❷ will equate to false, so the code will jump down and execute ❹, changing the frequency to 330 Hz, advancing time, and playing the sound for 3 seconds.

If you change the initialization of chance to 1 rather than 3 in ❶, then the if condition ❷ will be true and the first block of code ❸ will execute, playing a sine wave of frequency 220 Hz for 1 second.

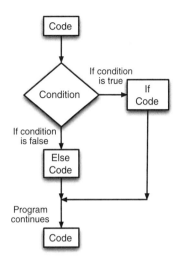

Figure 1.11 Flow chart of an if/else conditional. If the condition is true, then some ChucK code is executed. If the condition is false, then different code is executed.

Listing 1.14 if/else code example

```
// sound chain
SinOsc s => dac;            // Sine to dac, set frequency and gain.

// set frequency
220.0 => s.freq;
// set volume
0.5 => s.gain;              ❶ New integer named chance,
                              initialized to value of 3.
// chance logical variable
3 => int chance;

if (chance == 1)            ❷ If chance is equal to 1...
{
    // play first "twinkle" note if chance == 1
    1 :: second => now;     ❸ ...do this block...
}
else                        ❹ ...otherwise (else), set sine
{                             frequency to something different
    // otherwise, play other, higher twinkle note
                              and play for a longer time.
    330.0 => s.freq;
    // and play it for a much longer time
    3::second => now;
}

// set and play one note, an octave above "twinkle"  // After the if/else, play
440.0 => s.freq;                                      // another, much higher note
1 :: second => now;
```

Run the code in listing 1.14, changing chance to different values. You'll hear the low twinkle note followed by the much higher note only when chance==1, and for any other value you'll hear the twinkle2 note followed by the high one.

1.5.2 Logical operators and conditions

Just as you can have logical statements that combine or require multiple conditions ("My gas gauge is below half a tank, *and* gas is pretty cheap right now, so I'll buy gas"), it's also possible to have multiple conditions in an if statement. The && (known as and) operator means that all conditions must be true for the overall condition to be true. The || (known as or) condition means that only one of the conditions needs to be true to execute that block of code. An example of or might be "If my tank is really empty *or* gas is really cheap, then I'll fill up." ChucK code examples of these are shown in listing 1.15.

if/else/and/or statements will become increasingly useful as you learn more about ChucK and music programming.

Listing 1.15 More complex logical conditions

```
//conditional statements

if ( (chance == 1) || (chance == 5) )      ←   Or condition. If chance is equal to
{                                              1 or 5, then the condition is true.
    //code goes here
}.

if ( (chance < 2) && (chance2 >= 6))        ←   If chance is less than 2, and
{                                               chance2 is greater than or equal
    //code goes here                            to 6, then the condition is true.
}
```

1.5.3 The for loop control structure

You can make even more interesting music using the next control structure, called a for loop. As the loop name implies, this control structure is used to make loops and cyclical behaviors. In listing 1.16 and illustrated in figure 1.12, a for loop begins by setting an initial state with a variable ❶. It contains a condition ❷ that it checks to see if it's true (like an if statement). If it's true, it then executes a block (paragraph) of code ❹, and at the end it executes an update command ❸. Here the initial variable is updated to a new value, and then the condition is checked again. This process continues until the condition is false and the loop is over.

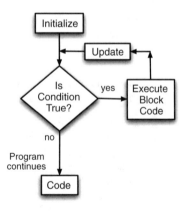

Figure 1.12 Flow chart of a for loop. Variable i is initialized to 0 and then counted up (++) until it reaches the value of 4. The code in the block is executed each time.

There are many musical cases where you might want to use a for loop, such as playing up the notes of a scale (next chapter) or sweeping gradually from one frequency to another by hitting all the frequencies in between. Here you're counting up and printing integers.

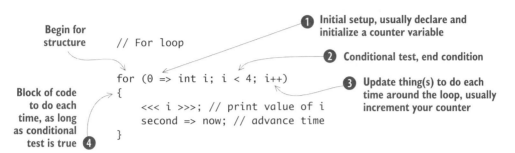

Listing 1.16 The for loop

In the example of the previous listing, the integer variable i is initialized to 0 ❶. The conditional test ❷ is of course true (0 is less than 4), so the block of code ❹ is executed (print i, wait 1 second); then i is incremented ❸ (i++ is the same as 1 +=> i, which is the same as i + 1 => i) and the for loop is run again with i equal to 1. The conditional test is still true (1 is less than 4), so the block is executed, i is incremented, and the for loop runs again. This continues until i is equal to 4, and the conditional test is now false, so the loop ends.

Let's add sound to this concept so you can start to hear what a for loop can do for you musically. In music programming, for loops can be used to play scales, repeat patterns such as bass lines or melodies, smoothly change gains, sweep frequencies up or down, and many other super-musical things.

In listing 1.17, you use a for loop ❶ to set frequencies of your SinOsc ❸ from values 20 Hz to 400 Hz (and print them out ❷) every 10 milliseconds ❹. Imagine having to write all these lines of code out one by one as you did in section 1.2! Looping allows you to make much more complicated sounds and compositions right away and saves you many lines of code. Already, as a composer, you're able to write music that you would have never been able to write without learning how to program.

Listing 1.17 Musical use of a for loop

```
// set up our patch
SinOsc s => dac;              Sine wave to dac

// loop                       A musical for loop
for (20 => int i; i < 400; i++)       ❶ For loop from 20 to 399
{
    <<< i >>>;    // print loop counter value    ❷ Prints out current value of i
    i => s.freq; // set freq to i         ❸ Sets frequency
    10::ms => now; // advance time        ❹ Waits 10ms, then loops again
}
```

1.5.4   *The while loop control structure*

The last control structure you're going to learn in this chapter is the while loop (figure 1.13), which you've already used to make an infinite loop. while is similar to a for loop but is written differently. You can rewrite the same for-loop program but using a while statement, as shown in listing 1.18.

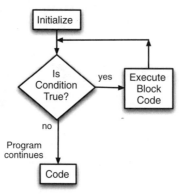

Figure 1.13   **Flow chart of a while loop. Integer variable i is first initialized to 0; then the block loops, incrementing i by 1 each time, until the condition is false (i reaches 400).**

Listing 1.18   Musical while loop

```
SinOsc s => dac;

// initialize variable i                    ❶ Initializes the counter/
20 => int i;                                    frequency to 20.

// while loop (instead of for loop)          ❷ The while loop only
while ( i < 400)                                has a conditional test.
{
    <<< i >>>;                               ❸ Block of code to
    i => s.freq;                                execute, including...
    10::ms => now;
    i++;    // update counter (very important!!)  ❹ ...increment counter
}
```

After setting up your usual sine wave, you initialize integer i to be 20 ❶. Then you set up your while condition ❷ (while i is less than 400). The name suggests that it's a condition, which can make it a little more obvious and easy to remember than the for loop. The while loop then continues inside its block ❸. Notice that you then add an update command ❹ similar to the for loop update. Running this code, you'll see that it makes the same sound as the for loop code of listing 1.15. It's important to learn both for and while loops because you'll use them in different ways throughout your ChucK learning journey.

Note that if you forgot to add the increment line ❹ in the block of code of listing 1.18 the program would run forever, with the value of i and the sine frequency always equal to 20. In most programming languages, the notion of an infinite loop (a conditional loop that never reaches a termination condition) is to be avoided at all costs. But this is less so in ChucK, and you've already intentionally used an infinite loop, while (true) in listing 1.12, to make really interesting music. The buttons at the top of the miniAudicle to add, replace, and remove shreds and clear the VM allow you to create and use infinite loops without fear. One attractive power of ChucK is that it can keep running while you add, modify, replace, and layer code to make really interesting sounds and music.

1.6   *Using multiple oscillators in your music*

So far in your programs you've played single notes and melodies using one oscillator. Because music involves more than melody and rhythm, you may wonder, how do you control and play multiple oscillators at the same time? This is easy in ChucK, as shown in the next listing.

Listing 1.19   Using more than one oscillator

```
// connect two oscillators to the dac          Your usual sine wave.
SinOsc s => dac;          ←
SinOsc s2 => dac;         ←          ❶ Another sine wave oscillator.

// set their frequencies and gains          ❷ Sets frequency of first sine.
220 => s.freq;            ←
1030 => s2.freq;          ←          ❸ Sets frequency of second sine.
0.5 => s.gain;            ←
0.5 => s2.gain;                      ❹ Sets gains to 1/2.

second => now;            ←          Lets time pass so you can hear the sound.
```

One nice aspect of ChucK is that when you connect more than one sound source to something, such as the dac, the sounds are automatically added together. Sound engineers call this mixing. In this example, when you connect the second SinOsc, s2, to the dac ❶, it will automatically be mixed with the other SinOsc, and you'll hear the sound of both oscillators. You set their frequencies to be different ❷, ❸, so you can hear that there are two oscillators. If you set their frequencies to be exactly the same, you'd hear one sound louder, because mixing two identical signals yields a louder version of those signals. In ❹, you set their gains to be 0.5, because you want to avoid overloading the audio output. A good rule of thumb when mixing together a number of sources is to scale their gains so that they all add up to about 1.0. If you added yet another SinOsc, s3, to this mix, you'd want to set all their gains to 0.3, or maybe one to 0.5 and the other two to 0.25.

1.7   *A final example: "Twinkle" with oscillators, variables, logic, and control structures*

Now it's time to bring everything together to make a composition using all the tools you've learned in this chapter. The example program in listing 1.20 shows you how to do just that, enhancing our "Twinkle" example to make some harmonies and do some really interesting things with loops. First, you'll declare two oscillators, one sine ❶ and one triangle ❷. Then you'll declare variables to hold pitch ❸ (melody) and your note on volume ❹. Finally in your initial setup, you'll define a duration variable to hold your note length ❺.

Listing 1.20a   Putting "Twinkle" all together, with two waves!

```
// Twinkle, with two oscillators!          ❶ Sine wave oscillator.
SinOsc s => dac;          ←
```

```
TriOsc t => dac;          ←——②  Another oscillator (triangle wave).

// our main pitch variable
110.0 => float melody;    ←——③  Sets initial pitch.

// gain control for our triangle wave melody
0.3 => float onGain;      ←————————④  Gains for note on.

// we'll use this for our on and off times
0.3 :: second => dur myDur;   ←————————⑤  Notes duration.
```

Continuing with the two-oscillator "Twinkle" example (listing 1.20b), you first play only the triangle oscillator ❻, setting the sine oscillator gain to 0.0 ❼. You begin the song by sweeping the triangle wave pitch upward from 110.0 to 220.0 using a while loop ❽. You then move the frequency up by 1 Hz each time around the loop ❾ and do it very quickly, updating every 1/100 of a second ❿.

Listing 1.20b   Putting "Twinkle" all together (part B, Sweeping Upward)

```
// only play t at first, sweeping pitch upward
onGain => t.gain;                        ←————————❻  Turns on triangle oscillator.
0 => s.gain;          ❼ Turns on sine osc.
while (melody < 220.0) {  ←——❽  Loops until pitch reaches 220.
    melody => t.freq;
    1.0 +=> melody;   ❾ Steps up pitch by 1 Hz.
    0.01 :: second => now;   ←——❿  Every 1/100 of a second.
}
```

Once you've swept the pitch upward, you begin playing your melody and harmony (listing 1.20c) by turning on the sine oscillator ⓫, setting the frequency to 110.0 ⓬, and playing two notes on the triangle oscillator using a for loop ⓭. To play these notes, you turn on the triangle oscillator (set gain to a non-zero value) ⓮, wait for a time ⓯, and then turn it off ⓰ and wait again ⓱. This plays the first "Twinkle" of the song.

Listing 1.20c   Putting "Twinkle" all together, first "Twinkle"

```
// turn both on, set up the pitches       ⓫ Now turn on sin osc too.
0.7 => s.gain;
110 => s.freq;        ←——⓬ ...and initialize its pitch.

// play two notes, 1st "Twinkle"
for (0 => int i; i < 2; i++) {  ←——⓭  Use a for loop to play two notes.
    onGain => t.gain;    ⓮ Turn on triangle.
    myDur => now;        ←——⓯ Let note play.
    0 => t.gain;         ⓰ Turn off triangle.
    myDur => now;
                         ←——⓱  Silence to separate notes.
}
```

For the second "twinkle," you set new pitches ⑱ and play two more notes ⑲ the same way, as shown next.

Listing 1.20d Putting "Twinkle" all together , the second "twinkle"

```
// new pitches!
138.6 => s.freq;                    ⑱ Sets up next "twinkle" frequency.
1.5*melody => t.freq;

// two more notes, 2nd "twinkle"
for (0 => int i; i < 2; i++) {      ⑲ Plays that twice (for loop).
    onGain => t.gain;
    myDur => now;
    0 => t.gain;
    myDur => now;
}
```

As shown in the next listing, to play "little," you set more new pitches ⑳ and play two more notes ㉑, again the same way. For "star," you need to play it only once, so you set the pitches ㉒ and play the notes ㉓, this time for 1 second ㉔.

Listing 1.20e Putting "Twinkle" all together, playing "little" and "star"

```
// pitches for "little"
146.8 => s.freq;                    ⑳ Sets up next frequency for "little".
1.6837 * melody => t.freq;

// play 2 notes for "little"
for (0 => int i; i < 2; i++) {      ㉑ Plays that twice (for loop).
    onGain => t.gain;
    myDur => now;
    0 => t.gain;
    myDur => now;
}

// set up and play "star!"
138.6 => s.freq;                    ㉒ Sets up next frequency for "star".
1.5*melody => t.freq;

onGain => t.gain;                   ㉓ Plays that note...
second => now;                      ㉔ ...for a second.
```

To conclude your song, shown next, you use a for loop ㉕ to sweep the frequencies of both oscillators all the way down to zero. Again, you update the oscillator frequencies by just a little (down 1 Hz every time around the loop) but very often (every 1/10 of a second ㉖).

Listing 1.20f Putting "Twinkle" all together

```
// end by sweeping both oscillators down to zero
for (330 => int i; i > 0; i--) {    ㉕ Uses a for loop to sweep
    i => t.freq;                       down from 330 Hz.
    i*1.333 => s.freq;
```

```
    0.01 :: second => now;     ←——— 26 Updates every 1/100 of a second.
}
```

Note that in this one example, you've used almost all of what you've learned in this chapter. You used sine and triangle waves, int and float variables, for and while loops, conditional tests, math, and the now keyword with durations to control time. We introduced one new aspect of the for loop here: you can count downward (from a higher number to a lower number) in a for loop. In this case, you sweep your oscillators downward by initializing your integer variable i and then count down to zero by using the decrement operator (i--, which is the same as 1 -=> i, which is the same as i - 1 => i).

Exercise

Try changing the number of times the notes are played by changing the conditions of the for loops (try i < 3 or 4, or more). Try changing the increment ❾ (listing 1.20b) and decrement ㉕ amounts (listing 1.20f) for your pitch-sweeping loops. Experiment!

1.8   Summary

Whew! We've covered a lot up to this point:

- You learned a little about sound waves in general, which are fluctuations traveling through the air.
- We discussed sine waves and oscillators and the built-in ChucK oscillator types (SinOsc, SqrOsc, SawOsc, and TriOsc).
- You learned about variables and data types: int(eger), float(ing point), dur(ation), and time.
- We showed you how to manipulate time in ChucK. No sound is made unless you, as the programmer, advance time (by ChucKing durations to now).
- You studied logical conditions and reserved words such as if, else, &&&, true, and false.
- You experimented with looping structures, for and while, which allow you to control your programs and sound/music without having to type out every event literally.

Congratulate yourself, because you're now a programmer and a digital artist! But ChucK offers you so much more power and invites you to learn more about programming as well as sound, acoustics, human-computer interaction, and more. For example, how in the world did we come up with those numbers for the pitches we used in this chapter? ChucK can help with that! And you'll learn that right away in the next chapter.

So continue on to learn more about ChucK's built-in libraries (useful functions you can use) and arrays (ways to organize and manipulate your musical/artistic data).

Libraries: ChucK's built-in tools

2

This chapter covers

- Library functions (methods)
- The ChucK Standard library, conversion of units
- Standard library type conversion
- The ChucK Math library
- Math library random number generation and sine function
- Using library functions to make your music more expressive

Now that you have your feet wet and have learned the basics of how to use ChucK, and you've created your first set of compositions, it's time to learn how to make even more expressive music and sound. You'll also be learning how to make your programming easier as well as your programs more readable. In this chapter we introduce libraries, which are sets of tools built into ChucK that will help you accomplish these goals.

In almost all programming languages there are general sets of utility functions that come in the form of libraries. These libraries handle basic functions that programmers have to use at one point or another. You can look at these functions as tools, and those tools are kept in toolboxes (each library) according to their type.

The individual tools are sometimes called methods or functions, which you'll learn more about in chapter 4.

We'll look at two libraries, or collections of functions: the ChucK Standard library (called Std) and the ChucK Math library. By learning about the Standard library functions that convert numbers and units, you'll be able to control pitch and loudness much more easily. You'll also learn ways to convert between data types, from strings to numbers and back, for example. In the Math library, you'll learn more about generating and using random numbers and how to round floating-point numbers to integers. You'll also use some cool math procedures, like computing values of a sine function explicitly using the built-in sin() function of the Math library, to control synthesis parameters in musically interesting ways. Specifically, in section 2.3 you'll use a sin() function to smoothly pan a signal left and right in the stereo sound field.

2.1   *The Standard library: tools for pitch, loudness, and more*

Initially, we're going to focus on the Standard library's methods that allow you to do unit conversion (such as from Fahrenheit to Centigrade temperatures, or numbers representing the notes on a musical keyboard into frequencies for our oscillators), and show how these can help you in your compositions.

Remember from chapter 1, in order to play our "Twinkle" song you had to type in lots of numbers for pitches? Some of those, like 220 and 330, were easy. But how did we come up with those? Others, like 415.305 Hz, might have caused you to ask, "Where in the world did that come from?" Well, one of the most useful Standard library functions allows you to quickly figure out the frequency of any musical note. And the Standard library has loads of other useful functions, such as one that helps you compute a gain that's related to your perception of loudness, and other functions to convert between different data types. Armed with a couple of Standard library functions, you'll be able to play our "Twinkle" song much more easily, and your code will be more friendly and readable. So let's dig in and look at some of the functions in the Standard library!

2.1.1   *Deriving musical frequencies from MIDI note numbers*

The first method you're going to learn about is the MIDI note-to-frequency converter, known in ChucK as Std.mtof() (mtof stands for MIDI to frequency). As with variable names,

> ### The Musical Instrument Digital Interface
>
> The Musical Instrument Digital Interface (MIDI) was adopted in the 1980s by nearly all makers of electronic keyboard synthesizers, organs, and digital pianos and then by computer makers and others. MIDI lets electronic musical instruments, controllers, computers, computer music notation programs, and more communicate musical things to each other, using the same set of agreed-upon codes and numbers. For example, a computer can instruct a synthesizer to play a note by sending a NoteOn message or bend the pitch by sending a PitchBend message.

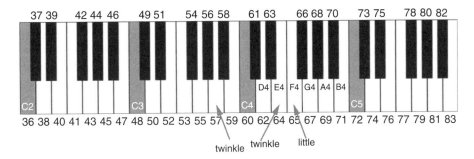

Figure 2.1   MIDI numbers labeled on a standard musical keyboard

you'll find that library functions almost always have meaningful, if somewhat cryptic at first, names. All Standard library functions are invoked by using the Std prefix (called a namespace), followed by a dot and the name of the method (function).

To convert from MIDI note numbers to frequencies, you first have to know how MIDI note numbers work. MIDI note numbers are integers that correspond to the individual keys of the musical keyboard, as shown in figure 2.1. The MIDI notes (keyboard keys) are designated by integer numbers ranging from 0 to 127 (which is the standard range for most MIDI parameters). The MIDI note numbers are arranged so that middle C (also called C4) is number 60, near the middle of the MIDI note range.

The standard piano-style musical keyboard

This type of black-and-white arranged keyboard is often called the piano keyboard or musical keyboard. This is helpful to differentiate it from other keyboards, like the QWERTY computer keyboard that you type on.

Some manufacturers decided that middle C should be C3, thus MIDI #48, so you might encounter octave differences between various devices and software programs. We're going to go with the music-theory-correct middle C = C4 = 60.

MIDI note numbers, combined with the Std.mtof() function, make it easier to create melodies, play scales, and do other musical tasks. To try it out, type in and run this code:

```
<<< Std.mtof(57) >>>;
```

And you should see printed in the Console Monitor window

```
220.000000 :(float)
```

which is the frequency of your first "Twinkle" note!

FUNCTIONS: ARGUMENTS AND RETURN VALUES   The number in the parentheses (57 in this case) is called the argument to the function. Using a function is referred to as invoking or calling the function. The value that results from using the function is called the return value.

Now try typing in

```
<<< Std.mtof(60), Std.mtof(62), Std.mtof(64), Std.mtof(65), Std.mtof(67) >>>;
```

which should yield in the Console window

```
261.625565    293.664768    329.627557    349.228231    391.995436
```

These are the frequencies of the first five notes of a musical C scale: C, D, E, F, G. Looking back at the keyboard of figure 2.1, you can see that if you count every key (both white and black), starting with 60 at C4, the white keys of the C scale are associated with the numbers 60, 62, 64, 65, and 67.

ChucK coding note

Just as with much of computer programming, there are multiple ways to achieve the same result. So ChucK functions can be used in two different ways: by calling with parentheses and an argument (in this case 64) such as

```
<<< Std.mtof(64) >>>;
```

or by ChucKing the argument to the function

```
<<< 64 => Std.mtof >>>;
```

These will do the same thing and yield the same result (return value).

Now, let's use a for loop to play lots of notes using the Std.mtof function. The code in listing 2.1 shows a program in which you play the entire chromatic scale (every note on the musical keyboard, both white and black) using a Triangle Wave oscillator (TriOsc). You do this by creating a for loop that goes from 0 to 127 (covering every MIDI note), which gets stored in variable i. Notice that variable i gets used as the input (sometimes called the argument to the function) into Std.mtof() ❶. So on the first time through the for loop, MIDI note 0 is converted to 8.175799 Hz., which is a C note that's too low to hear, five octaves below middle C (also called C_{-1}).

Listing 2.1   Playing a chromatic scale using Std.mtof()

```
// sound chain
TriOsc t => dac;
0.4 => t.gain;

// loop                                          ❶ Use Std.mtof
for (0 => int i; i < 127; i++)                      to convert
{                                                   note number
    Std.mtof(i) => float Hz; // MIDI to Hertz frequency   to frequency
    <<< i, Hz >>>; // print out result
    Hz => t.freq; // update frequency    ❷ Set oscillator frequency to Hz
    200::ms => now; // advance time
}
```

On the second iteration, MIDI note 1 is converted to 8.661957 Hz. Each time around the loop, the program prints the corresponding MIDI note value and converted frequency value in Hertz. The frequency value is ChucKed to the oscillator t.freq ❷ on each iteration so you can hear the scale. On the third iteration, MIDI note 2 becomes 9.177024 Hz. You won't be able to hear the first many low notes, because they're too low in frequency for your speakers to reproduce. Even when you begin to hear or feel the sound, your ears won't perceive the very low frequencies as having pitch.

> **TRY THIS** Run the code in listing 2.1 a number of times, and try to determine the lowest frequency that you can hear. Try it both with speakers and with headphones. At what frequency do you really start to hear pitches versus just feeling that there's sound? The human ear is more sensitive to some frequency ranges than others. Which frequency sounds the loudest to you?

> **TRY THIS** Rewrite the for loop to play the chromatic scale, using a while loop instead. Remember to increment that counter inside the loop!

As you can imagine, the Std.mtof() method is going to play a large role in creating melodies from now on. It's also possible to go the other direction and use the Std.ftom() method to convert frequency to MIDI notes. This could be useful if you have some particular frequency and want to know the musical note closest to that, or if you're using an external synthesizer or other software or hardware that accepts MIDI notes. You'll learn more about how to send MIDI notes to synthesizers and other things connected to your computer in chapter 11.

> **NOTE FOR MUSICIANS** Std.mtof() can also take in floating-point values to help you with microtonal scales and pitches, so Std.mtof(60.5) gives you a quarter tone between C and C#.

The Standard library also has functions (also called methods) to convert between units of gain, level, volume, loudness, and power—all terms that relate to levels, some perceptual and some physical, mathematical, or engineering in nature. These are covered in detail in appendix B, "Library functions: Std, Math, other."

2.1.2 *Converting between data types: float to int*

The next Standard library method will help you convert from floating-point numbers to integers. When you first realized you needed floating-point numbers to accurately express frequencies and gains, you might have typed in something that yielded an error because of trying to store a float into an int. The simplest example of that is

```
220.0 => int myFreq;
```

which yields an error printed to the Console Monitor window:

```
line(1): cannot resolve operator '=>' on types 'float' and 'int'...
```

This is just ChucK protecting you in a way, telling you that something might be lost in the conversion from floating point to integer. An example of that would be

```
220.5 => int myInt;
```

where the .5 part would be thrown away and you might not realize it. Thus, ChucK refuses to do it and prints an error. ChucK as a language is strongly typed, meaning that the data types are held relatively pure, and converting from one to the other can require a little work on your part. Interestingly, storing an int into a float requires no work, because no data could be lost in the process. So

```
220 => int myFreq;
myFreq => float myFloatFreq;
```

works just fine, because 220 gets changed into 220.0, no data is lost, and precision is actually gained, for use later.

But going the other way, from float to int, requires what's called a *conversion* or *type cast*, which means taking data of one type and casting it in the best way possible to another data type. The most common one you'll need as a ChucK programmer is going from float to int, which is accomplished using Std.ftoi (float to integer), in this way:

```
220.5 => Std.ftoi => int myFreq;    (or Std.ftoi(220.5) => int myFreq; )
```

Note that in this case, the fractional part is truncated (thrown away), yielding 220. Even if you specified

```
Std.ftoi(220.999999999) => myFreq;
```

you'd still get 220, because any fractional part is thrown away.

2.1.3 Obtaining an int from a number expressed as text

Another example of data type conversion might be if you had a string variable that held the string "128.7" but you wanted to use it as a float to set a frequency or something else. Many programs accept user input in the form of information typed into the computer, and ChucK can also read data from files on your computer, some of which might contain text. Fortunately, there are also Std library methods for converting strings (known sometimes as ASCII, that's where the *a* in *atoi* comes from) to and from integers and floating points. So you can do this using Std.atoi("128.7");, as shown in table 2.1.

Table 2.1   ChucK Std library functions to convert string, float, and int data types

Method	Output	Description
Std.atoi(string value)	int	Converts ASCII (string) to integer
Std.atof(string value)	float	Converts ASCII (string) to float
Std.itoa(int value)	string	Converts integer to ASCII (string)
Std.ftoa(float value)	string	Converts float to ASCII (string)

There are more useful functions in the Std library, all of which are listed and described in appendix B, including ones to take the absolute value of numbers (absolute value turns negative numbers into positive ones, leaving positive numbers alone) and return the sign, negative or positive, of numbers.

Standard isn't the only library available in ChucK, so let's leave it for now and turn to another super-useful library, called Math.

2.2 *The ChucK Math library*

Remember how cool it was when you used `Math.random()` to set the frequencies and durations of notes in an infinite loop? In the next few subsections, we'll be diving into another library, known as Math, which has a large number of utility functions that will allow you to make your programs much more powerful and expressive.

2.2.1 *Math library random functions*

The first set of Math library methods is used for generating random numbers. You used these in chapter 1 to play an infinite stream of notes of random frequencies and durations, so here we'll look into exactly how those functions work. Random numbers are very useful in making digital art. It's quite tedious for a programmer to set every single parameter value over time when exploring a sound with many parameters, for example. But using random functions allows you to hand such tasks over to the computer, while you listen for the parts you like, just as you did with the random notes in chapter 1.

Although ChucK isn't really a gaming language (but many people have written games in it), let's say you want to simulate the rolling of a single die. You'd need some way of randomly generating a number that can be 1, 2, 3, 4, 5, or 6. In the example in listing 2.2, you use the Math library to generate random integers between 1 and 6 using the `Math.random2()` method. This program runs forever (the `while (true)` condition is always true) and generates a random number every half second. The 2 on `random2` means you're going to specify two numbers, a minimum and a maximum, between which the function will generate random numbers. The specified numbers are also allowed, so in this case 1 and 6 will appear with equal probability for all integers 1 through 6.

Listing 2.2 Random integer generation using the Math library

```
// random integer number generation
// simulates the roll of a die
while (true)
{
    <<< "Dice Roll =", Math.random2(1,6) >>>;
    second / 2 => now;
}
```

The Math library has four ways of creating random numbers, as shown in table 2.2. Integers are made with the `Math.random2()` and `Math.random()` methods.

Table 2.2 Chuck Math library functions to create random numbers

Method	Output	Description
`Math.random()`	`int`	Generates random integer between 0 and `Math.RANDOM_MAX`
`Math.random2(int min, int max)`	`int`	Generates random integer in the range [min, max]
`Math.randomf()`	`float`	Generates random floating point number in the range [0, 1]
`Math.random2f(float min, float max)`	`float`	Generates random floating point number in the range [min, max]

Floating-point random numbers are created using `Math.randomf()`, which gives a number in the range 0.0 to 1.0, and `Math.random2f()`, which generates random floats in a range. Again, you as the programmer get to specify the minimum and maximum values.

> **NOTE** `Math.random()` isn't used very often, but it's built into ChucK to be more compatible with other programming languages.

The program in listing 2.3 demonstrates how random numbers can be used in the composition process. As you can see, you set up a for loop to play a total of 16 notes ❶. In each step of the loop, a random integer between 48 and 72 is created and stored in integer variable myNote ❷, and a random floating-point number between 0.05 and 0.9 is generated and stored in the float variable myGain ❸. After printing both out to the console, myNote is used to set the frequency of oscillator s via your old friend Std.mtof(), and myGain is used to set the volume. ❹ Thus, a new MIDI note (frequency) ❺ and volume are generated every fifth of a second ❻, making a composition that randomly generates notes. Although this generates no known melody, we think you'll agree that it sounds somewhat musical, because of the note-by-note changes in volume (called accents by musicians and composers) and the ever-changing frequencies. Run it a few times, and you'll hear that the notes and volumes generated are different each time. The only thing that's guaranteed is that there will be exactly 16 notes.

Listing 2.3 Random music using the Math Library

```
// Some random square wave music!        Makes a SinOsc to play
SqrOsc s => dac;                         your random notes.

for (0 => int i; i < 16; i++)      ❶ for loop plays 16 notes.
{
    Math.random2(48,72) => int myNote;      ❷ Random integer note
    Math.random2f(0.05,0.9) => float myGain;   number (C3–C5).
    <<< myNote, myGain >>>;              ❹ Prints current note and gain.
    Std.mtof(myNote) => s.freq;
    myGain => s.gain;                   ❺ Sets oscillator frequency and gain.
    0.2 :: second => now;
}
```

Random gain from .05 to .9. ❸

Lets each note sound for 1/5 second. ❻

Random number generators allow you to write musical programs that never sound exactly the same, but you can do so in a fairly controllable way, which can be an exciting technique as a modern composer. There's a way to make sure that a sequence of random numbers is always the same but different from all other such sequences. Say you don't want to write out what the notes are specifically, and you want them to be randomly generated, but you want the composition to be the same every time you play it. How do you accomplish this?

The key to controlling random number generation, along with specifying the range, is generating a seed, which the random number generator uses to start the sequence of random numbers it will generate from then on. The seed usually is created using something that's constantly changing, like your computer's system clock. Thus, every time you run the program of listing 2.3, a different seed is generated and the program generates a completely new set of notes and volumes. But starting with the same seed would ensure that the sequence of random numbers would be exactly the same across different executions of the same program. So how can you set the seed yourself? Type in the following new line of code and insert it into listing 2.3, right before the for loop at ❶:

```
Math.srandom(134); // set seed
```

The number 134 in this example was chosen arbitrarily. Try playing around with the seed value. Change it to 133 and see what happens. Contrary to what you might think, changing the seed just a little bit doesn't change the sequence just a little bit. Each seed value generates a completely new sequence, basically unrelated to all others.

> **TRY THIS** Change the seed value in Math.srandom to a few different numbers, and notice what it does to your composition. You should hear a particular pattern for any single seed value but a different pattern for each seed. Also change the numbers in the specified range where you set the note number (❷ in listing 2.3). For example, increase the higher number, and note that you begin to hear occasional higher notes than before.

2.2.2 Rounding numbers: being more fair about float-to-int conversion

Now you've begun to see the power of the Math library, and there are many more useful tools in it. Remember when you cast your floats to integers, and the fractional parts were lost due to truncation? Remember that 220.9999 got truncated to 220, which doesn't seem fair. The solution is to round, meaning that any fractional part greater than or equal to 0.5 gets rounded up, and any less than that gets rounded down (truncated). Math provides a function called round, which takes care of that. Try it with this line:

```
<<< Math.round(220.501), Math.round(220.49) >>>;
```

There are other Math functions, including logs, exponents, and trigonometry (sine, cosine, and tangent). If you're familiar with such functions, you should find the list of them in appendix B familiar. You'll be using some of them in later chapters as you get to more advanced programming and signal-processing techniques.

2.3 Stereo and panning

Let's take a break from math (but a very brief one, because you're going to use a Math function pretty soon) to look at a fun audio technique known as *panning*. Panning comes from the word *panorama*, meaning a "view of a region surrounding an observer." In audio, panning is a way audio mixers place sound in the stereo sound field between the left and right speakers. In modern music/sound production, many of the sound sources are recorded on

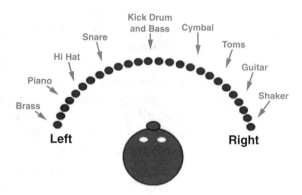

Figure 2.2 **Panning is used to position the instruments in a stereo sound field.**

different channels and often at different times and locations. The mixer (both the device called a mixer and the person operating that device, also called a mixer) has to blend things to artificially create a sense of space. As shown in figure 2.2, when mixing a song, audio engineers often place certain instruments in discrete regions (for example, horns to the left and guitar more to the right).

We're going to introduce three methods (shown in listings 2.4, 2.5, and 2.6) you can use to achieve panning in ChucK, which will give you more parameters to compose with. The first example shows two oscillators, one being hard panned to the left speaker and the other to the right speaker (or left and right ear headphone elements) using dac.left ❶ and dac.right ❷. Yep! dac has some extra functions hidden inside, including hooking to different audio channels. When you play this example, you'll hear two sine tones that are different in pitch ❸, ❹ on either side of your stereo field (one sine left and one right).

Listing 2.4 Using dac.left and dac.right to connect to left and right speakers

```
// two sine waves in stereo
SinOsc s => dac.left;          ❶ Connects one SinOsc to the left channel...
SinOsc t => dac.right;         ❷ ...and another to the right channel.

// set frequencies
220 => s.freq;                 ❸ Sets the frequency of the left osc...
361 => t.freq;                 ❹ ...and sets the right osc to a different frequency.

// advance time
second => now;
```

The second technique for panning is similar, but it can be used to do multichannel audio (like the 5.1 surround sound in movie theaters and in many home theater/game systems). If you have a setup in your studio with more than two speakers, and you have a multichannel sound card or external interface that supports more than two channels, then you can use the dac.chan() method to set what you want to play in each speaker. The next listing shows the multichannel connection of four oscillators.

Listing 2.5 Using dac.chan() to connect to multiple speakers

```
SinOsc s0 => dac.chan(0);
SinOsc s1 => dac.chan(1);
SinOsc s2 => dac.chan(2);
SinOsc s3 => dac.chan(3);
```

The third panning method is the one we like the most, because it allows us to use our programming skills and the power of ChucK to do things we generally can't do in commercial audio programs.

There's a cool UGen object called Pan2, which you can insert into the audio signal chain (between your SinOsc source and the dac), as shown in listing 2.6. We've named this object p, and you connect it to the dac (audio output) **1**. The nice thing about connecting Pan2 to dac is that ChucK knows that they're stereo, so the two outputs of Pan2 automatically get connected to dac.left and dac.right. Panning for the Pan2 object is controlled with a floating-point number from –1.0 (left) to 1.0 (right), using the .pan method. As you can see in the following listing, you set variable panPosition to –1.0 (leftmost) **2**. The panning position is set by updating p.pan with the panPosition current value. **4** You slowly increase that variable (rightward) by .01 **5** until it gets to 1.0 **3**. You can hear this example well with headphones.

Listing 2.6 Using a Pan2 object to connect a SinOsc to stereo dac output

```
// panning example
SinOsc s => Pan2 p => dac;              ← 1 Runs the oscillator through a Pan2 object

// initialize pan position
-1.0 => float panPosition;             ← 2 Sets initial pan to hard left...

// loop to vary panning
while (panPosition < 1.0) {            ← 3 ...until panPosition hits hard right.
    panPosition => p.pan;
    <<< panPosition >>>;               ← 4 Sets new pan position...
    panPosition + 0.01 => panPosition; ← 5 ...and increments it a little.
    10 :: ms => now;
}
```

To make panning even more interesting, we're going to return to the Math library and look at another example using the Pan2 object with a new sound-producing object called Noise. The Noise object generates white noise (random values at every point in time and equal energy at every frequency), which is really close to the "sss" sound from "see" of figure 1.1.

So you connect the `Noise` source n to the `Pan2` panning object to the *dac*. In an infinite `while` loop, you use another new method called `Math.sin()`. This method uses a sine function to create parameters for the panning object. Notice how this sounds. The white noise moves between left and right, back and forth, in the pattern of a sine wave, forever. This can be a powerful tool for making expressive compositions.

Listing 2.7   Automatic panning using `Pan2` and the `Math.sin()` function

```
//sound chain: white noise to pan2 to dac
Noise n => Pan2 p => dac;

//noise can sound quite loud
0.2 => n.gain;

// infinite loop
while (true)
{
    //oscillate pan between 1.0 and -1.0
    Math.sin(now/second) => p.pan;
    //do it pretty often, to make it smooth
    ms => now;
}
```

There are many other trigonometry-based mathematical functions in the Math library, which are listed along with all other Std and Math library functions in appendix B. What's the difference between `Math.sin()` and the `SinOsc` object? The `SinOsc` object is a sound-producing UGen type of object. As such, `SinOsc` automatically produces a sine waveform when connected to the *dac*, but `Math.sin()` requires you to call it with an argument, and then it returns a specific point within a sine wave. Math library functions are for computing math and also for parameters, like controlling `.pan` or `.gain` methods. Compositional uses of Math functions can include adding vibrato or even generating pitches.

Now that you've acquired a lot of new tools, the functions of the Std. and Math libraries, you should use them to make some music. So let's do just that

2.4   *Example: random music with two voices and panning*

To wrap up this chapter, you'll make a random music generator using a lot of the cool library methods we've talked about. For this example, you'll have one solo voice, an oscillator playing up and down the MIDI keyboard randomly, and you'll have an accompaniment voice randomly stick on notes that the solo voice plays but an octave lower. And you'll pan your melody randomly, using the Math library. So let's get to it!

As shown in listing 2.8, you first declare and add panning to your melody oscillator using the `Pan2` object ❶. Next, you make another oscillator for harmony and connect it to the *dac* ❷. Of course, the *dac* takes care of mixing these sources together automatically.

Then you make gain variables to use for turning your notes on and off ❸. As a last setup step, you declare a MIDI note number for your melody to start on ❹.

Listing 2.8 Two-part random walk music with panning

```
// 2-part Random Music with Panning
// by ChucK Team, September 25, 2020          ❶ SinOsc through
                                                Pan2 so it can
                                                move around       ❷ TriOsc fixed at
// two oscillators, melody and harmony                               center location
SinOsc s => Pan2 mpan => dac;
TriOsc t => dac;

// we will use these to separate notes later       ← Float variables
0.5 => t.gain;                                         to control your
0.5 => float onGain;                               ❸ note gains
0.0 => float offGain;

72 => int melodyNote;                              ← Int variable to control
                                                   ❹ your melody
while (true)
{
    // set melody pitch somewhat randomly, with limits
    Math.random2(-3,3) +=> melodyNote;
                                                   ← Randomly
    if (melodyNote < 60)                              changes melody
    {                                              ❺ up, down, or not
        60 => melodyNote;
    }
    if (melodyNote > 84)
    {
        84 => melodyNote;                          ❽ Sets solo SinOsc
    }                                                 pitch
    Std.mtof(melodyNote) => s.freq;                ←

    // melody has a random pan for each note
    Math.random2f(-1.0,1.0) => mpan.pan;

    // On a "dice roll," change harmony note
    if (Math.random2(1,6) == 1)
    {
        Std.mtof(melodyNote-12) => t.freq;         ←
    }                                                 Randomly sticks
                                                   ❾ TriOsc on a pitch
    // Pick one of three random durations
    Math.random2(1,3)*0.2 => float myDur;

    // note on time is 80% of duration
    onGain => s.gain;
    (myDur*0.8)::second => now;

    // space between notes is 20% of array duration
    offGain => s.gain;
    (myDur*0.2)::second => now;
}
```

Lower limit on melody ❻

Upper limit on melody ❼

In the infinite while loop block, you randomly increase or decrease your MIDI melody note by between -3 and +3 notes (keys on the MIDI keyboard) ❺. This is called a *random walk*, where rather than setting the note itself to a random number, you randomly walk up or down the keyboard (or stay still if the random number is 0). To make sure you don't walk too far left or right, thus playing notes that are too low or too high in pitch, you test the new MIDI note to make sure it's between middle C ❻ and two octaves above that ❼. Once you've set your new note, you use `Std.mtof` to turn that into a pitch for your `SinOsc` ❽. You also set a random panning for your melody (via `Pan2`) between left (–1.0) and right (1.0).

Next, on a dice roll (number between 1 and 6 inclusive), you decide whether to change the pitch of your harmony `TriOsc` ❾. So there's a one-in-six chance of it changing. If it does change, it's given the same pitch as your melody oscillator but one octave lower (+/-12 in MIDI notes is up or down one octave).

Finally, you compute a random duration of either 0.2, 0.4, or 0.6 seconds (1, 2, or 3 times 0.2) for your melody note to last before the loop runs again. You turn on your melody for 80% of that time and turn it off for 20%. Then the loop executes again, forever, until you click Remove Shred or Remove All Shreds.

> **TRY THIS** Add a call to `Math.srandom()` to seed the random number generator before the main `while` loop. Change the seed value a few times, noting that each number generates a different song but the same each time you run it with the same seed. Find a seed that generates your new, original, favorite song.

2.5 *Summary*

Wow, huh? You just made a pretty musical-sounding composition, but you chose to leave most of the actual decisions about the notes and durations and the synchronization of the melody and harmony completely up to the computer. You were able to accomplish this by using almost all of the things you've learned so far:

- Using Standard library functions like `Std.mtof`
- Converting between `int`s and `float`s (and back) and rounding
- Using Math library functions like `Math.random`
- Panning using the `Pan2` UGen
- Making random music and controlling the randomness (range and seed)

You'll do a lot more with library functions in the future, and you'll learn how to write your own functions from scratch (chapter 5).

The next chapter will dive into arrays, which are collections of data that you can use to organize your notes, pitches, durations, parameters, even strings of text, or whatever. Once you know how to make and use those, you'll be able to code whole songs much more easily, with much less typing, and also make your programs even more readable for you and others.

Arrays: arranging and accessing your compositional data

3

This chapter covers

- Declaring and initializing arrays
- Retrieving and modifying data in arrays
- Storing different types of data in arrays
- Using arrays to control musical parameters for a song

Now that you've been introduced to the power of the Standard library and Math utilities, you're going to learn one more important thing in order to make the coding of your melodies and compositions much easier and more expressive and to allow you to create longer songs without excessive typing. This chapter covers arrays, which are super-powerful mechanisms that allow you to make collections of data that you can use for all sorts of things. Arrays are fundamental to how almost all computer programs work. They're how email, pictures, sound/music files, and everything else get stored and accessed inside computers, smartphones, tablets, and on the web.

An *array* is a collection of data stored in memory. For composer-programmers, one use for arrays is to store lists of musical parameters that you want to use to control your songs over time, such as musical pitches (or MIDI note numbers), volumes, times, and/or durations. Another use for arrays is to store lists of character strings such as song lyrics. Arrays can store any type of data, and you can even make arrays of unit generators like SinOsc or Noise, which you'll do in the next chapter.

So far you've generated melodies by using loops to increase or decrease frequencies or pitches, or you've made long programs that specify each note you want, line by line. Wouldn't it be great if you could make a list of the notes you want to play at the beginning of the program? What if you could somehow store your compositional parameters in memory, making it easier to write whole songs? That's exactly what arrays allow you to do.

3.1   *Declaring and storing data in arrays*

Here you'll begin to learn how to play the notes of our "Twinkle" song by storing all of them in a single array. In this case, you'll store your melody as a list of MIDI note numbers. To start out, let's visualize what an array is conceptually.

In figure 3.1 you see seven boxes containing integers. These boxes are seven pieces of memory attached to your array. Inside the boxes are integer numbers; in this case they represent the MIDI notes of our "Twinkle" melody. Beneath each box, you see numbers that are the indices to the boxes. Notice that the index starts at 0. All arrays start at index 0. The array at index 3 will give you the data in that box, in this case MIDI note number 64, the fourth note of "Twinkle."

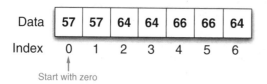

Figure 3.1   **An array stores data in individual locations, accessed by an index number.**

Now let's see how to represent this concept in code. You represent an array with square brackets ([]), with the number in the square brackets being the number of elements in the array. In this case there are seven MIDI notes, so you declare array *a* as int a[7] ❶ in the following listing. Notice that the array is of type integer (you can make arrays of any type, as you'll see later on). Next, you have to store your melody into the array. You do this by putting each integer into its own location in the array, one at a time, as shown in the lines between ❷ and ❸.

Listing 3.1   Declaring and filling an array of integers the long way

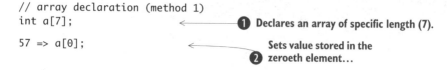

```
57 => a[1];
64 => a[2];                              ...and all locations...
64 => a[3];
66 => a[4];
66 => a[5];
64 => a[6];         ◄——— ❸ ...up to and including the last element.

<<< a[0], a[1], a[2], a[3], a[4], a[5], a[6] >>>;
```

You now have your MIDI notes in the array, but this took way too many lines of code. Isn't there a shortcut? Of course there is! As shown in listing 3.2, you can store your MIDI notes all on one line of code. Notice that you use a new operator, @=>, which is a special ChucK operator used to store all of the data into your array *a*, all at once. @=> is called the at-ChucK operator or the explicit assignment operator. You can use this operator to copy other objects in ChucK, but by far the most common use is for copying lists of elements into arrays.

> **Listing 3.2 Declare and initialize an array all at once**

```
[57, 57, 64, 64, 66, 66, 64] @=> int a[];

<<< a[0], a[1], a[2], a[3], a[4], a[5], a[6] >>>;
```

The other part of this new way of declaring and initializing an array is that now your declaration of array *a* doesn't have the preassigned [7] as the number of elements. This is part of what the @=> operator allows you to do. The *a* points to the beginning of your list of MIDI notes, but the size needn't be determined during declaration. ChucK figures this out for you, making it easy to add and subtract notes to make the melody longer or shorter by typing extra numbers into the list, without having to count how many notes you have each time.

3.2 *Reading and modifying array data*

Now you know a couple of ways to put data into an array: one element at a time or by copying a list through @=>, the at-ChucK operator. But how do you retrieve this data? Listing 3.3 shows how this is done. Here you read one element of the array in line ❶ and print the result in ❷. But what does this print? Think about it. Did you say 57? Remember that the index starts at 0! So the answer is really 64 (the third item in the array).

> **STARTING WITH ZERO** You might have been wondering why this book began with chapter 0 rather than chapter 1. That's because we're computer scientists, and we wanted to get you thinking right off the bat about things like array indices starting with zero rather than one. Interesting fact: many computer science buildings at universities number the ground floor as floor zero.

What if you want to change your melody from within your program? No problem; an array contains variables, so you can change what's in the array at any time by setting a new integer into the array a[2] location (or any location) ❸.

Listing 3.3   Accessing (reading and writing) data in an array

```
// declare and initialize an array
[57, 57, 64, 64, 66, 66, 64] @=> int a[];

// array look up by index                    ❶ Looks up note in array
a[2] => int myNote;                              by integer index

// print it out to check
<<< myNote >>>;                              ❷ Prints it

// want to change data?  no problem! (print too)
61 => a[2];
<<< myNote, a[2] >>>;                        Changes array element
                                          ❸ value at index
```

This code would print in the Console window

```
64 :(int)
64 61
```

This output reflects the fact that you changed the data in that one element of your array (to 61), but the data you previously read from there and stored into the myNote variable is unchanged (still 64). The myNote variable is stored separately from the array data, so you can change one without affecting the other at all.

You might be wondering by now, "What if I want to change the size of the array after I've declared it?" It's possible to do that, as described in detail in appendix B, section B.6. But that's a bit advanced for the task at hand, so we'll move on.

3.3   *Using array data to play a melody*

You know how to make and fill arrays, so now you can finally use your array to control sound, playing the melody you've stored. You start out in listing 3.4 by declaring and connecting a SqrOsc as the source of your audio signal chain ❶. Then you set up some gains to turn your notes on and off (0.7 for on and 0.0 for off) ❷. Next you declare and initialize an array just as you did before, but this time it has more data (more notes of your song!) ❸.

Now it's time for a new method: a.cap() (short for capacity), which tells you the total size of array a[]. In this case the size is 14. You can then use that number in a for loop to cycle through every element in array a[]. You print the value of index i and then the contents of the array at that index a[i] ❹. Notice that when running the code, it matches the array picture from figure 3.1.

Everything comes together musically when your MIDI note from array a[i] is converted to frequency with the Std.mtof() method ❺. After that, it's the standard means of playing notes: set the gain to something non-zero ❻, advance time ❼, and turn the note off for a while ❽ before going back to play the next note. This ends when i reaches 14 and there are no more notes to play.

Listing 3.4   Playing a melody stored in an array

```
// Let's Twinkle with a square wave
SqrOsc s => dac;                                    ❶ Square wave oscillator for melody

// gains to separate our notes
0.7 => float onGain;                    ❷ Note on/off gains
0.0 => float offGain;
                                                    ❸ Array of MIDI notes
// declare and initialize array of MIDI notes          (int) for melody
[57,57,64,64,66,66,64,62,62,61,61,59,59,57] @=> int a[];

// loop for length of array
for (0 => int i; i < a.cap(); i++)
{                                       ❹ Prints index and
                                            array note
    <<< i, a[i] >>>;

// set frequency and gain to turn on our note
    Std.mtof(a[i]) => s.freq;                       ❺ Sets pitch for melody notes
Note on ❻ ──>  onGain => s.gain;
    0.3::second => now;                             ❼ Duration for note on

// turn off our note to separate from the next
Note off ❽ ──>  offGain => s.gain;
    0.2::second => now;
}
```

3.4   *Storing other types of data in arrays*

You might have noted that the version of "Twinkle" produced by listing 3.4 is nearly complete, except for some problems with timing. For example, the notes corresponding with "star" and "are" should be longer than the others. Next, you're going to learn that you can store pretty much any type of data in arrays, including `ints`, `floats`, `strings`, and even durations.

3.4.1   *Using an array to store durations*

The "Twinkle" melody requires some notes to be longer than others. Those who write and read music call the note durations associated with "little" *quarter notes* and the longer note durations ("star") *half notes*. These are shown in musical notation in figure 3.2.

The reason quarter notes are called that is because there are four of them per musical *measure*; likewise, there are two half notes, twice as long, per measure.

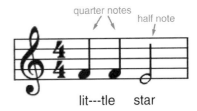

Figure 3.2   **Quarter notes and a half note denote the different durations for our "Twinkle" song.**

To account for this in your code, you could change your program to use logic, so that it holds those two notes longer. If you replace line ❼ in listing 3.4 with the `if/else` statement shown in listing 3.5, then the two notes will be held twice as long. The `noteOff` time of 0.2 seconds is the same in all cases. This time, added to a `noteOn` time of 0.8 seconds ❶, give you half notes of one second. And the 0.3 second noteOn time plus a 0.2 second noteOff gives you the desired 0.5 second quarter notes ❷. Try it and you'll hear the difference!

Listing 3.5   New logic to control note durations

```
if (i==6 || i==13)
{
    0.8::second => now;          ⟵  ❶ Some notes are longer
}
else
{
    0.3::second => now;          ⟵  ❷ The rest are shorter
}
```

We've also said that arrays can store any type of data, which is really powerful for making music or any kind of programming in general. If you think of all the things you'd like to manipulate in order to make a proper song, you might come up with pitch, duration, loudness, and other things (even lyrics!). You could store any or all of those in arrays.

Let's store your note durations in an array, as shown in listing 3.6. Here you perform the very same setup as in listing 3.4. You first declare and connect the square wave oscillator ❶. Then you declare and initialize the gains for noteOn and noteOff ❷ and create your array of MIDI notes ❸ (now called myNotes, remembering what you learned about meaningful names for variables). You declare two variables of type duration, one for quarter notes called q ❹ and one for half notes called h ❺. You then use those shorthand variable names to declare and initialize an array of durations called myDurs ❻.

Once all that has been declared, you can drop into a for loop to play your song, accessing the note array the same way ❽, turning each note on by using the onGain variable you declared ❾. But now you can use your myDurs array to play each note for the correct duration by ChucKing the proper duration to now ❿. After time passes, you turn each note off ⓫ and ChucK your off-time duration to now. You repeat that for each note; then the loop ends when your counter variable i reaches the size of your note array myNotes.cap() ❼.

Listing 3.6   Storing durations in an array

```
//  Let's Twinkle with a square wave
SqrOsc s => dac;                    ⟵  ❶ Square wave oscillator for melody

// gains to separate our notes
0.7 => float onGain;                ⟵  ❷ Note on/off gains
0.0 => float offGain;
                                                                ❸ Array of
// declare and initialize array of MIDI notes                     MIDI notes
[57,57,64,64,66,66,64,62,62,61,61,59,59,57] @=> int myNotes[];  ⟵ (int) for
                                                                   melody
```

```
// quarter note and half note durations          4  Duration for quarter notes
0.3 :: second => dur q;                  ←
0.8 :: second => dur h;                  ·········  5  Duration for half notes
[q, q, q, q, q, q, h, q, q, q, q, q, q, h] @=> dur myDurs[];   ←   Array of
                                                                   durations
// loop for length of array                                        for melody
for (0 => int i; i < myNotes.cap(); i++)  ←                     6  notes
{                                             For loop iterates over
                                           7  length of note array

    // set frequency and gain to turn on our note
    Std.mtof(myNotes[i]) => s.freq;        ←————  8  Sets pitch for melody notes
    onGain => s.gain;
    myDurs[i] => now;                      ←                  For duration stored
                                                          10  in array for that note
    // turn off our note to separate from the next
    offGain => s.gain;
    0.2::second => now;
}
```

Note on ⑨ → `onGain => s.gain;`

Note off ⑪ → `offGain => s.gain;`

3.4.2   *Arrays of strings: text can be musical too*

Now that you're on a roll with storing things in arrays, let's put some words into an array of strings. Listing 3.7 shows just how to do this. As with your other arrays, you use the same square brackets [...] to hold your list of strings ❶. You separate each element by commas and use the @=> copy form of the ChucK operator ❷ to store that list into a newly declared array of type string, which you call words[] ❸. Note here that each element can have a different length as an individual string ("Twin" versus "kle"), and ChucK just figures it all out for you, allocating just the right amount of storage to hold what you've declared.

> **Extending code across lines**
>
> Note here that you used a feature of ChucK coding wherein a single line of code can extend across multiple lines of text. The semicolon is what terminates an executable line of code in ChucK, so you can put half of your list of words, notes, and whatever on one line and the other half on the other (or even extend over many lines), and ChucK puts it all together when it finds the first semicolon.

Listing 3.7   An array of strings (the "Twinkle" lyrics)

```
// make an array to hold words and syllables            1  Declare and initialize
["Twin","kle","twin","kle","lit","tle","star,",           array of strings for lyrics.
  "how", "I","won","der","what","you","are."] @=> string words[];   ←
```

❷ Object copy form of ChucK operator.

❸ ChucK figures out how big to create words[] array.

3.5 *Example: a song with melody, harmony, and lyrics!*

To wrap up this chapter, we want to give you a more fleshed-out example of how to make a whole composition using all the things we've talked about so far. You'll make a much longer version of "Twinkle," using two MIDI note arrays for melody and harmony. You'll use a float array to hold the note durations. You'll also use an array of strings to print out the words as the song plays! And you'll pan the melody randomly, using the Math library. So let's get to it!

In listing 3.8, you first declare and add panning to your melody oscillator using the Pan2 object ❶. Next, you make another oscillator for harmony and connect it to the dac ❷. As you've learned, the dac takes care of mixing these sources together automatically. Then you make some gain variables to use for turning your notes on and off ❸.

Next, you have the same melody array that you've been working with ❹, and you make another array to control another oscillator for harmony ❺. You make an array of floats that you'll use for durations ❻ and yet another array of type string that holds your words ❼.

Be careful to make all of these arrays the same length, or you might encounter an error when you ask for the [i–th] element if it doesn't exist because one of the arrays is shorter than the others.

You continue on to the same for loop as you had in the last example using the .cap() function to determine the size of the arrays you're using ❽. In the loop block, you print out the value of your counter index i, along with your melody/harmony MIDI note numbers and, most important, your word or word fragment corresponding with that particular note of the song ❾.

You then set the frequencies of your two oscillators ❿, but you add variety for the melody line, setting a random panning value for each note ⓫. You turn on your two oscillators by setting their gains to your previously defined onGain ⓬; then you advance time by reading and using the values in the durs[] array ⓭, ⓮.

> **NOTE** In listing 3.8 you use a shorthand method ⓬ of setting the values of multiple things to a common single value. onGain => t.gain => s.gain; works just fine, because first onGain is ChucKed to t.gain, which then has this new value, which is then ChucKed to s.gain.

Listing 3.8 "Twinkle" with melody, harmony, and lyrics!

```
// by ChucK Team, July 2050

// two oscillators, melody and harmony
SinOsc s => Pan2 mpan => dac;
TriOsc t => dac;

// we will use these to separate notes later
0.5 => float onGain;
0.0 => float offGain;
```

❶ SinOsc through Pan2 for melody

❷ TriOsc fixed at center for harmony

Note on/off gains ❸

```
// declare and initialize our arrays of MIDI note #s
[57, 57, 64, 64, 66, 66, 64,
62, 62, 61, 61, 59, 59, 57] @=> int melNotes[];
[61, 61, 57, 61, 62, 62, 61,
59, 56, 57, 52, 52, 68, 69] @=> int harmNotes[];

// quarter note and half note durations
0.5 :: second => dur q;
1.0 :: second => dur h;
[ q, q, q, q, q, q, h, q, q, q, q, q, q, h] @=> dur myDurs[];

// make one more array to hold the words
["Twin","kle","twin","kle","lit","tle","star,",
 "how", "I","won","der","what","you","are."] @=> string words[];

// loop over all the arrays
//        (make sure they're the same length!!)
for (0 => int i; i < melNotes.cap(); i++)
{
    // print out index, MIDI notes, and words from arrays
    <<< i, melNotes[i], harmNotes[i], words[i] >>>;

    // set melody and harmony from arrays
    Std.mtof(harmNotes[i]) => s.freq;
    Std.mtof(melNotes[i]) => t.freq;

    // melody has a random pan for each note
    Math.random2f(-1.0,1.0) => mpan.pan;

    // notes are on for 70% of duration from array
    onGain => s.gain => t.gain;
    0.7*myDurs[i] => now;

    // space between notes is 30% of array duration
    offGain => s.gain => t.gain;
    0.3*myDurs[i] => now;
}
```

4 Melody (int) MIDI note array

5 Harmony (int) MIDI note array

6 Duration (dur) array

7 Lyrics (string) array

8 Plays through all notes in array

9 Prints note data, including lyrics

10 Sets frequencies from array MIDI notes

11 Random pan for melody oscillator

12 Turns on both oscillators

13 70% of array duration is note on time

14 30% of array duration is off time

3.6 Summary

Arrays can make life much easier and more organized for you:

- Arrays can be used not only for storing integers, like melodies as note numbers, but also to store any sequence of floating-point numbers, such as gains or frequencies.
- Arrays can be used to store durations and strings, including words, directions, and even filenames, or any type of data—unit generators, pretty much anything!
- You can find the size of any array using the .cap() method, so you don't have to count elements each time you change something.

Now that you've learned quite a bit about the ChucK language, we can turn our attention to making sounds and music richer and more realistic. Our next chapter will dive into working with sound files (essentially arrays that hold sound) and how you can use and manipulate them to make your music even more awesome.

Sound files and sound manipulation

This chapter covers

- Storing sound in computers
- Loading and playing sound files in ChucK using SndBuf
- Working with stereo files
- Modulo, a cool new, musically useful, arithmetic operator
- Making your own drum machine using samples

So far you've used only oscillators and noise to make your sounds and compositions. But there's much more to music composition and production than just these sounds. There are countless types of sounds in the world and in music. In this chapter, we'll show you how to use sound files in ChucK. Sound files, such as .wav, .aif, or other files you have on your computer or have seen on the internet, are sometimes called *samples*, for reasons you'll see soon. Samples are a quick and effective way to build sonic and musical elements with lots of variety and realism. By using samples, you can draw from the huge collection of existing sounds that people have recorded and synthesized over the years.

In later chapters you'll learn to synthesize your own sounds from scratch. But in this chapter, you'll use samples to get to the point where you can build your own beat-rockin' techno drum machine with many new programming skills. First, we'll take a quick look at how sound is turned from waveforms in the air into digital numbers for computer storage and transmission, called sampling. Then we'll dig into using samples in ChucK. We'll also look at new ways to use arrays and also introduce a new math operator called modulo.

4.1 *Sampling: turning sound into numbers*

First, let's talk a bit about sound. We define *sound* as the traveling of fluctuating air compressions through the air, from some source to our ears. In computer systems, sound is stored and played back in various digital formats as numbers. Although you don't need to know the specifics of all this to use sound files in ChucK, it's important to know some things as you load and play sound files and as you look forward to synthesizing sounds in the future.

To get sound into a format that your computer and ChucK can understand, sound is turned into a stream of numbers, called a digital signal. The process of turning a sound waveform into a digital signal is called analog-to-digital conversion. The device that does this is an analog-to-digital converter (ADC), which is essentially the opposite device of the digital-to-analog converter (DAC) that you've been using all along to get digital signals synthesized by ChucK out to your speakers or headphones. The ADC works by inspecting electronically the incoming waveform (this is called sampling) at regular intervals, called the sampling period (which is 1/sampling rate) and rounding the value to the nearest integer available to represent and store that amplitude. Figure 4.1 shows this process, zoomed into one "eee" period of our earlier "see" sound. We further zoom into the beginning of the waveform and show a few of the individual integers that represent the first few sample values.

In the previous chapter, when we talked about arrays, we said that arrays can hold anything, and anything that's in your computer is stored in an array. The process shown in figure 4.1 is doing exactly that, turning the values of a waveform into a sequence of numbers and storing those into an array. Here the indices (0, 1, 2, ...)

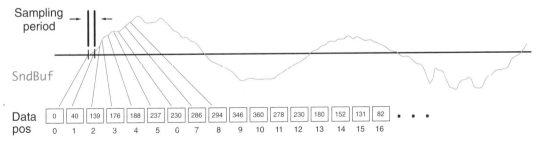

Figure 4.1 Sampling of one period of an "eee" sound. Pressure at a microphone is turned into voltage, which is turned into a number by a process known as analog-to-digital conversion.

represent increasing time, one count for each sample period (1/sampling rate). The levels corresponding to each point in time (sample) are integers in most sound file formats like .wav and .aiff, but ChucK converts them into floating point numbers in the range +1.0 to -1.0.

All of the waveforms you've seen, including the one in figure 4.1, require both positive and negative values because the line through the middle is zero. This is generally true for audio, which is the traveling through the air of compressions (air pressure higher than normal) and rarefactions (less than normal), so you need positive numbers for pressures higher than ambient air pressure and negative for lower pressures.

So, each number representing each value in time of a waveform is called a sample, and—perhaps confusingly—once a whole sound is turned into a stream of numbers, that collection of values, indexed in time, is also called a sample. When that collection of numbers is written out to be stored on disk, or as a link from a web page, or burned on a CD/DVD, it's called a sound file. One more term you should know is that when a sound file is loaded into your computer or synthesizer, it's sometimes also called a wavetable.

To play back audio, you need a DAC, which turns the numbers back into continuous waveform samples, usually voltages, in your speakers or headphones. You've used the dac object in ChucK a lot already in your compositions, to hook your oscillators and noise generators up to your speakers. ChucK, combined with your computer's audio hardware, takes care of turning sound files back into the voltages needed to drive your headphones or speakers.

> ### Sampling, word size, and sampling rate
> Engineers need to consider many issues when creating and working with sound files and especially when designing hardware for ADCs and DACs. These include how much computer storage should be allotted for each individual sample value (called word size, typically 16 bits or 24 bits per sample) for music and often 8 bits for speech sounds. Also, they must choose how often the waveform is sampled (typically 44100 samples per second). These have implications for quality and memory/disk space. For example, higher sample rates and more bits per sample are generally better, up to a point. CD-quality sound, at 2 bytes per sample, 2 channels, and 44100 samples per second, consumes about 10 megabytes per minute.
>
> For more information on sampling, sound file formats, and so on, see the references at the end of this chapter.

Now you know a little about how sound gets into your computer. Let's dig in right now and play sound files using ChucK's built-in unit generator called SndBuf.

4.2   *SndBuf: loading and playing sound files in ChucK*

SndBuf, shortened from *sound buffer*, is the built-in ChucK UGen that allows you to load sound files. To do this you must start out with a sound file or perhaps a folder full of sound files. We've provided you a series of sound files that you can use to start composing and that we're using throughout this book, so all the examples work without you having to change anything. It's also possible to add your own sound files and get things to work as you see fit. First you'll be setting up a file structure on your computer so ChucK can find the sound files. Then you'll learn lots of ways to load, play, and manipulate sound files using SndBuf.

4.2.1 *Organizing your sound files*

For you to start using sound files in ChucK, we first have to help you get your computer file structure set up so you can follow all the examples in this book, as well as adopt good habits for organizing your code, sounds, and songs.

As shown in figure 4.2, we recommend that you first create a chuck folder on your computer to save all your files. In this folder you also need to make a folder called audio that hosts all your samples. Included in the installed version of ChucK on your computer you'll find a folder called audio. Copy and paste this folder to your new chuck folder so you can use those sound files as you're reading through this chapter and the rest of the book.

Now that you've set up a file structure on your computer that makes it easy to use sound files, you can use ChucK to try it out by using prerecorded samples of playing a drum located in the audio directory. Listing 4.1 shows just how to do that, using SndBuf, which is a new sound-making UGen that helps you load and play samples. Although you connect it to the dac just like you have with other UGens so far, when compared with our oscillator (SinOsc, TriOsc, and so on) and noise unit generators, there are a number of new things about SndBuf that you need to know in order to use it.

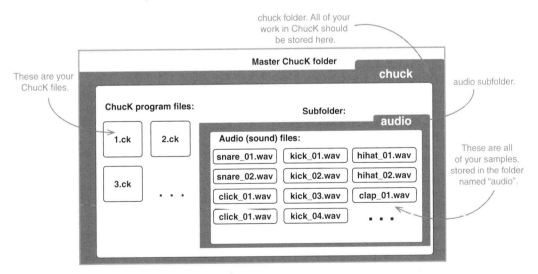

Figure 4.2 Recommended file structure for your ChucK projects. Make a new folder called chuck. Save (or move) all of your .ck code files into it, and copy the audio folder with all of its contents into it also. Now ChucK can know where to look for things!

First, you need to tell SndBuf to load a sound file and from where, or else it won't make any sound. You do that by assembling a complete file path and filename. You can think of this as an address on the file system of your computer, just as you have to use menu navigation to load documents, spreadsheets, or any other type of files on your computer into other programs. With ChucK, as long as you have things set up right (as shown in figure 4.2), you can load files from within ChucK programs using just ChucK code and without needing menus.

Type in the ChucK code of listing 4.1 and save it as UsingSndBuf.ck (or whatever you like; just remember what you named it) into the chuck directory you previously created. The code on line ❶ asks ChucK to return the complete file path to where your ChucK file resides. me is a keyword, and me.dir() returns the current directory where this ChucK file resides. That's why it's important to save your file somewhere in the chuck directory. You store the file path in a string called path to use later. In the next line you make a new string variable and initialize it with the name of the sound file you're going to play, including the audio folder name where that sound file resides.

Then you make another string variable called filename ❷ to hold the name of the sound file you're going to play. This name should include the audio folder holding your sound files. Note here that you use the + symbol in a new way, to attach the two strings named path and filename together to make a new string, which you store back into the filename variable. This is another cool feature of ChucK, where the plus sign can add numbers together or attach strings together automatically based on the data type in question.

Listing 4.1 Loading and playing sound files with SndBuf

```
// Using SndBuf to play a sound file
// by ChucK Programmer, December 2050
SndBuf mySound => dac;

// get file path
me.dir() => string path;                    ❶ Gets current working
// sound file we want to play                  directory.
"/audio/snare_01.wav" => string filename;

// + sign connects strings together!         ❷ Builds a full path/name
path+filename => filename;                      to a sound file.

// tell SndBuf to read this file
filename => mySound.read;                     ChucKing a string to the
                                              .read member of SndBuf
// set gain                                 ❸ causes it to load that file.
0.5 => mySound.gain;

// play sound from the beginning              ChucKing a number to the .pos (for
0 => mySound.pos;                             position) member of SndBuf causes it to
                                              start playing from that position in the
// advance time so we can hear it             array (in this case, from the beginning).
second => now;
```

NOTE   You can't use the + sign to add a `string` to a `float`, even though the string might look like a number. So `"123.7"+ 6.3` isn't legal, but depending on whether you want the final result to be a `string` or a `float`, you could use `Std.atof("123.7 ") + 6.3` to get a float. Remember that `Std.atof()` converts an ASCII string into a floating-point number. You could also use `"123.7" + Std.ftoa(6.3)` (float to ASCII) to get a `string`, although a somewhat nonsensical one, because it would have two decimal points in it.

Once you've assembled the complete path and filename, you can ChucK that to your SndBuf using the `.read` method ❸, and it will automatically load the file from disk and store it in your SndBuf's internal array. If things didn't work out, such as the file couldn't be found because the path wasn't correct or you mistyped something in the filename, then ChucK will print an error to the Console window.

Sound file formats and file extensions

Among the many types of audio file formats, the most common are .wav (from wave or waveform) and .aif (from audio interchange file or format). SndBuf understands these and other file formats just fine. Just tell your SndBuf to `.read` it, and ChucK will figure out the rest, or it will give you an error if it can't find the file or read the particular format. ChucK doesn't yet read .mp3 compressed files, so if you try to load one, you'll get a "Format not recognized" message in the Console Monitor window.

You can set the volume of your SndBuf using the `.gain` method. As you recall, every UGen in ChucK obeys the `.gain` method, so you can always use that to change volume. Finally, to make your SndBuf play, you use a new method called `.pos` (for position) to point the SndBuf's internal pointer to the first sample, indexed zero, just like with any array. After that, you just ChucK some duration (in this case 1 second) to now, to allow time to pass and sound to be generated. SndBuf takes care of the rest, handing individual samples over to the dac for playback over your speakers or headphones.

   Assuming you typed everything in correctly and all the files are in the right places, if you click the Add Shred button on the miniAudicle, you should hear a snare drum hit! Click that button a few times. Every time you do, you'll hear that same sound. You could even perform this live as the snare drummer in a band. Clicking in time is somewhat difficult—just like hitting a drum at exactly the right time—but doable.

4.2.2   Looping (automatically repeating) your samples

As you've seen, the SndBuf object has a number of different methods to control sound. Remember that our oscillators had `.gain` and `.freq` methods, and you've seen that SndBuf has a `.gain` object as well, but it doesn't have a `.freq` method. The reason for this is that because a SndBuf holds a recording, you have no idea what frequency, if any, that recording contains. You'll see soon how to make the pitch of the sound of a SndBuf go up or down.

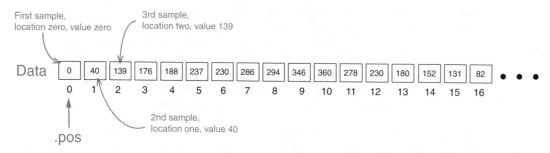

Figure 4.3   The .pos method of SndBuf sets the point from which the sound will start playing. This is also called the playhead.

You've also seen that SndBuf also has a .pos method, which is used to set the location where you start playing the sound file, called the playhead. One way to think about this is to imagine your sound file as a vinyl record. The .pos method would be where you place the stylus on the record. Looking at the samples stored in the SndBuf of figure 4.3, note that each successive sample going rightward matches up exactly with the sample values of our "eee" waveform of figure 4.1. Another way to think about it is to remember that your sound file is stored in a big array, and the .pos method tells you which array index to start at, as shown in figure 4.3.

In figure 4.3, the zero position (with sample value zero) is the beginning of the sample, time zero in the sound file. The position labeled 1 (value 40) holds the wave sample one T (sampling period) later. Each position is the sample one T later, so on until the end of the sound file.

What if you wanted to play your SndBuf sample over and over again, maybe in a repeating loop? You can do that by repeatedly setting the playhead to zero using the .pos method. While you're at it, you're going to add other expressive features, such as a panning object, which you remember from chapter 2. As you've done in the past, you'll place your sound control into a while loop, as shown in listing 4.2. Save this file to your ChucK directory once you've typed it in. In listing 4.2, you use random numbers for setting the volume/gain of your sound file ❶, and you set a random panning position ❷. As usual this will create a new volume and spatial position for every hit ❹.

For even more musical variety, you'll use one more method built into the SndBuf object. One of the most expressive aspects of working with sound files is getting to control the sample playback rate. Imagine again the record player: when a record plays faster than it was intended to, the sound is higher pitched. Likewise, when a record plays slower than normal, the sound is at a lower pitch. Through a single line of code, you can alter and experiment with this parameter to get a large variety of expression for your compositions. You do this using the .rate method, to set a random value from .2 to 1.8. The original playback speed is 1.0 ❸. Above 1.0 will go faster and thus higher, and below 1.0 will go slower and thus sound lower.

You set a time to wait **5** before repeating the loop. Here you wait 500::ms (1/2 second) between each new strike. You can make this number greater and see that your looping playback gets slower, make it less and hear your looper get faster.

Listing 4.2   Using a loop to repeatedly play a sound file

```
// Play a sound file repeatedly in a loop
// by ChucK Programmer, January 12, 2017
SndBuf mySound => Pan2 pan => dac;          ← Connects a SndBuf through a
                                              Pan2 panner object to the DAC

// get file path and load file all in one line!
me.dir()+"/audio/cowbell_01.wav" => mySound.read;

// play our sound over and again in an infinite loop
while (true)                                ← Infinite loop to play this
{                                             sound over and over
    // random gain, rate (pitch), and pan each time
    Math.random2f(0.1,1.0) => mySound.gain;   ❶ Random gain for
    Math.random2f(-1.0,1.0) => pan.pan;           sound file
    Math.random2f(0.2,1.8) => mySound.rate;   ← Random rate
                                              ❸ (speed and pitch)
    // (re)start the sound by setting position to 0
    0 => mySound.pos;                         ← Sets pos to zero to
                                              ❹ start it playing
    // advance time so we can hear it
    500.0 :: ms => now;                       ← Hangs out a bit
}                                             ❺ while it plays
```

Random pan position ❷ points to `Math.random2f(-1.0,1.0) => pan.pan;`

Controlling and stopping your loops with Replace Shred and Clear VM

Remember that to make a change, such as the range of the random numbers or the time you ChucK to now to control the timing of your looping sounds, you need to click the Replace Shred button to stop the old infinite loop and replace it with your new one. Because this is an infinite loop (while (true)), when you're finished and ready to move on, you have to stop what's running by clicking Clear VM.

4.2.3   *Playing your samples backward*

Because that sounded so incredibly cool, let's not stop there in messing around with samples. What if you wanted to play a sample in reverse? This is a useful technique that can add a further expressive motif to your compositions, and it's used for sound effects, special musical effects, movie sound design, and so on.

Listing 4.3 shows how to do this, using a different sound, a type of cymbal called a hi-hat. After first making a SndBuf and connecting it to the dac, you load your hi-hat sound file using me.dir() and other methods we've already covered ❶.

To play a sound file backward, you need to do two things. The first is to set the playhead position at the end of the file, an array built into SndBuf. But how do you know how many samples are in your sound file? SndBuf provides a method called

.samples(), which returns the number of samples in your sound file, and you store that in an integer variable called numSamples ❷. Another way to look at this is that you're asking SndBuf, how big is that array inside holding that sound file (similar to the .cap() method for actual arrays)? You first play the sound file once forward and at normal speed; note that you're using numSamples here to advance the time by exactly the right amount ❸. Using .samples(), you can now use that number as an upper limit with the .pos method to set where your playhead position starts ❹, as shown in figure 4.4.

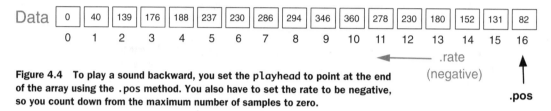

Figure 4.4   To play a sound backward, you set the playhead to point at the end of the array using the .pos method. You also have to set the rate to be negative, so you count down from the maximum number of samples to zero.

The second thing you must do to play a sound backward is to set .rate to go backward instead of forward. As you might have guessed, you do this by making the rate value negative –1.0 ❺ for reverse at the correct speed. Or you could use –.2 for slowly in reverse, –2.0 for double speed in reverse, and so on.

Listing 4.3   Playing a sound file backward

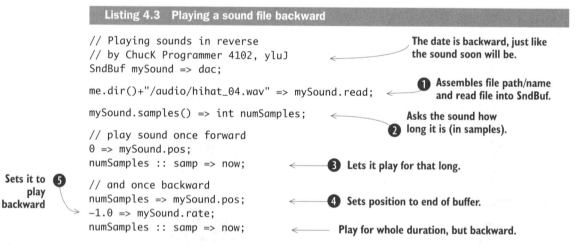

```
// Playing sounds in reverse
// by ChucK Programmer 4102, yluJ            The date is backward, just like
SndBuf mySound => dac;                        the sound soon will be.

me.dir()+"/audio/hihat_04.wav" => mySound.read;   ❶ Assembles file path/name
                                                     and read file into SndBuf.
mySound.samples() => int numSamples;          ❷ Asks the sound how
                                                 long it is (in samples).
// play sound once forward
0 => mySound.pos;
numSamples :: samp => now;                    ❸ Lets it play for that long.

// and once backward
numSamples => mySound.pos;                    ❹ Sets position to end of buffer.
-1.0 => mySound.rate;
numSamples :: samp => now;                    Play for whole duration, but backward.
```

Sets it to ❺ play backward

4.2.4   Managing multiple samples at a time

The final skill to learn in this section is how to play multiple SndBufs at the same time. There are two ways to do this, depending on how long your sounds are and what your compositional needs are. One way is to reload a single SndBuf with different sound files. Let's say you have three different snare drum recordings, and you want to interchange them throughout a composition. You can do this by making an array of strings to store the file paths and names ❶, as shown in listing 4.4. Now at any time you can access the paths to the sound files and load them into memory at any point during the program. As a simple example here, in an infinite loop, you generate a random number ❷ and use that to decide which file will load and play back ❸.

Note here you're doing something slightly different to play these files, in that you don't explicitly set the `.pos` pointer to zero. Inside SndBuf, loading a file automatically sets the `.pos` pointer to zero and the `.rate` to 1.0. So all sound files automatically play once when they're loaded, as long as time is advanced.

Listing 4.4   Playing different sound files with a single SndBuf

```
// Playing multiple sounds
// by ChucK Programmer July, 2023
SndBuf snare => dac;                              ❶ Makes and fills an
                                                     array of sound file
// make and fill an array of sound file paths+names  names.
string snare_samples[3];
me.dir()+"/audio/snare_01.wav" => snare_samples[0];
me.dir()+"/audio/snare_02.wav" => snare_samples[1];
me.dir()+"/audio/snare_03.wav" => snare_samples[2];

// infinite loop
while (true)
{                                                 ❷ Picks a random
                                                     number between
    // pick a random number between 0 and #files     1 and 3.
    Math.random2(0,snare_samples.cap()-1) => int which;

    // load up that file
    snare_samples[which] => snare.read;       ← Loads the random file
                                              ❸ associated with that.
    // let it play
    0.5 :: second => now;
}
```

The method of listing 4.4 can work fine, but it can also cause clicks if other processes running on your computer get in the way of the files being loaded in time to play or if the files are too long. There's a better way. Remember in chapter 3 we said that you can make arrays to hold any type of data? Here you exploit that by declaring an array of SndBufs instead ❶ and preloading them with different sound files ❷, as shown in the following listing. This way, all sound files are loaded before you enter the main loop, and you can avoid clicking by not trying to load files while sound is playing.

Listing 4.5   Playing different sound files (method 2) using multiple SndBufs

```
// Playing multiple sound files (method 2)
// by ChucK Programmer, August, 2023        ❶ Declares an array of
SndBuf snare[3];                               three SndBufs...

// for fun, let's pan them to left, right, center
snare[0] => dac.left;       ←              ...connects them to left,
snare[1] => dac;                           center, right...
snare[2] => dac.right;

// pre-load all sound files at the beginning
```

```
me.dir()+"/audio/snare_01.wav" => snare[0].read;
me.dir()+"/audio/snare_02.wav" => snare[1].read;
me.dir()+"/audio/snare_03.wav" => snare[2].read;

// infinite loop
while (true)
{
    // pick a random number between 0 and #files
    Math.random2(0,snare.cap()-1) => int which;

    // play that sample
    0 => snare[which].pos;

    // let it play
    0.5 :: second => now;
}
```

❷ …loads them with three different sound files.

Picks a random file to play

Play it!

You might have noticed that the sonic results of the code of listing 4.5 are the same as those of listing 4.4. This is common in programming, where, as with the for and while loops, you saw that there were multiple ways to achieve the same results. There are cases where the method of listing 4.5 might not be desirable, however. One example might be if you're using sound files that are very large (like whole songs, which we don't recommend for now) or you're running ChucK on a machine with little RAM. ChucK runs on some pretty small machines, such as really old Macs and PCs, and even the Raspberry Pi, a cheap and tiny Linux computer. In cases such as these, preloading all the files you might need ahead of time might be impossible. You could run out of memory before everything gets loaded. But you now know both methods and can choose which one to use!

We've looked at how to use Pan2 (listing 4.2) and how to accomplish hard panning—direct connection to left, center, or right, as shown in listing 4.5—to get stereo effects using SndBuf. But what about stereo files? No problem! Read on.

4.3   *Stereo sound files and playback*

The code we've looked at so far has treated sample files as single-channel, or mono (short for monaural, meaning "of one ear"), files. But you have two ears and usually listen to sound and music using two speakers or headphones with two ear cups/buds. Remember that you've already used a Pan2 unit generator to move noise back and forth between your left and right speakers/headphones. But you'll also want to be able to use two-channel, or stereo, sound files. Stereo sound files, in a sense, come pre-spatialized, so you don't need to use Pan2 to place them in the spatial sound field. A well-produced stereo sound file will have a more authentic sense of space than can be provided by a mono sound file processed by Pan2. But it's harder to change the spatialization after the file has been recorded, making dynamic panning adjustments in code more difficult.

Loading stereo sound files in ChucK is much the same as with mono files, but instead of using SndBuf, you use SndBuf2, as shown in listing 4.6. The addition of the 2 in the name indicates that the unit generator is stereo, that is, it has two output channels. Everything should look fairly standard by now, except for a new function/method you use ❶ to obtain a duration for advancing time. The .length() method for SndBuf and SndBuf2 returns a duration that's exactly equal to the time required to play that sound file. Thus, you can just use it to ask SndBuf2 how long to play and ChucK that immediately to now!

Listing 4.6 Loading and playing stereo sound files using SndBuf2

```
// Loading and playing stereo sound files        Makes a stereo SndBuf2
// by ChucK Programmer, September, 2023           and connects it to the dac
SndBuf2 myStereoSound => dac;                     (stereo is automatic!).

// load up a stereo file                          Loads a stereo
me.dir()+"/audio/stereo_fx_01.wav" => myStereoSound.read;   file using .read.

// and let it play for the right amount of time   ❶ New function/method!
myStereoSound.length() => now;                       .length returns the exact
                                                     duration of the sound file.
```

Note that you're no longer using a Pan2 object to control spatialization because SndBuf2 produces a two-channel output. Connecting it to the dac automatically does the correct things (left to left, right to right, just like the two outputs of Pan2).

Note also that if you had connected your SndBuf2 to a Gain unit before going to dac, the result would have been different. When a two-channel output is connected to a single-channel input, the two channels are mixed together to match the input. This throws away any spatialization effects in the original stereo signal, so mixing the output of SndBuf2 generally defeats the purpose of using SndBuf2. If you want to accomplish that, you can load a stereo file into a regular SndBuf, and the two channels will be mixed together internally within the SndBuf object and stored in the built-in mono array.

But you can still use Gain UGens to control the stereo sound field in other ways, as shown in listing 4.7. Here you combine your knowledge of arrays and unit generators to create an array of UGens, one for each channel. Using an array of two Gain UGens, you create a stereo balance control, which is a way of adjusting the panning of a stereo signal. So how does this work?

After making a stereo SndBuf and loading up a stereo file ❶, you make an array of two Gain UGens, to be used for left/right volume ❷. You then connect the left channel of your SndBuf to the zeroeth Gain (bal[0]) and then to the dac.left channel ❸. You do the same with dac.right and bal[1].

Listing 4.7 Stereo panning with stereo sound files using SndBuf2

```
// Loading and panning stereo sound files
// by ChucK Programmer, October, 2023
                                                    ❶ Makes a stereo
// declare and load up a stereo file                  SndBuf2 and
SndBuf2 myStereoSound;                                 loads a stereo
me.dir()+"/audio/stereo_fx_03.wav" => myStereoSound.read;   sound file.
```

```
// We'll use these for Stereo Panning
Gain bal[2];
```
❷ Makes a Gain UGen array for stereo volume control.

```
// connect everything up in stereo
myStereoSound.chan(0) => bal[0] => dac.left;
myStereoSound.chan(1) => bal[1] => dac.right;
```
❸ Connects left to left, right to right.

```
// set our soundfile to repeat forever
1 => myStereoSound.loop;
```
❹ Repeats automatically.

```
while (true)  {
    // pick a random playback rate and a random panning
    Math.random2f(0.2,1.8) => myStereoSound.rate;
    Math.random2f(-1.0,1.0) => float balance;
```
❺ Sets a random rate (pitch and time).

Sets a random balance (pan). **❻**

```
    // turn balance into left/right gain between 0 and 1.0
    (balance+1)/2.0 => float rightGain;
    1.0 - rightGain => float leftGain;
    leftGain => bal[0].gain;
    rightGain => bal[1].gain;
```
❼ Implements the stereo balance control.

```
    0.3 :: second => now;
}
```

Then you do something new **❹** with your SndBuf2, which you can also do with regular mono SndBuf. By ChucKing 1 to the .loop method, you tell SndBuf that you want it to play in a loop forever. Normally any SndBuf plays just once and sticks at the end, waiting for you to reset the play .pos (position) to zero. But by setting .loop to 1, you're telling the innards of SndBuf that when the position pointer reaches the end of the array, and all samples have been played, it should reset to 0 automatically and start playing again. Note that you could also use this for backward playback (negative rates), and when the pointer counts down to 0, it automatically resets to the last sample and repeats playing backward forever.

Now to the stereo panning stuff. Inside the infinite loop, you set a random playback rate **❺**, and you create and set (randomly) a new variable called balance **❻**. Just as with Pan2, as you set your balance variable toward -1.0, the left channel becomes more prominent; if balance tends toward 1.0, it makes the right channel more prominent. Once balance is randomly set between -1 and 1, you do the math to turn that into gains, between 0 and 1, for controlling the left and right channels **❼**.

> **TRY THIS** On paper, set balance to -1.0; then work through the math to arrive at leftGain and rightGain. Do the same for balance set to 0.0 and balance set to 1.0. See how moving balance from -1.0 to 1.0 causes the actual panning to move from left to right? Do this in ChucK code too so you can hear the difference as you change balance.

As you saw before when you preloaded an array of SndBuf UGens, arrays of UGens are a common technique for creating and manipulating multichannel synthesis patches in ChucK.

4.4 Example: making a drum machine

Now that you've seen ways to use sample playback in ChucK, let's put it all together to make a rockin' dance beat drum machine, with multiple sound files. Let's start out with a kick drum (bass drum in a drum set, played with a pedal) and a snare drum, connected to the dac ❶, via a mixer Gain UGen we call master, as shown in listing 4.8. The Gain UGen object allows you to make a gain control anywhere in your audio chain, in this case before the output to the dac, so that you can control the volume of your entire composition now by changing master.gain. You might remember that all UGens obey the .gain method, but you can use a Gain UGen not only to enable gain control but also to provide a nice named patch point for mixing multiple sources and other functions that you'll learn about later on.

Once it's created and connected in your code, you need only connect additional new SndBufs to the master Gain UGen ❷. This is because you've already connected that master Gain to the dac. After connecting your SndBufs, you can load them with the appropriate sound files ❸. Then you enter an infinite loop and play the kick drum (0 => kick.pos) by itself on Beat 1 ❹, and you play both drums on Beat 2 ❺ by ChucKing 0 to both kick.pos and snare.pos.

Listing 4.8 Making a drum machine with SndBufs in ChucK

```
//  Drum Machine, version 1.0
//  by block-rockin programmer, Dec 31, 1999

// SndBufs for kick (bass) and snare drums
SndBuf kick => Gain master => dac;        ❶  SndBuf into a
SndBuf snare => master;                       master mixer
                                              Gain into dac
// load up some samples of those
me.dir()+"/audio/kick_01.wav" => kick.read;   ❷  Another SndBuf
me.dir()+"/audio/snare_01.wav" => snare.read;     into master mixer

while (true)                                  ❸  Loads your
{                                                 sound files
    // Beat 1, play kick drum alone
    0 => kick.pos;                            ❹  Every even beat,
    0.6 :: second => now;                         play kick only

    // play both drums on Beat 2
    0 => kick.pos;                            ❺  All beats, play both
    0 => snare.pos;                               kick and snare
    0.6 :: second => now;
}
```

4.4.1 Adding logic for different drums on different beats

Already you're making music! But you can do oh so much better by using a for loop and some logical statements. Remember those? We told you they'd be increasingly important later. Change the previous while loop to that shown in the next listing. Also add a new tempo duration variable ❹, and replace the while loop with one that uses a for loop ❺ and logical tests ❻ ❼.

Listing 4.9   Improving the while loop of your drum machine

```
// Drum Machine, version 2.0
// by block-rockin programmer, Dec 32, 1999

// SndBufs for kick (bass) and snare drums          ❶ Kick to
SndBuf kick => Gain master => dac;                     master mixer
SndBuf snare => master;                                Gain to dac.
                                                    ❷ Snare also to
// load up some samples of those                       master mixer.
me.dir()+"/audio/kick_01.wav" => kick.read;
me.dir()+"/audio/snare_01.wav" => snare.read;       ❸ Loads your kick and
                                                       snare drum sound files.
// declare a new tempo variable
0.15 :: second => dur tempo;                        ❹ Tempo duration is
                                                       time between beats.
while (true)
{
    for (0 => int beat; beat < 16; beat++)          ❺ Loops over a
    {                                                  "measure" of 16 beats.
        // play kick drum on beat 0, 4, 8, and 12
        if (beat==0 || beat==4 || beat==8 || beat==12)  ❻ Plays kick only on
        {                                                  specific beats.
            0 => kick.pos;
        }
        // play snare drum on beat 4, 10, 13, and 14
        if (beat==4 || beat==10 || beat==13 || beat==14)  ❼ Plays snare only
        {                                                    on other specific
            0 => snare.pos;                                  beats.
        }
        tempo => now;
    }
}
```

NOTE You can change the if (beat==N) numbers to see how the overall pattern changes.

In listing 4.9 you use a for loop ❶ to play 16 beats at a time. Musicians and composers might call that a measure. You use logical operators and expressions such as if and || (or) to play the different drums on different beats within your measure; you play kick on some beats ❷ and snare on others ❸. Try changing the numbers in the beat==# conditions, click the Replace Shred button, and see how your pattern changes. You may get pretty good at clicking the button in time, so that your drum pattern changes but the basic timing is preserved. In later chapters you'll learn techniques for using ChucK's strong sense and control of timing to accomplish this type of on-the-fly drumming exactly.

> ### Loops and other control structures can be nested
> Note that in listing 4.9, we've nested a for loop within a while loop, and we've done that in prior examples in other chapters. This is totally cool to do, of course, and is really powerful. You can nest for loops within for loops, while loops within while or for loops, ifs within ifs, ifs within elses, as deep as you'd like. As long as you keep your curly braces straight and aligned, which the miniAudicle greatly helps you with, you can tell where each block begins and ends.

4.4.2 *Controlling when drums play using logic arrays*

Use your knowledge of arrays to control when the drums play, as shown in listing 4.10. And add another drum sound ❶, a hi-hat cymbal sound, while you're at it. Here you change your for loop into a while loop; again, there are multiple ways to solve problems in ChucK. You define two arrays ❷ that contain logical values, either 1 or 0, to tell the drum whether to play or not play on that beat. So here the index into the array is the beat number. That makes your logic pretty simple; instead of all those || or conditions tied together, you read the logic variable from the array at the right beat index, and that tells you whether or not to play that drum. You use one array for kick and one for snare, while your new hi-hat sound plays on every beat. But it would be really easy to introduce a third hatHits[] array and subject that drum to its own conditional statement as well. Note that you again use the .cap() function to determine the size of one of your arrays.

Listing 4.10　Using arrays to further improve your drum machine

```
//  Drum Machine, version 3.0
//  by block-rockin programmer, Dec 31, 1999

// SndBufs for kick (bass) and snare drums
SndBuf kick => Gain master => dac;          ❶ kick, snare, and hihat
SndBuf snare => master;                        SndBufs into mixer to dac
SndBuf hihat => master;

// load up some samples of those
me.dir()+"/audio/kick_01.wav" => kick.read;
me.dir()+"/audio/snare_01.wav" => snare.read;
me.dir()+"/audio/hihat_01.wav" => hihat.read;
0.3 => hihat.gain;

0.15 :: second => dur tempo;
                                            ❷ Arrays to control
// scores (arrays) to tell drums when to play    when kick and
[1,0,0,0,1,0,0,0,1,0,0,0,1,0,0,0] @=> int kickHits[];    snare play
[0,0,1,0,0,0,1,0,0,0,0,0,1,1,1,1] @=> int snareHits[];

while (true)
{
    0 => int beat;
    while (beat < kickHits.cap())
```

```
{
    // play kick drum based on array value
    if (kickHits[beat])
    {
        0 => kick.pos;
    }
    if (snareHits[beat])
    {
        0 => snare.pos;
    }
    // always play hihat
    1 => hihat.pos;
    tempo => now;
    beat++;
}
}
```

Checks array at location beat to see if you should play the kick drum now.

Checks array at location beat to see if the snare drum should play now.

Play hihat on every beat for now.

Advance time; lets sound synthesize.

Increments to next beat, and goes back and does the inner while loop again.

TRY THIS   Add a `hatHits` array full of 1s and 0s and add the code to play the hihat, conditional on each entry of the array. Change the 1s and 0s in all the arrays to make your own drum patterns. Further, try changing the lengths of the patterns by changing the lengths of the arrays. Be sure to make them all the same length after you've made your changes, or you might get an "Array index out of bounds" error.

You've improved your drum machine by using logic and looping structures and by arranging logical variables into arrays, corresponding to drum patterns that your inner loop(s) can play automatically. But there's more that you can do. Next, you'll learn about a mathematical operator that can be extremely useful for making musical patterns.

4.5   *A new math/music tool: the modulo operator*

Say you wanted to play a particular drum only on every fourth beat, or every other beat, or every *N*th beat for some arbitrary *N*? To give you another ChucK tool to make your drum machine—and compositions in general—even more flexible, we're going to introduce a math operator called *modulo*. Denoted by the % symbol, modulo is a type of division. Unlike normal division, modulo returns the remainder of a long-division operation. For example, 9 % 4 would return the number 1, because 9 divided by 4 is 2 with a remainder of 1. Similarly 14 % 4 would return the number 2 (3 with a remainder of 2, but modulo returns only the remainder).

The program in listing 4.11 prints and "sonifies" your modulo numbers to help you better understand how the modulo operator works. *Sonification* is the display of data or process state through sound, which ChucK is really good for. Here you use a couple of click sounds (one high pitched, one low) loaded into SndBufs ❶. You also define and assign a variable called MOD ❷, which we'll use (and you can change later on) to demonstrate the modulo operator.

A note on programming style

In listing 4.11, you define and assign an integer called MOD that you use for the rest of the program, without modifying it while the program runs. You can change the initial definition, which changes the sound, but MOD is said to be constant during any run of the program. It's common in programming to name such constant variables using all capital letters. Thus MOD is the name we selected for that variable. In our last example of this chapter, we'll make and use another constant variable called MAX_BEAT. Watch for it, and remember that you can do this in your own programs to make them more readable.

In a for loop that counts a variable called beat upward from zero ❸, you play the higher-pitched click sound on every beat ❹. But you play the lower-pitched click sound only under the condition where beat % MOD (in this case beat % 4, read "beat modulo four" or "beat mod four") is equal to zero ❺. This will be true on each MODth beat (every fourth beat in this case). Run this a few times, but change the number assigned to MOD, and see how the sonified result changes. Count along, and look at the results printed into the console.

Listing 4.11 Using the modulo operator

```
// Modulo math for music
// by musical math dude, 11/11/11

// make and load a couple of SndBufs to "sonify" modulo
SndBuf clickhi => dac;                              ← ❶ Loads two different
SndBuf clicklo => dac;                                  sound files
me.dir()+"/audio/click_02.wav" => clickhi.read;
me.dir()+"/audio/click_01.wav" => clicklo.read;

// define a number for our modulo
4 => int MOD;                          ← ❷ Modulo limit MOD

for (0 => int beat; beat < 24; beat++) {   ← ❸ 24-beat "measure"
    // print out beat and beat modulo MOD
    <<< beat, "Modulo ",  MOD, " is: ", beat % MOD >>>;

    // click this on every beat
    0 => clickhi.pos;                  ← ❹ High sound on every beat

    // but only click this on every "MODth" beat
    if (beat % MOD == 0) {             ← ❺ Low sound only every MOD beat
        0 => clicklo.pos;
    }

    0.5 :: second => now;
}
```

Listening to how this sounds, it should be clear that modulo could have musical uses; otherwise we wouldn't have introduced it. Modulo can play an important part in building drum machines, sequencers (loops that play drums, notes, whatever), and compositions in general. So you have yet another tool to use for determining when drums or other things might play and also for computing cyclic indexes, like the ones you might need to read through arrays over and over.

4.6 *Tying it all together: your coolest drum machine yet*

Let's tie together everything we've covered and make one last awesome drum machine example for this chapter. You'll use a number of drum sounds via SndBufs, and you'll do stereo panning using both Gains and the Pan2 object. The next listing shows the beginning of your program, where you set this all up.

Listing 4.12a SndBufs and panning connections for your big drum machine

```
// Drum Machine, version 4.0
// by block-rockin programmer, Jan 1, 2099
// Here we'll use Modulo % and random to play drums


// Define Gains for left, center, right
Gain master[3];
master[0] => dac.left;
master[1] => dac;
master[2] => dac.right;


// Declare SndBufs for lots of drums
//       hook them up to pan positions
SndBuf kick => master[1];
SndBuf snare => master[1];
SndBuf hihat => master[2];
SndBuf cowbell => master[0];


// Use a Pan2 for the hand claps,
//       we'll use random panning later
SndBuf claps => Pan2 claPan;
claPan.chan(0) => master[0];
claPan.chan(1) => master[2];


// load up some samples of those
me.dir()+"/audio/kick_01.wav" => kick.read;
me.dir()+"/audio/snare_01.wav" => snare.read;
me.dir()+"/audio/hihat_01.wav" => hihat.read;
me.dir()+"/audio/cowbell_01.wav" => cowbell.read;
me.dir()+"/audio/clap_01.wav" => claps.read;
```

Annotations:
- Declares an array of master gains, one for left ([0]), center ([1]) and right ([2]).
- Connects left ([0]) to dac.left.
- Connects center ([1]) to dac (both left and right automatically).
- Connects right ([2]) to dac.right.
- Connects kick drum SndBuf to center master gain.
- Connects snare drum to center also.
- Connects cowbell SndBuf to left master gain.
- Connects hihat to right master gain.
- Connects clap SndBuf to a Pan2 object.
- Connects the left (0) channel of the Pan2 to master gain left.
- Connects the right (1) channel of the Pan2 to master gain right.
- Loads all the sound files.

Once you have all of your drums declared, connected to gains, panning objects, and the dac, and once you've loaded all of your sound files, you need to declare variables that you'll use in your main loop to control your drums. In the following listing you declare an array to logically control your cowbell strikes ❶. Then you declare other global variables that all drums will use.

Listing 4.12b Setting up variables for your big drum machine

```
// array for controlling our cowbell strikes
[1,0,1,0, 1,0,0,1, 0,1,0,1, 0,1,1,1] @=> int cowHits[];
```
❶ Array to control cowbell strikes.

```
// controls the overall length of our "measures"
cowHits.cap() => int MAX_BEAT;     // all caps, remember?
```
Determines the maximum number of beats in your measure. Define this using all capital letters.

```
// modulo number for controlling kick and snare
4 => int MOD;
```
Constant for **MOD** operator— you'll use this to control kick and snare drum hits.

```
// overall speed control
0.15 :: second => dur tempo;
```
Master speed control (tempo)—you'll use this to advance time each beat.

```
// counters: beat within measures, and measure
0 => int beat;
0 => int measure;
```
Two counters, one for beat and one for measure number.

In the main loop, shown in the following listing, of your big drum machine, you're going to use a mixture of all of the techniques you've used so far: a loop, a beat counter, conditionals and logic, arrays, and the modulo operator.

Listing 4.12c Main loop to actually play drum patterns

```
// Main infinite drum loop
while (true)
{
    // play kick drum on all main beats (0, 4, ...)
    if (beat % 4 == 0)
    {
        0 => kick.pos;
    }
    // after a time, play snare on off beats (2, 6, ...)
    if (beat % 4 == 2 && measure %2 == 1)
    {
        0 => snare.pos;
    }
    // After a time, randomly play hihat or cowbell
    if (measure > 1) {
        if (cowHits[beat])
        {
            0 => cowbell.pos;
        }
        else
```

❶ Uses MOD 4 to play kick drum every four beats

❷ Plays snare only on specific beats

Plays ❹ cowbell, controlled by array

❸ Plays cowbell and hihat only after measure 1

❺ If not cowbell, then hi-hat

```
        {
            Math.random2f(0.0,1.0) => hihat.gain;          ⑥  Hi-hat has
            0 => hihat.pos;                                   random gain
        }
    }
                                                           ⑧  Claps have
    // after a time, play randomly spaced claps at end of measure    random
    if (beat > 11 && measure > 3)                                    pan
    {                                                      ⑦  Plays claps only on
        Math.random2f(-1.0,1.0) => claPan.pan;                certain measures
        0 => claps.pos;                                       and beats...
    }
    tempo => now;                                          ⑨  ...waits for one beat...
    (beat + 1) % MAX_BEAT => beat;
    if (beat==0)
    {                                                      ⑩  ...and then updates beat
        measure++;                                            counter (MOD MAX)
    }
}                                                          ⑪  Increments
                                                              measure counter
                                                              at each new
                                                              measure
```

You use an array to control the cowbell strikes ❶ in listing 4.12b. You'll use modulo to play kick drum on beats 0, 4, 8, and 12 ❷ and snare drum on beats 2, 6, 10, and 14 ❸, but you play snare only during odd measures—more on that soon. To give your drum song compositional structure, you use more conditional logic (if statements), checking your measure number, which counts up once for each MAX_BEATS beats, to see if you should be playing other instruments. For example, once the measure number is greater than 1 ❹ you begin playing either cowbell strikes ❺, as determined by the array ❺, or ❻ random gain ❼ hi-hat strikes. Once the measure number is greater than 3, you add in your randomly panned ❾ handclaps, but only on beats 12–15 ❽.

After advancing time by your duration tempo ❿, so all those drums can sound, if you've triggered them by ChucKing 0 to .pos, you use modulo math to update your beat counter ⑪. By incrementing beat, and then taking that number modulo MAX_BEAT and storing that back into beat, you automatically reset beat to zero when it reaches MAX_BEAT. If the result of that modulo operation on beat is zero ⑫, then you increment your measure counter, so you can use that in your logic to give your song that increasing compositional tension ❸, ❹, ❽.

4.7   *Summary*

Now you know how to make realistic sounds in ChucK, by using SndBuf to load and play back sound files, or samples. You learned how to load and play back sounds using the following:

- SndBuf's .read method, along with me.dir(), to load a sound file from memory
- The .pos method to set your playback position
- The .rate method to control how fast and how far forward/backward a sound file plays back
- SndBuf2 for stereo files

- One or multiple `SndBufs` for multiple sound files
- The modulo math operator

And now that you've coded your first drum sequencer, your compositional coding can advance to an entirely new level of fun and expression. That was a fairly involved example, but it built on everything you've used so far in your journey of learning ChucK. The results were decidedly awesome. We encourage you to put together more items that you've learned so far and modify this expressive techno beat to solidify the knowledge you've gained up to now.

You might be wondering if there's a way to factor out some of that code, some sort of shorthand or method of grouping things, to make your code both more readable and reusable. It turns out that's where we'll be going next. We've been talking about methods (functions) all along, such as when you set `.gain` or `.freq` or `.pos`. Next, you're going to learn how to write your own functions to make your life easier and give your programs super-powers. See you in chapter 5.

For further reading

Ken Pohlmann, *Principles of Digital Audio,* 6th Edition (McGraw Hill, 2010).

Perry Cook, *Real Sound Synthesis for Interactive Applications* (A K Peters LTD, 2002).

Ken Steiglitz, *A Digital Signal Processing Primer* (Addison Wesley, 1996).

Robert Bristow-Johnson, "Wavetable Synthesis 101, A Fundamental Perspective," AES 101 Conference, 1996. Available at http://musicdsp.org/files/Wavetable-101.pdf.

Functions:
making your own tools

5

This chapter covers

- Writing and using functions in ChucK
- Defining and naming functions
- Function arguments and return types
- Functions that can call themselves
- Using functions for sound and music composition

Now that you've had fun building a drum machine using the SndBuf UGen, it's time to learn how to write and use functions. You've already used a number of functions, which we've also called methods, ranging from changing the .freq and .gain of oscillators, to using Std.mtof() for converting MIDI note numbers into frequencies, to generating random numbers using Math.random2() and Math.random2f(). All of these are examples of functions.

Often in writing programs you need to do the same types of things multiple times and in multiple places. So far you've retyped or copied and pasted blocks of code, possibly changing them just a little. You've seen how using ChucK's built-in Standard and Math library functions help you get lots of work done by calling them with an argument or two. What if you could create and call your own functions? That's what you'll learn how to do in this chapter.

Adding functions to your programs will allow you to break up common tasks into individual units. Functions let you make little modules of code that you can use over and over. Modularity helps with reusability and with collaboration with other programmers and artists. It also makes your code more readable.

In this chapter you'll learn how write functions, define and name them, pass values into them, and specify what they return. We'll also look at functions that can call themselves, called recursive functions. We'll always have an eye toward using functions to make music and make your compositions even better.

5.1 Creating and using functions in your programs

Initially, you'll be creating new functions inside a single main file, looking conceptually like figure 5.1. You'll have a file, saved as myProgram.ck, for example, that contains the main program that executes your code, and from that main program you'll call your functions, boxes labeled Function 1 and Function 2, which are defined in the same myProgram.ck file. Because they're defined in the same file, you can use them by name as needed for your program and composition. Once you've defined and tested your functions, you usually move them to the end of your program file, but you can define your functions anywhere.

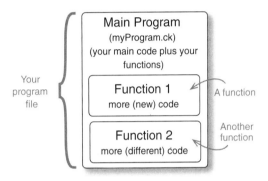

Figure 5.1 For now, one program file will contain all of your code, including the functions that the main program uses.

NOTE It's possible to define functions and save them in their own files, and you'll be doing that later, but for now you'll keep everything in the same file.

5.1.1 Declaring functions

Functions are like variables, so you have to declare them in order to use them, just as you did with ints, floats, SinOscs, and the like. We'll begin by discussing how to declare a function. There are four main parts to function declaration, as shown in figure 5.2. You begin the line with the word function, or shortened as fun. Next, you declare the return type, or what type of data the function will give

```
fun int fname( int arg, int arg2 )
{
    int result;

    // do something

    return result;
}
```

Figure 5.2 Parts of function code labeled

back after it finishes running. For example, this function will return an integer when it's complete; this is like `Std.ftoi()`, which returns an integer from a `float`.

NOTE Using a function is also sometimes called calling or invoking a function.

Next, you give the function a name. Just like with variables, you can name functions whatever you choose, although it's helpful for those names to be meaningful and imply the utility of the function. Finally, you list the input arguments, which are optional. These are variables that you pass into the function for it to use while executing. There can be many different input arguments, all of varying types, based on your design choices as a programmer.

5.1.2 *Your first musical function*

Now let's look at a musically useful function, one that returns the interval between two MIDI note numbers:

```
function int interval(int note1, int note2)
{
    note1 - note2 => int result;
    return result;
}
```

Yes, this is fairly trivial, because you could just subtract the two note numbers, but doing it in a function serves two purposes; you can use it over and again and you can name it something that reminds you why you're doing it in the first place, in this case, interval.

As you can see from figure 5.3, you can view a function like a module of code with input values and an output value. This one has two integer input variables named note1 and note2. The function uses these values and creates a *result* as an integer value

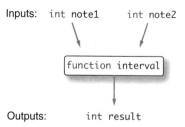

Figure 5.3 **A function is a block of code that takes arguments and returns a result.**

that's output back to the calling program. For example, if you passed in (72,60) for the arguments, the interval function would return 12 (72–60), the number of steps in an octave.

To better understand this process, let's start with an even simpler example, a function that adds an octave to any MIDI note number you pass to it, as shown in listing 5.1. You first create a function named addOctave ❶ with an input argument of an integer you name note and declare a return type of int. Then you create an integer named result ❷, which you use to store your final answer. You add 12 (one octave) to your variable note ❸ and store this new value in your variable result. The result is returned to the main program ❹.

When the program begins, it always starts in the main program and doesn't run the function until it's called. The program starts where `addOctave()` is called ⑤. Notice that `addOctave()` has a set of parentheses, and here you can enter any input you want (but it must be an integer). In this case you start by passing the number 60, and the function is executed, using 60 as the argument and running the function. At the end of the function, the result is returned, sending 72 as the `answer`. ⑥

Listing 5.1   Defining and testing a function that adds an octave to any MIDI note number

```
// A Simple Function example

// Declare our function here          ❶ Function declaration
fun int addOctave( int note )
{
    int result;                        ❷ Result to return
    note + 12 => result;
    return result;                     ❸ Calculates the value to return
}
```

`Returns it` ❹

```
// Main addOctave Test Program, call and print out result
addOctave(60) => int answer;          ❺ Uses the function

<<< answer >>>;                       ❻ Checks the result
```

`answer` prints this out in the console:

```
72 :(int)
```

Calling `addOctave` with an argument of 72 would return 84, 90 would yield 102, and so on. Defining a function such as `addOctave` lets you use it over and again, and because it has a meaningful name, you know what it's doing each time you use it or see it in code.

Two ways to call functions in ChucK

Functions with one argument can be called in two ways:

`addOctave(60)`

or

`60 => addOctave;`

These two ways of invoking a function work exactly the same way.

Let's do a simple sonic/musical test of the `addOctave` function and also test two ways of calling functions, by adding these lines to listing 5.1. In listing 5.2 you play a sine tone ❶ on middle C (MIDI note 60, as assigned to an integer variable called note ❷). You first use the parentheses form of calling the `Std.mtof` ❸ and then use the "ChucK-to" form of the `addOctave` function and the `Std.mtof` function ❹. As you can hear, either works fine.

Listing 5.2   Testing the addOctave function with sound

```
// Let's use addOctave for music               ❶ Oscillator so you can hear
SinOsc s => dac;                                   addOctave function
60 => int myNote;                              ❷ Initial note

Std.mtof(myNote) => s.freq;                    ❸ Plays initial note
second => now;

myNote => addOctave => Std.mtof => s.freq;     ❹ Plays one octave up
second => now;
```

Now let's go back and test the `interval` function. You pass two input arguments to the function, `note1` and `note2`, as shown in the following listing. The function is executed twice, with two different pairs of numbers, which then computes the `result`, twice, returning it to the main program to be printed out, yielding this in the console:

```
12   -7
```

Listing 5.3   Defining and testing a MIDI interval function

```
// Function definition
fun int interval( int note1, int note2)
{
    note2 - note1 => int result;
    return result;
}

// Main program, test and print
interval(60,72) => int int1;
interval(67,60) => int int2;

<<< int1, int2 >>>;
```

5.1.3   *Local vs. global variables*

In the modified version of the program shown in listing 5.4, it's important to understand that global variables can be accessed everywhere, including inside the functions or any structure with a set of { }; the local variables from the function, in this case, `result`, can't be called outside that scope.

Every variable has a scope based on where it's defined, called the *locality*. In every function, there is a set of curly brackets { }. This defines the area of the local scope. So in the programs of listings 5.4 and 5.5, the `interval` function has local scope variables `note1`, `note2`, and `result`. The main program, as shown in listing 5.4, has global scope variables `int1`, `int2`, `glob`, and `howdy`.

The program in the following listing will give an error, "line 16: undefined variable result." But if you delete that last line, or comment it out by inserting // at the beginning, the program will run just fine.

Listing 5.4 Local vs. global scope of variables

```
// Define some global variables
"HOWDY!!" => string howdy;
100.0 => float glob;
int int1, int2;

// Function definition
fun int interval( int note1, int note2)
{
    int result;
    note2 - note1 => result;
    <<< howdy, glob >>>;
    return result;
}

// Main program, test and print
interval(60,72) => int1;
interval(67,60) => int2;

<<< int1, int2 >>>;

<<< result >>>; // This line will cause an error
```

Thus far you've made and used some simple functions that operate on integers interpreted as MIDI note numbers. Now you'll make and use some new float functions for gain and frequency.

5.2 Some functions to compute gain and frequency

Now that you've seen the basics of functions and used them to solve a few simple problems, let's put them into action to help control sound. You'll define functions that operate on floats, interpreted as gains (0.0 to 1.0) and frequencies, and then use those to make your programs more musically expressive. You'll set oscillator gains and frequencies using your new functions. You'll then look at defining and using a function to gradually ramp gain up and down, creating a smooth amplitude envelope for each note you play. You'll then go back to using a SndBuf to play a sound file, but with the addition of a function to chop up that file randomly, or *granularize* it, as it plays.

Let's begin with a simple program, shown in listing 5.5, that has a function called halfGain() ❷, which takes a floating point input value named originalGain and yields a floating point output. As you can see, this function is extremely simple, just dividing the input in half before it's returned to the main program. To use this, you make a SinOsc s connected to the dac ❶. Next you jump to the main program; execution skips the function definition until the function is explicitly called. You then print the current value of s.gain() ❸. Notice that when you call s.gain() with an empty set of parentheses, a method built into SinOsc returns the current value of the .gain of s. You wait for one second, letting the sine play at this initial volume. Then you call the function p with the input s.gain() ❹. The function executes, dividing originalGain in half and returning the new value of 0.5 to set s.gain. Again you wait for 1 second while object s is played at the new lower volume.

Listing 5.5   Function to cut gain (or any float) in half

```
SinOsc s => dac;                              ←        ❶ Oscillator to test halfGain function

// our function                              ←
fun float halfGain( float originalGain )
{                                                       ❷ Defines the halfGain function
    return (originalGain*0.5);
}

// remember that .gain is a function built into SinOsc
<<< "Full Gain: ", s.gain() >>>;             ←
second => now;                                          ❸ Prints initial gain of SinOsc

// call halfGain()
halfGain(s.gain()) => s.gain;                ←
<<< "Gain is now half: ", s.gain() >>>;                 Prints new SinOsc gain
second => now;                                        ❹ after cutting it in half
```

5.2.1 *Making real music with functions*

Next, you're going to build a real musical example that uses three different square wave oscillators: s, t, and u. This time you want to use functions to help set frequencies for all oscillators. First, you define two functions, octave() and fifth():

```
// functions for octave and fifth
fun float octave( float originalFreq )
{
    return 2.0*originalFreq;
}
fun float fifth( float originalFreq )
{
    return 1.5*originalFreq;
}
```

Notice that both of these functions have the same name, originalFreq, for the input argument. Because the scope of both variables is local only to each of the functions, it's okay! The originalFreq in function octave() can be seen only within its own local scope, just like the originalFreq in function fifth() can be seen only locally to that function. But to avoid confusion, you probably wouldn't want to label any global variable originalFreq.

If you dig a bit deeper, you'll see that the new octave() function is different from the previous one (which accepted a MIDI integer note number). This one takes the input variable and multiplies it by 2.0. The function expects a frequency value in Hertz. Acoustical theory says that an octave leap up occurs for every doubling of frequency. The fifth() function multiplies by 1.5 giving a musical interval called a "just fifth" (named because it's the fifth note in a standard musical scale) above any frequency argument.

Let's now look at a complete program that uses those two functions, to create a very rich-sounding ascending frequency sweep, as shown in listing 5.6. You first make three oscillators and connect them to the left, center, and right dac channels ❶. Then you set the gain of all oscillators ❷, so that when the sounds add together, the total won't exceed 1.0, which could cause the dac/speakers to overload and sound bad. Note that you take advantage of a feature of ChucK to set all three oscillators to the same value ❷; setting a parameter or variable value also returns that same value. The main program revolves around a for loop that increases from 100 to 500 by increments of 0.5 ❸. Each time around, the value of the for loop variable freq is used to set the frequency of SqrOsc s ❹. Then you use the return value of the octave() function to set the frequency of t ❺, and you use the fifth() function to set the frequency of u ❻.

Listing 5.6   Using functions to set oscillator frequencies

```
// three oscillators in stereo          ←───  Three square waves,
SqrOsc s => dac.left;                       ❶ panned left, center, right
SqrOsc t => dac;
SqrOsc u => dac.right;

// set gains so we don't overload the dac
0.4 => s.gain => t.gain => u.gain;     ←────── ❷ Sets gains of all three

// functions for octave and fifth
fun float octave( float originalFreq )
{
    return 2.0*originalFreq;
}

fun float fifth( float originalFreq )
{
    return 1.5*originalFreq;
}
                                              ❸ Sweeps frequency
                                                from 100 to 500 by
                                                ½ Hz each step
// Main program
for (100 => float freq; freq < 500; 0.5 +=> freq )  ←─┘
{                                             ❹ Sets left square wave to freq
    freq => s.freq;                    ←─────
    octave(freq) => t.freq;            ←───── ❺ Sets center square wave to octave above
    fifth(freq) => u.freq;             ←─
    <<< s.freq(), t.freq(), u.freq() >>>;     Sets right square
    10::ms => now;                          ❻ wave to fifth above
}
```

You've seen two examples of how functions can be used to help manipulate .gain and .freq methods of your oscillator unit generators. But you've been controlling .freq and .gain so far without using your own functions, right? It's nice, however, to have meaningfully named functions, even if they only do something that you could do otherwise, because anyone reading your code (including you in the future) can guess what the octave and fifth functions are doing.

5.2.2 Using a function to gradually change sonic parameters

In this next example we'll show you how to do something that would be much harder and less flexible to do without using a function. We're going to define a function to gradually change the volume of an oscillator, ramping it up and down at an arbitrary rate. If you look at the program in listing 5.7 you'll see our new swell() function ❶. Notice that it has four arguments: a UGen called osc and three floating-point inputs: begin, end, and step. The latter three variables are used to control two loops, one to increase ❷ and then another to decrease ❸ the volume of the oscillator osc.

> **NOTE** The swell function has a return type of void, which means it doesn't return a value at all, because it doesn't need to. Remember in chapter 1 when we introduced data types, and we promised you that we'd use void later on? Well, here we are. You can also make functions with void arguments, like you used for s.gain() in listing 5.6, because they don't need data input to do their thing. Some functions like this return a value, others do useful work without either needing or yielding data. These might work on global variables, advance time, or do other things.

Listing 5.7　Using a swell function to ramp oscillator volume up and down

```
// swell function, operates on any type of UGen
fun void swell(UGen osc, float begin, float end, float step)
{                                                          swell function
    float val;                                             definition ❶
    // swell up volume
    for (begin => val; val < end; step +=> val)            for loop to ramp
    {                                                      ❷ up volume
        val => osc.gain;
        0.01 :: second => now;
    }

    // swell down volume
    while (val > begin)
    {                                                      while loop to ramp
        val => osc.gain;                                   ❸ it back down
        step -=> val;
        0.01:: second => now;
    }
}
```

> **NOTE** When we defined our swell() function, we specified the first argument to be a UGen, which means that you can pass absolutely any type of unit generator into the function in that place. This takes advantage of a property called inheritance, which you'll learn more about in a later chapter. For now, you can exploit it to make your functions extremely flexible and much more reusable. You'll also learn about many more kinds of UGens, beginning in the next chapter.

If you look at our main program, shown in listing 5.8, which uses swell, you'll see an oscillator => dac sound chain ❶ and an array you'll use to play a melody ❷. Then you enter a loop to play all of the notes in the array ❸. Each time, the swell() function is called ❺. Note that swell() has time advancing inside it. It's important to understand that the main program jumps into the function at ❹ and procedurally executes every line of code. Time passes in this function as the volume changes, and when the function is complete, the function returns to the main program, which executes the next trip around the loop.

Listing 5.8   Main program uses `swell` to expressively play a melody

```
// Main program
// our sound "patch"
TriOsc tri => dac;                              ❶ Triangle oscillator to test
                                                   swell function

// global array of notes to play
[60,62,63,65,63,64,65,58,57,56] @=> int notes[];   ❷ Array of notes to play

// Swell through all notes                          ❸ Iterates through notes array
for (0 => int i; i < notes.cap(); i++)  {
    Std.mtof(notes[i]) => tri.freq;
    swell(tri,0.2,1.0,0.01);                    ❺ Calls swell function
}
```

Sets frequency ❹

As you can see, this is a highly expressive function that can be used to turn a simple oscillator into a musical instrument with smooth-sounding individual note beginnings and endings.

5.2.3   *Granularize: an audio blender function for SndBuf*

In a final example for this section, you'll use concepts you learned in chapter 4 (about samples and sound files) but now using a function. The program in listing 5.9 loads and plays a SndBuf ❶ but constantly chops it up, playing random pieces using the .pos() ❺ method. This is a form of sound synthesis and manipulation called *granular synthesis*, which has been around for a long time; even before digital, people cut and spliced pieces of audio tape to do granular synthesis.

In listing 5.9, you first make a SndBuf2 named click, connect it to the dac ❶, and load a nice stereo sound file ❷. Remember that the audio directory containing your sound files must be in the same place as this program. To exploit functions, you make a new one called granularize() ❸, which takes an argument called myWav (any SndBuf) and an integer called steps. This function uses steps to make random grains (little clips) of sound from myWav. To do that, it takes the total number of samples in the sound file and divides it by the steps variable to get a grain size ❹. You then select a random play position within the sound file ❺. You then advance time by grain and return to the main loop, which will be executed again forever.

Listing 5.9   Creating and using a cool `granularize()` function to chop up a sound file

```
SndBuf2 click => dac;                              ← ❶ Makes and connects
                                                       a stereo SndBuf2
// read soundfile
me.dir() + "/audio/stereo_fx_01.wav" => click.read;   ← ❷ Loads it with a
                                                           stereo sound file
// function to hack up any sound file
fun void granularize(SndBuf myWav, int steps )    ←
{                                                  ❸ Defines granularize function
    myWav.samples()/steps => int grain;
    Math.random2(0,myWav.samples() - grain) + grain => myWav.pos;   ←
    grain :: samp => now;
}                                                  Sets play pointer to
                                                   random grain
// Main Program                                    location in buffer ❺
while (true)
{
    // call function, time passes there
    granularize(click, 70);
}
```

Calculates grain size ❹

Aside from the awesome sounds your `granularize` function makes, the wonderful thing about this function is that it can take any sound file and chop it up, so it can be reused over and over again. All you have to do is load a different sound file.

TRY THIS   Load different sound files into the `click` SndBuf2 object in listing 5.9. There are other stereo and longer files in the audio directory you've been using, so try them out. Try changing the `steps` argument and hear the difference. Also, find other sound files (.wav, .aiff) on your computer, copy them into the audio directory, load them into `click`, and hear what they sound like when they're granularized.

5.3   *Functions to make compositional forms*

You've begun to see how you can use functions to give you lots of expressive control and in ways that you can use repeatedly. In this section you'll look at how functions can be used to help create new compositional forms. You'll first create a melody pattern, then learn how you can use functions to operate on arrays, both reading and modifying the internal elements. Finally, you'll make a super-flexible drum machine using functions and arrays.

5.3.1   *Playing a scale with functions and global variables*

Let's explore how functions and global variables can work together by writing a program that walks up and down a little scale pattern, rising in pitch forever. In listing 5.10, you'll use a new sound-making UGen, a `Mandolin`, and connect it to the `dac` ❶. The `Mandolin` is a complete "instrument" that you can play with simple commands like `.freq` (like SndBuf) and `.noteOn` (which essentially plucks the `Mandolin`). We'll talk more about `Mandolin` and many other UGens starting in the next chapter. Continuing with listing 5.10, you also define a global variable called `note` and initialize it to 60 (middle C) ❷. Both mand and note are global, because you declare them at the top of your program, outside any braces. Next, you define two functions: noteUp() ❸ and noteDown() ❼, which have no input arguments, because they operate only on global variables. Also notice that the output types are set to void (denoting no return value). If you now look more closely at noteUp() ❸, you'll see that it updates the global variable note, by adding one ❹, and prints out the new note value ❺. noteDown() ❼ has similar functionality but this time subtracts 1 from note ❽ You define one more function called play() ❾, which sets the pitch of your mand ❿, plucks it with noteOn ⓫, and advances time by 1 second ⓬. The two functions noteUp() and noteDown() call ❻ the play() function ❾ to cause the mandolin to play.

Listing 5.10 Void functions on global variables, for scalar musical fun

```
// global variables          ❶ Makes and connects a
Mandolin mand => dac;            Mandolin instrument UGen.
60 => int note;        ❷ Global note variable

// functions                 ❸ noteUp function definition
fun void noteUp()
{
    1 +=> note;     // note half-step up     ❹ Adds 1 to global note variable
    <<< note >>>;   // print new note value  ❺ Prints it out.
    play();         // call play function    ❻ Plays it.
}

fun void noteDown()          ❼ noteDown function
{
    1 -=> note;     // note half-step down
    <<< note >>>;   // print new note value  ❽ Subtracts 1 from global note variable
    play();         // call play function
}

// play global note on global mand UG    ❾ Defines play function
fun void play()
{                                          ❿ Sets global Mandolin frequency using global note
    Std.mtof(note) => mand.freq;
    1 => mand.noteOn;       ⓫ Plays note on Mandolin
    second => now;          ⓬ Hangs out for a second before returning to main loop
}
```

Now let's look at listing 5.11, which is the main infinite-loop program ❶ that uses our noteUp() and noteDown() functions. Notice that the loop doesn't have any advancement of time in it. In many cases, this means the program wouldn't work and ChucK would hang! But as you saw in the previous swell() and granularize() examples, time can be advanced inside functions. In this case, remember that when noteUp() is called ❷, after it does its work, it calls the play() function (❾ in the previous listing), which does its work and advances time by 1 second. After this is complete, play returns to noteUp(), which immediately returns to the main program, where noteDown() is called ❸. noteDown() decrements note, prints it out, calls play(), and then returns. This process continues for the remaining calls to noteUp() and noteDown().

Listing 5.11 Using the noteUp and noteDown functions in a main loop

Calls
noteUp... ❷

...calls
noteDown. ❸

```
// Main Program, gradually rising "melody"
while (true) {
    noteUp();      // execute noteUp, and when it's done
    noteDown();    // execute noteDown, and so on
    noteUp();
    noteUp();
    noteDown();
}
```

❶ Main program to test noteUp
and noteDown functions.

Then calls noteUp twice.

Then calls noteDown and loops.

This process keeps repeating, and this program plays the notes and prints out the following:

```
61 :(int)
60 :(int)
61 :(int)
62 :(int)
61 :(int)
62 :(int)
61 :(int)
62 :(int)
63 :(int)
62 :(int)
63 :(int)
… etc …
```

5.3.2   *Changing scale pitches by using a function on an array*

You'll now learn how you can use arrays with functions. Just as you passed UGens as arguments to functions, arrays are valid arguments as well. For example, you can define a function called arrayAdder that modifies one member (index) of an array (temp), to have a new value (add one to it). You'll use this shortly to change the pitches of a note array called scale.

```
fun void arrayAdder( int temp[], int index )
{
    1 +=> temp[index];
}
```

The following listing tests this new function, declaring a global array ❶ and our arrayAdder() function ❷ and then testing it out a couple of times, modifying two elements of the array.

Listing 5.12 Functions on arrays

```
// global array
[60,62,63,65,67,69,70,72] @=> int scale[];

// function to modify an element of an array
fun void arrayAdder( int temp[], int index)
```

❶ Global note array

❷ arrayAdder function to modify it

```
{
    1 +=> temp[index];
}
```

```
// test it all out
<<< scale[0], scale[1], scale[2], scale[3] >>>;
arrayAdder(scale, 2);
<<< scale[0], scale[1], scale[2], scale[3] >>>;
<<< "scale[6] = ", scale[6] >>>;
arrayAdder(scale, 6);
<<< "scale[6] = ", scale[6] >>>;
```

The console prints out

```
60 62 63 65
60 62 64 65
scale[6] = 70
scale[6] = 71
```

showing that the elements of the global array were indeed modified; array[2] went from 63 to 64, and array[6] went from 70 to 71.

More on scope: temporary copies of int and float arguments inside arrays

When you pass an int or float into an array, the variable inside the function is a copy of the value passed in, local only to that function. So this program

```
// global integer variable

60 => int glob;

// function adds one to argument

fun void addOne(int loc)

{

    1 +=> loc;

    <<< "Local copy of loc =", loc >>>;

}

// call the function

addOne(glob);

// nothing happens to global glob!!

<<< "Global version of glob =" , glob >>>;
```

prints out in the console

```
Local copy of loc = 61

Global version of glob = 60
```

clearly demonstrating that even though the local variable loc gets modified, the global variable passed in as the argument is not modified. For computer science techies, this is called *passing by value*, where the value of glob is copied into a locally declared variable, loc. Arrays are different, because they're passed into functions by reference, and the local array variable name is just a reference to the exact same array that was passed in.

> *(continued)*
>
> In other words, when you pass most data types into a function, you need to explicitly use the return keyword to get a result. But when you pass an array to a function, the contents of the array are modified directly.

Now let's put our `arrayAdder()` function to work for a musical purpose. Listing 5.13 makes a `Mandolin` ❶ on which to play a scale ❷, then uses the `arrayAdder()` function ❸ to convert the original scale array to a different scale. Using a new `playScale()` function ❹ you create to play the notes of any integer array passed in as an argument, you play the scale as it's originally defined ❺, then move the second and sixth elements up by one ❻, and then play the scale again ❼. Note that you call the `arrayAdder()` function twice ❻ and could call it any number of times with different arguments. This is the powerful aspect of functions, because they can be used over and over.

NOTE   For music theory types, we converted a Dorian minor mode scale into a standard major scale.

Listing 5.13   Using the `arrayAdder()` function to convert a scale from minor to major

```
// make a mandolin and hook it to audio out
Mandolin mand => dac;                          ←❶ Mandolin instrument.

// global scale array
[60,62,63,65,67,69,70,72] @=> int scale[];     ←❷ Scale array of note numbers.

// function to modify an element of an array
fun void arrayAdder( int temp[], int index)    ←❸ arrayAdder function definition.
{
    1 +=> temp[index];
}

//play scale on mandolin
fun void playScale(int temp[])  {              ←❹ playScale function definition.
    for (0 => int i; i < temp.cap(); i++)
    {
        Std.mtof(temp[i]) => mand.freq;
        <<< i, temp[i] >>>;
        1 => mand.noteOn;
        0.4 :: second => now;
    }
    second => now;
}

// play our scale on our mandolin
<<< "Original Scale" >>>;
playScale(scale);                 ←❺ Tests playScale.

// modify our scale
arrayAdder(scale,2);              ←❻ Call arrayAdder to change two elements.
arrayAdder(scale,6);
```

```
// play scale again, sounds different, huh?
<<< "Modified Scale:" >>>;
playScale(scale);
```

7 When we call playScale again. It's different!

5.3.3 Building a drum machine with functions and arrays

Now that you know how to use both global variables and arrays with functions, let's start looking at how you can make a program that builds form into your compositions. In listing 5.14, you start out by setting up bass drum and snare drum sound buffers **1**. Then you read in the sound files **2** and set their pointers to the end **3** (so they don't make any sound initially). Then you define arrays that you'll use to control your drum sample playback sequences **4**. In the function playSection() **5**, wherever you place a 1 in these arrays, you'll hear a sound, and a 0 will be silence. The main loop **6** calls playSection() with different pattern arrays **7** to make a drum loop.

Listing 5.14 Drum machine using patterns stored in arrays

```
// sound chain: two drums
SndBuf kick => dac;
SndBuf snare => dac;
```

1 SndBufs for kick and snare drum sounds

```
// load the sound files for our drums
me.dir() + "/audio/kick_01.wav" => kick.read;
me.dir() + "/audio/snare_03.wav" => snare.read;
```

2 Load kick and snare wave files

```
// set their pointers to end, to make no sound
kick.samples() => kick.pos;
snare.samples() => snare.pos;
```

3 Set initial positions to end so they don't play yet

```
// drum patterns as logical variables
[1,0,0,0,1,0,0,0] @=> int kickPattern1[];
[0,0,1,0,0,0,1,0] @=> int kickPattern2[];
[1,0,1,0,1,0,1,0] @=> int snarePattern1[];
[1,1,1,1,0,1,1,1] @=> int snarePattern2[];
```

4 Arrays to hold logical values play=1/not play=0

```
// function to play pattern arrays
fun void playSection(int kickA[], int snareA[], float beattime)
{
    for (0 => int i; i < kickA.cap(); i++)
    {
        if (kickA[i])
        {
            0 => kick.pos;
        }
        if (snareA[i])
        {
            0 => snare.pos;
        }

        beattime::second => now;
    }
}
```

5 Define playSection function, array arguments control patterns

```
// Main program, infinite loop
while (true)                          ←—— ❻ Infinite test loop
{
    playSection(kickPattern1,snarePattern2,0.2);
    playSection(kickPattern2,snarePattern2,0.2);        ❼ Calls playSection
    playSection(kickPattern1,snarePattern2,0.2);           with different
    playSection(kickPattern2,snarePattern1,0.2);           patterns
}
```

> **EXERCISE** Customize your drum machine! Change the 1s and 0s in the arrays, change the contents of the arrays used in the calls to playSection(), and change the tempo by changing the last argument in the calls to playSection(). Add more drums—you're the composer and the programmer!

So far in this chapter, using functions and arrays, you've greatly expanded your expressiveness and also made your code more flexible and readable. But you can go farther, of course.

5.4 *Recursion (functions that call themselves)*

You've learned the basics of functions and how they can transform your music and program architecture. Now it's time to learn advanced techniques that can result in very interesting sonic and structural materials. You've seen how functions can call other functions (like when noteUp() and noteDown() called play() in listing 5.10). But can functions call themselves? And why would you want to do that? There are many musical structures (like scales) and figures (like trills and drum rolls) that are really repeated events or transformations. Many of these might benefit from a function that can call itself.

Here we introduce the concept of *recursion*, which in programming means that useful things can happen because a function can call itself. Because functions let you get lots of useful work done, sometimes repeatedly, then a function calling itself might multiply its power dramatically. The classic example of recursion taught in nearly every programming book is that of the mathematical function factorial, but because we're artists, we'll put that off and jump right into a musical example. Listing 5.15 shows a mandolin ❶ that gets played by a function recurScale() ❷. After setting frequency ❸, plucking with noteOn ❹, and advancing time ❺, the function calls itself, with a lower note (subtract 1) and a shorter duration (90%) ❼. But it does this only if the argument is above some lower value (stops at note 40) ❻. Otherwise the function would keep calling itself forever.

> **Listing 5.15 Recursive (function that calls itself) scale-playing function**

```
// sound chain, mandolin to audio out
Mandolin mand => dac;                    ←——————— ❶ Mandolin instrument

// recursive scale player                          ❷ recurScale function definition
fun int recurScale(int note, dur rate) {  ←
    Std.mtof(note) => mand.freq;          ←——— ❸ Sets frequency of mandolin note
```

```
    1 => mand.noteOn;              ←————————— ④ Plays note using noteOn
    rate => now;                   ←————————— ⑤ Waits for duration rate

    // only do it until some limit is reached
    if (note > 40)                      ←————— ⑥ Limit for recursion
    {
        // here's the recursion, it calls itself!
        recurScale(note-1, 0.9*rate);   ←——
    }                                          ⑦ recurScale can call
}                                              recurScale!

// now play a couple of scales
recurScale(60, 0.5 :: second);
recurScale(67, 1.0 :: second);
```

So for a very small amount of code, you're able to play lots and lots of structured (non-random) notes, by exploiting the power of recursion. You could, of course, accomplish this same thing using a `for` loop or by explicitly coding each and every note, but recursion gives you yet another new and powerful technique for controlling your sound and music.

> **NOTE** We should warn you that, while extremely powerful, programming recursions can be a bit dangerous, because you always have to build the stopping conditions (`if note > 40`) into your recursions. Otherwise, they'll wind into themselves infinitely and never end. You always have the Remove Last Shred and Clear VM buttons on the miniAudicle to kill off any undead zombie processes, though.

5.4.1 *Computing factorial by recursion*

Let's go back to the mathematical factorial function, but very shortly you'll add a musical twist. The factorial function (written in math as N!, but we'll write it here as a function, `factorial(N)`) computes the product of an integer with every other integer less than it, down to integer 1. For example, `factorial(3)` is 3 * 2 * 1 = 6, and `factorial(4)` is 4 * 3 * 2 * 1 = 24. Factorial has real-world applications in statistics, counting things, and other areas. The number of four-letter combinations (permutations) of the letters ABCD (like ABCD, ACBD,....) is 24 (`factorial(4)`). Note that `factorial(4)` = 4 * `factorial(3)`, which is also 4 * 3 * `factorial(2)`, and so on. This allows you to use recursion to compute all factorials, just by writing one function, as shown in listing 5.16. The `factorial()` function calls itself unless the argument is less than 1, in which case it returns 1. So `factorial(4)` returns 4 * `factorial(3)`, which returns 3 * `factorial(2)`, which returns 2 * `factorial(1)`, which returns 1. All that returns the final value, 24.

Listing 5.16 Computing factorial by using recursion

```
fun int factorial( int x )
{
    if ( x <= 1 )
```

```
    {
        // when we reach here, function ends
        return 1;
    }
    else
    {
        // recursive function calls itself
        return (x*factorial(x-1));
    }
}

// Main Program, call factorial
<<< factorial(4) >>>;
```

5.4.2   *Sonifying the recursive factorial function*

For musical fun, let's *sonify* (turn data or process information into sound) the recursive factorial function, as shown in listing 5.17. Here you'll use a SinOsc ❶ but add a line inside the factorial function ❷ to sonify() ❸ the current value. That function adds half that number to 60 (middle C) ❹ and plays the associated frequency on your SinOsc ❺. In the main program you sonify the calls to factorial ❻, so what you actually hear is a number of low descending pitches. You hear one note for each (recursive) call to factorial, followed by the final higher pitch of the result. Listen carefully; you may hear that factorial(2) is equal to 2 (same note at beginning and end) and that factorial(5) yields a result that's almost too high to hear. This demonstrates, through sound, that the factorial function grows quickly in value for increasing argument value. This is one of the cool things about sonification and about ChucK.

Listing 5.17   Sonifying the factorial() function

```
// sound chain, SinOsc to audio out
SinOsc s => dac;                        ←   ❶ SinOsc so you can
                                              hear factorial
// our recursive factorial function
fun int factorial(int x)                ←       factorial function
{                                           ❷   definition
    sonify(x);                          ←
    if (x <=1) return 1;                    Call the sonify function
    else return (x*factorial(x-1));     ❸  within factorial
}

// a function to sonify numbers            ❹  Definition of the
fun void sonify(int note) {             ←      sonify function
    // offset above middle C
    Std.mtof(60+(0.5*note)) => s.freq;  ←
    1.0 => s.gain;                      ←          Sets frequency as
    300 :: ms => now;                          ❺  function of note
    0.0 => s.gain;                      ❻ Turns on Osc
    50 :: ms => now;
}
```

```
// try it out!
sonify(factorial(2));
second => now;
sonify(factorial(3));
second => now;
sonify(factorial(4));
second => now;
sonify(factorial(5));
second => now;
```

5.4.3 *Using recursion to make rhythmic structures*

Let's look at one more example in listing 5.18, similar to our factorial examples, this time to make a drumroll pattern but using only an `Impulse` unit generator ❶. The `Impulse` UGen generates a click each time you tell it to. In the `impRoll()` function ❷, you use the `index` argument as your counter to determine how many times the function will call itself recursively ❹, and you also use the `index` as your delay between impulses for advancing time ❸. The result is an ever accelerating roll, whose starting tempo and total length are determined by the argument to the call to the `impRoll()` function from the main program ❺.

Listing 5.18 Recursive drum roll using only an `Impulse` UGen

```
Impulse imp => dac;                       ❶ Impulse (click) generator to dac.

fun int impRoll(int index) {
    if (index >=1)                        ❷ impRoll function definition.
    {
        1.0 => imp.next;                  ❸ Duration is the recursion variable.
        index::ms => now;
        return impRoll(index-1);          ❹ Recursive call from impRoll to impRoll.
    }
    else {
        return 0;
    }
}

impRoll(20);
second => now;
impRoll(40);                              ❺ Tests all with different starting durations.
second => now;
impRoll(60);
second => now;
```

So you've seen that although they are powerful, functions that can call themselves can be super powerful. You can play many notes or sounds and compute complex mathematical results by exploiting recursion. But you also need to be careful in designing recursive functions, to make sure that they have a guaranteed stopping condition.

5.5 *Example: making chords using functions*

To wrap up this chapter, we want to give you one more musical example using functions, giving you the ability to play different types of chords (multiple simultaneous notes in harmony). To start, we're going to show you an advanced way to declare your UGen sound network, which is to declare an array of unit generators. Any data type or object can be declared and put into an array, so you'll use this to declare an array of SinOsc UGens named chord[] in the first line of listing 5.19 ❶. You want your chord to have three notes. You use a for loop to ChucK each element in your chord[] array to dac ❷, and then you set the .gain of each SinOsc so that they add up to 1.0 ❸.

The function playChord() takes in a *root* MIDI note number as an integer value, a chord quality (major or minor), and a duration of time that the chord will play, named howLong. Those of you who are musicians will know that major and minor chords consist of three notes: a root note ❹, a note a third above, and another note a fifth above. In both major and minor chords, the root and the fifth are the same. The fifth is seven MIDI notes higher than the root ❺. The difference comes with the third. A major third is four MIDI notes above the root ❻, sounding brighter; a minor third is three MIDI notes above the root ❼, sounding darker. You control all of this with simple if/else logic. You also do one more test to make sure the user has specified one of the legal chord qualities, major or minor ❽.

> **Listing 5.19 Playing chords on an array of SinOsc UGens, using a function**

```
// Sound Network
SinOsc chord[3];                    ❶ Three oscillators for a chord.

for (0 => int i; i < chord.cap(); i++)
{
    // connect each element of our array to dac
    chord[i] => dac;                ❷ Connects them to the dac...

    // adjust gain so we don't overload
    1.0/chord.cap() => chord[i].gain;   ❸ ...and sets their gains so
}                                        you don't overload.

fun void playChord(int root, string quality, dur howLong)
{
    // set root of chord
    Std.mtof(root) => chord[0].freq;    ❹ Root of chord.

    // set fifth of chord
    Std.mtof(root+7) => chord[2].freq;  ❺ Fifth of chord.

    // third sets quality, major or minor
    if (quality == "major")             ❻ Major chord.
    {
        Std.mtof(root+4) => chord[1].freq;
    }
    else if (quality == "minor") {      ❼ Minor chord.
        Std.mtof(root+3) => chord[1].freq;
    }
```

```
    else
    {
        <<< "You must specify major or minor!!" >>>;
    }
    howLong => now;
}
```

Prints error
message in case of
8 illegal argument.

The main program, shown in the following listing, is an infinite loop that calls the playChord() function **1**, generating a random number for the root value and playing a minor chord based on that note. Then you call playChord with two fixed chords, a C minor chord **2** and a G major chord **3**.

Listing 5.20   Using playChord

```
// Main program: now let's use playChord!!
while (true)
{
    playChord(Std.rand2(70,82), "minor", second/2);
    playChord(60, "minor", second/2);
    playChord(67, "major", second/2);
}
```

1 Plays a minor chord on a random note

2 Plays a C minor chord

3 Plays a G major

Exercise

Change the parameters to the calls to playChord, including root, quality, and duration. Add more calls to playChord() in the while loop. If you're really musically ambitious, try coding up a whole set of chord changes for a song. Hint, "Twinkle" might start like this:

```
playChord(60,"major", second/2);
playChord(60,"major", second/2);
playChord(72,"major", second/2);
playChord(60,"major", second/2);
playChord(65,"major", second/2);
playChord(65,"major", second/2);
playChord(60,"major", second/2);
```

5.6   *Summary*

In this chapter you learned how to write and use your own functions, including the following facts.

- Functions allow you to better organize and document your code.
- Functions are declared by name (unique, like variables), return type (int, float, UGen, any type, even void), and arguments (values passed in for the function to operate upon).

- Well-designed functions can be used over and over again between programs.
- Functions can call themselves. This is called recursion.
- Variables have scope, which is local to a function or curly brace context or global, visible to all code.

You made lots of interesting sounds and musical structures with your new skills and knowledge of functions. Going through all these examples on functions should give you a strong grasp on how to organize your code into modules and, in essence, make your programs much more expressive, readable, and reusable.

In the next chapter, we'll open the doors to creating new sounds in ChucK, looking at a variety of unit generators, which are the building blocks of sound synthesis and processing.

Part 2

Now it gets really interesting!

Now that you know the basics, part 2 will cover more advanced topics and features of the ChucK language. Chapter 6 introduces a number of new Unit Generators (UGens), which are ChucK's built-in audio processing and synthesis objects. UGens cover many models and techniques for sound synthesis and audio effects, so you'll know even more ways to make interesting sounds. Chapter 7 continues our coverage of UGens, introducing many of the physical, modal (resonant), and particle synthesis UGens available via the Synthesis ToolKit (STK).

Chapter 8 introduces multithreading and concurrency, the ability to run many programs or functions at the same time. Chapter 9 introduces object-oriented programming (OOP) and how you can create your own *objects* and *classes* to use in your code. By the end of this chapter, you'll know how to create smart musical instruments, and even play objects in code, which you can then in turn use to do your musical bidding.

Chapter 10 covers Events, which allow ChucK programs to signal each other. Events also allow ChucK to respond to signals and data from the "outside world," such as using your keyboard, mouse, or joystick for real-time control over your programs and compositions.

Chapter 11 looks at ways that ChucK can communicate with other programs, computers, and control devices. We briefly cover how MIDI can be used with ChucK, both using an external MIDI device (such as a keyboard) to play ChucK as a synthesizer, and how ChucK can control other synthesizers, both software and external hardware synths. We also introduce Open Sound Control (OSC), which is another standard way for music programs and devices to communicate. We then look at Serial Input/Output, which allows us to talk to even more devices. We conclude by talking about ways to extend ChucK itself.

Unit generators: ChucK objects for sound synthesis and processing

6

This chapter covers

- More ChucK oscillators
- Envelope generators
- Frequency modulation synthesis
- More about sound and acoustics, to motivate and inspire
- Intro to physical modeling synthesis

Okay, here's where it really gets good. Having covered much of how ChucK works, we can start digging into the specifics of synthesis and processing in ChucK. At the heart of the power of ChucK for audio synthesis and processing is the concept of UGens. You've already used UGens, starting with our "Hello Sine" example, where you ChucKed a SinOsc UGen to the dac to hear your first sound. You continued to use UGens in pretty much every program you've written so far. The nice thing is that you don't have to worry about how each UGen makes or processes sound; the designer of that UGen took care of that part. You only need to know what they can do and how to use them.

In this chapter, we'll introduce some of the UGens built into ChucK that you can use to make your music/sound making and processing very easy. You'll use a new type of oscillator (PulseOsc) to make sci-fi techno sounds. Up until now you've used gain to turn your sounds and musical notes on and off abruptly, but in this chapter you'll learn about and use *envelope generators*, which generate smooth functions in time. With envelopes, you'll be able to turn your notes on and off smoothly, like a DJ fading the sounds of turntables in and out, or a violinist starting and stopping the bowing of a note, which isn't abrupt, but has smooth ramps at the start and end. We'll introduce frequency modulation (FM) synthesis as well as sound synthesis and processing by *physical modeling*, where rather than synthesizing a desired output waveform, you model and compute the physics of waves as they vibrate and propagate (travel) inside instruments and rooms. In this chapter you'll build simple physical models of a plucked string and of the reverberation patterns in a room. We'll set the stage for the next chapter where we look at a lot of ChucK's built-in physical modeling instrument UGens. So let's get started!

Synthesis history: unit generators

The UGen idea goes far back, dating to analog synthesizer days when oscillators, noise sources, and other signal generators were patched through filters and other processors into mixers and eventually to amps and speakers. In 1967, when many synth pioneers were working with analog synthesis, Max Mathews (called by many the Father of Computer Music) at Bell Laboratories posed (and implemented) the idea of synthesizing sound and music digitally by connecting UGens to form instruments and using other programs to read scores to control it all to make music. Most computer music languages (ChucK included) since then have held to this basic idea.

6.1   *ChucK's special UGens: adc, dac, and blackhole*

You've been using the dac UGen throughout this book, to allow you to connect other UGens to the outside world of your speakers or headphones via your sound hardware. ChucK has two such special UGens that connect you to the outside world via your audio hardware. The reason they're special is that these three UGens (adc, dac, and blackhole) are always there, meaning that you don't have to declare them like other UGens such as SinOsc, SndBuf, or Impulse. Recall that when you used these other types of unit generators, you had to declare them in this manner:

```
SinOsc s => dac;
```

or

```
Impulse imp => ResonZ filter => dac;
```

But you didn't need to declare a dac variable name, because dac is always there, and there's only one of them. So you just call it simply dac.

The other special outside world UGen is called adc (for analog-to-digital converter), and it allows you to get sound into your computer from a built-in microphone, a mic-in or line-in jack, or other inputs via an externally connected sound card. To test this, you can make a connection from the input to the output on your computer. You might use the code in the following listing.

Listing 6.1   Connecting audio input to output using adc and dac

```
//connect audio input to audio output through Gain UG
adc => Gain g => dac;

//let it run for 10 seconds
10.0 :: second => now;
```

> **CAUTION! CAUTION! CAUTION!**   Be extremely careful before you execute this code, making sure that there won't be an ear-splitting feedback loop (as can happen when sound from your speakers gets back into your microphone). Plug in headphones, or turn your speaker volume way down before hooking the adc to the dac (running this code).

Strictly speaking, you don't need the Gain UGen between the adc and the dac, but you should always avoid connecting the adc to the dac directly. The reason for this is that adc and dac are the only persistent UGens in all of ChucK, and once connected they stay connected until explicitly disconnected (by unChucKing using =<). In listing 6.1, however, the Gain UGen you named g will disappear after the code has finished executing, thus breaking the connection from input to output. Note that you didn't have to declare a variable of type adc and give it a name, as you had to for the Gain UGen, and you didn't have to name your dac. Both adc and dac are unique in this way. All other unit generators require you to make a variable and give it a name if you want to use one.

So now you know how to listen to a mic connected or built into your computer, but what if you want to use a microphone to detect if there's a loud sound nearby, so you can do interesting things based on that, but you don't want to listen directly to that microphone sound? ChucK has one more special UGen called blackhole, which acts like a dac that isn't connected to any sound device. There are many reasons why you might want to connect sound to an output that doesn't make sound, but the main one is if you want to do signal processing of some type (like pitch detection) or to inspect a signal (like the loud sound detector we mentioned previously), without connecting that path directly to any sound output. The blackhole UGen serves to suck samples from any and all UGens that are connected to it. Those UGens wouldn't compute any new sound otherwise, because ChucK is clever about being efficient and not computing any samples that don't get used somewhere. The blackhole serves to use those samples, even though you never hear them.

Listing 6.2 is an example of using blackhole to do something useful, specifically to keep an eye on the input from the adc and print out a message if things get too loud ❶. The g.last() in the if conditional ❷ returns the last sample passed through the Gain UGen. You can change the value that's compared (0.9) to any value you like. For example, changing it to 0.001 means the program will print out for even quiet inputs (maybe all the time), and changing it to 10.0 means it may never print out at all. This kind of audio peak detector is useful for lots of things in real life, such as automatic gain control or art installations that respond to sound.

> **Listing 6.2   An audio peak detector in ChucK**

```
// suck samples through Gain UGen into blackhole
adc => Gain g => blackhole;           ← ❶ blackhole sucks samples
                                          from adc through Gain
while (true)
{
    if (g.last() > 0.9)               // if it's loud enough   ←
    {                                                          .last() gets last
        <<< "LOUD!!!", g.last() >>>;  // print it out          sample from
    }                                                        ❷ any UGen
    samp => now;                      // do this for every sample
}
```

NOTE   This code takes advantage of your ability to manipulate time in ChucK in a completely flexible way, in this case advancing time by one sample, each and every sample, so you can look at the individual values as they come in from the adc.

6.2   *The pulse width oscillator: an electronic music classic*

Remember when you wrote your very first ChucK program to make sound ("Hello Sine!")? You used a SinOsc UGen, hooking it to the dac to make your first note (pure pitched sound). We also talked about and used a few of the other oscillator-type UGens: TriOsc, SawOsc, and SqrOsc. ChucK has more oscillator-type UGens, and you're going to use one of those now to make great electronic dance-type sounds and music.

The PulseOsc UGen generates a square pulse (like SqrOsc), but you can also control the fraction of each period that's high versus low (this is called the pulse width, or the duty cycle). You can set or vary the duty cycle of PulseOsc anywhere between 0.0 and 1.0, to create varied spectral sounds (a small duty cycle yields a very bright spectrum; 0.5 yields less bright). Figure 6.1 shows the output of PulseOsc for two different widths: 0.1 (high only 10% of the time) and 0.5 (equal 50% high and low times, like a square wave).

The 0.5 setting, also called 50% duty cycle, generates the same waveform that SqrOsc does. Such oscillators with varying pulse widths are commonly used in electronic dance music, often changing the pulse width in rhythm to the music. Sweeping the pulse width dynamically can make cool science-fiction sound effects as well.

The code in listing 6.3 generates a techno dance bass line, using a PulseOsc connected to the dac as a sound source. In the main infinite loop, you set the pulse width randomly between 0.01 (really spikey, therefore really bright sounding) and 0.5 (square, more mellow sounding). You also use Math.random2(0,1) to flip a coin, to

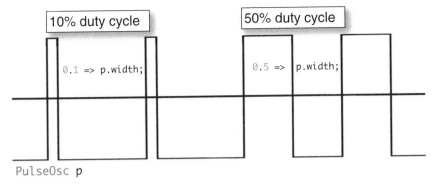

Figure 6.1 `PulseOsc` waveforms for 0.1 (10% text high time) and 0.5 (50%) duty cycles

determine one of two pitches for your pulse wave. The lower frequency of 84 Hz is close to a musical E2 (the lowest string on a guitar), and the frequency of 100 is close to the note G2 above that. To get rhythm, you switch your oscillator on and off every tenth of a second, on for 60 milliseconds (0.06 seconds) and off for 40 milliseconds (0.04 seconds).

Listing 6.3   Sci-fi techno dance bass line using the `PulseOsc` UGen

```
//PulsOsc for techno-bass, by ChucK Programmer, 2014
PulseOsc p => dac;                           // connect a new PulseOsc to dac

// infinite loop of sci-fi techno!
while (true)
{
    Math.random2f(0.01,0.5) => p.width;      // set random pulse width
    if (Math.random2(0,1))                   // pick a pitch randomly
    {
        84.0 => p.freq;                      // from one of
    }
    else
    {
        100.0 => p.freq;                     // two different pitches
    }

    1 => p.gain;                             // turn on oscillator
    0.06 :: second => now;                   // hang out a bit

    0.0 => p.gain;                           // turn off oscillator
    0.04 :: second => now;                   // hang out a bit
}
```

6.3   *Envelope (smooth slow function) unit generators*

So far in your programs, to separate repeated notes or to make sounds with rhythm, you've turned your oscillators on and off by changing a gain somewhere in your sound chain. You set it to zero for silence and non-zero for sound making, switching between those to play individual notes. But most sounds and musical notes don't work that way in nature: When you blow into a clarinet or trumpet, or start bowing a violin, or begin to sing, the notes don't switch on instantly. When you stop blowing, bowing, or singing, you don't hear a click because the sound stopped instantly. For most instruments, you can choose to start a note softly and get louder or start loud and get softer. There must be a better way to turn your notes on and off more gradually, and indeed there is.

Envelope UGens built into ChucK gradually ramp up and down to control volume or other parameters you might want to change slowly. The Envelope UGen ramps from 0.0 to 1.0 in response to a .keyOn message, over a time set by the .time method. The Envelope UGen ramps back to zero in response to a .keyOff message.

6.3.1   *Making a clarinet sound using SqrOsc and Envelope*

In chapter 1 we talked about how a square wave can sound somewhat like a clarinet and how the stick-slip physics of bowed strings generate something like a sawtooth wave. Now, by applying an Envelope to a SqrOsc, you can build a super-simple clarinet that more properly (gradually) starts and stops notes.

Listing 6.4 shows a simple example of using the Envelope and SqrOsc UGens to make a clarinet sound. Note that you connect the oscillator through the Envelope to the dac ❶. After setting an initial frequency ❷, you use a while loop ❸ to play individual notes by triggering the Envelope ❹, waiting a bit to let it smoothly rise, and then turning the Envelope off ❺ (again waiting a bit to let it ramp down). We use a loop to play what's called a "harmonic series," increasing the pitch by 55 Hz. each time ❻.

Listing 6.4   Simple clarinet synthesis with Envelope applied to SqrOsc

```
// Simple Clarinet Synthesis
// Envelope applied to SqrOsc
SqrOsc clar => Envelope env => dac;          ❶ Square wave mimics
// initial note frequency (musical A)           Clarinet waveform.
55.0 => clar.freq;                           ❷ Sets initial pitch.
// play up the overtone series
while (clar.freq() < 441.0)                  ❸ Loops over three octaves of pitches.
{
    // trigger envelope
    1 => env.keyOn;                          ❹ Envelope.keyOn starts note.
    // hang out a bit
    0.2 :: second => now;
    // tell envelope to ramp down
    1 => env.keyOff;                         ❺ Envelope.keyOff ends note.
    // hang out some more
    0.2 :: second => now;
    // next note up the overtone series
    clar.freq() + 55.0 => clar.freq;         ❻ Increases pitch, climbing
}                                               up harmonic series.
```

The left side of figure 6.2 shows the waveform generated by a single note of the code of listing 6.4. Note that the note starts and ends gradually, rather than switching on and off (shown for comparison on the right side of figure 6.2).

Figure 6.2 Envelope UGen applied to SqrOsc (left), compared to no Envelope (right)

There are other methods you can use with `Envelope`, such as causing it to move to an arbitrary target value in response to the `.target` message, or you can set the output immediately using the `.value` method. For example, `0.5 => env.target` causes the envelope value to ramp to `0.5` (no matter what its current value) and stay there once the value of `0.5` is reached. Invoking `0.1 => env.value` causes it to immediately begin putting out that value, forever, until a `keyOn`, `keyOff`, `target`, or a new `value` message is sent.

6.3.2 *Making a violin sound with SawOsc and the ADSR Envelope UG*

Moving to a new instrument model, if you wanted to make a violin-like sound, you could swap the square wave for a sawtooth oscillator in the previous example. But let's do some more interesting things to make it sound even more like a bowed fiddle. Violinists tend to use specific gestures to attack the notes, often shown in their physical motions when playing. There's a more advanced and useful type of envelope generator in ChucK, the `ADSR` (which stands for attack, decay, sustain, release). Figure 6.3 shows a typical function generated by an `ADSR` UGen, in this case with attack, decay, and release set to `0.1` seconds and sustain level set to `0.5`. You can set all of those individually using the `.attackTime`, `.decayTime`, `.sustainLevel`, and `.releaseTime` methods/functions, or you could do it all by using the `.set` method like this:

```
myEnv.set(0.1 :: second, 0.1 :: second, 0.5, 0.1 :: second);
```

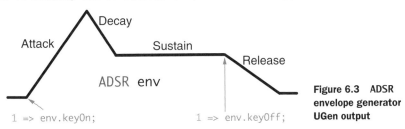

Figure 6.3 ADSR envelope generator UGen output

Note in figure 6.3 that both decay and release took only half as long as the attack, even though their times were set to the same duration. This is because they have to go only half as far, from 1.0 to 0.5 for decay down to the sustain level and from `0.5` to `0.0` for the release phase.

To make your simple violin synthesizer, you can combine an `ADSR` envelope generator with a `SawOsc`, like this:

```
SawOsc viol => ADSR env => dac;
```

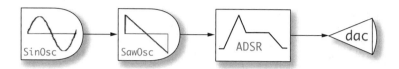

Figure 6.4   A simple violin patch uses sine wave vibrato oscillator, sawtooth oscillator, and ADSR.

But there's more to a violin sound than a sawtooth wave. Violins are famous for their vibrato, so you might want to do something about that as well. This is a perfect time to talk about a feature of the `Oscillator` UGens, and that's that you can ChucK a signal into them to modulate things like frequency or phase. This is very good news indeed, because you can use a `SinOsc` to generate vibrato for your violin synthesizer, something like what's shown in figure 6.4.

```
SinOsc vibrato => SawOsc osc => ADSR env => dac;
```

But that won't exactly work yet, because you first need to tell your `SawOsc` to interpret the sine wave input as a frequency modulation. To do that you use the `.sync()` method ❶, as shown in listing 6.5. And you need to set the frequency of your vibrato to something reasonable, like 6 Hz, using the `.freq()` method ❷. You can set all envelope parameters at once ❸, define a scale in an array ❹, and then play up that scale using a `for` loop ❺, setting the pitch of the violin ❻ and playing each note using the ADSR. Finally, you increase the vibrato and play the last note longer ❼.

Listing 6.5   Simple violin using `SawOsc`, `Envelope`, and `SinOsc` for vibrato

```
// Simple SawOsc-based violin with ADSR envelope and vibrato
SinOsc vibrato => SawOsc viol => ADSR env => dac;
// Tell the oscillator to interpret input as frequency modulation
2 => viol.sync;
// set vibrato frequency to 6 Hz
6.0 => vibrato.freq;
// set all A D S R parameters at once
env.set(0.1 :: second, 0.1 :: second, 0.5, 0.1 :: second);
// define a D Major Scale (in MIDI note numbers)
[62, 64, 66, 67, 69, 71, 73, 74] @=> int scale[];

// run through our scale one note at a time
for (0 => int i; i < scale.cap(); i++)
{
    // set frequency according to note number
    Std.mtof(scale[i]) => viol.freq;
    // trigger note and wait a bit
    1 => env.keyOn;
    0.3 :: second => now;
    // turn off note and wait a bit
    1 => env.keyOff;
    0.1 :: second => now;
```

Sets vibrato frequency ❷

Makes a scale note array ❹

Tells the SawOsc to interpret vibrato input as ❶ frequency modulation

Configures ADSR envelope ❸ parameters

Plays through whole ❺ scale using for loop

Sets frequency ❻ for each note

```
}
// repeat last note with lots of vibrato
1 => env.keyOn;
10.0 => vibrato.gain;          <—————— 7 Uses more vibrato for last note
1.0 :: second => now;
0 => env.keyOff;
0.2 :: second => now;
```

There are other oscillator types, including a whole family of GenX table generators, such as exponential, polynomial, line-segment, and UGens that automatically add together harmonic sine waves. All of these function as lookup tables (value in yields value out) but can also be used as oscillators by driving them with a special Phasor UGen. All of these, and more, are covered more in depth in appendix C.

6.4   *Frequency modulation synthesis*

If you set the frequency of the vibrato oscillator in figure 6.4 to much higher in the audio range, you'll hear something quite odd. That's exactly what happened to composer John Chowning at the Stanford Center for Computer Research in Music and Acoustics (CCRMA) when he typed in 100 instead of 10 for the frequency of a vibrato oscillator. He was using sine waves for both oscillators, but what he heard sounded a lot more interesting than just a wiggly sine wave or two. He asked around and discovered that what he was hearing was a complex spectrum created by frequency modulation (FM).

If you change the viol SawOsc oscillator in listing 6.5 to a SinOsc, set vibrato.freq to 100.0, and set the vibrato.gain to something larger, like 1000.0, you'll hear something a lot like what Chowning heard in 1967. What you're hearing is a whole bunch of sine frequencies that are created when the one wave (called the *modulator*) modulates the frequency of the other (called the *carrier*). One way to view this is that by changing the frequency of the carrier rapidly, the sine wave shape is distorted into a different shape. In fact, FM is part of a class of synthesis algorithms called wave shaping.

Now change the line inside the loop (6 in listing 6.5 and repeated here) so that the viol and vibrato oscillators get set to the same frequency, and change the vibrato.gain so you get more modulation:

```
// set both frequencies according to note number
   Std.mtof(scale[i]) => viol.freq => vibrato.freq;   <—— 6
   100 => vibrato.gain;
```

You'll note that it sounds sort of like a brass instrument playing a scale. Now change the single line of 6 to two lines:

```
// set carrier and modulator freq randomly
   Math.random2f(300.0,1000.0) => viol.freq;
   Math.random2f(300.0,1000.0) => vibrato.freq;
```

Run it a few times. You'll notice that each note has a different character, generally inharmonic bell-like tones (but minus the decay characteristics that bells have).

Chowning worked out that if the carrier and modulator frequencies aren't related by simple integer ratios (C:M ratio of 1:2, 2:1, 2:3, 1:3, …), then the resulting spectrum will be inharmonic. He went on to synthesize bells, brass, voices, and other interesting sounds, all using just sine waves! Adding and combining more modulators and carriers can yield even more interesting sounds.

ChucK has a number of built-in FM UGens and presets for those to model the spectra of a variety of instruments, including electric pianos (Rhodey and Wurley). The following listing is a simple program for testing the Wurley electric piano.

Listing 6.6   Simple FM test program

```
// FM Unit Generator Instrument Test Program
// by FM Dude, March 4, 1976

// make an FM instrument and connect to dac
Wurley  instr => dac;                        ←———————————— ❶ FM electric piano

// play it forever with random frequency and duration
while (true) {
    Math.random2f(100.0,300.0) => instr.freq;

    // turn note on (trigger internal ADSR)
    1 => instr.noteOn;                       ←—————— ❷ Turns on note, waits a (random) bit
    Math.random2f(0.2,0.5) :: second => now;

    // turn note off (ramp down internal ADSR)
    1 => instr.noteOff;                      ←—————— ❸ Turns off note, waits a (random) bit
    Math.random2f(0.05,0.1) :: second => now;
}
```

Exercise

Other STK FM instruments include an organ (BeeThree), FMVoices, orchestra chimes (TubeBell), flute (PercFlut), and distorted guitar (HevyMetl). Switch out the Wurley UGen in ❶ for some of the others (TubeBell, PercFlut, Rhodey, and so on). Because these UGens are complete self-contained instruments, they respond to noteOn ❷ and noteOff ❸ messages, which turn on and off the internal ADSR envelope generators that control the levels of the internal carrier and modulator oscillators.

6.5   *Plucked string synthesis by physical modeling*

It's probably time to observe that the clarinet and violin you've built so far don't sound very realistic, which might be fine for many purposes, but you can do better by looking at the physics involved in instruments like the clarinet, violin, and trombone. Physical modeling (PM) synthesis solves the equations of waves in and around sound-making objects to automatically generate the sounds. This differs greatly from what you've done so far, where you synthesized a waveform or noise of some type. In PM, you emphasize the physics of the instrument, with faith that the resulting waveform will come out right.

In this section, you'll be building an increasingly realistic string model, starting with the absolute simplest model (an impulse-excited delay line, to model the pick sound traveling down and back along the string), then adding a better excitation (noise), then improving the delay line to allow for better tuning, and finally adding even more control over the pick excitation. Let's begin with one of the first historical computer string models.

6.5.1 *The simplest plucked string*

One of the earliest, most basic physical models for sound synthesis is that of a plucked string. The simplest version of this involves a *delay line* (a UGen that delays the signal from input to output, so that anything going in comes back out unmodified, but later in time), fed back into itself, and excited with an impulse as input. Of course, ChucK has all of these elements built in as UGens. This code shows the Impulse UGen fed into a delay line and then to the dac; then the delay line is hooked back up to itself to form a loop:

```
Impulse imp => Delay str => dac; // impulse feeds a delay line
str => str;                      // loop the delay back into itself
```

The Impulse UGen generates a single sample of output whenever you set its .next method to any value other than zero. That is, the line 1.0 => imp.next; ❶ in listing 6.7 causes imp to put out 1.0 on the next sample and then 0.0 forever after until you use the .next method again.

Why is an impulse fed into a delay line and then fed back into itself a physical model? Because this sound chain is a valid physical simulation of a plucked string, where traveling waves move up and down along the string, with slight losses for each trip.

> ### Synthesis history: physical modeling
> The Plucked String synthesis algorithm (also called the Karplus-Strong algorithm) was discovered in 1982 by Stanford computer scientists Kevin Karplus and Alan Strong. That same year, Julius Smith and David Jaffe (an electrical engineer and a composer, working together at Stanford CCRMA) explained the model scientifically and improved it. Smith called the structure a "waveguide filter," because the string (delay) guides the wave (impulse) back and forth along the string. Physical modeling synthesis is often called waveguide synthesis.

If you set the round-trip string gain to something less than 1.0 (to represent the slight losses) and set the string length (delay time) to some reasonable value for the round-trip time (the period of oscillation of the string), then you've built a primitive string model, as shown in the following listing.

Listing 6.7   Simple plucked string physical model

```
// Super simple Karplus-Strong plucked string
Impulse imp => Delay str => dac;
// connect string back into itself
str => str;
// round-trip string delay, 100 Hz At 44.1k SRATE
441.0 :: samp => str.delay;
// set round-trip string gain to less than 1.0
0.98 => str.gain;
// "pluck" the string
1.0 => imp.next;                          ← ① Tells the impulse to output a
// let the string "ring" a bit                1.0 (only for the next sample)
5.0 :: second => now;
```

This makes a sound that's vaguely string-like, in that it starts suddenly, decays more slowly, and has a pitch. But you can do better, by exciting the string with something more interesting than an impulse.

6.5.2   *Exciting the plucked string with noise*

The original plucked string model inventors actually excited (plucked) their string with noise rather than an impulse. This corresponds to a really energetic pluck, but it sounds bright and very cool. Fortunately, ChucK has a built-in Noise UGen, but it puts out noise constantly, unlike the Impulse, which spits out a pulse whenever you set the .next value. So you need to *gate* (switch on) the output of the Noise UGen to excite the delay line string when you pluck, then shut off the noise after a very short period of time. To do this, you can switch on the noise (set its gain to 1.0) for the number of samples equal to the length of the delay line, then switch it off (set the noise gain to 0.0), as shown in the next listing.

Listing 6.8   Better plucked string physical model, excited with noise

```
// Better Karplus-Strong plucked string
Noise pluck => Delay str => dac;
// hook string back into itself
str => str;
// round-trip string delay, 100 Hz At 44.1k SRATE
441.0 :: samp => str.delay;
// set round-trip string gain to less than 1.0
0.98 => str.gain;
// "pluck" the string for the right amount of time
1.0 => pluck.gain;
441.0 :: samp => now;
// shut off the noise generator
0.0 => pluck.gain;
// let the string "ring" a bit
5.0 :: second => now;
```

You need to do one more thing to copy what Karplus and Strong were doing, which will also make your simple plucked string sound even better. That is to add a filter in the string loop (delay line) to model the fact that the losses experienced by the waves traveling up and down the strings are frequency-dependent, where for each trip around the string, high frequencies experience more losses than low frequencies.

6.5.3   *Modeling frequency-dependent decay with a filter*

To model the frequency-dependent decay, you need only modify the line where you hook the string to itself by adding a low-pass filter, which reduces the gain of high frequencies more than low frequencies.

```
str => OneZero filter => str;
```

With this filter added, your string will instantly sound better and more realistic. OneZero is a very simple filter UGen, which we'll talk more about very soon.

6.5.4   *Modeling fractional (tuning) delay*
and adding an ADSR for plucking

You can also add one thing; the Delay line needs to support fractional samples of delay, so you can tune your string to arbitrary frequencies. Remember, in chapter 1 you learned that you needed floating-point numbers to express some pitches because integers wouldn't do. For the string model, fractional delay is especially important for high frequencies, because the delay line gets pretty short and the difference between 44 samples and 45 samples at 44.1 kHz sample rate is 980 Hz versus 1002.27 Hz. If you needed exactly 995 Hz, then you'd need a delay of 44.3216 samples. Fortunately, ChucK has built-in interpolating delays, named DelayL (for linear interpolation between samples) and DelayA (for allpass, an odd type of filter that can yield fractional samples of delay). So all you'd have to do is replace Delay with DelayL or DelayA to enable fractional delay and thus arbitrary tuning. These delay UGens accept a floating-point number for delay, so you can set them to any length, such as this:

```
44.3216 :: samp => str.delay;
```

You can also use an ADSR to let your noise pluck into the string, which means you don't have to turn it on and off explicitly. Once you've configured the attack, decay, sustain, and release parameters, you can use ADSR's .keyOn method to accomplish your plucking. All of this is shown in figure 6.5 and the following listing.

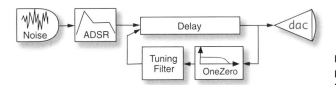

Figure 6.5   Karplus-Strong plucked string model with noise pluck and loop filters

---

Listing 6.9   Even better plucked string, with enveloped noise and low-pass filter

```
// Even Better Karplus-Strong plucked string
Noise nois => ADSR pluck => DelayA str => dac;          Noise through ADSR into
                                                        interpolating delay line

// hook string back into itself
str => OneZero lowPass => str;                           Feedback delay through
                                                        a low-pass loop filter

// set ADSR noise envelope parameters
pluck.set(0.002 :: second, 0.002 :: second, 0.0, 0.01 :: second);   Sets ADSR parameters to pluck
                                                                    rapidly and then stick at 0.0
// Play random notes forever
while (true)
{
    Math.random2f(110.0, 440.0) :: samp => str.delay;   Can now set
    // turn on note (pluck string) and wait a bit       delay length to
    1 => pluck.keyOn;                                    any arbitrary
    0.3 :: second => now;                                float number
}                           Plucks by sending keyOn to
                            ADSR, gates noise into string
```

6.6   *Intro to filter UGens: frequency-dependent gain*

What was that magic OneZero UGen you just used to provide the frequency-dependent gain in your string loop? The OneZero UGen uses simple math that adds its current input sample to its last input sample and divides the result by 2, thus computing an average of those samples. Another name for this filter is Moving Average.

```
(thisInput + lastInput) / 2 => output;
```

Averaging tends to smooth out rough signals, reducing high frequencies, while emphasizing smoother, lower-frequency signals. This is precisely what happens in a real stringed instrument as the waves travel down and back on the string. The frequency response of the OneZero UGen illustrated in figure 6.6, shows a gain of 1.0 for the lowest frequency (0.0 Hz), less gain for increasing frequencies, and a gain of 0.0 for the frequency at half the sample rate. This gain of zero at one frequency is the "one zero" in this filter name.

One other type of filter UGen we like to use a lot is ResonZ, shown in listing 6.10, which creates a single resonance (higher gain at one selectable frequency) on any

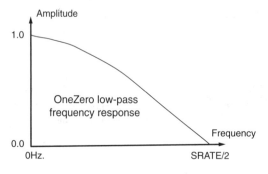

Figure 6.6   The OneZero moving average filter exhibits a simple low-pass frequency response.

signal passed through it. ResonZ responds to .freq, which sets the resonance frequency, and .Q, which stands for "quality factor" and determines the amount of emphasis at the resonant frequency. If you set .Q very high, ResonZ can oscillate as a sine wave; if you set .Q to 100 or so ❷ and feed the filter with an Impulse excitation ❶, you get a pitched ping or pop sound at the resonance frequency each time you fire the impulse ❸.

Listing 6.10 Simple resonant-filtered impulse makes for cool computer music

```
// Computer music!!  Impulse through resonant filter
Impulse imp => ResonZ filt => dac;

// Set the Q (Quality) fairly high, to yield a pitch
100.0 => filt.Q;

while (1)
{
    // pick a random frequency
    Math.random2f(500.0,2500.0) => filt.freq;

    // fire our impulse, and hang out a bit
    100.0 => imp.next;
    0.1 :: second => now;
}
```

❶ Impulse excites resonant filter.

❷ Q (quality) is amount of resonance.

❸ Tells impulse to output 100.0 (only on next sample).

For shaping sounds and special effects, there are filter UGens for doing high-pass (HPF), low-pass (LPF), band-pass (BPF), and band-reject (BRF). These all are controlled using the .freq and .Q methods. The frequency range that can get through these filters is called the *passband*, and frequencies that receive decreased gain are called the *stopband*. The boundary between the passband and the stopband is called the *cutoff frequency*, which is set by the .freq method. Again, Q stands for "quality" and determines the amount of emphasis at the cutoff frequency and the rolloff (gain slope down into the stopband).

Figure 6.7 shows the frequency response (gain versus frequency) of an LPF unit generator, with Q set to 1, 10, and 100. Passband, stopband, and rolloff regions are labeled.

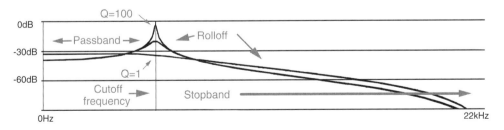

Figure 6.7   LPF low-pass filter frequency response for Q=1, Q=10, and Q=100

The following listing shows the use of the LPF (passes all frequencies below the cutoff set by the `.freq` method) UGen (resonant low-pass filter) to filter noise.

Listing 6.11   Testing the LPF resonant low pass filter with noise input

```
// pass noise through low pass filter
Noise nz => LPF lp => dac;

// set frequency and Q
500.0 => lp.freq;
100.0 => lp.Q;
0.2 => lp.gain;

second => now;
```

Exercise

Change LPF to HPF in listing 6.11. In the LPF case you should hear low frequencies up to the resonance frequency. In the HPF case you should hear high frequencies down to the resonance frequency. Try BPF and BRF. What do you hear? Change the `.freq` and `.Q` values and note how the sound changes.

6.7   *More on delays: room acoustics and reverberation*

When a sound is produced, the waves propagate (travel) outward from the sound source. Sounds made in rooms travel outward and bounce off the walls, floor, ceiling, and objects in the room (see figure 6.8). You might know that a single reflection of a sound off one boundary, such as a wall or building, is called an echo if the time delay is long enough for you to hear that reflected sound by itself (greater than 50 ms or so).

In a reasonable-size room, the reflections are shorter in time than echoes and add back together at the ears of a listener (or a microphone), to create reverberation. Because sound waves take time to travel, those trips around the room, bouncing off walls and other obstacles, take different times to eventually reach your ears (where all of the reflections add together). Remember when we were talking about the speed of sound, wavelengths, and stuff like that? Now that you know about Delay UGens, you can put all of that to work to make a simple model of the acoustics of a room. You'll be able to feed any signal (like our microphone in through the adc) through this room acoustics patch and give it the sound of being in that room.

Let's assume you want to model a room measuring 40-by-50 feet, with a 30-foot-high ceiling (figure 6.8). I know that's a high ceiling, but the 3 x 4 x 5 dimensional trick is well known to designers of speakers, concert halls, and other acoustical things. If you assume the walls of your room are parallel and pretty reflective, then the path between each pair of parallel walls is much like our string that we developed in section 6.5.1 where waves travel back and forth, being reflected and absorbed a little each trip. Because you have three primary sound reflection paths, between the two pairs of walls and from the ceiling to the floor, you can use three delay lines to model the gross acoustics of your box-shaped room. The round-trip time between the wall pair spaced

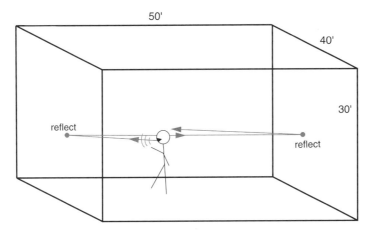

Figure 6.8   Sounds travel and bounce off (reflect from) walls before reaching your ears. If one of those reflections comes back significantly later in time, it's called an echo. Lots of shorter time reflections from all the walls, ceiling, and floor combine to become reverberation.

at 50 feet is 100 ms (an approximate rule of thumb of 1 ms per foot, and it's a round trip, so 2 x 50 feet), the other wall pair delay would be 80 ms, and the ceiling/floor delay would be 60 ms.

The code in listing 6.12 creates a *reverb* (signal processing that models reverberation is often called a reverberator, or reverb) by connecting the adc through three delay lines, in parallel ❷, and to the dac ❶. Then you connect each delay line back to itself ❸ and set its gains to something reasonable of typical room dimensions and delays ❹. Then you must set the delay time for each delay. Delay times/lengths that use much memory (longer than a few dozen milliseconds) require you to tell the Delay UGen how long you expect it to be, so it can allocate memory. This is done using the .max method. You can set .max and .delay all in one line ❺. Because you're connecting the adc to the dac through some delays, be really careful about feedback (use headphones).

Listing 6.12   Simple reverb using three Delay UGens

```
// Direct sound
adc => Gain input => dac;
1.0 => input.gain;

// Delay lines to model walls + ceiling
input => Delay d1 => dac;
input => Delay d2 => dac;
input => Delay d3 => dac;

// Hook delay lines back to themselves
d1 => d1;
d2 => d2;
d3 => d3;
```

❶ Direct signal from adc to dac (through Gain)

❷ adc to dac via three delay lines in parallel

❸ Closes each delay loop (hook output to input)

```
// set feedback/loss on all delay lines
0.6 => d1.gain => d2.gain => d3.gain;
```
④ Can set all three delay
gains in one line

```
// allocate memory and set delay lengths
0.06 :: second => d1.max => d1.delay;
0.08 :: second => d2.max => d2.delay;
0.10 :: second => d3.max => d3.delay;
```
Can set max and delay
⑤ all in one line

```
// Enjoy the room you built!
while (1)  {
    1.0 :: second => now;
}
```

The results are pretty magical, but you might notice annoying ringing at a low pitch. That's because 60, 80, and 100 ms all share some common factors, and those tend to pile up and cause resonances. This is easily fixed by changing the delay lengths to relatively prime (no common factors) numbers, like 61, 83, and 97 ms.

Assignment

Change the numbers to different values to see the effects. Change the delay gains from 0.6 to something else (but never greater than 1.0, because this causes sound to build infinitely). You'll note that for smaller numbers, the reverb rings for less time, and for greater numbers, longer. This is called reverb time, and you get to control it because you're a programmer! This reverb still sounds somewhat bright and ringy, but you could fix that by putting filters in the feedback loops just like you did with the plucked string. Try putting a simple OneZero low-pass filter in the loop of each delay where it connects to itself, like this: d1 => OneZero lp1 => d1;.

Okay, by now you're thinking that designing and building reverberators that sound really good might be difficult. And it is, but once again you're in luck, because ChucK has some built-in reverberator UGens: PRCRev (named after Perry R. Cook, who wrote it to be the most computationally efficient reverb that still sounds somewhat good), JCRev (named after John Chowning of FM fame), and NRev (*N* stands for *New*, which it was in the 1980s). These are really easy to use, as shown in the following listing.

Listing 6.13   Using ChucK's built-in NRev reverberator UGen

```
// make a new reverb and hook it up
//   (Again, Beware Feedback!
//        Turn down the volume or wear headphones)
adc => NRev rev => dac;

// set reverb/dry mixture
0.05 => rev.mix;

// kick back and enjoy the space
while (1)  {
    1.0 :: second => now;
}
```

You might notice that this reverb sounds really nice compared to our three-delay one. That's because it has lots of delay lines and filters, interconnected in ways that give it properties considered desirable for acoustic spaces. It was designed by really smart folks who know a great deal about simulating reverb, but you get to use it without worrying about all the inner workings. If you're really into this type of thing, you could implement any reverberator of your choosing using ChucK. That's the beauty of knowing how to program and having a powerful, expressive language.

6.8 *Delay-based audio effects*

From your experience so far with the plucked string, and with echoes and reverberation models using delays, you can see that delay line UGens do really well at modeling lots of interesting physical things. All of those delay lines were fixed in length once you set their initial delay. But interesting things also happen when delays vary in time. The Doppler pitch shift that happens when a car, train, or plane is moving toward or away from you happens because the delay time between the source and you is changing. So a delay line that changes length causes the pitch of what's going through it to shift, upward if the delay is getting shorter and downward for elongating delay. You can exploit this to make a chorus effect, which uses delay lines that shift length slowly up and down to create delayed copies of any input signal, with slightly changing pitch. The pitch shifts up slightly while the delay is getting shorter and down while the delay is growing longer. And this all cycles slowly up and down. ChucK has a built in Chorus UGen, which you can use like this:

```
adc => Chorus chor => dac;
```

There are parameters you can play with for Chorus, such as .modFreq (rate at which the pitch is shifted up and down, the default is 0.25 Hz) and .modDepth (default is 0.5), and .mix (same function as in the reverberation UGens).

> **Exercise**
> Put a Chorus UGen into one of the examples from this chapter. Try it on the plucked strings, violin, Clarinet, Wurley, and so on.

If you wanted to constantly shorten a delay line in order to shift pitch up by some constant amount, you'd eventually run out of delay and reach 0.0. But if you made a bank of delay lines and cross faded (gradually faded in one delay while fading out another) between them as each one got too short, then you could make a pitch shifter. Well, ChucK has a UGen called PitShift that does exactly that. The next listing shows code that demonstrates how it works.

Listing 6.14   Using ChucK's built-in pitch shifter UGen, `PitShift`

```
// run mic input through pitch shifter
adc => PitShift p => dac;
// set mix to all pitch shift (no dry signal)
1.0 => p.mix;

// forever shifting pitch
while (1)
{
    // pick a random shift across +/- 1 octave
    Math.random2f(0.5,2.0) => p.shift;
    0.2 :: second => now;
}
```

We'll introduce one more super-useful effect here called `Dyno`, for dynamics processor. `Dyno` has loads of features, including

- *Limiting*—Don't let the signal get over a certain volume level.
- *Compression*—Make loud sounds softer and soft sounds louder, to yield a smaller dynamic range between loudest and softest.
- *Noise-gating*—Don't let very soft sounds such as ambient/background noise through, but open up above some threshold and let louder sounds through.
- *Ducking*—Modify the level of the signal, but do it based on the loudness of some other, external signal.

Those of you who know about some of these effects will find the settings familiar, and you should look up all of them in the ChucK unit generator reference (appendix C). Even if you don't know about compression, noise-gating, and ducking, one thing that `Dyno` is perfect for is protecting your ears and speakers. The compressor and limiter defaults are pretty good for doing that, because if the sound gets too loud, `Dyno` keeps it in check. Many ChucK programmers we know always put a `Dyno` before the `dac` in nearly every patch they make, especially experimental ones that they think might blow up, such as feedback. Using `Dyno` is, of course, as easy as this:

```
adc => Dyno safety => dac;
```

6.9   *Example: fun with Filter and Delay UGens*

To use all you've learned in this chapter, we'll finish up with an example that expands on our `ResonZ` UGen example from listing 6.10 and our three-delay UGen reverberator from listing 6.12. In listing 6.15, you use the same impulse UGen-excited `ResonZ` filter to give you pitched pings ❶. Then you make an array of three `Delay` UGens ❷ (yep, you can make arrays of pretty much anything), and connect those between your input and the left, center, and right `dac` channels ❸. You do the rest of the delay line connections, setting of delay times, and gains in a for loop ❹. You make the delays quite long, on the order of a second or more, to create a multichannel stereo echo effect. If you look at the math in ❺, you can work out that the three delay lines will be given delays of 0.8, 1.1, and 1.4 seconds. You then declare a MIDI note number array ❻ that you'll use to set the pitches of the ResonZ filter.

After setting everything up, you drop into an infinite while loop, setting random pitches from the allowed notes of the table ❼ and firing the Impulse UGen to make sound ❽. Note that there's only one sound-producing object in this whole program (the Impulse), but interesting polyphonic (multisound) and rhythmic music results, because of the delay lines and their lengths.

Listing 6.15   Musical fun with a resonant filter and three delay lines

```
// Fun with UGens!  By UG dude, Oct 14, 2020
// Impulse-excited resonant filter drives
// three delay lines, fed back to themselves        ❶ Direct path of resonant
Impulse imp => ResonZ rez => Gain input => dac;         filtered impulse.
100 => rez.Q;
100 => rez.gain;
1.0 => input.gain;

// We can make arrays of UGens, too
Delay del[3];                               ❷ Array of three delay lines.

// Let's have some stereo
input => del[0] => dac.left;                ❸ Left, right, center delay outputs.
input => del[1] => dac;
input => del[2] => dac.right;

// Set up all the delay lines
for (0 => int i; i < 3; i++) {              ❹ Setup for all delays.
    del[i] => del[i];
    0.6 => del[i].gain;
    (0.8 + i*0.3) :: second => del[i].max => del[i].delay;   Each delay time
}                                                             is different but
                                                          ❺ related.
// Define note array for our song
[60, 64, 65, 67, 70, 72] @=> int notes[];
notes.cap() - 1 => int numNotes;                  Array of notes that
                                              ❻ you'll draw from.
//  Let the fun begin! (and continue forever)
while (1)  {
    Std.mtof(notes[Math.random2(0,numNotes)]) => rez.freq;   Plays a random
    1.0 => imp.next;         Fires impulse (output           note (resonant
    0.4 :: second => now;  ❽ 1 on next sample).            ❼ filter frequency).
}
```

6.10   Summary

In this chapter you elevated your sound synthesis and processing abilities to a new level, by learning about a lot more ChucK unit generators. UGens are built into ChucK to make sound synthesis and processing easy. Important points to remember include:

- Envelope and ADSR UGens make slowly changing values to control volume and other things.

- You can generate sound by frequency modulation synthesis either from scratch, using one sine wave to modulate another, or using ChucK's built-in FM UGens.
- Physical models, like the plucked string, can be implemented using `Delay` UGens and refined using filters, noise, and `ADSR` UGens.
- Delay lines can simulate echoes, reverberation, chorus effect, and pitch shifting.
- ChucK has lots of built in UGens to do many effects!

In the next chapter, you'll meet (more of) the STK (Synthesis ToolKit) UGens, expanding your knowledge of ChucK's instrument UGens, including a number of physical models, and other flexible and great sound synthesis models and instruments.

Synthesis ToolKit
instruments

7

This chapter covers

- New physical modeling instrument unit generators, such as
  - Wind instruments, including clarinet, brass, and flute
  - Better stringed instruments, including mandolin and sitar
  - Rigid objects, including metal/wood bars and glass
  - Particle models, like maracas, tambourines, and wind chimes
  - Voice acoustics and vocal models in ChucK
  - UGens for classic analog and digital synthesizer sounds

In this chapter you'll expand your arsenal of unit generators, covering many self-contained instrument UGens. We say *instrument* because these UGens make sound in response to frequency, noteOn, noteOff, messages, and other parameters, depending on the type of model implemented. By the end of this chapter, you'll be able to build a band to play Indian classical music automatically.

You'll learn to use and make sound with models as diverse as clarinet, brass, flute, mandolin, sitar, marimba, maraca (shakers), and voice. We'll touch on the physics of those instruments and what differentiates individual members within a particular instrument family. We'll also look at the acoustics of the human voice and how to model that using ChucK UGens. We'll also cover UGens that can be used to make sounds reminiscent of classic analog and digital synthesizers, organs, and more. It's especially cool to be able to make these classic analog sounds in ChucK, because you can exploit the power of computer programming to control and compose with them.

In the previous chapter, we introduced the idea of synthesis by physical modeling (PM), looking at the plucked string, and also explored using delays to model room acoustics and some other physical phenomena such as the Doppler pitch shift. Many of the new UGens you'll see in this chapter are physical models as well. The exciting thing about PM synthesis is that the simulated instruments respond to many of the same controls that actual players use to control the real physical instruments. Bowing pressure and position, blowing pressure, lip tension, the stiffness of a reed, and the number of beans in a maraca or other shaker all are available control parameters in the ChucK PM instrument UGens.

> ### Synthesis history: the Synthesis ToolKit in C++
> Many of the UGens in ChucK came from the Synthesis ToolKit in C++, created beginning in 1995 by Perry R. Cook when he was at the Stanford Center for Computer Research in Music and Acoustics. He was trying to unify all of the instruments he had created in lots of different computer languages and bring them into a common, open source, publicly available code collection that others could use easily. Most of the STK is included in ChucK.

At this point, we can note again that the clarinets (and violins) you've built so far don't sound very realistic, even though you keep improving them by adding vibrato, ADSR envelopes, and so on. The lesson of the plucked string is that perhaps you can do better by looking at the actual physics involved in instruments like the clarinet, flute, and trombone. And that's what you're going to do in this chapter, which introduces many instruments and some of the parameters you can use to control them. We won't belabor the physics too much, nor will we dive deeply into all of the available parameters. The goal here is to give you a sampler of the many things ChucK and STK provide to make new sounds and more interesting music.

7.1   STK wind instruments

ChucK has many built-in UGens that model the physics of various instruments and sound-producing objects. You'll look first at the clarinet, which uses a delay line to model the tube (waveguide) along which sound waves travel up and down, a filter to model the wave reflections and transmissions at the bell (open end), and a nonlinear spring simulation to model the reed. The clarinet model block diagram of figure 7.1 looks pretty close to what you built for your plucked string model in the previous chapter: a delay line, a filter, a bit of noise, and so on. The differences here are that instead of waves traveling up and down a string, you're using the delay line to model

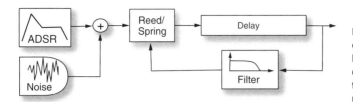

Figure 7.1 The clarinet model contains excitation (ADSR + `Noise` for blowing pressure), a delay line to model the bore, a filter in the loop, and a nonlinear reed/spring model.

sound waves traveling up and down the clarinet bore (tube). There's an envelope generator to model the player's blowing pressure, and you add noise to that to model the rush of air through the reed. The biggest difference in this model from your plucked string is that it has an additional box that models the springiness of the reed, responding to the player's blowing pressure (the `ADSR`) and the pressure inside the bore (coming back from the delay line, through the low-pass bore filter).

The best news is that even though you could build a clarinet by making these individual UGens and hooking them all together, you don't have to because the `Clarinet` UGen has all of these things built in! And, because it's a physical model, you can play the STK `Clarinet` by just declaring one and "blowing" it, as shown in the following listing.

Listing 7.1 Playing the ChucK STK `Clarinet` physical model unit generator

```
// STK Physical Clarinet Model
Clarinet clar => dac;

0.2 => float blow;                        Gradually increases from
                                          initial blowing pressure
while ((0.05 +=> blow) < 1.0)      ←
{
                                          Alternately blowing
    blow => clar.startBlowing;     ←      and not blowing
    0.2 :: second => now;
    1 => clar.stopBlowing;
    0.2 :: second => now;
}
```

Running this code, you'll hear that the `Clarinet` doesn't start making musical sound until you blow it hard enough. This is sometimes called the *speaking threshold*. After that point, every new note played around the loop, each time with increasing pressure, has a different quality, just like a real clarinet. That's the power of physical models.

The `Clarinet` has other parameters you can change and control, such as `.reed` (stiffness), `.noiseGain`, `.vibratoGain`, and `.vibratoFreq` (internal sine wave modulation of breath pressure). Because it's an instrument, you can also blow it using `.noteOn` (identical to `.startBlowing`) and turn it off with `.noteOff`.

7.1.1 The STK brass instrument physical model UGen

Once you've made a wind instrument, you can make others by adding extra physics and controls. By giving the reed/spring some mass, it becomes more like the lip of a brass player. The tube remains basically the same, and if you want to play just a note, you can use the .freq method, as shown in the next listing, which plays a little trumpet exercise on the STK Brass UGen, which is a self-contained UGen that models a brass instrument.

Listing 7.2   Playing the ChucK STK Brass PM UGen

```
// Playing a PM UG trumpet in a nice space
Brass trump => NRev rev => dac;
0.1 => rev.mix;

// notes for our "exercise"
[82,84,86,84,82,84,86,84,82,77,86,86,89] @=> int notes[];

// play through the exercise, except for the last note
0 => int i;
while (i < notes.cap()-1)
{
    0.8 => trump.startBlowing;
    Std.mtof(notes[i]) => trump.freq;
    0.1 :: second => now;
    1 => trump.stopBlowing;
    0.05 :: second => now;
    i++;
}
// add a little breath vibrato for last note
0.4 => trump.vibratoGain;
0.8 => trump.startBlowing;
Std.mtof(notes[i]) => trump.freq;
second => now;
1 => trump.stopBlowing;
second => now;
```

The Brass UGen also gives you even more control via the independent controls via the .lip and .slide methods.

7.1.2   The STK Flute physical model UGen

A flute is just a waveguide tube too, so if you change the properties of the reed, you can use a similar model to mimic the air jet of flute-like instruments. The STK Flute UGen does that, providing extra access to the properties of the flute jet via the .jetDelay method. This parameter controls the speed of the air across the blowing hole of the flute and can be used to make the flute overblow to other harmonics, as is typical of flute-like instruments when blown really hard. There are other parameters as well, which you can look up in the ChucK UGen reference (appendix C). Listing 7.3 sets the .jetDelay method randomly to show the flexibility and realism of this physical model. If you want to play notes to sound like a regular flute, use the .freq method as with most other sound-producing UGens.

Listing 7.3 Noodling around with the STK Flute PM UGen

```
// Noodling around with the STK Flute UGen
Flute pipe => dac;

while (true)
{
    // pick a random MIDI note to play
    Std.mtof(Math.random2(60,80)) => pipe.freq;
    1 => pipe.noteOn;
    0.8 :: second => now;

    // then randomly mess around with the jetDelay
    for (0 => int i; i < 4; i++) {
        Math.random2f(0.0,1.0) => pipe.jetDelay;
        0.2 :: second => now;
    }
    1 => pipe.noteOff;
    0.1 :: second => now;
}
```

Other STK wind instruments include:

- BlowHole models a clarinet with one tone hole (via .tonehole) and one register hole (via .vent).
- BlowBotl models a simple pop-bottle-like instrument.
- Saxofony models a variety of reed instruments (including sax) mostly by accessing the .blowPosition method.

Try this

Try playing a scale using the Flute, BlowBotl, or Saxofony instruments. Make one of these instruments and hook it to the dac. Put your notes in an array, and using a for loop, set the frequency using Std.mtof and play notes in that loop using .noteOn and .noteOff. Remember to advance time for both the note-on and note-off segments!

After looking at quite a few STK wind instruments and exploring their parameters, it should be pretty clear that there's quite a bit of expressiveness in these instruments. You can play notes on them fairly easily by using the .freq and .noteOn methods, but you can go much deeper if you actually control the parameters.

7.2 *Better stringed instruments*

When you built your plucked string model in the previous chapter, it made a string-like sound but didn't particularly sound like a guitar, banjo, or other stringed instrument. Aspects that separate certain stringed instruments from others include the overall length (mostly affects pitch range), the shape and size (and materials) of the body, and the type and number of strings. Classical guitars have nylon strings, where folk and electric guitars have steel strings. The steel strings sound brighter, because they're stiffer than the nylon ones. Smith and Jaffe described how to modify the Karplus-Strong model to mimic the effects of string stiffness, which serves to stretch the higher harmonics upward. This shifting upward of the upper harmonics gives the characteristic brighter sound of steel. You can model this by adding allpass filters in the string loop (special filters that change delay differently for different frequencies). The ChucK STK StifKarp UGen shown in the following listing ❶ does just that, with access to the amount of stiffness and spectral stretching via the .stretch method ❷.

Listing 7.4   Playing strings of different stiffness using the StifKarp UGen

```
StifKarp skarp => dac;          ←——  ❶ Stiff string model
while (1)
{
    Math.random2f(0.3, 1.0) => skarp.stretch;   ←——
    1 => skarp.noteOn;                                ❷ .stretch method
    0.3 :: second => now;                                controls stiffness
}
```

7.2.1   *The STK Sitar physical model UGen*

The Indian sitar, shown in figure 7.2, is characterized by a nonlinear string/bridge interaction (the bridge is where the strings connect to the resonating body). The shape of the bridge causes the strings to chatter when they vibrate, giving a characteristically bright, buzzy quality to the sitar. The STK Sitar UGen models this nonlinear buzz and mimics the pitch bends that sitar players perform on nearly every note. Listing 7.5 shows how to play a *raga*, or *rag*, ❷ (Indian scale, rhymes with *frog*) on the Sitar UGen ❶.

Figure 7.2   Nonlinear buzzing bridge (left) of the Indian sitar stringed instrument (right)

```
Sitar sit => dac;                                    ← ❶ Sitar instrument model

[50,51,54,55,57,58,61,62] @=> int rag[];            ←   Indian scale is called a
                                                      ❷ rag (rhymes with frog)
for (0 => int i; i < rag.cap(); i++)
{
    Std.mtof(rag[i]) => sit.freq;
    1 => sit.noteOn;
    0.5 :: second => now;
}
```

7.2.2　*The STK Mandolin physical model UGen*

The STK `Mandolin` UGen instrument ❶ in listing 7.6 adds many improvements over all of your string models so far, including a body model (which can be made virtually larger or smaller via the `.bodySize` method), `.pluckPos` ❷, `.stringDamping`, and `.stringDetune` ❸. The code in the listing experiments with this instrument, randomly setting body size, damping, and the other parameters to different values between 0.0 and 1.0.

```
Mandolin mand => dac;                               ←       Mandolin physical
                                                     ❶      instrument model
[79, 78, 74, 78, 76, 72] @=> int solomio[];

for (0 => int i; i < solomio.cap(); i++)  {
    Std.mtof(solomio[i]) => mand.freq;
    Math.random2f(0.2,0.8) => mand.pluckPos;          ❸ Random detune
    Math.random2f(0.05,0.11) => mand.stringDetune;  ←   between strings
    for (0 => int trem; trem < 12; trem++)  {          in a pair
        1 => mand.noteOn;                           ←   Tremolo strumming
        Math.random2f(0.06,0.09) :: second => now;      gesture
    }
}
```

Random plucking position ❷

Try this

Write a program to play a scale on the `Mandolin` UGen, like the many scales you've played before, using an array and a `for` loop. Before the `for` loop, set one of the parameters of `.bodySize`, `.stringDetune`, or `.pluckPosition` to a value between 0.1 and 0.9. Play the scale, add shred, and then change this parameter and play the scale again. Can you hear the difference? Do this for all of these parameters, one at a time. Experiment!

7.2.3　*The STK bowed string instrument UGen*

Bowed strings are a little trickier than plucked strings, but science and digital signal processing (DSP) have provided efficient techniques for modeling them using waveguide techniques. Shown in the following listing, the built-in ChucK Bowed UGen ❶ can be used easily. You can tell it to play notes by setting the frequency ❷ and sending it .noteOn messages ❸. You also add a little flourish at the end, as you did with the Brass example, by increasing the vibrato on the last note ❹.

Listing 7.7 Playing a scale on the STK Bowed string model

```
// Bowed string demo
Bowed viol => dac;                            ①  Bowed string physical model

// define a D Major Scale (in MIDI note numbers)
[62, 64, 66, 67, 69, 71, 73, 74] @=> int scale[];

// run through our scale one note at a time
for (0 => int i; i < scale.cap(); i++)
{                                             ②  Sets pitch with
    // set frequency according to note number    .freq, just like
    Std.mtof(scale[i]) => viol.freq;             other UGens
    // note on for a while, then note off
    1 => viol.noteOn;                         noteOn starts it
    0.3 :: second => now;                     bowing
    1 => viol.noteOff;                        ③  automatically
    0.1 :: second => now;
}
// repeat last note with lots of vibrato
1 => viol.noteOn;
0.1 => viol.vibratoGain;                      A little extra
2.0 :: second => now;                         vibrato on the
0 => viol.noteOff;                            ④  last note
0.2 :: second => now;
```

You might recognize the code of listing 7.7 as similar to our first SawOsc-based violin patch (listing 6.5), but it's much shorter and simpler. If you play this a few times, you'll hear that each note sounds a little different each time. This again is one of the benefits of PMs. The Bowed PM UGen lets you control meaningful things like .bowPressure ❶, .bowPosition ❷, rate of bowing, and so on, as shown in listing 7.8. But if you fiddle with those, don't be surprised if the instrument doesn't make sound at all or sounds odd. With the benefits of PMs come some of the real-world side effects: they're hard to play by varying all the parameters by hand. A good rule is to make small changes, maybe in a loop (or two), to see how each parameter changes the behavior, as shown in the following listing. Note the variety of sounds available from this instrument.

Listing 7.8 Fiddling around with the STK Bowed UGen

```
// Test some Bowed parameters
Bowed viol => dac;

for (1 => int i; i <= 5; i++)  {              ①  Gradually
    for (1 => int j; j <= 5; j++)  {             increases
        i*0.2 => viol.bowPressure;               bowPressure...
```

```
    j*0.2 => viol.bowPosition;
    <<< "pres=", i*0.2, "pos=", j*0.2 >>>;
    1 => viol.noteOn;
    0.3 :: second => now;
    1 => viol.noteOff;
    0.1 :: second => now;
    }
}
```

...and changes
❷ bowPosition.

Now you know that there are many stringed instrument physical models built into ChucK as unit generators. Each models a particular physical attribute, like stiffness or nonlinear buzzing, and/or models a specific instrument like the sitar or mandolin. The available parameters give you a lot of expression to play with and use in your compositions. But are there more instrument families you can synthesize using PM? Yep!

7.3 *Bars and other rigid things*

John Chowning discovered that modulating one sine wave with another could yield complex sounds, including bell-like tones, which he noted have "inharmonic spectra." *Inharmonic* means that the sounds are composed of sine waves, but the frequencies of those sines are not related by simple integer ratios like the frequencies 100, 200, and 300, are. Also recall that stiff strings have stretched harmonics, because high frequencies travel up and down the string faster than low frequencies. Smith and Jaffe showed how to use allpass filters to model that in the Karplus-Strong plucked string.

For really stiff structures like rigid bars, even though waves travel up and down just like in the string, using allpass filters to model the stiffness might not be very efficient because you have to use really big filters to get enough stretching of the spectrum. Also, stiff structures such as metal plates and glass objects don't have clear waveguide paths up and down. But all of these, as well as objects such as drumheads, exhibit sine wave modes of oscillation, just not usually harmonic or in a regular spectral pattern.

Fear not, because there's a synthesis method called *modal synthesis* that uses resonant filters like the ones you used in section 6.6 to model the individual resonant modes of the sounds of objects. ChucK's `ModalBar` UGen was created to model the sounds of bars but can be used to model a variety of modal sounds. It has a number of built-in settings for vibraphone, marimba, woodblock, agogo bell, and other bar-like sounds, as shown in the following listing.

Listing 7.9 Trying out the many presets of the `ModalBar` UGen

```
// Demo of modal bar presets
ModalBar bar => dac;

while (true) {
    // pick a random object type
    Math.random2(0,8) => bar.preset;
    // and random frequency
    Math.random2f(200.0,1000.0) => bar.freq;
    // Then whack it!!
```

```
    1 => bar.noteOn;
    0.4 :: second => now;
}
```

This example shows the sounds you can get from just one model, changing the filter settings to more closely match metal bars, wood bars, and other rigid things.

If you want to make a new model, you can also use the ModalBar UGen but explicitly set the modal frequencies and amount of resonance (Q) for the four modes built into ModalBar. If you look at the spectrum in figure 7.3 of the sound of whacking a water glass with a wooden pencil, you can see four clear modes that dominate. The modal frequencies are marked as 1206, 2240, 3919, and 5965 Hz, and their amplitudes are roughly 0, -7, -3, and -8 dB.

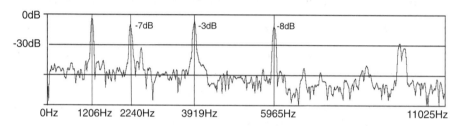

Figure 7.3   Spectrum of sound produced by striking a water glass clearly shows four dominant modes.

With just a little bit of code, you can reprogram the modes of ModalBar to match those shown in figure 7.3 exactly in frequency and amplitude, and with more work, you can figure out what the resonance parameters should be to match the decay times of each mode (listing 7.10). Modal frequencies are set as ratios (.modeRatio ❶), relative to the first (0ᵗʰ) mode. Each .modeGain ❷ is set using the convenient ChucK built-in Std.dbtorms() function, which converts dB gain to linear amplitude. The .modeRadius ❸ parameter is a little tricky, but 1.0 means that the mode would never decay (essentially making that filter into a sine wave oscillator, like setting the Q to infinity); 0.9999 causes the mode to die away over a period of about 2 seconds; 0.999 dies in about 1/8 second. Smaller numbers decay more rapidly. The next listing shows how to make ModalBar match our struck water glass quite closely.

Listing 7.10   Spectral modeling using the ModalBar UGen: a struck glass sound

```
// Synthesize a modal glass sound from spectral model
ModalBar glass => dac;

[1206.0,2240.0,3919.0,5965.0] @=> float modeFreqs[];
[100.0,93.0,97.0,92.0] @=> float modeGainsdB[];
[0.9999,0.9997,0.9998,0.9996] @=> float modeRadii[];

for (0 => int i; i < 4; i++)  {
    i => glass.mode;
    modeFreqs[i]/modeFreqs[0] =>  glass.modeRatio;
```

❶ Sets frequency of each mode as ratio with zero-eth mode.

```
    Std.dbtorms(modeGainsdB[i]) => glass.modeGain;
    modeRadii[i] => glass.modeRadius;
}

// set to first mode frequency, set gain too
1206 => glass.freq;
0.2 => glass.gain;

// whack it!!!
1 => glass.noteOn;
3.0 :: second => now;
```

② Uses dbtorms() to get a gain from a dB magnitude.

③ Radius sets decay time.

ChucK has another type of physical model for rigid/stiff objects called `BandedWG`, which models each mode as a waveguide (a delay line; you should remember this from our plucked string explorations) with a band-pass filter (a filter that allows only part of a signal, within a specified frequency range, or band, to pass through) for each mode, to match other properties. The inclusion of delay gives more physical control than just modeling the sinusoidal modes with resonant filters, as `ModalBar` does. You can actually bow the `BandedWG` model, in this case to match the characteristics of a Tibetan prayer bowl, as demonstrated in the following listing.

Listing 7.11   Bowing a rigid bar using the BandedWG UGen

```
// Test some Banded WaveGuide parameters
BandedWG bwg => dac;
// set to model Tibetan prayer bowl
3 => bwg.preset;
// whack the "bowl" to get it started
1 => bwg.noteOn;
// bring the bow to the surface
1 => bwg.startBowing;

// then bow it with increasing pressure
for (0 => int i; i <= 7; i++)
{
    <<< "bowPressure=", i*0.1 => bwg.bowPressure >>>;
    second => now;
}
// then bow it with decreasing pressure
for (6 => int i; i > 0; i--)
{
    <<< "bowPressure=", i*0.1 => bwg.bowPressure >>>;
    second => now;
}
```

You've learned about the acoustics and synthesis of the sounds of rigid objects like bars of metal and wood. You've also learned that you can tweak the parameters of the `ModalBar` and `BandedWG` models to simulate a large variety of such objects. Next, we'll move on to a completely different family of sound-making things: shakers, scrapers, crunchers, and other particle-based systems.

7.4   *Particle models*

There are other types of physical systems of musical interest, specifically ones that make sound by the interactions of lots of small particles or objects. Examples include maracas, tambourines, sleigh bells, wind chimes, things crunching beneath our feet (leaves, snow, sand, gravel), and general scraping and scratching sounds. The Shakers UGen in STK covers these and more with an algorithm called Physically Informed Stochastic Event Modeling (PhISM), which is fancy talk for using one or more resonant filters (like the ResonZ resonant filter you've used before), but exciting the filters at random times (*stochastic*) with impulses and tiny noise bursts. You can control the damping (how quickly the sound dies away after you "shake" the model), resonance (general center frequency of the resonances, roughly correlates with total object size), and how many objects are inside the virtual shaker. You can also just use the 22 presets. The following listing is a program that runs through all of the presets.

Listing 7.12   Testing all the presets for the Shakers UG

```
// Fun with particles, the Shakers instrument
Shakers shak => dac;
// Run through all the presets in order
for (0 => int i; i < 23; i++)  {
    i => shak.preset;
    1 => shak.noteOn;
    1.0 :: second => now;
}
```

The next listing is another program that picks one Shakers preset, the Quarters in a Coffee Mug instrument ❶, and randomly fiddles with the parameters, including the number of quarters in the mug ❷ and the damping (or decay time) of the whole system ❸.

Listing 7.13   Experimenting with the parameters of one particular shaker preset

```
// Mess with the parameters of the "Quarters in coffee mug" preset
Shakers shak => dac;
17 => shak.preset;                                        ❶ Quarters bouncing around
// then fiddle around with #objects and damping              in a coffee mug preset
while (1)  {
    Math.random2f(0.0,128.0) => shak.objects;             ❸ Random amount of
    Math.random2f(0.0,1.0) => shak.decay;                    damping (decay time)
    <<< "#Objects=", shak.objects(), "damp=", shak.decay() >>>;
    1.0 => shak.energy;
    1.0 :: second => now;
}
```

Random number of quarters ❷

A large number of sounds can be made with the Shakers UGen, and you can tweak the parameters (objects, decay, freq) to endless variety. Next, you'll leave the realm of the physical and enter the world of classic electronic sounds.

7.5 *Synth soundz*

In the last 60 years—or more—the music world has seen the introduction of many new sounds based on electronic circuits, ranging from electronic organs, through electric guitars and their amplifiers, to synthesizers, and of course computers. In this section, we'll look at some of ChucK's more electronic-sounding unit generators.

Many classic analog synthesizers combine oscillators with filters. One of the most popular synthesizers of all time was the Moog (pronounced like *vogue*, not like *Google*), named after synthesizer pioneer Bob Moog (1934–2005). The Minimoog, first produced in 1970 by R.A. Moog Inc., had three oscillators (each switchable to generate sine, triangle, sawtooth, square, or pulse) with an ADSR envelope generator, with the oscillators fed through a sweepable (time-varying resonance) filter, also driven by an ADSR. ChucK pays homage to the Moog synthesizers with the Moog UGen, which has an oscillator through a resonant filter that sweeps with each .noteOn, as shown in the next listing.

Listing 7.14 ChucK's shout-out to the Minimoog, the Moog UGen

```
// Homage to a classic analog synth sound
Moog mog => dac;

// table of pitches to use
[77,72,69,75,70,67,74,70,65,72] @=> int cars[];

// play first note;
play(cars[0],0.25);
// then play most of the rest
for (1 => int i; i < cars.cap()-1; i++)
{
    if (i % 3 == 0) play(cars[i],0.5);
    else play(cars[i],0.25);
}
// push up "mod wheel" for last note
0.25 => mog.vibratoGain;
play(cars[cars.cap()-1], 1.0);

// function to play notes on/off
fun void play(int note, float howLong)
{
    Std.mtof(note) => mog.freq;
    1 => mog.noteOn;
    (howLong - 0.05) :: second => now;
    1 => mog.noteOff;
    0.05 :: second => now;
}
```

There are some additional Moog parameters available, such as .filterSweepRate, .filterQ, and .vibratoFreq.

Try this

Write new code to test these out! Maybe something like this:

```
// Trying out the Moog parameters
Moog mog => dac;
200.0 => mog.freq;

while (1)  {
    Math.random2f(1.0,1.0) => mog.filterQ;
    Math.random2f(0.01,1.0) => mog.filterSweepRate;
    1 => mog.noteOn;
    if (Math.random2(0,10) == 0) {
        Math.random2f(1.0,20.0) => mog.vibratoFreq;
        0.5 => mog.vibratoGain;
        second => now;
    }
    else  {
        0.01 => mog.vibratoGain;
        0.125 :: second => now;
    }
    1 => mog.noteOff;
    0.125 :: second => now;
}
```

We also talked about FM synthesis in the previous chapter, which can be quite nice for making synthesizer-type sounds. For example, the PercFlut models a percussive flute sound, but it can sound pretty synthetic because it's FM. BeeThree pays tribute to the sound of the classic Hammond B3 organ, but again it can sound synthetic because it models an electronic organ. The HevyMetl FM UGen is modeled somewhat after the characteristics of a distortion guitar but definitely has the sound of classic oscillator-based synthesizers. Try the example in the following listing of using HevyMetl to play a song associated with a particularly famous electric guitar player (Jimi Hendrix playing the "Star Spangled Banner" at Woodstock, 1969).

Listing 7.15   Using the HevyMetl FM UGen to synthesize an electric guitar

```
// a brief FM electric guitar tribute
HevyMetl jimi => PRCRev r => dac;          ①  FM "guitar" through reverb...
jimi => Delay d => d => r;
0.3 => d.gain;
1.2 :: second => d.max => d.delay;                ...and a delay line (for
// sets us up for whammy bar bend later     ②  big, outdoor sound)
0.5 => jimi.lfoSpeed;

[[70.0,0.8,0.0],[67.0,0.4,0.0],[63.0,1.2,0.0],
 [67.0,1.2,0.0],[70.0,1.2,0.0],[75.0,2.4,0.2],
 [79.0,0.8,0.0],[77.0,0.4,0.0],[75.0,1.2,0.0],    ③  Table of notes,
 [67.0,1.2,0.1],[69.0,1.2,0.2]] @=> float banner[][];     durations, and
                                                          modulations
```

```
// play through our data table first
0 => int i;
while (i < banner.cap())  {
    banner[i][2] => jimi.lfoDepth;
    pick(banner[i][0],banner[i][1]);
    1 +=> i;
}
```
Plays all the notes
❹ in the table

```
// play last note longer, then
Std.mtof(82) => jimi.freq;
1 => jimi.noteOn;
2.0 :: second => now;
```

```
//  go nuts and sweep frequency downward
while (jimi.freq() > 100.0) {
    0.98 * jimi.freq() => jimi.freq;
    0.01 :: second => now;
}
1.0 :: second => now;
1 => jimi.noteOff;
2.0 :: second => now;
```
Big gliss (pitch
❺ sweep) downward

```
// function to play a note for a duration
fun void pick(float note,float howLong) {
    Std.mtof(note) => jimi.freq;
    1 => jimi.noteOn;
    (howLong - 0.1) :: second => now;
    1 => jimi.noteOff;
    0.1 :: second => now;
}
```
Function to
❻ pick each note

The code uses both a PRCRev ❶ and a Delay for echo ❷ to give it all a stadium sound. The array named banner ❸ contains elements specifying MIDI note number, duration, and modulation amount. You also use a function to play the individual notes ❻, and after you've played through all the notes in your array ❸ using a while loop ❹, you go a little crazy on the last note, sweeping the pitch downward (a digital whammy bar) using another while loop ❺.

7.6 *Voices*

If you look at the spectrum (figure 7.4) of our "eee" sound from "see" from chapter 1, you'll note that the spectrum is harmonic, with regularly spaced sine spikes, but you also might note that some of the sines have higher amplitudes than others. The way the voice works is that the vocal folds oscillate periodically for pitched sounds (vowels, ell, em, and so on), and the vocal tract consisting of a person's throat, mouth, tongue, and nasal passages serves to filter that sound and shape the spectrum. Depending on the shape of the vocal tract, some frequencies are emphasized (resonances) and others are deemphasized. The resonant peaks are called *speech formants*, and their locations determine whether you hear an "eee," an "ahh," or another sound from the variety you can make, all on the same pitch. The formants in the "eee" spectrum are shown in figure 7.4.

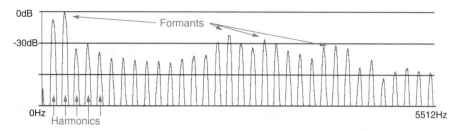

Figure 7.4   Spectrum of "eee" sound shows harmonics and resonant speech formants.

Because ChucK has both oscillators and resonant filter UGens, it's pretty easy to build a model that sounds like a human voice. The code of listing 7.16 uses a SawOsc UGen ❶ to model the vocal folds through three resonant filters ❷ ❸ (one for each of three formant resonances of the vocal tract) to make a pretty good singer model. You also add a SinOsc ❹ to modulate the SawOsc for vibrato. Once it's hooked up, the resonances are calibrated ❺, and you drop into an infinite loop ❻ to sing random vowels ❼ and pitches ❽.

Listing 7.16   Building a simple formant (resonant filter) voice model

```
// Simple singing voice model
// by Enrico C., August 1921
SawOsc folds => ResonZ formant1 => dac;          ❶ Sawtooth models vocal folds
folds => ResonZ formant2 => dac;                     through formant filter
folds => ResonZ formant3 => dac;                 ❷ 2nd formant (vocal
                                                     tract resonance)
❸ 3rd formant

// hook up a modulation (vibrato) oscillator
SinOsc vibrato => folds;
6.0 => vibrato.freq;                             ❹ Adds vibrato to voice source
1.5 => vibrato.gain;
2 => folds.sync;

// Set up filter resonance amounts                ❺ Sets resonance of all
20 => formant1.Q => formant2.Q => formant3.Q;        three formant filters

// Sing forever, randomly
while (1) {                                      ❻ Sings a random "song" forever
    Math.random2f(200,750) => formant1.freq;
    Math.random2f(900,2300) => formant2.freq;    Random "vowel"
    Math.random2f(2400,3600) => formant3.freq;   ❼ (formant frequencies)
    if (Math.random2(0,3) == 0)
    {
        Math.random2f(60.0,200.0) => folds.freq;  ❽ Random voice pitch
    }
    Math.random2f(0.2,0.5) :: second => now;
}
```

ChucK also has a built-in VoicForm (voice modeled with formant filters) UGen instrument, which includes a vocal fold oscillator (with vibrato), a noise source (whispering an "eee" means not letting the vocal folds make a pitch but pressing them together just enough to make noise), four formant filters, and presets for common vowels and consonants. As shown in listing 7.17, you can select the *phonemes* (individual speech sounds) by number ❶ or by name ❷ as a string.

Note that the transitions between vowels and pitches are smoothed, not making pops and clicks between new settings like your simple voice model of listing 7.15. That's because VoicForm has built-in smoothing envelopes that make the transitions gradual when moving to new oscillator and filter frequencies.

Listing 7.17   Using ChucK's VoicForm formant voice UGen

```
// Simple singing example using the VoicForm UG
VoicForm singer => dac;
0.05 => singer.vibratoGain;

[40,42,44,45,47,45,44,42] @=> int scale[];

// Start singing our first note
Std.mtof(scale[0]) => singer.freq;          ❶ Selects vowel by
11 => singer.phonemeNum;                        number
1 => singer.noteOn;

// sing through whole scale
0 => int note;                               ❷ Sings a diphthong
while (note < scale.cap()) {                    (transition between
    dipth("lll","ahh",scale[note]);             two vowels)
    1 +=> note;
}
// last note
dipth("lll","ahh",scale[0]);
0.15 => singer.vibratoGain;
2.0 :: second => now;
1 => singer.noteOff;
0.2 :: second => now;

fun void dipth(string phon0, string phon1, int note)  {
   phon0 => singer.phoneme;
    0.1 :: second => now;
   phon1 => singer.phoneme;
    Std.mtof(note) => singer.freq;
    0.4 :: second => now;
}
```

The VoicForm UG also gives you control of the mix of pitched voiced versus unvoiced noise sources to be filtered via the .voiceMix method, so you can whisper or make breathy voices. You can also control the vibrato amount via .vibratoGain, the vibrato rate via .vibratoRate, and the rate at which the oscillator moves from pitch to pitch via .pitchSweepRate.

There are more ways to synthesize voices. John Chowning figured out early in his experiments with FM that if he set the frequencies of a number of sine wave carrier oscillators near each formant frequency and modulated all of them with a sine wave at the fundamental pitch, he could generate voice-like sounds. The ChucK FMVoices instrument UGen does just this.

There are more UGens that we haven't talked about yet. You can read about those in appendix C and try them out for your music making.

7.7   *Example: Indian music*

For a final example, called ragajam, you're going to make a band to play Indian music. In all of the code that follows, you'll use a sitar as your primary solo instrument. You'll have other instruments, so, as shown in listing 7.18, you'll make a Gain called master for mixing before the dac ❶. For a little echo, you'll connect the sitar to a Delay UGen ❷, connect the Delay to itself (through a feedback gain), and connect the whole thing to the master mixer ❸. You'll then set the parameters for the sitar echo, including setting the feedback gain so the echo decays.

> **NOTE**   All of the code from here until the end of the chapter is a continuation of listing 7.18. So it all goes into one .ck file before you run it.

Listing 7.18   Ragajam Indian music in ChucK

```
// we'll play our melody on sitar

Sitar sitar => Gain master => dac;                    ❶ Sitar instrument,
                                                         master mixer Gain

sitar => Delay delay => Gain sitarFeedback => delay;  ❷ Delay line to
                                                         give Sitar an
delay => master;              ❸ Connects delay line      echo
                                to output mixer
```

You need accompaniment for your sitar player, so you use some very low singers as drones. First, you declare an array of four singers (VoicForm UGens) ❹ and an NRev reverberator ❺ for them to sing through. Using a for loop, you connect them all to their reverb ❻ and set their gains ❼. Then you set the parameters for each drone singer: vibrato ❾, the vowel they will sing ❿, and their pitches ⓫ (from an array ❽).

```
// drone "singers" to accompany
VoicForm singerDrones[4];              ❹ Uses four "singers"
NRev droneRev => master;                 as low drones.
for( 0 => int i; i < singerDrones.cap(); i++)   ❺ Drones get their own reverb...
{
    singerDrones[i] => droneRev;       ❻ ...connect the singers...
    (.5/singerDrones.cap()) => singerDrones[i].gain;  ❼ ...and set their gains
}                                                        appropriately.

// singer parameters (drone)
[26,38,45,50] @=> int drones[]; // global pitch array   ❽ Pitches for low
.5 => droneRev.mix;                                        drone singers.
for( 0 => int i; i < singerDrones.cap(); i++)
{                                      ❾ Gives droners a
    .02 => singerDrones[i].vibratoGain;   little vibrato.
```

Sets their
pitches. **11**
```
    "lll" => singerDrones[i].phoneme;
    Std.mtof(drones[i]) => singerDrones[i].freq;
}
```
Sets the "word"
10 they're singing.

You'd like some percussion as well, so for that you can use the Shakers UGen **12**. You'll also define a shake function **13** to control the sitar player's pretty random playing. That way you can tell him to shake (call the function), and he'll set up parameters randomly and do his own .noteOn to make sound.

```
// Shaker percussion, and control function
Shakers shaker =>  master;

fun void shake()
{
    // drum control
    Math.random2(1,2) => shaker.preset;
    Math.random2f(60.0,128.0) => shaker.objects;
    Math.random2f(.8,1.0) => shaker.decay;
    shaker.noteOn(Math.random2f(0.0, 4.0));
}
```
12 Shaker percussionist,
connects to output mixer

Function to cause the shaker
13 to play a "note"

As is traditional in many kinds of music, you need to pick a musical scale, called a raga in Indian music:

```
// global raga scale
[62,63,65,67,69,70,72,74] @=> int raga[];
```

and you need to pick a tempo, called a *lay* (or *laya*).

```
// global timing/tempo parameter
.2 => float beattime;
```

Now that you've set the tempo, you can set the Sitar delay parameters to help reinforce the rhythm:

```
// sitar echo parameters
beattime::second => delay.max;
beattime::second => delay.delay;
.5 => sitarFeedback.gain;
```

Finally, before you teach this band to play, you need to realize that you have six instruments playing (four drones, a sitar, and a shaker), so you might want to scale down your master gain:

```
// master volume parameter
.7 => master.gain;
```

Time to play! You let the drones start it all off for a few seconds **14**; then the sitar **16** and shaker **18** join in, playing at random multiples **15** of the basic tempo. The sitar player selects random notes **17** from the raga[] array, and the shaker plays along (randomly too **19**). The result is pretty magical, all thanks to ChucK:

```
// MAIN PROGRAM, ragajam.ck

// warm up with a drone solo            ←————⑭ Drones begin the piece.
5::second => now;

// main loop, add Sitar and Shaker
while (true)
{
    // time variation                        ⑮ Random timing for
    Math.random2(1,3) => float factor;  ←————   each new "measure".

    // loop
    for( 0 => int i; i < raga.cap(); i++ )
```

Sitar
player. ⑯ →

```
    {
        // sitar control
        Std.mtof(raga[Math.random2(0,raga.cap()-1)]) => sitar.freq;  ←
        sitar.noteOn(Math.randomf());

        // play a percussion sound
        shake();                        ←————⑱ Tells the shaker to play on beat...

        // advance time by 1/2 our basic beat
        (0.5*beattime)::second*factor => now;

        // an occasional half-time percussion hit for flavor
        if (Math.random2(1,3) == 1)
        {
            shake();       ←————⑲ ...and lets him play on off-beat every so often.
        }

        // advance time by the other 1/2 beat
        (0.5*beattime)::second*factor => now;
    }
}
```

Random note ⑰
from raga array.

7.8   *Summary*

In this chapter we introduced a lot more unit generators, specifically ones that are self-contained instruments, meaning that they respond to messages like .freq, .noteOn, and .noteOff to make sound. You learned about a lot of physical (and physically inspired) models, specifically:

- Stiff and nonlinear strings, and the Sitar and Mandolin
- Wind instruments such as the Clarinet and Flute
- Rigid bars and hard objects like glass and metal via ModalBar and BandedWG
- Particle models to make the sounds of Shakers, scrapers, wind chimes, and the like
- The human voice, synthesis from scratch using filters, and the VoicForm UGen

You also learned about STK UGens that implement other synthesis models and how to use them:

- FMVoices and other FM algorithms
- Electronic and synthesizer sounds, via the Moog, Wurley, and other UGens

You learned that almost all of these instrument UGens have control parameters that are similar to those of the real instruments. You now know a lot of new ways to make sounds and music and can use these UGens in your compositions. In our final Indian music example of this chapter, you built a band made up of vocal drones, a shaker percussionist, and a solo sitar player.

In the next chapter, you'll learn how to make your bands more flexible, break up the individual players into separate ChucK files, and run them individually, in parallel, from a master conductor program. This is called *concurrency*, and it will make your programs and music-making even more powerful.

For further reading

To learn more about PM synthesis and the STK and how all of the instrument models work, check out *Real Sound Synthesis for Interactive Applications*, by Perry R. Cook (CRC Press, 2003). And see Julius O. Smith's excellent web resources on PM: https://ccrma.stanford.edu/~jos/pasp/.

Multithreading and concurrency: running many programs at once

8

This chapter covers

- Using spork to turn functions into concurrent shreds
- Using `Machine.add()` and other virtual machine functions
- Composing music using separate, concurrent shreds
- Using concurrency to control multiple aspects of objects
- Organizing your concurrent ChucK files and projects

In your ChucK journey so far, you've learned how to write single ChucK programs that create sound and music. But many of you may wonder how you can get ChucK to run multiple files and processes concurrently. You might have clicked the Add Shred button a few times and noted that multiple programs can happily run and make sound at the same time. Or, you might be curious what the advantages of running multiple programs at once might be. Running multiple shreds at once, or *concurrency*, is what this chapter is all about.

As a real-life example of concurrency, imagine you've been really busy and haven't had time to do your laundry. Imagine that you have many loads of laundry to do—whites, darks, sheets, and towels—and you start by running your whites in the washing machine and then transfer them to the dryer. After they dry, you continue by washing and drying your darks, and then your sheets, and finally your towels. This would take a long time!

Now imagine you took the concept of concurrency to your laundry (which most of you already do). After you wash your white clothes, you put them into the dryer. But then you put the darks into the washing machine. So two things are now happening at the same time! If you run a process in your washing machine at the same time as running a process in your dryer, you'll get your laundry done much faster. Concurrency in programming is like going to a Laundromat, where you can do all four of your loads in four separate machines, all at the same time.

In this chapter we explore how concurrency works in ChucK. This is an advanced topic in computer science, known as *multithreading*. ChucK was designed to rethink how programming languages deal with multithreading, including control and timing between running processes. ChucK's way of dealing with concurrency and multi-threading, combined with its on-the-fly coding architecture and capabilities, make these topics much easier to use and understand.

8.1 Programming with concurrency

Manipulating time and concurrency are two core concepts in the ChucK language. Taking full advantage of these, and in tandem, is the key to unlocking the full potential of the language.

So, what is concurrency, and why is it useful? *Concurrency* means having more than one thing happening at the same time. If you've ever run more than one ChucK program at a time, you've already used a basic form of concurrency. More broadly speaking, concurrent programming is the ability to specify two or more independent and potentially related pieces of code and run them at the same time with mechanisms for synchronizing their behaviors.

We've talked throughout this book about the fundamental relationship between time and sound. Similar to how sound, music, and time are interrelated, music is often about the simultaneity of many processes, all happening in parallel. Doing your laundry in parallel helps you save time, but the different instrument parts in music *must* all take place in parallel, simultaneously, for them to fit together and make up the whole song. Concurrency lets you model this in code.

Concurrency lets you break down complicated processes and deal with them individually, without having to constantly consider the full picture. For example, one concurrent module can deal with sound synthesis, another can control pitches, and yet another might handle real-time input from an external controller, such as a keyboard or joystick. In ChucK, concurrency builds on top of and works closely with time. Concurrent processes normally don't need to worry about how other modules work; they need only to control time in their own way and can share data and synchronize with each other only when desired.

Let's start by looking at a simple concurrency example, as shown in the following listing, where you'll create and run two concurrent functions that each print a unique message (the string "foo!" for one function and "BAAAAAAR!!!" for the other) and make a unique sound (an 800 Hz pop sound for one function and a 700 Hz pop for the other). Each function advances time but by different amounts (1/4 second in one, 1 second in the other).

Listing 8.1 Basic concurrency example, print with sound

```
// function foo                            1  Defines a function foo.
fun void foo()
{
    // sound for foo process
    Impulse foo => ResonZ rez => dac.left;    2  foo will make pops at 800 Hz...
    800.0 => rez.freq;
    50 => rez.Q;

    // infinite time loop
    while( true )
    {
        // print and make sound
        <<< "foo!", "" >>>;                   3  ...and print itself out...
        100 => foo.next;
        // advance time
        250::ms => now;                       4  ...every ¼ second.
    }
}
fun void bar()          // function bar          5  Function bar...
{
    // sound for bar process
    Impulse bar => ResonZ rez => dac.right;   6  ...will make pops at 700 Hz...
    700.0 => rez.freq;
    50 => rez.Q;

    while( true )  // infinite time loop
    {
        // print and make sound
        <<< "BAAAAAAR!!!", "" >>>;            ...and print out something
        100 => bar.next;                       7  different from foo...
        // advance time
        1::second => now;                     8  ...every second.
    }
}
// spork foo() and bar() each on a child shred    9  Starts foo by sporking it.
spork ~ foo();
spork ~ bar();                                10  Starts bar by sporking it.

// infinite time loop to serve as a parent shred
while( true ) 1::second => now;               Infinite parent loop,
                                              so children foo and
                                              11  bar can run.
```

The example shows a simple concurrent program, where you define two functions, foo() ❶ and bar() ❺, each of which continually prints a different string ❸ ❼ and synthesizes a little tuned pop ❷ ❻. Each function loops at two different rates (250::ms ❹ and 1::second ❽). Attempting to run these functions one after another will result in only the first actually running, because each contains an infinite time loop. Thus the first function called would just run forever, never returning to the point where another function could be called. But this program does something a bit different: it runs foo() and bar() on two separate concurrent processes ❾ ❿. After sporking these two shreds, the main program is a simple infinite loop that actually doesn't do anything but advance time ⓫.

But how do you do this? What is this spork ~ operation?

8.2 *Shreds and sporking*

In ChucK, each running process is called a *shred*, which you can think of as a strand or thread of code. So far, you've been running a single program (creating a single process) by clicking the Add Shred button. But new shreds can also be created from functions by executing specific ChucK code, through a special ChucK operation called a *spork*. In listing 8.1, which we show part of here again, you *sporked* (ChucK-speak for spawning new shreds) function foo() on a new shred with the syntax spork ~ foo() ❾, and then you sporked function bar() on another shred ❿. The spork operations don't actually run the functions, but the new shreds will begin running automatically when the existing code advances time. This happens down in the main infinite loop ⓫, where the two child shreds then begin running as well:

```
// spork foo() and bar() each on a child shred
spork ~ foo();                                    ❾
spork ~ bar();                                    ❿

   // infinite time loop to serve as a parent shred
while( true ) 1::second => now;                   ⓫
```

So, when you start the main program by clicking the Add Shred button, you create what's called the *parent shred*, as shown in figure 8.1. The sporking operations ❾ ❿ set up the *child shreds*, which begin as soon as the infinite loop is entered ⓫. This relationship between the parent and the child shreds is shown in figure 8.1 If, for some reason, the parent shred terminated, the children would be automatically destroyed. But in this case, you have an infinite loop, so you have to explicitly stop the shreds by clicking the Clear VM button.

One cool thing about shreds is that as long as each shred takes care of time in its own way, ChucK coordinates and synchronizes all shreds properly with respect to time. It all just works!

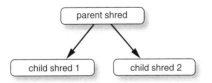

Figure 8.1 Parent shred (running program) can spork functions as child shreds.

Spork?

Spork comes from the idea of forking a parallel process from other programming systems, except that ChucK shreds (called threads in other languages), have some key differences from parallel processes in those languages. Shreds are deterministic (predictable) and heavily dependent on time, so in ChucK, you *spork shreds* to create concurrent behaviors, which are handled by the *shreduler*, which is called a scheduler in other languages.

To better see what has happened inside the ChucK VM, look at the console and VM monitors from the miniAudicle (figure 8.2). The Console Monitor shows the two processes printing out their text messages, one "BAAAAAAR!!!" for each four "foos!" The VM monitor shows that we have three shreds running: one parent (the file containing all the code, and two children (foo and bar). Note that all three shreds have been running for the same total time, because they were started at the same instant.

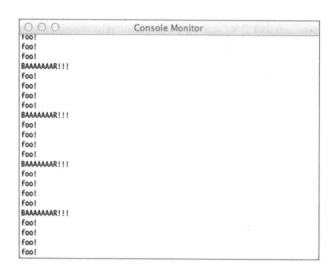

Figure 8.2   Console monitor and VM resulting from running the code of listing 8.1. The VM shows three shreds: the parent first, then two children.

A little more on parent and child shreds

You might be wondering why the last line ⑪ of listing 8.1 (while(true) 1:: second => now;) is necessary. This has to do with an implicit relationship between new shreds that get sporked (child shreds) and the shred from where they're sporked (the parent shred). ChucK automatically gets rid of child shreds when their parent shred ends; for example, when it reaches the end of its code. So without the infinite loop in the last line, the children would be shreduled to run but would never run, because they would have no parent. For this reason, where the parent ends or potentially ends before any child shred you still need, the parent shred should be kept running.

Now that you know how to run current processes (programs) using spork ~, you can unlock a whole new dimension of power in your musical programming. For one, you can start to approach your music making even more compositionally, such as factoring different instruments into different processes.

8.3 *A parallel, multithreaded, concurrent drum machine*

So, now that you know a little about concurrency, let's put it to work immediately to make a smarter drum machine, as shown in listing 8.2. You first make a few global duration variables that all of your shreds can share ❶. Then you make three functions, one for each drum sound: kick ❷, snare ❸, and hihat ❹.

Listing 8.2 Parallel, multithreaded, concurrent drum machine

```
// by Drummond Base, October 2020
// First define some global durations                    ❶ Defines whole, half, and
                                                            quarter note durations
1 :: second => dur whole;
whole / 2 => dur half;
whole / 4 => dur quarter;

// Kick drum function
fun void kick()  {                          ❷ Function to play kick drum
    SndBuf kick => dac;
    me.dir()+"/audio/kick_01.wav" => kick.read;

    // only play every whole note
    while (true)  {
        whole => now;
        0 => kick.pos;
    }
}

// Snare drum function
fun void snare()  {                         ❸ Function to play snare drum
    SndBuf snare => dac;
    me.dir()+"/audio/snare_01.wav" => snare.read;

    // play with half note tempo
    while (true)  {
        half => now;
        0 => snare.pos;
    }
}

// Hi hat drum function
fun void hihat()  {                         ❹ Function to play hi-hat
    SndBuf hihat => dac;
    me.dir()+"/audio/hihat_01.wav" => hihat.read;
    0.2 => hihat.gain;

    // play every quarter note
    while (true)  {
        quarter => now;
```

```
        0 => hihat.pos;
    }
}
// Main program to spork our individual drum functions
// start off with kick drum for two measures
spork ~ kick();
2*whole => now;
```
⑤ Sporking kick function starts it playing

```
// then add in hi hat after two measures
spork ~ hihat();
2*whole => now;
```
⑥ Sporks hi-hat after a time

```
// add snare, but on off beats (quarter delayed start)
quarter => now;
spork ~ snare();
```
⑦ Sporks snare starting on off beat

```
// let it run for four more measures
4*whole => now;
```
⑧ Lets it all run for four more measures

Once your functions and global tempo variables are defined, you can spork them at will in your main program. First, you spork the kick() drum function and advance time by two measures (2*whole) ⑤. Then you add in the hihat() function and let both of those run for two more measures ⑥. Finally, you add in the snare() function but delayed by a quarter note ⑦. You let it all run for four measures ⑧; then the program ends, ending all of the children shreds too. If you watch the VM window while everything runs, you'll see the shreds appear as they begin and disappear together at the end.

From this somewhat simple example, some of the power of concurrency should be becoming clear. Already you might be seeing the power of being able to create a function for each instrument and then spork those as shreds, in arbitrary orders and at arbitrary times, to make a musical composition. You could change the function for any individual instrument or the order in which they're sporked to tweak your composition in really flexible ways.

You've seen how to create different instruments and players that can run on independent shreds, cooperating and synchronizing to make very cool music. Concurrency is great for factoring out different drums in a drum kit or different instruments

Exercise: make your own even better drum machine

Modify the drum machine example to make your own composition. Change the order and timings of when the drum functions are sporked and removed. Change the durations used within individual drum functions, like changing half to quarter, or define an eighth duration, and use that for the hi-hat timing. Change the snare code to randomly play on either quarter- or half-note durations. Use what you learned in previous chapters about using arrays, logic, and the modulo operator to make this parallel drum machine even better. Give some drum functions an array to control when they play. Use modulo in a different drum function to control when it makes sound. Add more instruments. Play with the tempo variables. Express yourself!

of an ensemble. But you can do more with shreds and concurrency, such as using them to control parameters for a single synthesis model or sound. Next, you'll learn how to do that.

8.4 Using concurrency to control aspects of common objects

Now we'll look at a different application of concurrency: using two different shreds to control one or more shared objects, as shown in figure 8.3.

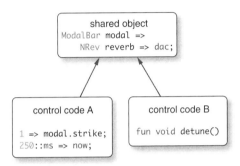

Figure 8.3 Shreds can be used to control different aspects of common objects. For example, control code A might play notes at one rate, while control code B might control detuning, vibrato, or other expression.

In the example in the following listing, you create two functions that both operate on a global `ModalBar` UGen ❶ that makes your sound. The main shred controls articulation via `.strike` ❸, and another shred detunes your global `ModalBar` over time, using a sine function. This tuning shred is the sporked ❷ `detune()` function ❹.

Listing 8.3 Controlling different aspects of a single global object using concurrency

```
// sound chain
ModalBar modal => NRev reverb => dac;
// set reverb mix
.1 => reverb.mix;
// modal bar parameters
7 => modal.preset;
.9 => modal.strikePosition;

// spork detune() as a child shred
// note: must do this before entering into infinite loop below!
spork ~ detune();

// infinite time loop
while( true )
{
    // first note! then wait
    1 => modal.strike;
    250::ms => now;
    .7 => modal.strike;     // another note! then wait
    250::ms => now;
    .9 => modal.strike;     // one more note! then wait
    250::ms => now;
```

❶ Modal bar through reverb to dac

❷ Sporks a function called detune()

❸ Plays notes (strikes bar).

```
    repeat( 4 )          // now play four quick notes
    {
        // note!  and wait                    ❸ Plays notes (strikes bar).
        .5 => modal.strike;          ←
        62.5::ms => now;
    }
}

// function to vary tuning over time     ❹ detune function
fun void detune()                    ←      definition
{
    while( true )  // infinite loop
    {
        // update frequency sinusoidally
        84 + Math.sin(now/second*.25*Math.PI) * 2 => Std.mtof => modal.freq;
        // advance time (controls update rate)
        5::ms => now;
    }
}
```

When you run the code of listing 8.3, you hear a repeating drum pattern played on the ModalBar in the main loop, but you also hear the pitch of the bar change slowly up and down due to the sporked detune() function. You could write and spork even more functions to control the same ModalBar object, giving you more flexibility over the sound. Concurrency!

Now you know that you can use concurrency in a number of ways, including synchronizing many independent instruments or controlling a single global instrument from separate shreds. Before we go on, let's note a few important things about shreds and concurrency:

- A shred is a ChucK process, a strand of sequential code.
- A new shred can be created by using spork ~ on a function.
- Shreds don't necessarily need to know about each other and only need to deal with time locally.
- There's no limit on the number of shreds (so spork away!).
- Parent shreds must be kept alive to keep child shreds running.

The use of time and concurrency together is a simple and powerful way to get a whole lot more out of ChucK. As always, we recommend that you experiment freely. So far, we've introduced the most precise and direct way to introduce concurrent behavior into your music-making programs, but it's not the only way. Up next, you'll take a look at a higher-level way to organize and run many programs at once.

8.5   *Machine commands: adding ChucK files as new shreds*

So far in this chapter you've worked with sporking shreds as functions from within a single program. But there's a way to add entire ChucK files saved on disk as new shreds. This allows you to factor and control your code, reuse files you like, and generally create music in super-flexible ways. To do this you'll use a set of functions associated with the VM object, which is really the running part of the ChucK language. Similar to our Std and Math functions from those libraries, the VM functions are called using the Machine prefix. First you'll see how to use `Machine.add()` to spork new processes from ChucK files; then you'll use that to further structure your programs and compositions.

8.5.1 *ChucK Machine commands for adding and running files*

The first and most important function is `Machine.add(filePath)`, which adds the code found at `filePath` as a new shred in the VM. `Machine.add()` returns a unique integer if it can successfully find and run the program specified in the argument and returns 0 if there's a failure of some kind. Figure 8.4 shows how the `Machine.add()` function is used.

Figure 8.4 `Machine.add()` function adds a new ChucK program specified by `filePath`, returning a unique integer if it's successful and 0 if it fails for any reason (can't find file, file has an error, and so on).

Note that you might need to use `me.dir()` or other file path techniques that you learned in chapter 4 to make sure that ChucK can find the file you're trying to add. If there's an error, ChucK will return a zero and inform you in the Console Monitor window:

```
[chuck](VM): sporking incoming shred: 1 (Main.ck)...
[myFile.ck]: no such file or directory
```

Another useful Machine function is `Machine.remove(ID)`, which removes any shred numbered ID from the VM, terminating any shreds associated with it (if it's a parent that sporked any shreds while running). If ChucK can't find the specified shred, it returns an error number but doesn't stop any other shreds from running. Figure 8.5 shows this function.

Figure 8.5 The `Machine.remove` function removes shreds associated with the integer argument.

`Machine.replace()` takes two arguments. The first is an integer pointing to a running shred, and the second is the name of a new ChucK file that you'd like to replace the running shred with. Figure 8.6 shows this function.

Figure 8.6 The `Machine.replace` function removes a shred associated with an integer argument and replaces it with a new shred created by running the file associated with the second argument.

8.5.2 *Using Machine functions for composition*

As an example of how to use your new Machine functions, let's assume you've saved the programs associated with listings 8.1–8.3 as Listing8.1.ck, Listing8.2.ck, and Listing8.3.ck. Now create one more file from the code in listing 8.4, and save it as score.ck in the same directory where your other three files are located. If you load and run score.ck, you'll hear all of the examples from this chapter so far, all arranged into a composition!

The code first loads, runs, and sporks your foobar program (Listing8.1.ck) ❶ and waits 2 seconds and adds your concurrent drum machine ❷ (Listing8.2.ck). After letting that run for 6 seconds, the score program adds the bending modal bar from Listing8.3.ck ❸. The drum machine will stop by itself, because it contains no infinite loops. But then the code explicitly stops the modalbend shred by using `Machine.remove()` ❹. The score.ck code then replaces foobar with modalbend ❺, lets that run for 4 seconds, and then removes modalbend ❻, stopping all sound. Watch the VM window while all of this runs, and you'll see each amazing event, with all associated shreds, as they happen.

Listing 8.4 Using `Machine.add`, `Machine.remove`, and `Machine.replace`

```
// Example of using Machine functions
// by Sporkie Griswold, June 2014

Machine.add(me.dir()+"/Listing8.1.ck") => int foobar;
2.0 :: second => now;
Machine.add(me.dir()+"/Listing8.2.ck") => int drumnbass;
6.0 :: second => now;
Machine.add(me.dir()+"/Listing8.3.ck") => int modalbend;
4.0 :: second => now;
Machine.remove(modalbend);
2.0 :: second => now;
Machine.replace(foobar,me.dir()+"/Listing8.3.ck") => modalbend;
4.0 :: second => now;
Machine.remove(modalbend);
```

❶ Adds foo/bar program from listing 8.1...

❷ ...then adds code of listing 8.2...

❸ ...adds 8.3 code (modalbend program)...

❹ ...removes 8.3...

❺ ...replaces foobar with modalbend code...

❻ ...then removes it.

Clearly you've unlocked an incredible new source of power for organizing your code and controlling your compositions. So let's finish this chapter with an even more musical example, a jazz combo!

8.6 *Example: building a multithreaded jazz band*

To conclude, let's combine some of the cool instrument UGens you learned about in the previous two chapters with your newfound tools of sporking and `Machine` functions to create a really musical example. The code of listings 8.5–8.10 assembles and controls a jazz quartet, consisting of an electric piano player (FM Rhodey instrument), a bass player (STK `Mandolin` with tweaked parameters), a `SndBuf` drummer, and a flute solo. Each runs in its own separate files, with its own knowledge and agenda, but together they make up a pretty good band, playing a nice improv.

Because you're going to put the code for each of your jazz band players in a separate file, first we'll talk about file organization. Next, you'll hire your players (write your individual programs for each instrument), and then we'll introduce an architecture for running your concurrent code. At the end, you'll hear some cool jazz.

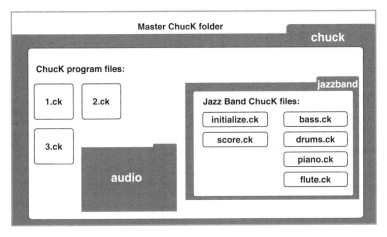

Figure 8.7 Suggested file architecture for our jazz band example. A directory called jazzband holds all of your files, one for each player/instrument, along with your score (where you Machine.add() your players), and a file called initialize.ck, the only file you need to run.

8.6.1 *A file organization structure for your jazz band*

To keep all of this organized, you should make a new directory called jazzband, where you'll save all of the individual player files, along with the master score.ck file and a file called initialize.ck, which kicks everything off. You'll use this file architecture (shown in figure 8.7) from now on in the book, because now that you know about spork and Machine.add(), you'll likely be creating multiple files for each new project.

8.6.2 *Programming the individual players*

The first instrument you'll hire for your band is an electric piano, using the FM Rhodey electric piano UGen, shown in listing 8.5. You'll make four of them in an array ❶, so you can play four-note chords, and you'll connect those four notes to different channels in your stereo dac soundfield ❷ ❸. You then define two chords via a two-dimensional array ❹. In an infinite loop ❺, you play one chord for a bit ❻ and then the other chord for a bit ❼, looping forever.

Listing 8.5   Jazz band: piano.ck

```
// piano.ck
// sound chain                    ❶ Four notes' worth
Rhodey piano[4];                     of electric piano
piano[0] => dac.left;
piano[1] => dac;                  Connects them to left...
piano[2] => dac;               ❷ ...and center...
piano[3] => dac.right;            ❸ ...and right dac channels

// chord 2D array                            ❹ Array to hold two chords
[[53,57,60,64],[51,55,60,63]] @=> int chordz[][];   of four notes each
```

Infinite loop ⑤

```
// loop
while( true )
{
    // build first chord
    for( 0 => int i; i < 4; i++ )
    {
        Std.mtof(chordz[0][i]) => piano[i].freq;
        Math.random2f(0.3,.7) => piano[i].noteOn;
    }
    1.0 :: second => now;
    // build second chord
    for( 0 => int i; i < 4; i++ )
    {
        Math.mtof(chordz[1][i]) => piano[i].freq;
        Math.random2f(0.3,.7) => piano[i].noteOn;
    }
    1.4 :: second => now;
}
```

⑥ **Plays first chord...**

⑦ **...then second chord**

Your next player (listing 8.6) is a bassist, made by using a Mandolin ① with parameters adjusted to make the strings ring for a long time ② and to have a really big body ③. You then define a jazz scale in an array ④ and a pointer into that array that you'll modify to walk up and down the scale ⑤. This will make the bass player do a characteristic walking bass line in an infinite loop ⑥, as she randomly moves up the scale, down the scale, or stays on the same note ⑦. Since they could walk off either end of the array, you have to check to make sure the walk pointer doesn't become less than zero ⑧ or greater than the size of the array ⑨. Finally, you set the note ⑩ and pluck the bass at a random string position ⑪.

Listing 8.6   Jazz band: bass.ck

```
// bass.ck
// sound chain (mandolin for bass)
Mandolin bass => NRev r => dac;

// parameter setup
0.1 => r.mix;
0.0 => bass.stringDamping;
0.02 => bass.stringDetune;
0.05 => bass.bodySize;
.5 => bass.gain;

// jazz scale data
[41,43,45,48,50,51,53,60,63] @=> int scale[];
4 => int walkPos;

// loop
while( true )
{
    Math.random2(-1,1) +=> walkPos;
    if (walkPos < 0) 1 => walkPos;
    if (walkPos >= scale.cap()) scale.cap()-2 => walkPos;
```

① **Mandolin bass player through reverb.**

② **Makes strings ring a long time.**

③ **Gives it a really big bass-sized body.**

④ **Scales array for walking bass line.**

⑤ **Pointer for position within scale.**

Walks ⑥ forever.

⑧ **Makes sure position doesn't go outside the array...**

Adds 1 or -1 or 0 to scale position. ⑦

⑨ **...on the top end too.**

```
Std.mtof(scale[walkPos]-12) => bass.freq;        ← ⑩  Sets pitch from scale note.
Math.random2f(0.05,0.5) => bass.pluckPos;        ←
1 => bass.noteOn;                                      Random plucking
0.55 :: second => now;                           ⑪  position.
1 => bass.noteOff;
0.05 :: second => now;
}
```

Your next band member (listing 8.7) is a drummer who will play a pretty random
hihat sample using SndBuf ①. Because you're using SndBuf, you'll need to load a sample, so it's important that your /audio directory live at the same level as the jazzband
directory. You use the me.dir(-1) function ② to point up one directory level so you
can find the /audio directory. Once all of that's set, you drop into a loop ③ and play
with random parameters ④ ⑤ ⑥ and go back and loop forever ⑦.

Listing 8.7   Jazz band: drums.ck

```
// drums.ck

// sound chain                           ①  Hi-hat sound for
SndBuf hihat => dac;                    ←     percussion.

// me.dir, one level up to find the /audio directory
me.dir(-1) + "/audio/hihat_01.wav" => hihat.read;   ← ②  Reads the wave file.

// parameter setup
.5 => hihat.gain;

// loop
while( true )                       ← ③  Infinite loop.
{                                                          ④  Random
                                                              volume...
    Math.random2f(0.1,.3) => hihat.gain;    ←
    Math.random2f(.9,1.2) => hihat.rate;    ← ⑤  ...and pitch (rate).
    (Math.random2(1,2) * 0.2) :: second => now;   ←
    0 => hihat.pos;                        ←          Waits either .2 or
}                                    ⑦  ...then plays and loops.  ⑥  .4 seconds...
```

Your final band member (listing 8.8) is the headliner, a famous cool STK flute player ①
with lots of delay effects added ② ③. The flautist uses the same jazz scale that the bass
player walks around ④ and in an infinite loop ⑤ plays random coolness ⑦ at random
time intervals ⑥, sometimes playing very hip, introspective rests ⑧.

Listing 8.8   Jazz band: flute.ck

```
// flute.ck
// Our famous headliner flute solo (with EFX)   ①  Flute soloist through reverb...
Flute solo => JCRev rev => dac;             ←
0.1 => rev.mix;                                  ②  ...also through a delay line.
solo => Delay d => d => rev;                 ←
0.8 :: second => d.max => d.delay;           ←
0.5 => d.gain;                               ③  Sets delay to 0.8 seconds.
0.5 => solo.gain;
```

```
// jazz scale data
[41,43,45,48,50,51,53,60,63] @=> int scale[];          ← ④ Jazz scale array.

// then our main loop headliner flute soloist
while (1)  {                                            ⑥ Waits 0.2, 0.4, 0.6, 0.8,
    (Math.random2(1,5) * 0.2) :: second => now;   ←        or 1.0 seconds.
    if (Math.random2(0,3) > 1) {                   ←
        Math.random2(0,scale.cap()-1) => int note;         Occasionally
        Math.mtof(24+scale[note])=> solo.freq;             (50% of time)
        Math.random2f(0.3,1.0) => solo.noteOn;      ⑦      picks a new note...
    }
    else 1 => solo.noteOff;         ← ⑧ ...otherwise turns note off.
}
```

Infinite loop. ⑤

The score program (listing 8.9) controls all of your players, acting as a conductor to add them in a compositionally meaningful way. The piano starts it all out ❶, and after a bit the drummer joins ❷. After some more time, the bass player starts their walk ❸, and then the flute headliner saunters on stage and begins to play ❹. After a short while you remove the drummer ❺ and add him back in after a little while ❻.

Listing 8.9   Jazz band: score.ck

```
// score.ck

// start piano
Machine.add(me.dir() + "/piano.ck") => int pianoID;    ← ❶ Starts off with
4.8::second => now;                                         piano chords...

// start drums
me.dir() + "/drums.ck" => string drumsPath;        ❷ ...then adds hi-hat
Machine.add(drumsPath ) => int drumsID;       ←       percussion...
4.8::second => now;

// start bass                                         ❸ ...then adds in the
Machine.add(me.dir() + "/bass.ck") => int bassID;  ←    walking bass line...
4.8::second => now;

// start flute solo                                  ❹ ...then adds
Machine.add(me.dir() + "/flute.ck") => int fluteID; ←   the flute solo.
4.8::second => now;

// remove drums          ❺ Cuts the percussion
Machine.remove(drumsID);  ←  for a bit...
4.8::second => now;

// add drums back in      ❻ ...then adds it
Machine.add(drumsPath) => drumsID;  ←  back in.
```

Of course this code, or the players, could be modified as much as you like, adding, replacing, and so on. As programmer/composer, you get to decide. You can now run score.ck, and if all of your other files are in the right place and run fine, you should hear the jazz band. If you see any errors, fix them by running the individual file; then try again. Testing each player individually as you type and save is good programming practice. It's called modular development, testing, and debugging.

8.6.3 An architecture for running your concurrent code

While we're talking about creating and managing multiple files, we're going to introduce you to a suggested architecture for organizing and running your code. We talked about making a directory for each new composition or project, depicted in figure 8.7. One extra file in that directory is initialize.ck, shown in the next listing, which you'll use from now on as your master program that runs everything else. The file score.ck will still take care of most of your compositional things, such as adding instruments and timing. But you'll use initialize.ck to do things you need to before the song begins.

> **Listing 8.10 Jazz band: initialize.ck**

```
// initialize.ck

// Important things will go here soon,
// like Classes, which we learn about in the next chapter

// for now, we just add our score.ck
me.dir() + "/score.ck" => string scorePath;        ❶ Adds score file
Machine.add(scorePath);                                 for jazz band
```

For now, the initialize.ck file shown in listing 8.10 only adds score.ck ❶, which in turn adds all of your jazz band instrument files. The whole chain of Machine.add() function calls is shown in figure 8.8. Yes, it's sort of dumb to have one file add one other file, but very soon you'll see why it's a good idea to have this file separated from the score or any other song-time ChucK files.

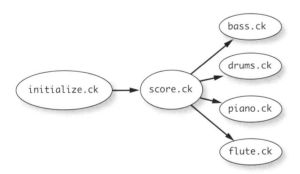

Figure 8.8   Suggested file architecture for your jazz band example. Initialize.ck adds score.ck, which then adds your instrument files. Soon, initialize.ck will do more interesting things.

Exercise: Expand your jazz band

Make the players better or different. Add more drums to the drummer. Use arrays to control the drumming. Change the scales (remember that flute and bass use the same scale, but they don't have to). Change score.ck to add the instruments at different times, or start them all together. Add another instrument of your choosing. Compose, explore, program!

8.7   Summary

Wow! You now know that you can run multiple programs at the same time (concurrency or multithreading) but in a very controllable way. You can now do the following:

- Make new shreds from within code, by sporking functions.
- Make new shreds from ChucK files, by using `Machine.add()`.
- Use `Machine.remove()` and `Machine.replace()` to control your shreds.
- Use structured code, like score.ck and initialize.ck, to compose music.

Frankly, this is huge. The sky is pretty much the limit now, because you can use code you've already written or code that others have written, reusing and borrowing functions, ideas, and entire compositions from yourself and others. You can run as many ChucK files as you like, actually as many as your CPU will support without clicking or distorting. Clicking or breaking up of the output audio is what happens when your computer finally runs out of horsepower to run your ChucK code. If this happens, you'll have to run fewer files at the same time.

But, it's not over yet. Next up you'll learn how to further expand your powers by learning how to make your own objects and classes, which are modules of encapsulated code that you can use, somewhat like functions, but objects and classes are much more powerful. So let's get to it, unless you want to compose for a while using shreds, which we wouldn't blame you for at all.

Objects and classes: making your own ChucK power tools

This chapter covers

- Data encapsulation and access, member variables
- Behavior of objects, functions, and methods
- Public vs. private classes
- Inheritance, overloading, and polymorphism
- Musical applications of objects and classes

As you keep adding to your bag of ChucK tricks and tools, you're able to be more expressive in your compositions, more succinct and efficient with your code, and generally more awesome as programmers and composers. In chapter 5, you learned how to make your own functions, opening up new capabilities for your programming, because you could reuse code and get a lot more work accomplished by calling functions with different arguments. In the previous chapter, you learned how to run programs and functions in parallel, again adding to your programming power and musical expressiveness. In this chapter, you'll learn how to make your own objects and classes, which can be viewed as super-functions but even more powerful. When you're through, you'll have even more ways to organize, use, and reuse your ChucK code. And your music and art will be even better.

9.1   Object-oriented programming: objects and classes

In this chapter, we'll will dive into the last major computer science topic in the book: OOP. The power that you'll gain from learning about and how to make and use objects and classes can make your programs and compositions even more flexible, readable, and expressive. First, we need to briefly define some terms, and then you'll be ready to learn about and use OOP in your programs.

> ### A little OOP history
> Beginning in the 1980s, a new notion called object-oriented programming began to revolutionize the computer world. Actually, OOP systems weren't so new, dating back to Simula, ALGOL, Lisp, and other languages in the late 1960s, but the ideas were new to production programming (commonly used programs and applications). Languages such as Smalltalk, Object Lisp, and others began to popularize OOP in the 1980s, but OOP really caught on with the introduction and adoption of C++, Objective C, and Java during the 1990s. Inspired by many of these pioneering languages, ChucK is an objected-oriented language that borrows from the object systems of C++ and Java but with some differences. You'll see in this chapter how powerful this philosophy, method, design, and style of programming can be, especially for music and media programming.

9.1.1   Objects in general

Say you want to put together a band, but in this case you'll be using ChucK code, as you did in the previous chapter with your jazz band. You might hire players (program them in ChucK), give the players music or tell them the song you want to play, and conduct them or somehow get them started at the same time with the same tempo. From your perspective, each player is essentially an object. The guitar player, drummer, and flute player all bring with them their own instrument and expertise. Each knows how to play their own instrument, knows how to read music, and/or knows their part for the song of interest. As a contractor/producer, you don't need all that special knowledge; you need to know only that each band member knows what they're doing. For each player, the instrument is itself an object (or collection of objects in the case of a drum set). The flute player doesn't have to know the physics of the materials that make up a flute, or the physics of the waves travelling inside, or the nonlinear fluid dynamics of the air jet they're blowing. So the flute player is an object playing an object, getting instructions or messages and data from other objects (conductor, score, and other players).

Just as you've used functions to encapsulate calculations (behaviors), you can make software objects that do the same. But objects are bigger and better than functions, because they can have knowledge in the form of internal data that persists over

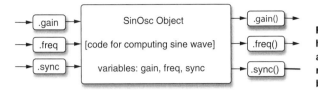

Figure 9.1 A SinOsc object contains hidden code for computing a sine wave and variables that you can modify or retrieve using the functions provided by the object.

time. Some object data can be private (as with the mysterious physics inside the flute), and some data can be public, accessible by all. Some things that objects do are also private (how the STK Flute model calculates each sample internally), whereas others are public, like the .freq and .gain methods you use to control pitch and volume. You'll see later why you might want to make some things private and others public.

You've been using objects in ChucK, because all unit generators are objects. Each variable you declare is an object, just a simple one. An array is an object composed of other objects. So when you declare something like

```
[0,0,1,1,0,1,0,1] @=> int nums[];
```

you're declaring an array object that holds integer variables inside.

When you make a new SinOsc, it has data inside it, including frequency, amplitude, how to interpret input (.sync), and the calculations to make the sine wave. Figure 9.1 depicts a SinOsc object that contains code for computing a sine wave (hidden from you, it just "works") and variables controlling gain, frequency, and sync. You can change the variable values by using the .gain, .freq, and .sync methods. You can also ask the SinOsc object for the current value of .gain(), .freq(), and .sync().

UGens are objects, and even the VM is an object, so you've already used lots of objects. But how do you make your own new types of objects? To do that, you have to know about classes.

9.1.2 *Classes*

In OOP, a class is a data type that encapsulates and abstracts data and behavior. This means that a class defines what an object will do and what it will contain, including variables and functions that you can call from outside to control and inspect the object. The class also defines any hidden code that the object will implement and/or variables that the object will contain.

When you want to use a SinOsc, you have to declare one, and you can declare and use as many as you like, as shown in figure 9.2. ChucK knows what a SinOsc is because the SinOsc class is already defined inside ChucK. When you declare SinOsc s1, ChucK creates a new one for you and associates it with the name s1 and similarly for SinOsc s2 and SinOsc s3. Each is a different copy of the basic SinOsc type, and you can modify its frequency, gain, and so on individually without changing the others. The individual SinOsc s1, s2, and s3 are instances of the basic SinOsc class. Declaring a new object and giving it a variable name is often called *instantiation* in OOP.

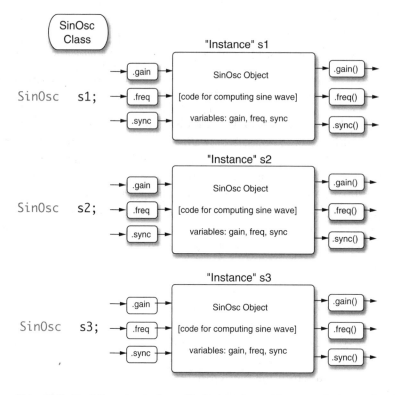

Figure 9.2   Each time you declare a SinOsc, you're making a new instance of the SinOsc class. You can use them individually without confusion, because you give each instance a unique variable name.

When we introduced variables in chapter 1, you learned that you can declare multiple variables like float x, y, and z; each is an individual float variable that can have its own value. Similarly, you can declare SinOsc s[4], and each member of that array is a separate SinOsc object. In OOP we say that a declared object is an instance of a class, and you can make (declare) as many of those instances as you like. As shown in figure 9.2 s[3] is one instance of SinOsc, and x and y are *instances* of float.

Let's take a specific example of a class that you've already used extensively, SndBuf. You can make as many instances of SndBuf as you like just by declaring them, but for now let's just declare one SndBuf, myBuff.

Usually, the function you first use with a new SndBuf is myBuff.read(FILENAME), in this case causing this particular myBuff instance to load a sound file into its internal memory. When you call that function, SndBuf automatically allocates the amount of memory needed to store the sound file you wish to load. You don't have to worry about that (as you do in the case of Delay objects, where you must tell them how much maximum delay you might need); the SndBuf class takes care of that automatically. In OOP, functions for accessing and modifying object data and causing computation within an object are called methods or member functions. Other SndBuf member functions include .rate and .loop.

You can use the built-in SndBuf member functions to change myBuff.rate to modify the speed and pitch of playback. You can set myBuff.loop to cause the sound to loop (set it to 1) or not (set it to zero). You can query myBuff to see how long the sound you've loaded is, either as an integer number of .samples() or as a duration using .length(). There are other member functions and variables built into SndBuf, specified within the class, and available to you via member functions called on any instance that you make.

Variables encapsulated within an object are sometimes called member variables. For example, member variables of SinOsc instances include .freq and .gain. There's lots of other lingo to describe how cool classes and objects are, but rather than expand on those, we'll show you how to make and use your own custom classes.

9.2 *Writing your own classes*

Your first class, called testData ❶, in listing 9.1, will show how objects can contain both data and functions. testData contains int ❷ and float ❸ member variables and a function ❹ (a method or member function). You can access the data easily by name and use the function as you might expect. Both are attached to the name of the instance of the class by a dot, so in this case you make an instance called d ❺ and access the internal myInt by using d.myInt ❻. You can invoke the internal class function by calling d.sum() ❻. This should all look familiar, because you've been making lots of objects such as UGens and accessing their innards by using the dot, as in the case of s.freq() and s.gain for a SinOsc called s.

Listing 9.1 Making and using your first new class, testData

Local int variable ❷

Local float variable ❸

```
// Simple Class to show data access
public class testData  {                    ←   Declares a public class
    1 => int myInt;                         ❶   called testData
    0.0 => float myFrac;

    // a simple function that adds the data
    fun float sum() {                       ←   Function to
        return myInt + myFrac;              ❹   add the two
    }
}

// make one of our new testData objects    ❺   Tests it all by
testData d;                                 ←   making a testData

<<< d.myInt, d.myFrac, d.sum() >>>;         ←
                                                Prints out default
// change the data, just like we would variables  ❻  initial testData values
3 => d.myInt;
0.141592 => d.myFrac;

// check to show that everything changed
<<< d.myInt, d.myFrac, d.sum() >>>;
```

Now let's do something musically useful with classes. In listing 9.2, we'll refer to our ResonZ example from listing 6.10. You declare the same chain of Impulse through the ResonZ filter into dac ❷, but you wrap it all in a class definition ❶, with some methods to set the frequency ❸, filter resonance (Q) ❹, and volume ❺. You also create a noteOn() function ❻ that behaves as any other instrument might, playing a note at the specified argument volume. The nice thing about encapsulating all this into a class is that you can then make any number of that type of object just as you make floats and ints and SinOscs, and use them without their internal variables (imp, filt) getting in the way of each other. You could even make an array of your new Simple objects.

Listing 9.2   Simple resonant pop class wraps UGens and functions for accessing them

```
// Simple example of a resonant pop sound-making class
public class Simple  {
    // our Simple instrument patch
    Impulse imp => ResonZ filt => dac;

    // some default settings
    100.0 => filt.Q => filt.gain;
    1000.0 => filt.freq;

    // set freq as we would any instrument
    fun void freq(float freq)
    {
        freq => filt.freq;
    }
    // method to allow setting Q
    fun void setQ(float Q)
    {
        Q => filt.Q;
    }

    // method to allow setting gain
    fun void setGain(float gain)
    {
        filt.Q() * gain => imp.gain;
    }

    // play a note by firing impulse
    fun void noteOn(float volume)
    {
        volume => imp.next;
    }
}
// Make an instance of (declare) one of our Simples
Simple s;

while (1)  {
    // random frequency
    Std.rand2f(1100.0,1200.0) => s.freq;
```

❶ Declares a new class called Simple

❷ Impulse through resonant filter to dac

❸ Frequency setting method

❹ Resonance (Q) setting method

❺ Gain setting method

❻ noteOn sets impulse to make a click

❼ Declares a new Simple instrument

❽ Infinite loop

❾ Random pitch frequency for pop

```
// play a note and wait a bit
1 => s.noteOn;                          ⑩  Triggers a simple pop sound
0.1 :: second => now;
}
```

Once your class is defined, you can make an instance of it ❼ and play it in an infinite loop ❽, where you change the frequency randomly ❾ for each note ⑩.

You've now created your first class that makes and controls sound! This class contained UGen objects, including an Impulse and a ResonZ filter. You can declare as many instances of your Simple objects as you like, and each one will contain unique instances of the Impulse and ResonZ filters. Next, you'll make your class definitions and functions even more flexible.

9.3 Overloading: different functions can share the same name

OOP allows you to overload functions, which means that functions can behave differently depending on the arguments. This allows you to interact with your classes using meaningful function names, and the class and object instance figures out what to do based on the argument. As an example of making a highly useful overloaded function, you might define some new functions for Simple, to set pitch either by MIDI note number (an int), frequency (a float), or even a musical note name (a string). Those three functions can all have the same function name (we'll use .pitch()), but because their arguments are different, the class will know what to do.

ChucK figures out which one you want by looking at the argument you pass to the .pitch() method. If it's a float, you use the .freq method you already have ❶. If it's an int, then the integer version is used ❷, with the argument treated as a MIDI note number. If it's a string ❸, some logic and math on string characters is used to convert that into a MIDI note number ❹, and then the int version of pitch is called ❺ by invoking the this keyword (meaning *this* object, *this* instance of the class). Try adding these three new pitch functions to Simple from listing 9.2, then calling it with different arguments. The code for this is shown in the following listing.

Listing 9.3 Add these overloaded pitch() functions to Simple

```
// three ways of setting pitch
//   one by float frequency          ❶  Sets pitch as a float
fun float pitch(float freq)              frequency in Hertz.
{
    return freq => filt.freq;
}

// another to set pitch by MIDI note number   ❷  Sets pitch using an integer
fun float pitch(int noteNum)                     MIDI note number.
{
    return Std.mtof(noteNum) => filt.freq;
}
```

Sets pitch using a note name (string). ❸

```
// another way to set pitch by noteName, capital A–G required
// Needs specific format: C4, D#5, Eb3, As3, Bf6
fun float pitch(string noteName)
{
    [21,23,12,14,16,17,19] @=> int notes[]; // Note numbers A thru G
    noteName.charAt(0) - 65 => int base;
    notes[base] => int note;
    0.0 => float freq;
    if (base > -1 && base < 7)  {
        if (noteName.charAt(1) == '#')  // either '#' symbol
            notes[base] + 1 => note;
        if (noteName.charAt(1) == 's')  //      or 's' counts for sharp
            notes[base] + 1 => note;
        if (noteName.charAt(1) == 'b')  // either 'b' or
            notes[base] - 1 => note;
        if (noteName.charAt(1) == 'f') //           'f' counts for flat
            notes[base] - 1 => note;
    }
    else {
        <<< "Illegal Note Name!!" >>>;
        return 0.0;
    }
    noteName.charAt(noteName.length()-1) - 48 => int oct;
    if (oct > -1 && oct < 10) {
        note + 12*oct => note;
        return this.pitch(note);
    }
    else {
        <<< "Illegal Octave!!" >>>;
        return 0.0;
    }
}
// Make a Simple, and test new pitch functions
Simple s;

// MIDI note number pitch
s.pitch(60);
1 => s.noteOn;
second => now;

// pitch as float frequency
s.pitch(440.0);
1 => s.noteOn;
second => now;

// pitch as note name string
s.pitch("G#5");
1 => s.noteOn;
second => now;
```

❹ Manipulates ASCII code to come up with array pointer.

❺ After figuring out note number, calls MIDI pitch function.

❻ Tests MIDI integer pitch setting function.

❼ Tests float pitch-setting function.

❽ Tests string note-name pitch-setting function.

Once you've added these functions to your Simple class, you can test it by calling pitch using each method, passing it an int ❻, a float ❼, and a note name string ❽.

> **Did you get an error when running your new Simple class?**
>
> When you tried to run your new `Simple` class example, you likely got an error from the miniAudicle. If it was a syntax error, as you so often get when first running any new code, you can fix the error and try again. But even with no syntax errors, you probably got an error that looked something like this:
>
> ```
> [Simple.ck] :line(2):  class/type 'Simple' is already defined in
>     namespace '[user]'
> ```
>
> Read on, because the next section will explain this and help you fix it.

When defining your own classes, you can declare multiple functions that have the same name but can do different things depending on the type and number of arguments. The same is true inside ChucK for many operators. You've already been using lots of ChucK operators that are overloaded. The ChucK symbol => itself is overloaded, because you use it to connect unit generators (SinOsc s => dac), to assign values to variables (0.1 => float x), and to advance time (0.1 :: second => now). ChucK figures out by the context and the data types of the arguments and destinations what the ChucK operator should be doing. Another example of overloading is the plus sign. You can use it to add integers, floats, or even complex numbers, and it can also be used to concatenate strings ("Hello "+"World" => string helloworld). As we said, functions can be overloaded as well, and you've already seen a musically useful reason for that with your Simple.pitch() functions.

9.4 *Public vs. private classes*

That error you probably got when running your new `Simple` class has to do with defining new classes as public, which means that every new piece of ChucK code can have access to and use the newly defined class. Having classes defined as public is great, as long as you know that your class works just the way you want it and you don't ever want to modify it. But for development, you need to be able to modify your class definitions, functions, and data on the fly. The problem the ChucK compiler ran into was that it already had a class defined called `Simple`, and running your new code told ChucK to define it again, which is illegal.

   The easiest way to fix this is to rename `Simple` to `Simple2` or something else, but that's not really the best way, because class definitions will pile up quite quickly and become confusing. Another way to deal with the public name-collision issue is to declare the class as private rather than public, meaning that only code within this file and shred, as you're running it, can see it and have access to any new private class. So for now, go to the top of your `Simple` code, and change the first defining line to read as follows:

```
// Simple example of a class, made private
private class Simple  {
    // our Simple instrument patch
```

```
Impulse imp => ResonZ filt => dac;
    // etc. etc. etc.
```

With Simple defined as private, you can now redefine, experiment, and fiddle with the new class all you like, even adding more of them on top of each other while the virtual machine continues running.

private classes are great, if you define and use them in the same .ck code file. But there are many reasons why you need and want public classes as well as private, and the next section will demonstrate just one of those reasons: communication between shreds via global (static) public variables.

9.4.1   *Useful applications for public classes*

Now that you know how to define classes and declare them as private so that you can incrementally improve them, you might wonder why you'd ever make a class public. Because they're global and visible to all, public classes can be really useful. As an example, let's define a public class that keeps track of tempo for an orchestra of players, as shown in the following listing. The job of the BPM class is to be a container for some related durations: quarterNote, eighthNote, and so on ❶. The tempo() method takes a floating-point argument specifying the beats per minute ❷, does a little math to figure out a base duration ❸, and sets the remaining durations ❹.

Listing 9.4   Public class BPM acting like a global conductor

```
public class BPM                                    Variables declared this way  ❶
{                                                   are accessible globally
    // global variables
  dur quarterNote, eighthNote, sixteenthNote, thirtysecondNote;

  fun void tempo(float beat)  {
      // beat argument is BPM, example 120 beats per minute
      60.0/(beat) => float SPB; // seconds per beat      Does a little math to
      SPB :: second => quarterNote;                      go from BPM to
      quarterNote*0.5 => eighthNote;                  ❸  seconds per beat
      eighthNote*0.5 => sixteenthNote;
      sixteenthNote*0.5 => thirtysecondNote;             Uses that to set
  }                                                   ❹  all durations
}

SinOsc s => dac;                                    ❺  Tests your BPM object
BPM t; // Define t Object of Class BPM                  by making one
t.tempo(300); // set tempo in BPM
                                                       Sets tempo of new
400 => int freq;                                    ❻  BPM object
while (freq < 800)
{
    freq => s.freq;
    t.quarterNote => now;           Uses .quarterNote
    50 +=> freq;                 ❼  method to advance time
}
```

Function to set tempo (all variables) ❷

To use the BPM class, you just need to make an instance of it ❺, set the tempo ❻, and then ask for the values you need (quarter, eighth, and so on) ❼. This example uses a duration within a BPM object ❺ to step the frequency of a SinOsc upward from 400 to 800 Hz every quarterNote ❼. If you run the code of listing 9.5 multiple times but change the tempo ❻, you'll hear the frequency step upward faster or slower.

9.4.2 *The Clear VM button*

Because you're using a public class for BPM, once you've defined the class and run the code again, you'll run into the same type of "already defined in namespace '[user]'" error message as you define and redefine the class. The way around this is to click the special Clear VM button, which causes ChucK to forget everything that's been defined previously. You might want to redefine one class while leaving all others in place, but this isn't possible. But very soon we'll show you a means of organizing your code that makes all this much easier to deal with.

9.4.3 *Static variables*

Our example of using BPM to step a SinOsc frequency upward is fine as an example, but you could have done that by just defining and using the quarter note duration. The true power of BPM as a public class is that many objects and functions can access it at the same time. To really take advantage of that, you need to make a little change to your BPM class definition in order to make its variables visible to other shreds of ChucK code, so everyone in your band can see the tempo values from everywhere. The way to do that is to declare the note duration values as static ❶, as shown in the following listing, meaning that those particular variables are shared and accessible across all instances of the class.

> **Listing 9.5 Redefining BPM's variables as static**

```
public class BPM                              Declaring variables as static makes  ❶
{                                             them global to all instances of this class
    // global variables
      static dur quarterNote, eighthNote, sixteenthNote, thirtysecondNote;

    fun void tempo(float beat)  {
        // beat argument is BPM, example 120 beats per minute

        60.0/(beat) => float SPB; // seconds per beat
        SPB :: second => quarterNote;
        quarterNote*0.5 => eighthNote;
        eighthNote*0.5 => sixteenthNote;
        quarterNote*0.5 => thirtysecondNote;
    }
}
```

If you make two instances of BPM, in two different ChucK files, or even two BPMs within the same file, and modify one BPM instance, the other BPM is modified automatically, because they share the same static duration variables. We'll use that in an example in the next two listings.

Listing 9.6   Make a BPM; setting tempo here affects all others

```
// This lives in file UseBPM.ck
SinOsc s => dac;
BPM t; // Define t Object of Class BPM
t.tempo(300); // set tempo in BPM
0.3 => s.gain;

400 => int freq;
while (freq < 800)
{
    freq => s.freq;
    t.quarterNote => now;
    50 +=> freq;
}
```

Listing 9.7   Make another BPM, but static variables are shared

```
// Lives in another file, UseBPM2.ck
SinOsc s => dac.right;
BPM t2; // Define another BPM named t2
0.3 => s.gain;

800 => int freq;
while (freq > 400)
{
    freq => s.freq;
    t2.quarterNote => now;
    50 -=> freq;
}
```

Save your BPM class definition in one ChucK file, BPM.ck. Save your first test program in a file called UseBPM.ck and your second test program in a file called UseBPM2.ck. Then you can add them in that order (BPM.ck, then UseBPM.c, and then UseBPM2.ck) and hear the first sine wave rising and the second one falling. The variables quarter-Note, eighthNote, and so on are now global, meaning that they're visible from everywhere within ChucK.

You might ask, "But can't I put all those in the same file and just run it?" As it is, the definitions of SinOsc s and int freq would collide, yielding an "already defined" error. You could change that, giving each a new name, but as the size of your orchestra grows, you're increasingly going to need a way to keep things straight and put instruments, class definitions, data, and the like in separate files so you can reuse them (another strength of OOP). Also, because you now know how awesome concurrency can be, you might as well get used to thinking in that way: putting different things in their own files and using Machine.add() and other VM functions to control your programs and compositions.

9.5   *Initialize.ck: an architecture for organizing your code*

To help keep things straight, you use a special file called initialize.ck, whose job it is to be the first and only file you run (using the Add Shred button). Once you've crafted

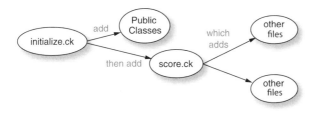

Figure 9.3 Suggested architecture for organizing code. Master file initialize.ck first adds any public classes and then adds score.ck, which then adds other files to make up the composition.

and saved your individual files (classes, score.ck, instrument files, and so on) initialize .ck can be the only file you open, and it adds everything to the ChucK VM. initialize.ck first adds any public classes and then adds the score.ck file, which in turn adds the other files. Figure 9.3 shows this architecture.

Just as with sounds and other files in previous chapters, the use of

```
me.dir()+"/FILENAME.ck" lets that run for 4 seconds,
```

allows ChucK to find your files, as long as they're in the same directory as initialize.ck. As shown in listing 9.8, initialize.ck first adds your public BPM class ❶ and then your two test files, UseBPM.ck and UseBPM2.ck ❷. Note that they're perfectly in sync, with one sine wave stepping upward and the other stepping downward. This is another way to start two or more independent instruments playing together at the same time. If you Machine.add() them together, they start together.

Listing 9.8 Initialize.ck file serves as the master program

```
// initialize.ck  manages classes and files
// add public classes first
Machine.add(me.dir()+"/BPM.ck");

// then add instruments, scores, etc.
Machine.add(me.dir()+"/UseBPM.ck");
Machine.add(me.dir()+"/UseBPM2.ck");

// wait a bit, then add some more!
4.0 :: second => now;
Machine.add(me.dir()+"/myScore.ck");
```

❶ Adds master BPM class definition

❷ Adds test files UseBPM.ck and UseBPM2.ck

❸ Waits a bit and then adds score file

After waiting a bit, initialize.ck adds one more file, myScore.ck ❸, which contains an endless loop that continuously adds UseBPM2.ck and a new file, UseBPM3.ck ❶, as shown in the following listing.

Listing 9.9 MyScore.ck file adds lots of other BPM users in an endless loop

```
// myScore.ck, endless loop to add some BPM users
while (true)  {
    Machine.add(me.dir()+"/UseBPM2.ck");
    1.0 :: second => now;
    Machine.add(me.dir()+"/UseBPM3.ck");        New file, UseBPM3.ck
    2.0 :: second => now;
}
```

UseBPM3.ck, shown in listing 9.10, modifies the tempo randomly each time it's added ❶, so any other files that are still running (UseBPM2 or UseBPM3) will change tempo as well. UseBPM3 also sweeps its own sine wave downward ❷.

Running initialize.ck, you should hear lots of sine waves sweeping downward at different rates, because it first runs UseBPM.ck and UseBPM2.ck ❷ and then adds myScore.ck after 4 seconds have passed. myScore.ck in turn runs UseBPM2.ck and UseBPM3.ck in an endless loop. Watching the VM monitor window, you'll see all of the new shreds being added and removing themselves after their individual sines have swept.

Listing 9.10   UseBPM3.ck randomly sets BPM tempo and sweeps another sine

```
// This lives in another file, UseBPM3.ck
SinOsc s => dac;
BPM t2; // Define another BPM called t2
0.3 => s.gain;

// and set tempo to a random number
Math.random2f(200.0,1000.0) => t2.tempo;    ←——❶ Sets random tempo

1000 => int freq;
while (freq > 400)          ←——————————❷ Sweeps sine frequency downward
{
    freq => s.freq;
    t2.quarterNote => now;
    50 -=> freq;
}
```

This example shows how you could use public classes and global static variables to communicate and synchronize between shreds, but because BPM is about tempo, you should do something more rhythmic, don't you think?

9.6   *Conducting a drum pattern using a time-varying BPM*

Let's put the BPM class to even more musical use, by constructing a drum pattern using different sounds controlled by different files, as shown in listing 9.11. Because of the flexibility of ChucK, and by crafting your individual programs well, you can easily adapt these to use BPM to control tempo globally. You'll use the very same BPM class definition you made and used previously. This example will also modify BPM on the fly as all of the drums are playing, using it as a global conductor, controlled by your score.ck file. You should put all these files in their own directory, named something like DrumBPM, at the same level as the /audio directory.

You need percussion instruments, so you'll start out with a kick drum. This file uses a SndBuf loaded with a kick drum sound file ❶. Then you define a BPM object ❷, but you don't need to set any parameters for it because that will all happen globally, controlled by your score.ck file (you'll make that later). The kick infinitely plays ❸ a four-beat pattern ❺, sounding each beat ❻ and refreshing its quarter-note duration at the beginning of each bar ❹. You'll be writing each instrument (player) so that it does its

thing for a four-beat bar and then refreshes its local duration from the global BPM
before starting the bar pattern over.

Listing 9.11   kick.ck kick drum file, conducted by BPM

```
// kick.ck, on the fly drumming with global BPM conducting
SndBuf kick => dac;
1 => kick.gain;                                        ❶ Reads a kick drum sound
me.dir(-1)+"/audio/kick_04.wav" => kick.read;             for this instrument

// make a conductor for our tempo
// this is set and updated elsewhere                   ❷ Makes a BPM to use
BPM tempo;                                                 to sync with others

while (1)  {
    // update our basic beat each measure             ❹ Uses quarter note
    tempo.quarterNote => dur quarter;                    from BPM

    // play a measure of quarter note kicks
    for (0 => int beat; beat < 4; beat++)  {          ❺ Four-beat measure
        0 => kick.pos;                                ❻ Plays on every beat
        quarter => now;
    }
}
```

Infinite loop ❸

To add more instrument players, snare.ck (listing 9.12) and cowbell.ck (listing 9.13)
look pretty much like kick.ck, except they play different patterns to make things interesting. Snare (listing 9.12) plays on off beats (beats two and four), with an extra eighth
note for accent. Tempo is updated at the beginning of each measure pattern ❶. The
off-beat playing pattern is accomplished by first advancing time by a quarter note ❷,
then playing a snare hit ❸, waiting two quarter notes ❹, and then playing another
hit ❺. You then advance time by a sixteenth note ❻, play a hit ❼, and then make up
the remaining time (three sixteenth notes) ❽.

Listing 9.12   snare.ck plays on beats 2 and 4 and more, conducted by global BPM

```
// snare.ck
// on the fly drumming with global BPM conducting
SndBuf snare => dac;
me.dir(-1)+"/audio/snare_01.wav" => snare.read;
0.5 => snare.gain;
snare.samples() => snare.pos;

// make a conductor for our tempo
// this is set and updated elsewhere
BPM tempo;

while (1)  {
    // update our basic beat each measure             ❶ Updates tempo at beginning
    tempo.quarterNote => dur quarter;                    of each measure...

    // play measure of: rest, snare, rest, sna-snare
    quarter => now;                                   ❷ ...waits a beat (quarter)...
```

```
0 => snare.pos;          ←——— ❸ ...plays a snare hit...
2.0*quarter => now;      ←——————— ❹ ...waits two beats...
0 => snare.pos;          ←——————————— ❺ ...plays another hit...
quarter/4.0 => now;      ←——— ❻ ...waits for a quarter beat...
0 => snare.pos;          ←————— ❼ ...plays another hit...
3.0*quarter/4.0 => now;  ←———————— ❽ ...waits for remainder of the measure.
}
```

Cowbell (listing 9.13) plays only on the last eighth note of the whole four-beat pattern, by first updating `tempo` from BPM ❶, then using a for loop ❷ of eighth-note time advances ❹, and only playing on the seventh (remember, you start counting at zero) eighth note ❸.

Listing 9.13   cowbell.ck plays only on last eighth note of measures, conducted by BPM

```
// cowbell.ck
// on the fly drumming with global BPM conducting
SndBuf cow => dac;
0.3 => cow.gain;
me.dir(-1)+"/audio/cowbell_01.wav" => cow.read;

// make a conductor for our tempo
// this is set and updated elsewhere
BPM tempo;

while (1)  {
    // update our basic beat each measure
    tempo.eighthNote => dur eighth;          ←  ❶ Synchronizes on
                                                  eighth notes.

    // play measure of eighths                  ❷ Measure is 8 total
    for (0 => int beat; beat < 8; beat++)  {  ←    eighth notes.
        // but only play on the last 8th
        if (beat == 7) {                         ❸ Plays only on the last
            0 => cow.pos;                ←          eighth note.
        }
        eighth => now;               ←——— ❹ Advance time by eighth.
    }
}
```

The hihat.ck player is similar, as shown in the following listing, but it plays all eighths except for the last one (when the cowbell plays). Note that the code is nearly identical to cowbell, except the logical condition check is changed from `if (beat == 7)` for the cowbell to `if (beat != 7)` for the hi-hat ❶. What a difference one character can make!!

Listing 9.14   hihat.ck plays on all eighth notes except the last, synced to BPM

```
// hihat.ck
// on the fly drumming with global BPM conducting
SndBuf hat => dac;
0.3 => hat.gain;
me.dir(-1)+"/audio/hihat_02.wav" => hat.read;
```

```
// make a conductor for our tempo
// this is set and updated elsewhere
BPM tempo;

while (1)  {
    // update our basic beat each measure
    tempo.eighthNote => dur eighth;

    // play a measure of eighth notes
    for (0 => int beat; beat < 8; beat++)  {
        // play mostly, but leave out last eighth
        if (beat != 7) {
            0 => hat.pos;
        }
        eighth => now;
    }
}
```

❶ Plays all eighths except the last one (the anti-cowbell)

The hand clapper clap.ck program, shown in the next listing, randomly claps ❶ on sixteenth notes ❷.

```
// clap.ck
// on the fly drumming with global BPM conducting
SndBuf clap => dac;
0.3 => clap.gain;
me.dir(-1)+"/audio/clap_01.wav" => clap.read;

// make a conductor
// this is set and controlled elsewhere
BPM tempo;

while (1)  {
    // our basic beat for this instrument
    // update this every measure
    tempo.sixteenthNote => dur sixteenth;

    // play a whole measure of 16 16th notes
    for (0 => int beat; beat < 16; beat++)  {
        // clap randomly on 16th notes
        if (Math.random2(0,7) < 3) {
            0 => clap.pos;
        }
        sixteenth => now;
    }
}
```

❶ Random claps (3/8 probability)...

❷ ...on sixteenth notes

So now you've created files to control kick, snare, hi-hat, cowbell, and hand claps. You still need a score file to add all of these into the VM and, most importantly, to control tempo using BPM ❶, as shown in the next listing. Your song starts out by gradually adding in each drum player file ❷. Then you change the tempo to 80 BPM ❸, then 160 BPM ❹, and then gradually decrease the tempo until it reaches 60 BPM ❺. Finally, you remove all the instruments ❻.

> **Listing 9.16   score.ck controls individual players and tempo via BPM**

```
// score.ck, on the fly drumming with global BPM conducting
//  Here we make our BPM instance that controls tempo
BPM tempo;
tempo.tempo(120.0);
```
❶ Makes a global BPM to control from here.

```
// Add in instruments one at a time, musically
Machine.add(me.dir()+"/kick.ck") => int kickID;
8.0 * tempo.quarterNote => now;
Machine.add(me.dir()+"/snare.ck") => int snareID;
8.0 * tempo.quarterNote => now;
Machine.add(me.dir()+"/hihat.ck") => int hatID;
Machine.add(me.dir()+"/cowbell.ck") => int cowID;
8.0 * tempo.quarterNote => now;
Machine.add(me.dir()+"/clap.ck") => int clapID;
8.0 * tempo.quarterNote => now;
```
❷ Adds instruments one at a time.

```
// now have some fun with tempo
<<< "Set tempo to 80BPM" >>>;
80.0 => float newtempo;
tempo.tempo(newtempo);
8.0 * tempo.quarterNote => now;
```
❸ Changes tempo to 80 BPM...

```
<<< "Now set tempo to 160BPM" >>>;
160.0 => newtempo;
tempo.tempo(newtempo);
8.0 * tempo.quarterNote => now;
```
❹ ...then changes it to 160 BPM.

```
/* if you want to run OTFBPM.ck to change tempo
   as these run, then comment out the lines below  */

<<< "Gradually decrease tempo" >>>;
while (newtempo > 60.0) {
    newtempo - 20 => newtempo;
    tempo.tempo(newtempo);
    <<< "tempo = ", newtempo >>>;
    4.0 * tempo.quarterNote => now;
}
```
❺ Gradually moves tempo down.

```
// bring out the instruments, gradually
Machine.remove(kickID);
8.0 * tempo.quarterNote => now;
Machine.remove(snareID);
Machine.remove(hatID);
8.0 * tempo.quarterNote => now;
Machine.remove(cowID);
8.0 * tempo.quarterNote => now;
Machine.remove(clapID);
```
❻ Pulls out instruments one at a time.

Finally, you need to create an initialize.ck file to load/declare the BPM class ❶ and load your score file to kick off the music ❷, as shown in the next listing.

Listing 9.17 Initialize.ck adds BPM.ck class and then turns it all over to score.ck

```
// initialize.ck

// our conductor/beat-timer class
Machine.add(me.dir()+"/BPM.ck");

// our score
Machine.add(me.dir()+"/score.ck");
```

1 Adds the BPM class definition...

2 ...then adds the score, which does the rest.

And that's it—a whole orchestra of individual percussionists, all controlled in perfect sync by BPM objects via common shared static variables! Having classes and objects makes it amazingly flexible to share and modify lots of information globally (using static variables), as you've done here with the BPM class.

9.7 *Making new classes from existing classes*

Possibly the most powerful aspect of classes and objects is the ability to model a new class after an existing one, adding to it or modifying how it behaves. In OOP, this is called *inheritance*, meaning that you can make classes that inherit from others. Just as human children have some features that look and/or act like those of a parent but also have their own behaviors, in ChucK programming so can a child class do whatever a parent class can do but also add to it or change some behaviors altogether.

9.7.1 *Inheritance: modeling and modifying parents*

As a simple example, you'll make a clarinet that knows a little more about playing notes than just the regular built-in `Clarinet` UGen. This is shown in figure 9.4, where the subclass `MyClarinet` inherits features (functions, data, and behavior) from its `Clarinet` parent.

All functions that are already defined in the parent `Clarinet` class are available to the child `MyClarinet` class, but new functions can be added (and parent methods can be overloaded as well) in the `MyClarinet` definition, as shown in the next listing.

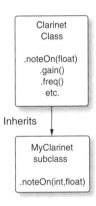

Figure 9.4 `MyClarinet` subclass inherits from parent class `Clarinet`. All functions, variables, and the like automatically become part of `MyClarinet`, and you can add your own functions such as a new `noteOn` that takes two arguments, MIDI note and volume.

Listing 9.18 A smarter `MyClarinet` that inherits from `Clarinet`

```
// A clarinet that understands MIDI note numbers in noteOn!!
public class MyClarinet extends Clarinet
{
    // here we define one new function
    fun float noteOn(int noteNum, float volume) {
```

1 Subclass of Clarinet UGen.

2 New noteOn function with two arguments.

```
        // we set frequency using MIDI note Number
        Std.mtof(noteNum) => this.freq;
        // then call the built-in inherited noteOn
        volume => this.noteOn;
    }
}

// make a new instance of our special clarinet
MyClarinet myclar => dac;

// test our new noteOn function
myclar.noteOn(60, 1.0);
second => now;
1 => myclar.noteOff;
second => now;
// test our old noteOn function
myclar.noteOn(1.0);
second => now;
```

3 Uses Clarinet's built in .freq method...

4 ...and uses Clarinet's noteOn to set volume

5 Tests it all out.

6 The old Clarinet noteOn still works too!

Note in listing 9.18 that you use a new word extends and the class (Clarinet) that you wish to extend or inherit from **1**. The MyClarinet class is a child of Clarinet, and Clarinet is a parent of the new class. In the class definition you define a new noteOn function/method that accepts two arguments, a MIDI note number and a velocity/volume **2**. These are then used to call the existing Clarinet .freq **3** and .noteOn **4** methods using the this keyword.

NOTE We've been talking about parent and child classes, but you'll find that if you learn another language, like Java or C++, you might hear the terms *superclass* used for parent and *subclass* used for child.

You're also exploiting overloading here, with two noteOn methods that take different numbers of arguments. When you call myclar.noteOn() with two arguments **5**, ChucK knows you want to use your new MyClarinet function. Then when you call myclar.noteOn() with only one argument **6**, ChucK looks up and uses the superclass Clarinet noteOn method. All other things that the Clarinet parent knows how to do you don't have to rewrite; they're inherited automatically. This is the beauty of inheritance, because you can use the built-in functionality of existing classes but customize them by adding your own data and methods.

Exercise: make an even smarter instrument

Add more new functions to MyClarinet, such as a noteOn that responds to a string note name and a float volume. Next, make a smarter subclass of any instrument of your choice. Give it new functions to understand more things that you want to do. Try overwriting at least one function that the instrument/class already has and add new functions you create yourself. For example, you could make a flute player that sweeps each note upward slightly as it's being played. You could do this by declaring a noteOn function that sweeps the pitch up from 0.9 times a target frequency until it reaches the target. (Note: you'd have to advance time in that function.)

Clearly, inheritance is a super-powerful aspect of OOP, allowing you to use classes that already exist or that you (or other programmers) have created and then modified in small or large ways, without having to type and implement all of the parts of the original class that you want to keep.

9.7.2 *Polymorphism: managing many children*

Now that you know about inheritance, you can also use it to group things and control them under a common base class. You did this in chapter 5 (listing 5.7) when you defined your `swell()` function to work on any UGen (listing reproduced here). Because all unit generators, whose parent class is called `UGen`, obey the `.gain()` method, you can pass absolutely any UGen into that `swell` function and it will work just fine. That's called polymorphism, but it's actually a very simple version of it.

> **Listing 5.7 (Repeated) Using a swell function to ramp oscillator volume up and down**

```
// swell function, operates on any type of UGen
fun void swell(UGen osc, float begin, float end, float grain){
    float val;
    // swell up volume
    for (begin => val; val < end; grain +=> val)
    {
        val => osc.gain;
        0.01 :: second => now;
    }

    // swell down volume
    while (val > begin)
    {
        val => osc.gain;
        grain -=> val;
        0.01:: second => now;
    }
}
```

For another example of polymorphism, you can make an array of objects that inherit from the existing `StkInstrument` class and fill that array with instances of various subclasses, to make them easier to access and control. Figure 9.5 shows the relationship of the `StkInstrument` superclass with some of its children. In this version of polymorphism, each instrument might interpret `.noteOn`, `.freq`, and the like in a different way based on how it works, but you can refer to them all using the same array.

Let's use this in a simple example in listing 9.19. Here you make an array of four `StkInstruments` and fill that array with four different types of instruments. When you drop into the main test loop, you don't have to know which instrument you're playing, because they all obey `.freq`, `.noteOn`, and `.noteOff`. The individual instruments (and ChucK) figure it all out, through polymorphism, because every one of those instruments has built-in `.freq`, `.noteOn`, and `.noteOff` methods. Inside, each does something different with each function, like setting the length of a delay line to model a

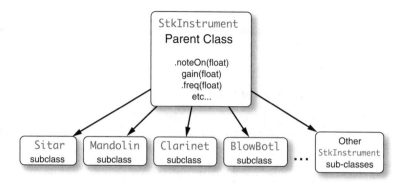

Figure 9.5   Sitar, Mandolin, Clarinet, BlowBotl, and all other StkInstrument UGens inherit from a parent class StkInstrument.

string or tube for Mandolin or Clarinet versus setting the center frequency of a filter for BlowBotl. Similarly, .noteOn plucks a string in Mandolin or Sitar but triggers an internal ADSR for Clarinet or BlowBotl. Polymorphism covers it all!

Listing 9.19   Polymorphism with an array of StkInstruments

```
// Example of polymorphism and base class use
// make an array of generic instruments
StkInstrument inst[4];

// make each instrument a different type
Sitar inst0 @=> inst[0] => dac;
Mandolin inst1 @=> inst[1] => dac;
Clarinet inst2 @=> inst[2] => dac;
BlowBotl inst3 @=> inst[3] => dac;

// take advantage of polymorphism to play them all
for (0 => int i; i < 4; i++)  {
    500.0 - (i*100.0) => inst[i].freq;
    1 => inst[i].noteOn;
    second => now;
    1 => inst[i].noteOff;
}
```

You can do even more with inheritance and polymorphism, but both of those can quickly become pretty advanced programming topics. At least you're now familiar with pretty much all of the possibilities (and buzzwords) of OOP. As you program more and more in ChucK, you might now easily think of cases where making your own classes, either from scratch or basing them on existing classes, will help you be more expressive and efficient with your code. Let's finish up by building and using a smart Mandolin player class.

9.8   *Example: building a smart mandolin player*

You've worked through much of the magic and power of OOP, classes, and objects. You know something about inheritance, overloading, and polymorphism, but there's a whole lot more that you can do with classes. You'll be using them for the rest of the book, and you'll see many more examples of their expressive capabilities.

For now, we'll conclude by extending our idea of making bands out of smart instrument players, by building a somewhat smart mandolin instrument and player class called MandoPlayer ❶, as shown in the following listing. This class bundles four Mandolin UGens in an array ❷, one for each string pair on a real mandolin (a mandolin has four pairs of strings; each string pair is tuned to the same note to give a richer sound than a single string). Each mandolin string pair is then connected to a single reverb and to the dac. ❸

Listing 9.20   Smart mandolin instrument and player class

```
// Four Mando "strings", plus some smarts
// by Perry R. Cook, March 2013                         ❶ Public MandoPlayer
public class MandoPlayer {                                  class definition.

    // make an array of four mandolin strings and connect them up
    Mandolin m[4];
    m[0] => JCRev rev => dac;                          ❸ Hooks them all up so
    m[1] => rev;                                           you can hear them.
    m[2] => rev;
    m[3] => rev;
    0.25 => rev.gain;
    0.02 => rev.mix;
    // set all four string frequencies in one function
    fun void freqs(float gStr, float dStr, float aStr, float eStr)
    {
        m[0].freq(gStr);
        m[1].freq(aStr);                               ❹ Sets all four string
        m[2].freq(dStr);                                   frequencies.
        m[3].freq(eStr);
    }
                                                       ❺ Sets all four string
                                                           note numbers...
    // set all four string notes in one function
    fun void notes(int gNote, int dNote, int aNote, int eNote) {
        m[0].freq(Std.mtof(gNote));
        m[1].freq(Std.mtof(dNote));                    ❻ ...using .mtof.
        m[2].freq(Std.mtof(aNote));
        m[3].freq(Std.mtof(eNote));
    }

    // a few named chords to get you started, add your own!!
    fun void chord(string which)  {
        if (which == "G") this.notes(55,62,71,79);     ❽ G Chord is G3,
        else if (which == "C") this.notes(55,64,72,79);    D4, B4, G5.
        else if (which == "D") this.notes(57,62,69,78);
        else <<< "I don't know this chord: ", which >>>;
    }
}
```

Contains four Mandolin UGens. ❷

Chords by name. ❼

Plays notes ⑪
one at a
time...

...with
rate
duration
between. ⑫

⑨ Chord roll (arpeggiate)
function.

Sets chord by string
using MandoPlayer
⑩ .chord function.

```
// roll a chord from lowest note to highest at rate
    fun void roll(string chord, dur rate) {
        this.chord(chord);
        for (0 => int i; i < 4; i++)  {
            1 => m[i].noteOn;
            rate => now;
        }
    }

// Archetypical tremolo strumming
fun void strum(int note, dur howLong)  {
    int whichString;
    if (note < 62) 0 => whichString;
    else if (note < 69) 1 => whichString;
    else if (note < 76) 2 => whichString;
    else 3 => whichString;
    Std.mtof(note) => m[whichString].freq;
    now + howLong => time stop;
    while (now < stop)  {
        Std.rand2f(0.5,1.0) => m[whichString].noteOn;
        Std.rand2f(0.06,0.09) :: second => now;
    }
}

// Damp all strings by amount
// 0.0 = lots of damping, 1.0 = none
fun void damp(float amount)  {
    for (0 => int i; i < 4; i++)  {
        amount => m[i].stringDamping;
    }
}
// END the MandoPlayer Class Definition
}
```

⑬ Strumming
function
(tremolo).

⑭ Figures out
which string
to strum.

⑯ Time to stop
strumming...

⑰ ...do it until
you get to
that time.

Sets
frequency. ⑮

Somewhat
random
⑱ volume.

Somewhat random time. ⑲

⑳ Damping function.

㉑ Whew! Finished defining the
smart Mandolin player class.

You then provide functions to set all four strings at once. The `.freqs()` function sets the string notes with four floating-point frequencies ❹. The `.notes()` function expects four integer MIDI note numbers ❺ and uses `Std.mtof()` ❻ to set the individual string frequencies. Because this `MandoPlayer` is more than just an instrument, you give it even more smarts by creating a function that knows the names of a few common mandolin chords ❼. This function expects a string specifying which of the standard G, C, and D chords to use ❽.

You then give `MandoPlayer` the knowledge and technique to perform gestures that are common to stringed instrument playing. The `roll()` function ❾ accepts a `string` argument specifying a chord and a duration specifying the rate (time spacing between playing each note). This function takes advantage of the `this` keyword and the `MandoPlayer` `.chord()` function to set the notes of each string pair ❿. Then it uses a for loop ⑪ to play the notes one at a time, delaying by the rate between each note ⑫. Another musical name for what the `roll` function accomplishes is *arpeggiation*.

With a `.strum()` function ⓭, you also give the `MandoPlayer` the ability to perform tremolo strumming, which is the rapid repeating of a single note, a very common mandolin playing technique. The function takes an integer MIDI note number and a total duration for which to strum. First, you use a bit of logic to sort out which is the correct string to play the note on ⓮. This is a subtle but important feature, because any strings still ringing from a previous note or chord will continue to ring. You then use the `this` keyword to set the frequency of the correct string ⓯, and you do math on `time` and duration to determine when the function should stop strumming ⓰. Then you drop into a `while` loop ⓱ and with somewhat random volume ⓲ play repeated notes for somewhat random durations ⓳. Building in this randomness, combined with the mandolin being a physical model, makes it sound more like a human player rather than a robotic computer program.

Finally, you define one more function to set the damping for all four string pairs at once ⓴. This completes the definition of the `MandoPlayer` class ㉑.

You can now put your `MandoPlayer` through its paces, testing all of the smart functions you've created, as shown in listing 9.21. First, you make a new `MandoPlayer` ❶. Then you declare chords and durations for the song you're going to play ❷. You also define strumming notes for later on in the song ❸. To play your song, you first use a `while` loop ❹ to roll through all of the chords in your song array ❺. You then strum through your strumming note array ❻. You end by setting the damping to `1.0`, meaning that the strings will ring for a very long time ❼, and roll a G chord ❽, letting that ring for 2 seconds. Finally, you damp the strings as a player might do at the end of a song ❾.

Listing 9.21 MandoScore.ck makes and plays your new `MandoPlayer`

```
// let's try all this out!!  Make a MandoPlayer object          ❶ Makes a smart
MandoPlayer m;                                                      MandoPlayer object

// and declare some data for chording and strumming             ❷ Array of string
["G","C","G","D","D","D","D","G"] @=> string chords[];              chord names
[0.4,0.4,0.4,0.1,0.1,0.1,0.1,0.01] @=> float durs[];
[79,81,83] @=> int strums[];                                    ❸ Array of things
                                                                   to strum...
// counter to iterate through the arrays
0 => int i;
// roll the basic chords, reading through the arrays
while (i < chords.cap())  {                                         ...through whole
      m.roll(chords[i],durs[i] :: second);                      ❹ chord name array
      i++;
}

// now strum a few notes
0 => i;
while (i < strums.cap())  {
      m.strum(strums[i++], 1.0 :: second);                         Strums through the
}                                                                ❻ array of strums
```

Rolls each chord ❺

```
// then end up with a big open G chord
m.damp(1.0);
m.roll("G", 0.02 :: second);
2.0 :: second => now;

// damp it to silence, letting it ring a little
m.damp(0.01);
1.0 :: second => now;
```

Rolls a G chord **8**

7 **Lets strings ring a long time**

9 **Damps strings at the end**

You could just run this score, provided that you remember to run the class definition of MandoPlayer.ck once (and only once) beforehand. But to keep with your new practice of keeping your code organized, you'll make a simple initialize.ck file that uses Machine.add() to first add the class definition **1** and then add MandoScore.ck **2** to start the music, as shown in the next listing.

Listing 9.22   initialize.ck adds MandoPlayer.ck class and then MandoScore.ck score

```
// initialize.ck for MandoPlayer class and demo MandoScore

Machine.add(me.dir()+"/MandoPlayer.ck");    ←——1 Adds MandoPlayer class definition...

Machine.add(me.dir()+"/MandoScore.ck");    ←——2 ...then adds score, which does the rest.
```

PUBLIC CLASSES AND CLEAR VM   Remember that you might get occasional errors because you're trying to redefine a public class that has already been defined. This is easily fixed by clicking the Clear VM button.

9.9   *Summary*

Your ChucK toolset keeps expanding, and now you know how to build your own tools in the form of classes. Object-oriented programming systems are a super-powerful means to organize and extend your code and to express yourself in really new ways. All this comes from knowing the following:

- *Classes* are code that encapsulate data and behaviors (functions). They can be either public (visible to all) or private (only locally visible).
- *Objects* are *instances* of classes. You declare them like variables.
- You can *overload* functions of the same name to do different things.
- You can use *static variables* to make them globally accessible.
- *Inheritance* lets you make new classes from a *parent* class by declaring *extends*.
- *Polymorphism* can be a powerful tool for your programming, allowing you to make and control multiple children of a single superclass through inheritance.

You've seen how shreds can communicate with each other via the use of public classes with static variables, but in the next chapter you'll look at events, which will let your ChucK code and programs be aware of many new things. You'll learn how to get events from the computer keyboard and how to listen for and send messages between shreds. Armed with that knowledge, you'll be able to make your programs more responsive to each other and the outside world.

Events: signaling between shreds and syncing to the outside world

This chapter covers

- Events: a different way to advance time
- Controlling ChucK in real time from your computer keyboard
- Inter-shred communication using events
- Broadcast events vs. notify events
- Creating your own event classes by subclassing

You've explored many topics and gained many skills throughout the book so far, including using logic, arrays, functions, multithreading, classes, and objects. If you've never programmed before, you can now look at almost any other language and be able to jump in and start understanding the basics right away.

One last step for you is to learn some new tools for live performance, so that you can take your compositions on stage as well as talk to other systems in the studio. You're going learn two ways of doing this: using the keyboard and mouse in this chapter and using MIDI controllers and Open Sound Control (OSC) in chapter 11. In the process of learning these new techniques and skills, you first need to learn about a new concept called events, which provide a means for shreds to talk to each other in real time and also a means for you to receive signals and information from the outside world.

10.1 What are events?

So far, we've worked with controlling time in ChucK as a mechanism to make everything happen in a strongly timed way. In all of these cases, we specified the precise durations by which to move time forward. For example, ChucKing 100::ms to now advances ChucK time by exactly that duration. This is useful for all kinds of situations, like specifying a rate, establishing a tempo, holding a note, waiting for time to pass, adding voices and instruments and sections sequentially in time, and more. Advancing time is fundamental to making any sound at all with ChucK.

But there are situations where it's useful to advance time for an indefinite period, until something happens, and you don't necessarily know in advance when that something is going to happen. You might be waiting to respond to real-time external input from a user pressing a button on a keyboard or joystick, or waiting on a message from the network, or waiting on an action from another concurrent shred.

This is where events come to your aid in ChucK. An event is simply a mechanism to notify a shred when something happens. Events have two sides:

- One or more shreds can wait on an event while time advances.
- An event can be triggered to notify waiting shreds that something has happened.

In the latter case, the event might be triggered by another concurrent process or by ChucK internally, in the case of specialized events such as via MIDI, mouse, or joystick.

Let's look at a basic code snippet of waiting on an event. Waiting on an event (in this case, myEvent is an Event) isn't much different than advancing time by some duration. If myEvent is of type Event, you can directly ChucK myEvent to now ❶. This advances time on the current shred, and you don't have to specify the precise duration.

```
// advance time by ChucKing an event to now
myEvent => now;
// Code resumes running only after myEvent is signaled
… some code here …
```

❶ Time is advanced indefinitely, until myEvent is signaled (somewhere else)...

❷ ...then code can resume running.

The most important thing to remember here is that the current shred advances time at the current line and *does not move past this line of code until the event is triggered* (from somewhere else in the system). When the event is triggered, this code resumes execution from the next line ❷.

Figure 10.1 shows that by ChucKing an event to now, a shred is associated with that event and won't run until the ChucK shreduler sees the event, which then notifies the shred that the event has occurred (figure 10.2). Only then can the shred continue executing.

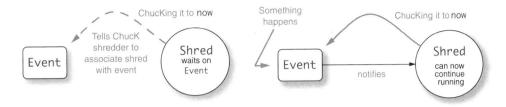

Figure 10.1   Shred ChucKs an event to now and then waits for event to be triggered.

Figure 10.2   Event is triggered. ChucK notifies the shred that it has occurred. Shred can continue running.

Events and event-driven programming aren't unique to ChucK; they can be found in most programming languages that support some notion of concurrency. But the way you use events in ChucK is rather unique, because like everything else in ChucK, you're always aware of time and the precision of timing. To make events concrete, let's look at an example of waiting on a keyboard event.

10.2   *Programming with events: keyboard input*

As mentioned previously, you can use events to allow you to respond to *asynchronous* (you can't predict when it will happen) real-time input from external devices. These may come from a connected MIDI device, a computer keyboard, a mouse, joysticks, or WiiMotes, as well as networked communication such as OSC (we'll get to this later). In all of these cases, ChucK provides specialized events tailored for those purposes.

In our first example of listing 10.1, you'll use an event to wait for and respond to computer keyboard input. To get input from the computer keyboard, you'll use a special ChucK event object, called Hid (stands for human interface device). Hid is responsible for getting input from computer keyboards, mice, and anything that considers itself a joystick/gamepad. You're going to create a Hid event and wait on it inside a loop. You'll then write code to specify what to do once that event is triggered (by ChucK, when the user presses a key). Let's first take a look at code that sets up the general structure for working with Hid events.

In this simple example, you first instantiate a Hid object ❶, called myHid, along with a HidMsg object ❷, called msg. HidMsg is an object that carries data from Hid whenever new information, such as a button press, arrives at the Hid object. You next hook myHid to your computer keyboard by using the openKeyboard() method ❸. You then check to see if this all worked, and if it didn't, you print an error ❹ and exit ❺. If everything worked out, you print a status message stating the name of the keyboard device ❻.

Listing 10.1   Standard code to create a Hid event

```
// Declare a new Hid object
Hid myHid;                                          ❶ Makes a new Hid.
// message to convey data from Hid device
HidMsg msg;                                         ❷ Makes a Hid message holder.
```

```
// device number: which keyboard to open
0 => int device;

// open keyboard; or exit if fail to open        ❸ Opens Hid on
if( !myHid.openKeyboard( device ) )    ←           keyboard device.
{
                                                        ❹ Error if it can't
    <<< "Can't open this device!! ", "Sorry." >>>;  ←    be opened.
    me.exit();                          ←
}                                          ❺ Exit, because nothing
// print status of open keyboard Hid          more can be done.
<<< "keyboard '" + myHid.name() + "' ready", "" >>>;  ←
// Testing the keyboard Hid                          ❻ If success, print
// Impulse keyboard "clicker"                           happy message.
Impulse imp => dac;                ←
                                       "Clicker" to hear
// infinite event loop              ❼ key strokes.
while( true )
{
    // wait for event              ❾ Wait here for
    myHid => now;        ←            a Hid event.

    // get message(s)                      ❿ Loop over all
    while( myHid.recv( msg ) )  ←             messages.
    {
        // Process only key (button) down events
        if( msg.isButtonDown() )        ←——⓫ If keydown...
        {
            // print ascii value and make a click
            <<< "key DOWN:", msg.ascii >>>;   ←  ⓬ ...then print which key...
              5 => imp.next;          ←
        }                              ⓭ ... and make click.
        else // key (button) up
        {
            // do nothing for now      ←
        }                        ⓮ Do nothing on keyUp
    }                              (you could add something here).
}
```

❽ Infinite loop. (annotation pointing to `while( true )`)

To use and test your new Hid keyboard event, you can make a simple click generator by using an impulse unit generator ❼. Then you drop into an infinite loop ❽, where you wait on the Hid event by ChucKing myHid to now ❾. This advances time indefinitely until the Hid event is triggered elsewhere in ChucK. Also, code execution suspends at this point in the current shred, which means that nothing beyond this line of code is yet executed.

When the user presses any key, ChucK internally receives this information and triggers any associated Hid events. Your shred is waiting on this event ❾ and wakes up, resuming execution. You then enter a while loop ❿, whose purpose is to receive and act on all available incoming data on the HidMsg object you declared at the beginning of the program. You use a while loop because more than one input data could be available (if the user pressed several keys simultaneously). Inside the loop, you check to see whether it was a key-down ⑪ or key-up event and print out a message with the ASCII code associated (a unique integer for each key) with the key that was pressed ⑫. You also use your `imp` Impulse UGen to make a little click ⑬. If the event was not a buttonDown message (key released), you don't do anything ⑭

> **USING KEYBOARD INPUT WITH MINIAUDICLE** Keyboard typing appears in the editor windows of miniAudicle, so you'll likely notice this happening when you test the programs of listing 10.1. One way to fix this is to move the focus of your computer away from miniAudicle, by clicking on an empty space on your desktop. Then keyboard messages won't enter text in miniAudicle, but your program will still receive and respond to the keystrokes.

With listing 10.1, we've demonstrated the basic form of getting data not only from `Hid` events but also from MIDI and OSC, which you'll learn about in chapter 11.

Exercise: figure out a little about ASCII

Look at the console output when you hit different keys, and see if you can determine the pattern of keyboard keys, the alphabet and other symbols, and the integers assigned to them. Can you start to think of writing a program that responds to particular keys only (using `if` statements)? Or one that responds differently for different keys (like the asdf row versus the qwerty row)?

Next, let's flesh out your keyboard event input program and add more interesting sound to create a keyboard organ! Note that the basic structure of listing 10.2 is largely the same as the code from listing 10.1. You make a new `Hid` ❶ and `HidMsg` ❷, open up the device ❸, and check to see if it's valid ❹, and if so, you print out some things about the specific keyboard device that was opened ❺. You might ask, "How many keyboards could a computer have?" Actually, more than one, because you're free to plug a USB keyboard into your laptop or plug two or more USB keyboards into any computer. That's why you have to specify a device number ❸, because the ChucK `Hid` class can take input from different ones.

Listing 10.2 Keyboard organ controlled by Hid event

```
// Hid object
Hid hi;                                        ❶ Makes a new Hid object...
// message to convey data from Hid device
HidMsg msg;                                    ❷ ...and Hid message holder.

// device number: which keyboard to open
0 => int device;                               ❸ Keyboard device number.

// open keyboard; or exit if fail to open
if( !hi.openKeyboard( device ) ) me.exit();    ❹ Opens it, exits if failed.
// print a message!
<<< "keyboard '" + hi.name() + "' ready", "" >>>;  ❺ Prints message if success.
```

```
// sound chain for Hid keyboard controlled organ
BeeThree organ => JCRev r => dac;
```
⑥ **Organ UGen through reverb to dac.**

```
// infinite event loop
while( true )
{
    // wait for event
    hi => now;
```
⑦ **Waits for keyboard event.**

```
    // get message
    while( hi.recv( msg ) )
    {
```
⑧ **Loops over all messages (keys pressed).**

```
        // button (key) down, play a Note
        if( msg.isButtonDown() )
        {
            // take ascii value of button, convert to freq
            Std.mtof( msg.ascii ) => organ.freq;
```
⑨ **If keyDown, set frequency from keycode...**

```
            // sound the note
            1 => organ.noteOn;
```
⑩ **...and play a note.**

```
        }
        else // button up, noteOff
        {
            // deactivate the note
            0 => organ.noteOff;
```
⑪ **End the note on keyUp.**

```
        }
    }
}
```

To complete the construction of your first playable ChucK instrument, you add code to set up a nice sound for synthesis, using the STK FM BeeThree organ UGen ⑥. In the main loop, you do the same ChucKing of your Hid event to now ⑦, and when you receive a key the code drops into the same while loop to service the messages ⑧. You also expand the code to activate/deactivate the sound in response to key-down and key-up events. The keyDown (called buttonDown in the Hid class) message treats the ASCII key codes as MIDI note numbers, using Std.mtof() to set the frequency ⑨; then you just send a noteOn to your organ ⑩. For keyUp (buttonUp) ⑪, you send noteOff. And that's it!!

How awesome is that? ChucK has allowed you to turn your computer into a playable organ with just a few lines of code! You can also do things like this with mice, joysticks, or other devices.

10.3 Inter-shred communication using events

In the previous examples you used Hid, a specialized ChucK event, to get real-time input from the computer keyboard. In this case, you only needed to worry about waiting on the event and responding when the event actually happened. The *triggering* of the event happened elsewhere in ChucK, behind the scenes.

It's also possible to create events and programmatically trigger them from your own ChucK programs. This is extremely useful for inter-shred communication, when

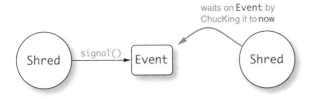

Figure 10.3 Event triggered with signal() in shred on left

one or more shreds need to know when something happens on a different shred. For example, one shred might be serving as a master clock or center of operations and wishes to tell related shreds when to perform various tasks. Alternatively, two shreds may simply want a handshake mechanism, where one shred synchronizes to (waits on) the actions of a second shred.

Let's say you have an event and a shred. As you've seen before, the shred can simply ChucK the event to now to wait on it. This is no different than you've done in the keyboard examples of listings 10.1 and 10.2. The shred in question is said to be waiting on the event, as shown in figure 10.3. The shred on the right ChucKs the event to now. Any other running shred can signal that event.

Next, let's say you have a second shred (on the left in figure 10.3), which has access to the same event as shown in figure 10.4. This shred can manually trigger the event by calling signal(). After the shred on the left triggers the event, the event in turn notifies and wakes up the shred on the right, resuming its execution. In the next section and in listing 10.3 we show how a shred can use the event .signal() method to synchronize with another shred.

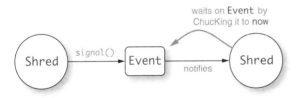

Figure 10.4 Event triggered with signal() in shred on left, thus advancing time in shred on right

10.3.1 *Using event.signal() to synchronize one shred to another*

For a simple example of using events, shown in listing 10.3, you begin by declaring a new Event called evnt ❶. Then you declare a function that takes an event as an argument ❷. That function is a simple endless loop ❹ that ChucKs the event to now ❺. If the function ever receives a notification to wake up, it prints a message and the current time in seconds ❻ and then repeats the loop, ChucKing the event to now and going back to sleep ❺. To make things interesting, and because it's ChucK, you include an Impulse connected to the dac ❸, which you sonify on each wakeup/print ❼. To test your new function, you spork one of them ❽ and then enter an endless loop ❾, signaling the event ❿ every second ⓫.

Listing 10.3   Simple event signaling

```
// Declare an event we will use for signaling
Event evnt;                                        ① Declare an event object.

// function that waits on an event               ② Declare a function to wait
fun void foo( Event anEvent)                          on any event.
{
    Impulse imp => dac;                             Sonify the function
                                                   ③ with a click.
    while( true )
    {
        // wait
        anEvent => now;                            ⑤ Wait on event...
        // action
        <<< "Hey!!!", now / second >>>;            ⑥ ...when event is sent, print out...
          5 => imp.next;                           ⑦ ... and make click.
    }
}

// spork a foo                                     ⑧ To test, spork your event-
spork ~ foo( evnt );                                  waiting function.

// then signal the event forever in a loop
while( true )                                      ⑨ Infinite loop...
{
    // fire the next signal
    evnt.signal();                                 ⑩ ...to signal the event...
    // advance time
    1::second => now;                              ⑪ ...every second.
}
```

Infinite loop. ④

10.3.2   Using signal to synchronize multiple shreds

In listing 10.4, you'll now use this same mechanism to use one shred, which we'll call the master shred, to signal() multiple slave shreds. They're called slaves because they can't do anything without a signal from the master. Still using the same globally declared Event ①, you'll modify the foo function from the previous listing and rename it bar ② to take three arguments; the first argument is still an event that you'll use to trigger the actions of the shred. The second argument is a string that will be printed out each time a signal notification is received. The third argument is a frequency for a strongly resonant ⑤ filter at a particular frequency ④ applied to the Impulse ③, so you'll be able to hear the difference between the different shreds.

The bar() function does the same thing internally as the previous foo() function, dropping into an infinite loop ⑥, waiting for anEvent ⑦, and then waking up when notified, printing out the string msg, the float freq, and the current time in seconds ⑧. You also fire the impulse ⑨; then the function goes back to sleep ⑥.

To test, you spork three bar() function shreds, each with a different string message and frequency ⑩ ⑪ ⑫. You then drop into the same infinite loop ⑬, signaling the event every second ⑭.

Listing 10.4 Using one shred to `signal()` multiple other shreds

```
// Declare an event we will use for signaling
Event evnt;                                            ←——①  Declares an event.

// function that waits on an event                     ②  New event-waiting function
fun void bar(Event anEvent, string msg, float freq) ←——    with extra arguments.
{
    Impulse imp => ResonZ rez => dac;    ←——④  Tuned pop sound
    50 => rez.Q;                         ←——
    while( true )                        ⑤  High resonance for tuned pop
    {
        // wait
        anEvent => now;         ←————————⑦  Sleeps until event is signaled.
        // action
        <<< msg, freq, now / second >>>;   ←——
        freq => rez.freq;                   ⑧  When event comes, print out.
        50 => imp.next;
    }
}

// spork a few bar shreds               ⑩  Spork one event-waiting function...
spork ~ bar( evnt, "Hi ", 500.0 );  ←——
spork ~ bar( evnt, "There ", 700.0 ); ←——  ⑪  ...and another, with different
spork ~ bar( evnt, "Sport! ", 900.0 ); ←——     string and frequency...

// then signal the event forever in a loop     ...and yet another, different
while( true )                       ←——     ⑫  from the other two.
{
    // fire the next signal          ⑬  Infinite loop to test
    evnt.signal();           ←——         sporked functions.
    // advance time
    1::second => now;       ⑭  Fire event using
}                               signal() method.
```

Labels at left margins:
- Frequency for pop. ③
- Infinite loop. ⑥
- Frequency for pop. ③
- Triggers pop sound. ⑨

Running this, you'll notice that each shred runs by itself, sequentially in turn, in response to each single `signal()` message. This is depicted in figure 10.5, which shows that each `signal()` triggers only the next shred in line (in the order in which it was sporked). So for the previous example, you'd first trigger the shred that prints "Hi" and sounds 500 Hz. Next you'd trigger "There" with 700 Hz and then "Sport!" with 900 Hz. The next event would trigger the first shred ("Hi" with 500 Hz) again, and so on cyclically forever.

That behavior might be what's desired, but you might want all three shreds to wake up at once. In the next section you'll see a couple of ways to do that.

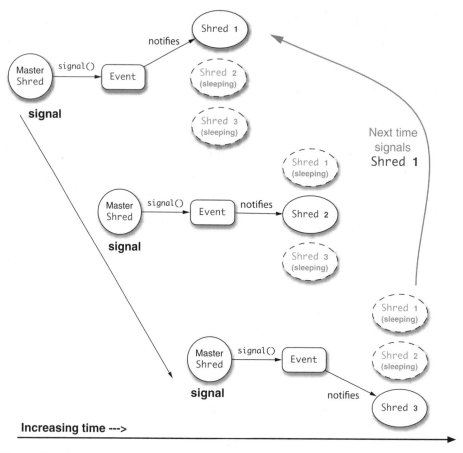

Figure 10.5 Triggering events with `signal()` within shred on left advances time in shreds on right but only one shred per `event()` message.

10.3.3 *Triggering multiple shreds at the same time using events*

One way to make your three shreds all trigger at the same time would be to signal the event three times with no time delay between them.

> **Exercise: use multiple signal() messages to wake up more than one shred**
> Copy and paste the following line (⑭ from listing 10.4) so that the event `signal()` message is sent a total of three times, followed by the 1-second delay. So your new program will have that identical line repeated three times:
>
>   evnt.signal();
>   evnt.signal();
>   evnt.signal();
>
> You'll now see all three messages print together, hearing all three sounds at once.

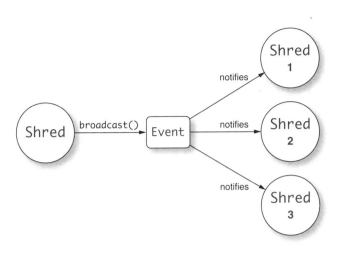

Figure 10.6 Event triggered with `broadcast()` in shred on left advances time in all shreds on right.

There is another way to notify and wake up multiple shreds with a single message. Event has a variant of `signal()`, called `broadcast()`, which wakes up all shreds currently waiting on the event, as shown in figure 10.6.

By using `broadcast()`, the master shred can notify all shreds (unlimited) currently waiting on that event. They wake up at the same time and do their respective things. Think of what this might mean for a drum machine or music composition!

Exercise: use a `broadcast()` message to wake up more than one shred

Go back to listing 10.4 and ⓮ and change the `signal()` message to `broadcast()`.

`evnt.broadcast();`

You'll now see all three messages print and hear all three sounds at the same time.

10.4 Customized events example: a multi-instrument gamelan

Because Event is a ChucK class, you can extend the functionality by subclassing (remember that from the previous chapter on classes and objects?). You can extend the Event class to make customized events that can contain additional data and behavior. In listing 10.5, you'll use custom events and polymorphism to synchronize a small orchestra of different StkInstruments. The result will be similar to the gamelans of Java and Bali, with different bells, pots, pans, and the like being struck in precise rhythm to create a rich musical texture of complimentary sounds.

To start, you create a new event type as a subclass of Event, called TheEvent ❶, which you'll use to pass MIDI `note` ❷ and `velocity` ❸ data between shreds. To use your new TheEvent class, you declare two of them called evnt and evnt2 ❹. You then declare a global reverberator and connect it to the dac ❺. Your polymorphic event-handling function called poly ❻ takes as arguments an StkInstrument (any kind, polymorphism!) and an event upon which to synchronize. The `poly` function does the usual things; after connecting the `StkInstrument` to the global reverberator ❼, you drop into an infinite loop ❽ and ChucK the event to now ❾, putting this shred to sleep. When it receives the event, it sets the note number ❿ and velocity ⓫ and then sleeps again.

Listing 10.5 Using a custom `Event` subclass, with polymorphism

```
class TheEvent extends Event                    ← ❶ Declares Event subclass with
{                                                    extra instance variables.
    int note;
    float velocity;              ← ❸ Float velocity instance variable.
}

TheEvent evnt, evnt2;            ← ❹ Declares two new TheEvent objects.

// patch
NRev globalReverb => dac;        ← ❺ Declares a global reverb for use by all.
.1 => globalReverb.mix;

// instrument function to spork
fun void poly( StkInstrument instr, TheEvent e, string s )   ← ❻ Declares an
{                                                                 event-waiting,
    // connect to output                                          instrument-
    instr => globalReverb;                                        playing
                                                                  function.
    // hang out waiting to receive an event to play
    while( true )                ← ❽ Infinite loop.
    {
        // wait
        e => now;
        // play
        e.note => Std.mtof => instr.freq;       ← ❿ When event comes, sets note frequency...
        e.velocity => instr.noteOn;             ← ⓫ ...and fires instrument with velocity.
    }
}

// spork a few polys, listening on "evnt"
spork ~ poly( new StifKarp, evnt, "StifKarp" );   ← ⓬ Sporks an evnt-waiting function with a StifKarp instrument...
spork ~ poly( new Mandolin, evnt, "Mandolin" );   ← ⓭ ...and another with a Mandolin instrument...
spork ~ poly( new Wurley, evnt, "Wurley" );       ← ⓮ ...and yet another with an FM Wurley instrument.

// spork one poly listening on "evnt2"
spork ~ poly( new Rhodey, evnt2, "Rhodey" );      ← ⓯ Sporks an evnt2-waiting function with a Rhodey instrument.

[60,62,64,67,69,72,74,76,79] @=> int notes[];

// play forever                 Notes scale for your gamelan
while( true )                    (a scale is called a laya). ⓰
{
    // fire the next signal, on a dice roll
    Math.random2(1,6) => int dice;     ← ⓲ Dice roll.
```

❷ Integer note instance variable.
❼ Connects the instrument to your global reverb.
❾ Waits for event to be signaled.
⓱ Infinite loop.

```
    if (dice != 1)
    {
        // pick a random note from our array
        notes[Math.random2(0,notes.cap()-1)] => evnt.note;
        Math.random2f( .2, .9 ) => evnt.velocity;
        // send the signal to only one instrument
        evnt.signal();
        // and advance time
        0.25 :: second => now;
    }
    else
    {
        // play a lower notes on evnt2, and all of the evnt instruments
        notes[Math.random2(0,notes.cap()-1)] - 24 => evnt2.note;
        notes[0] - 12 => evnt.note;
        1.0 => evnt2.velocity;
        // on all instrument shreds
        evnt.broadcast();
        evnt2.signal();
        // and wait longer
        second => now;
    }
}
```

⑲ Five times out of 6, pick a note from the laya.

Random velocity. ⑳

㉑ Signal event (one of StifKarp, Mandolin, Wurley)...

㉒ ...otherwise, pick a lower laya note and signal evnt2 (Rhodey)...

㉓ ...and broadcast to all evnt listener instruments.

To use your new class, you spork a few shreds on the evnt event, each using a different instrument ⑫ ⑬ ⑭. You also spork a shred to wait on evnt2, with yet another instrument ⑮. You next define an array of pitches to use for your composition ⑯.

In an infinite loop ⑰, you roll a random die ⑱, and depending on the result either you signal the next one of the three evnt-related shred/instruments ㉑ to play a random note ⑲ at a random velocity ⑳, or much less frequently you opt to play lower notes on all instruments by using signal() on evnt2 ㉓ and broadcast() on evnt ㉒.

So as you can see, events represent an extremely powerful programming construct in ChucK that you can use to synchronize shreds and wait on external real-time input, further adding to your arsenal of ChucK programming tools. As always, experiment and have fun with it!

Exercise: expand your gamelan orchestra

Start with the example of listing 10.5, and add more instruments or change the logic to have them play differently. Change the note numbers in the array to suit your taste. Try adding one or more percussion instruments by using SndBuf.

Note: SndBuf isn't a subclass of StkInstrument, so you'll have to write your own event function like poly but to accept a SndBuf as the first argument and a sound file name to load, in addition to an event to trigger it.

Exercise: write a whole event-driven drum machine

Rewrite one of the drum machines from the previous chapter to use events for triggering. This can be pretty hard, so do it slowly, starting with only one instrument, then adding more. You might also want to do it all in one file, especially when trying it out for the first time. Then you can split the instruments out to their own files and create a score.ck file to add everything as you like.

10.5   *Summary*

In this chapter you learned how to work with time in ChucK using events. You saw how important events can be for working with things like the computer keyboard to capture real-time gestural data from a user and for shreds to talk to each other. You even built your first playable musical instrument, a keyboard organ! Here are some important things to remember:

- Events can be waited on by one or more shreds while time advances.
- Events can be triggered to notify waiting shreds that something has happened.
- Events can be triggered by external events such as Hids; for example, a keyboard.
- Shreds can trigger events by using signal(), which triggers at most one listening shred, or broadcast(), which triggers all listening shreds.
- You can subclass Event to make your own event types, adding data or functions to them.

In our next chapter we'll expand the types of external devices and signals that can trigger events, looking specifically at MIDI devices and OSC.

Integrating with other systems via MIDI, OSC, serial, and more

11

This chapter covers

- The Musical Instrument Digital Interface
- MIDI messages
- Controlling ChucK with MIDI devices
- MIDI output to other software, synthesizers, robots, and more
- The Open Sound Control protocol for networked systems
- Serial interfaces in ChucK

So far we've covered a lot of concepts, all in a creative context, emphasizing composing music and controlling sound in real time. You've learned about arrays, logic, functions, multithreading, classes, objects, events, and more. If you were new to programming, you'll now be able to look at almost any other language and understand the basics right away. The fact that ChucK allows you to control sound and make music so easily and expressively is one of the things that sets it apart from other languages. One last step in your ChucK journey is to learn more tools that

217

you can use for live performance. This will allow you to take your compositions and code-built instruments on stage. In chapter 10, you learned about events and how to start using the keyboard. Now you'll learn about the Musical Instrument Digital Interface, how to use MIDI controllers with ChucK in real time, and how to use ChucK to control external MIDI synthesizers and devices.

We'll also briefly introduce the Open Sound Control (OSC) protocol, which allows you to use ChucK in a networked context, and we'll talk briefly about serial I/O in ChucK.

11.1 Using MIDI: history, basics, and advanced applications

In this section we cover the MIDI standard, including the hardware and connectors, some types of messages, and how you can use it with ChucK. You'll learn how to connect to things in the outside world such as MIDI-capable musical keyboards and synthesizers and even robots!

As a thought experiment, can you imagine if all of the manufacturers of cell phones, cameras, computers, DVD players, TVs, and other electronic devices adopted a single cable type and data standard so that all devices could talk over the exact same connections? The world would be so much easier to navigate. Well, in the 1980s, almost all of the electronic music manufacturers of the day drafted and adopted the MIDI standard, so that their devices could communicate with each other. If you think about it, it was (and still is) quite a miracle, because MIDI allows you to connect keyboards, synthesizers, computers, lighting controllers, and many other artistically interesting things.

Originally, the heart of MIDI was a specific type of connector called a five-pin DIN, or MIDI connector, and MIDI cable that could be used to plug one device into another. This wire and connector are still somewhat important today, and if you look on the back of a digital keyboard (electronic piano or organ) or synthesizer, you're still likely to see two or three round, five-pin, female MIDI jacks (figure 11.1). Being able to recognize these connectors will be important to you later, when we talk about how to connect to MIDI musical keyboards and synthesizers.

For those of you who make music primarily with your computers, physical MIDI cables and connectors are less important today than they were three decades ago, but they still can be used to connect to the outside world, to control computer programs

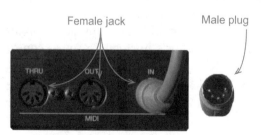

Female jack   Male plug

Figure 11.1   Female MIDI jacks commonly found on the back panel of keyboard synthesizers and other devices. A cable with the male MIDI plug is also shown.

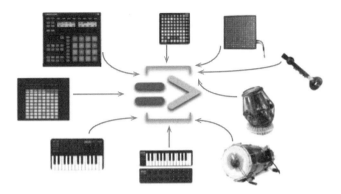

Figure 11.2 You can use a MIDI interface and cable to control ChucK from lots of MIDI devices, ranging from music keyboards (clockwise from bottom), to drum/ percussion controllers, to button matrix controllers such as the Monome (top) and Tenori-on by Yamaha, to custom-built controllers like the ESitar and ETabla (right).

(like ChucK) with a MIDI keyboard or other controller (figure 11.2). Physical MIDI interfaces, connectors, and cables can also be useful for connecting one computer to another.

To connect your computer in this way using MIDI, you first need a MIDI adapter, which usually plugs into a USB port, FireWire, Thunderbolt, or other device. The MIDI adapter might have female jacks, as shown in figure 11.1, or it might go directly from your computer to male plugs, also shown in figure 11.1, which can connect directly to MIDI devices. Some MIDI keyboard controllers and other devices can connect directly to USB.

MIDI hardware and cables can also be important because you can use ChucK to control outboard synthesizers and many other MIDI devices (figure 11.3).

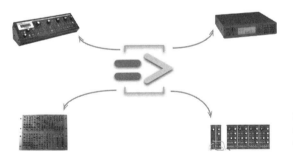

Figure 11.3 You can also control lots of external synthesizers and other MIDI cable devices from ChucK.

Even without a MIDI interface and cable, you can still use MIDI in ChucK to communicate between programs running at the same time, such as software sound synthesizers, virtual keyboards, DJ software, and digital audio workstations (DAWs), as shown in figure 11.4. Almost every commercial music program includes MIDI connectivity, so if you're running one of these programs on your computer, ChucK will be able to see it and communicate. You'll learn how to do this very soon.

Now that you know a little about the physical MIDI connectors and cables, you need to know something about the software specifications for MIDI, specifically, how musical and other parameters are transmitted from one device/program to the other.

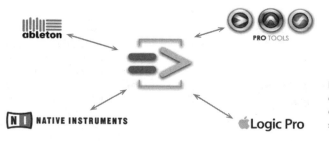

Figure 11.4   Via MIDI, ChucK can talk to lots of other MIDI-capable software programs and systems.

11.1.1 *MIDI messages*

To get started, you should first understand MIDI messages, most of which consist of three integer bytes of 8 bits each, as shown in figure 11.5. Each byte can take on values ranging from 0 to 255, and only the first byte, called the status byte, of any MIDI message can be greater than 127, ranging from 128 to 255. The next two bytes, called the data bytes, have a value less than 128, from 0 to 127. Having the status byte in a different range from the other two is the way MIDI can tell which one is the first byte.

Probably the most common MIDI message is the noteOn message (status byte equal to 144–159), but other messages types include noteOff, Control Change, and others. Control Change messages (status byte equal to 176–191) have many types, as determined by the value of the second byte, including sustain pedal, volume pedal, pitch bend, panning, reverb level, and many more.

To make this clearer, you'll create a little program to play random notes on an external MIDI synthesizer, as shown in listing 11.1. First, you have to open the MIDI device on which your target interface or synthesizer lives ❶, and you need a MIDI device to be present so you can open it. So make sure that you have some MIDI-compliant synthesizer to control from ChucK.

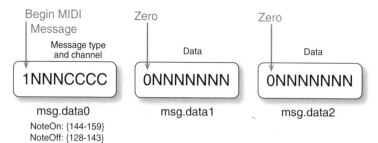

Figure 11.5   Almost all MIDI messages have three integer bytes. The first (status) byte has a value of 128–255, and the remaining (data) bytes have values between 0 and 127.

A MIDI synthesizer to play from ChucK

To play a MIDI device from ChucK, you can use a MIDI interface and cable to connect your computer to the MIDI input of an outboard synthesizer. Or you can locate or install and run a virtual MIDI synthesizer on your computer. Mac users can use a variety of such programs, including SimpleSynth (free), General MIDI Player (costs a little), and Logic (costs more). Windows users often find a built-in General MIDI synthesizer already installed on their computer. Windows users can also use VirtualMIDISynth, MidiPiano, Anvil Studio, Cakewalk, and many other programs. Linux users can use LMMS, Qtractor, Schism Tracker, and others.

Once you have a MIDI interface and synthesizer connected, or a software synthesizer loaded and running on your computer, you can use the Device Browser window in the miniAudicle to see your MIDI device(s), using the menu item for MIDI.

Note: You must exit and restart miniAudicle when connecting and disconnecting MIDI devices; otherwise new ones won't show up.

Now that you have a MIDI device connected/installed and identified, you should be able to inspect it in the miniAudicle, as shown in figure 11.6, by selecting Window > Device Browser and then selecting MIDI from the tool in that window.

Once you have a MIDI device successfully connected and identified, you can play it using the code of listing 11.1. You first make a `MidiOut` object ❶ and try to open it ❸ on the appropriate MIDI port number ❷. Note: You might need to change the number to match the particular synthesizer you're trying to play. If the device opens correctly, you then make a `MidiMsg` holder for `noteOn`/`noteOff` messages you're going to send ❹. You define a `MIDInote` function ❺ for sending either `noteOn` messages (argument `onoff=1` ❼) or `noteOff` (`onoff=0`) ❻. That function packs the numbers into the correct message holders (`data1`, `data2`, `data3`) and sends the message.

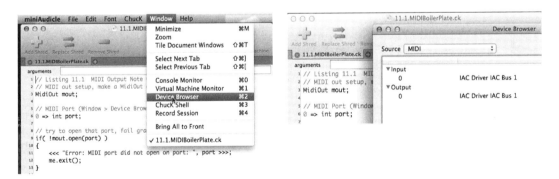

Figure 11.6   Selecting the Device Browser in the miniAudicle Window menu brings up that browser window (upper left). Then you can select MIDI and inspect the inputs and outputs (lower right). You then use these port numbers in ChucK to connect to those devices.

Listing 11.1   MIDI output note on/off boilerplate

```
// MIDI out setup, make a MidiOut object, open it on a device
MidiOut mout;                          ① Makes a new MidiOut.

// MIDI Port (Window > Device Browser > MIDI > Output)
0 => int port;                         ② MIDI port number (varies).

// try to open that port, fail gracefully
if( !mout.open(port) )                 ③ Tries to open the MIDI port.
{
    <<< "Error: MIDI port did not open on port: ", port >>>;
    me.exit();
}

// Make a MIDI msg holder for sending    ④ Makes a MIDI
MidiMsg msg;                              message holder.

                                          ⑤ Function to send
                                            MIDI noteOn/Off.
// utility function to send MIDI out notes
fun void MIDInote(int onoff, int note, int velocity)
{
    if (onoff == 0) 128 => msg.data1;      If noteOff, set status
    else            144 => msg.data1;   ⑥ byte to 128...
    note => msg.data2;                     ...else set status
    velocity => msg.data3;              ⑦ byte to 144.
    mout.send(msg);
}

// loop
while( true )
{
    Math.random2(60,100) => int note;    ⑧ Test noteOn with
    Math.random2(30,127) => int velocity;   random note and
    MIDInote(1, note, velocity);             velocity...
    .1::second => now;
    MIDInote(0, note ,velocity);         ⑨ ...and test noteOff.
    .1::second => now;
}
```

To test everything, you set the MIDI note and velocity to appropriate random numbers and send a noteOn by calling your function ⑧. It's pretty important to turn off ⑨ every note that you turn on in MIDI; otherwise you get possible stuck notes, which are one of the common criticisms of MIDI systems.

Exercise: play "Twinkle, Twinkle Little Star" on your MIDI synthesizer

Instead of playing random notes, change the infinite while loop to a for loop, and iterate through the notes and durations for the "Twinkle" song (reproduced here) that we used in chapter 4. Note that you don't have to do Std.mtof(myNotes[]) here because you can just send the MIDI note number, and your synthesizer will take care of the rest.

```
// declare and initialize array of MIDI notes
[57,57,64,64,66,66,64,62,62,61,61,59,59,57] @=> int myNotes[];

// quarter note and half note durations
0.3 :: second => dur q;
0.8 :: second => dur h;
[ q, q, q, q, q, q, h, q, q, q, q, q, q, h] @=> dur myDurs[];

// loop for length of array
for (0 => int i; i < myNotes.cap(); i++)
{
    MIDInote(1, myNotes[i], 100);
        myDurs[i] => now;
        MIDInote(0, myNotes[i], 100);
        0.2 :: second => now;
}
```

Try playing a different song, by coding different note and duration values.

When we first introduced noteOn, we noted that the status byte could range from 144 to 159. This is because the status byte for noteOn is the value 144 plus the channel number, which can have any value from 0 to 15, for a total of 16 channels. By exploiting different channel numbers, a MIDI sender can control multiple devices, each of which can listen on a different channel number.

11.1.2 *External MIDI controllers for ChucK*

Just as you controlled a MIDI synthesizer using ChucK code, you can also use external controllers or software to control things going on inside ChucK code. This can unlock the true potential of ChucK's real-time synthesis, concurrency, and event-driven design. MidiIn is an object that can be ChucKed to now as an event, and whenever a message comes in over that port, the event is signaled, causing time to pass.

Using a MIDI controller to play and control ChucK code

Just like playing a synthesizer from ChucK, you'll need a MIDI interface and cable to connect your computer to the MIDI output of an outboard keyboard or other MIDI controller. Or you can locate or install and run a virtual MIDI keyboard. One excellent software MIDI keyboard that's available for all platforms is Virtual MIDI Piano Keyboard (VMPK). Mac-specific virtual MIDI keyboard programs include MidiKeys and Chirp, as well as virtual keyboards available in other music programs such as Logic, Pro Tools,

(continued)

and many others. Windows users can use FreePiano, MidiPiano, and many others. In addition to VMPK, Linux users can use jack-keyboard and others.

Once you have a MIDI interface and keyboard/controller connected, or a software keyboard/controller loaded and running on your computer, use the Device Browser window in the miniAudicle to see your MIDI device(s), using the MIDI menu item.

Listing 11.2 shows a simple monophonic (one note at a time) piano synthesizer that can be played using MidiIn. After you make a MidiIn object ❶ and open it ❷, remembering to set the port number appropriately, and make a MidiMsg holder for incoming messages ❸, you declare and connect a Rhodey FM electric piano to use as your synthesizer ❹.

In an infinite loop ❺, you ChucK the MidiIn object min to now, as an event, suspending time until a message is received on that port ❻. When you press a key on your MIDI keyboard, ChucK time is allowed to advance and the program continues executing.

Listing 11.2   Simple piano synthesizer controlled by MIDI input

```
// Setup MIDI input, set a port number, try to open it
MidiIn min;                                    ❶ Makes a MidiIn object

// MIDI Port (ChucK Menu: Window > Device Browser > MIDI > Input)
0 => int port;

// open the port, fail gracefully      ❷ Tries to open it on
if( !min.open(port) )                      port, handles failure
{
    <<< "Error: MIDI port did not open on port: ", port >>>;
    me.exit();
}

// holder for received messages    ❸ Makes object to hold
MidiMsg msg;                           MIDI messages

// make an instrument to play   ❹ Rhodey piano to play
Rhodey piano => dac;               with MIDI controller

// loop
while( true )              ❺ Infinite loop
{
    min => now; // advance when receive MIDI msg   ❻ Sleeps until a MIDI
                                                      input message comes
```

```
    while( min.recv(msg) )
    {
        <<< msg.data1, msg.data2, msg.data3 >>>;
        if (msg.data1 == 144)  {
            Std.mtof(msg.data2) => piano.freq;
            msg.data3/127.0 => piano.gain;
            1 => piano.noteOn;
        }
        else  {
            1 => piano.noteOff;
        }
    }
}
```

When time advances, you test to see if the incoming message is a noteOn on channel 0 (data1 == 144), and if so, you set your piano frequency and gain and play a note. If the message is a noteOff, you send your piano a noteOff message.

> ### Exercise: make your own software synthesizer using your MIDI controller
> Rock out using your MIDI controller and ChucK. Make an array of Rhodey piano UGens, and cycle through it using a counter. Use BeeThree UGens to make an organ or Mandolins to make a mandolin, or whatever you like. ChucK makes it pretty easy to build your own playable instruments by using the StkInstrument UGens available or by making your own instrument classes.

11.1.3 ChucK to ChucK using a virtual MIDI port

One other interesting thing you can do with MIDI is to use it to talk between ChucK shreds, using one process to control another. For that, you need a virtual port. On Mac computers, you can make a virtual port in the Audio Midi Setup application, found in the /Applications/Utilities folder. Basically you have to enable the IAC driver, as shown in figure 11.7 (left), by selecting Window > Show MIDI Window from the top menu, clicking the IAC Driver icon, and then selecting the Device Is Online check box.

Windows users can use loopMIDI or virtualMIDI from Tobias Erichsen (see figure 11.7, right) or music software programs such as Cakewalk or Pro Tools. To use loopMIDI, you need to download, install, and run it. Click the + button in the lower left of the window that appears. Now when you run the miniAudicle (remember, you have to stop it and restart it so that new devices can show up), that device should appear.

Once you've created a virtual MIDI port, you can use the miniAudicle Device Browser to see it in the MIDI Devices window. Using that port number, you should now be able to run the code of listing 11.1 and listing 11.2 and hear your monophonic Rhodey electric piano responding to your random note sender. ChucK to ChucK via MIDI!

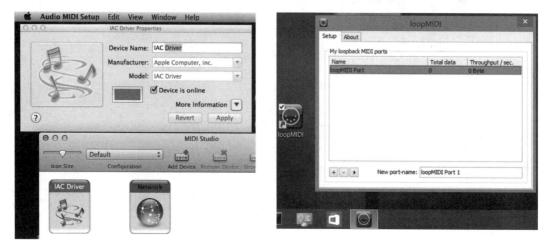

Figure 11.7   Audio MIDI Setup (left) on a Mac and loopMIDI (right) on Windows let you set up a virtual MIDI port, which you can then use to connect ChucK to other programs or itself.

11.1.4 *Controlling robots via MIDI*

One amazing thing to do with MIDI is to control things other than synthesizers. These can include lighting controllers (available from music and theatrical supply stores), special effects like fog machines and pyrotechnics, and robots, as shown in figure 11.8.

"Wait a minute," you might say, "I don't have a robot to control via MIDI." Actually, one might be closer and more available than you think. A number of manufacturers make MIDI player pianos, such as the Yamaha Disklavier shown in figure 11.8.

MIDI player pianos can often be found in the lobbies of hotels, in department stores, in churches, and in other public spaces. You might be able to call up your local piano store and ask if you can plug into their MIDI player pianos and control them

Figure 11.8   ChucK can control many physical objects in the real world such as robots (left), including commercially available MIDI player pianos like the Yamaha Disklavier (right).

using ChucK! The nice thing about MIDI player pianos is that they respond to noteOn and noteOff just like a synthesizer, so any code you write that works with your synthesizer should work with a MIDI player piano. Some electronic organs (and even some large church organs) respond to MIDI as well, and you can control those from ChucK just as you would any synthesizer.

Wow! You've learned that MIDI allows you to use ChucK to control external synthesizers, theatrical effects, and even robots. MIDI also lets you control ChucK synthesis from external devices such as musical keyboards. ChucK shreds can talk to each other using MIDI within a single computer or between computers using MIDI interfaces and cables. MIDI also lets you connect ChucK to other programs. The power and ubiquity of MIDI is one of the reasons that it has stuck around for 30 years and will likely be with us for a long time to come.

Let's now look at a newer and even more flexible way to communicate between programs and computers, called Open Sound Control.

11.2 *Open Sound Control: networking music*

Another protocol for passing musical information between programs and devices is OSC, developed and announced in 1997 to address shortcomings of MIDI and to take advantage of the increasing connectedness of computers made possible by local area networks. Today, most musical programs and languages, including commercial systems, allow for the use of OSC, and some controllers can even send and receive OSC. Mobile apps also can send and receive OSC, making it possible to control musical and artistic events and systems in many flexible ways. The birth and proliferation of laptop orchestras, mobile orchestras, interactive art installations, and many other things (see chapter 0) have been enabled and pushed forward by the availability of networks (especially wireless) and OSC.

Appendix D gives a more complete introduction to OSC, but to demonstrate the potential, let's make a simple conductor (sender) and player (receiver, client) that use OSC. First, you'll build the sender, as implemented in listing 11.3. OscOut ❶ is an object that can send OSC messages on a port number of your choosing ❷. You use the special name localhost ❸ to indicate that you want to send and receive on the same computer. This is all that's required to set up and send OSC! Then you drop into an infinite loop ❹ to conduct the receiver that you're going to create soon.

At the heart of any OSC message is the specification of how the message starts, the *address*, a unique string that you make up, and the arguments that come after that ❺. In this case, we chose /myChucK/OSCNote as our message address and specified that the arguments coming after will be one int, one float, and one string. All of these must be present, in exactly this order, for the message to be complete and sent and to be received at the other end. After you've started and specified your message ❺, you compute some values ❻ ❼ ❽ and then add the arguments you want to send with the message ❾ ❿ ⓫. You can add any combination of ints, floats, and strings, but it's a good idea to use the same combination with every message of a given address so the receiving end knows what to expect. When you've finished adding arguments, you tell the OscOut object to send the message ⑫.

Listing 11.3   Simple OSC sender

```
// First, make an OSC send object and set port #
OscOut xmit;                                    ← ① Makes an OSC output object.
6449 => int port;                               ← ② Port number to send OSC on.
xmit.dest ( "localhost", port );     ←
                                         ③ Sets network destination
// infinite time loop                        to this computer.
while( true )                   ← ④ Infinite loop.
{
    // start the message, after prefix (our choice)
    //     expects one int, one float, one string    ⑤ Starts OSC output.
    xmit.start( "/myChucK/OSCNote" );    ←

    Math.random2(48,80) => int note;            ← ⑥ Computes integer note number.
    Math.random2f(0.1,1.0) => float velocity;
    "Hi out there!!" => string message;         ← ⑧ Makes a string message

    // a message is kicked as soon as it is complete
    // - type string is satisfied and bundles are closed
    note => xmit.add;
    velocity => xmit.add;               ← ⑩ Adds velocity to output.
    message => xmit.add;    ←

    xmit.send();        ← ⑫ Send it!    ⑪ Adds string to output.

    // hang a bit, then do it again
    0.2 :: second => now;
}
```

Computes float velocity. ⑦

Adds note to output. ⑨

Now that you've created your sender, you need a receiver, as shown in listing 11.4. Here you make an OscIn object ① and set the same port number ② (very important). You also create an OscMsg object ③, which will store each message that you receive. In the next line, you add an address in your receiver that exactly matches the format of the messages that the sender will be transmitting ④.

After making a new Rhodey object and connecting it to the dac ⑤, you drop into an infinite loop ⑥ to wait for your messages to come in. Note that an OscIn object is an event, so it can be ChucKed to now just like any other event ⑦, suspending time until a message is received. Once this event fires, you retrieve the message itself ⑧ and then get the arguments using the appropriate functions ⑨ ⑩ ⑪, use those to control your notes ⑫ ⑬, and print it all out just to verify things arrived okay ⑭.

Listing 11.4   Simple OSC receiver

```
// Make a receiver, set port#, set up to listen for event
OscIn oin;                    ←──── ❶ Makes an OSC input object
6449 => oin.port;             ←──── ❷ Port number to receive OSC on
OscMsg msg;                   ←────
                              ❸ Makes an OSC message holder

// create an address in the receiver, store in new variable
oin.addAddress( "/myChucK/OSCNote" );
                              ←── ┌ Sets beginning of
                              ❹   └ message to listen for

// Our synthesizer to be controlled by sender process
Rhodey piano => dac;          ←── ┌ Rhodey piano to play with
                              ❺   └ received OSC messages

// Infinite loop to wait for messages and play notes
while (true)                  ←──── ❻ Infinite loop
{
    // OSC message is an event, chuck it to now
    oin => now;               ←──── ❼ Sleeps until OSC received


    // when event(s) received, process them      ┌ Deals with potentially
    while (oin.recv(msg) != 0)  {   ←──── ❽       └ multiple messages
        // peel off integer, float, string
Gets note →  msg.getInt(0) => int note;
number ❾     msg.getFloat(1) => float velocity;  ←──── ❿ Gets velocity
             msg.getString(2) => string howdy;   ←──── ⓫ Gets string

        // use them to make music                ┌ Sets piano frequency
        Std.mtof(note) => piano.freq;  ←──── ⓬    └ from note
Sets gain →  velocity => piano.gain;
for noteOn ⓭ velocity => piano.noteOn;

        //  print it all out                     ┌ Prints out message received
        <<< howdy, note, velocity >>>;  ←──── ⓮   └ from sender via OSC
    }
}
```

This little demonstration should convince you of the power of OSC, letting you control one ChucK shred from another. It would also let you communicate between ChucK and other music software and languages, other graphics programming languages such as Processing, and anything else that uses OSC.

The real power kicks in when you use OSC between different computers over a network. We don't have the space or time to fully get into that here, but the clue is in the dest() line of the sender program of listing 11.3 ❸. If you changed localhost to another machine name on your network, such as GeWang.local, or an IP address of the form 192.168.0.2, then you could run the receiver on that machine, and you'd have the beginnings of a multi-machine orchestra!

> ### Exercise: make your own LOrk (Laptop Orchestra)
> Do as we just described, changing localhost to another machine name or IP address on your network. Use your own knowledge of networking, or get a friend who knows networking, and trade them your knowledge of ChucK for their help. Run the sender on one machine and the receiver on the other. Create two senders and two receivers, one for each machine. Perform a networked ChucK duet over your local wireless network.

OSC is super powerful, and we've barely cracked the surface here. There's more in-depth documentation in appendix D and many online resources, such as documentation for specific pieces by the Princeton Laptop Orchestra and Stanford Laptop Orchestra, that talk about how OSC can be used to communicate between computers and programs.

Just as with MIDI, many commercial programs also support OSC, so you could use ChucK to move the virtual volume and effects sliders on a digital audio workstation program such as Reaper, Pro Tools, Logic, or Cakewalk. Connecting ChucK to other such systems via OSC means that you're no longer limited to things the manufacturer provides, because your ChucK programs become part of those systems!

We'll now turn briefly to one more outside-world communication method: serial ports and connections.

11.3 Serial input/output to the outside world

Serial communication means that the individual binary digits (bits) of a message or value go over a wire one at a time. MIDI is actually a form of serial communication, because all of those messages are transmitted over a single wire, one bit at a time. So the first (status) byte of a MIDI noteOn (channel 0) would be transmitted as the individual bits:

1 0 0 1 0 0 0 0 (binary for the number 144)

Even though MIDI is a form of serial communication, usually when people talk about serial, they're talking about a protocol called RS-232 or one related to it. Not long ago, computers talked to each other via modems, over phone lines, using RS-232 serial. Although it's pretty outdated and most people don't use it regularly, serial is still good for connecting to many things, like Arduino microcontrollers, older development boards (BasicStamp, DSP boards from Texas Instruments, Analog Devices), and some older interfaces and systems, as shown in figure 11.9. As an example, listing 11.5 shows a simple ChucK program to accept text information as strings via a serial interface ❶ configured to the specific settings for an Arduino board ❷. Each time the Arduino sends a new string, the .onLine() event is triggered ❸, allowing you to getLine() the string ❹ and print it out ❺. Serial I/O is covered in much more detail in appendix F.

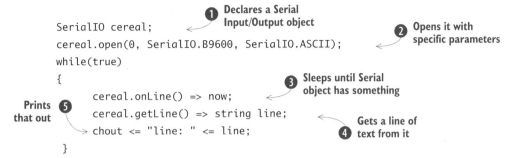

Listing 11.5 Receive lines of strings from an Arduino via a `SerialIO` object

```
SerialIO cereal;                                         ❶ Declares a Serial
                                                            Input/Output object
cereal.open(0, SerialIO.B9600, SerialIO.ASCII);          ❷ Opens it with
                                                            specific parameters
while(true)
{                                                        ❸ Sleeps until Serial
                                                            object has something
    cereal.onLine() => now;
    cereal.getLine() => string line;                     ❹ Gets a line of
                                                            text from it
    chout <= "line: " <= line;
}
```

❺ Prints that out

> **ANOTHER WAY TO PRINT IN CHUCK** Note that the example of listing 11.5 uses a different method to print to the console from the one you've been using (`<<< "Print this" >>>;`). The `chout <=` technique is another way of printing that's more compatible with Java and some other languages.

Many things that you can connect to your computers via USB are actually using, or emulating, the old RS-232 serial protocol.

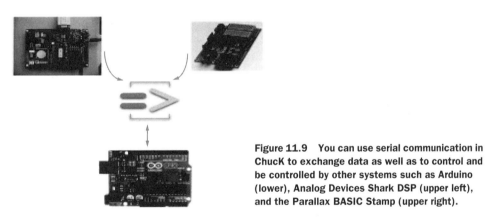

Figure 11.9   You can use serial communication in ChucK to exchange data as well as to control and be controlled by other systems such as Arduino (lower), Analog Devices Shark DSP (upper left), and the Parallax BASIC Stamp (upper right).

We're not going to cover any more specific serial examples here, because it's a pretty specialized topic and highly dependent on the hardware being used. But serial is, of course, supported in ChucK, and for more examples of how to use it, see appendix F.

11.4 Summary: looking outward and forward

You've done a whole lot, but ChucK lets you do so much more. In this chapter you learned how to connect to things in the outside world using MIDI, OSC, and serial. MIDI is a time-honored means for electronic musical devices to talk to and control each other. MIDI can be used to connect a huge number of devices and systems, ranging from musical keyboards, to drum controllers, synthesizers, computers, theatrical lights and effects, and even robots. OSC is a more modern protocol for computer systems to communicate with each other about music and sound. Serial is even older than MIDI, but it's still around and in use for many do-it-yourself types of systems such as Arduino. ChucK can speak all of these: MIDI, OSC, and serial.

Throughout the book you've learned about ChucK's types, logic and control structures, arrays, objects, classes, events, and more and how to use them for your music making. But there's more to ChucK than we could ever cover in just one book. Even though you know quite a lot about ChucK's built-in unit generators, there are more of them that you've never used, but they're all described in appendix C.

And, we didn't use or talk about all of the functions available in the ChucK Standard, Math, Machine, and other libraries and classes, but they're documented in appendix B.

ChucK can also open, read, and write computer files such as text files containing scores, lyrics, and whatever. The specifics of dealing with files are covered in appendix E.

Appendix G tells you how to use ChucK in the command line (terminal, shell, DOS box, or other text-only interface), without needing the miniAudicle at all. If this doesn't make sense to you, don't worry about it. We include it so that all types of computer users can enjoy and use ChucK.

ChucK isn't limited to what's built in. You can do even more, like extending the ChucK language itself, creating your own unit generator classes via three mechanisms:

- *Chugens*—ChucK code encapsulated in a function that acts like a UGen.
- *Chubgraphs*—New UGen classes that are composed of existing unit generators connected together.
- *ChuGins*—External objects written in the C or C++ languages, which are loaded when ChucK runs and show up as native unit generators.

All three of these, with examples, are covered in appendix H .

What's clear is that if you've worked through all of the examples and exercises, you're now a ChucK programmer and a digital artist who is capable of creating amazing works of art, limited only by your inspiration and imagination. ChucK is a powerful tool, and it's now in your toolbox. So, as we like to say in the ChucK community,

```
The time is now;
// Let's make music!!
```

appendix A
Installing ChucK and
miniAudicle

This appendix tells you how to download and install miniAudicle, ChucK's integrated development environment (IDE), and other components of ChucK onto your computer. To start, navigate to the ChucK website at http://chuck.stanford .edu/ and click Download ChucK, as shown in figure A.1. This takes you to the

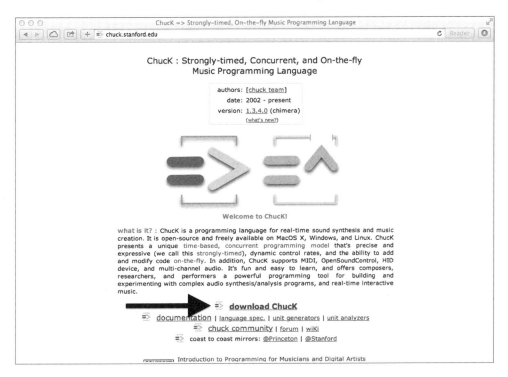

Figure A.1 Main download page for ChucK and miniAudicle (located at http://chuck.stanford.edu/)

233

ChucK : Release page, where you can see download links for each platform that ChucK supports. For Mac users, the following section covers the process from here. Windows users can skip to the next section, "Installing on Windows," and Linux users can jump to the last section, "Installing on Ubuntu Linux."

Installing on Mac OS X

From the main ChucK : Release download page, shown in figure A.2, click the Installer link under the MacOS X subheading, and a file called chuck-W.X.Y.Z.pkg will start to download (where W, X, Y, and Z are version numbers that will vary as new versions of ChucK are released). On Mac OS X, a single installer application installs both miniAudicle (the editor and graphical development application for ChucK) and the chuck command-line program.

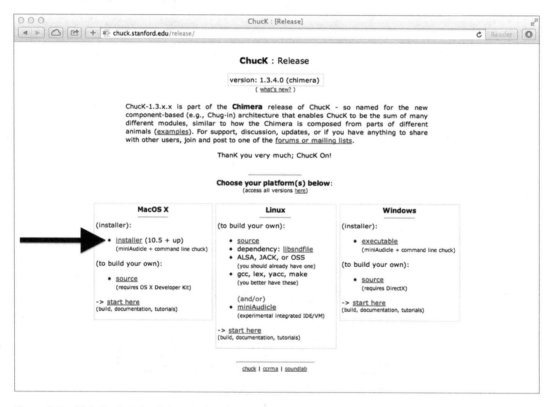

Figure A.2   Click the Installer link under MacOS X.

Open this file when it has finished downloading, and the standard Mac OS X installer dialog, shown in figure A.3, will appear.

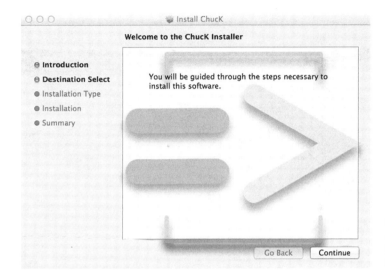

Figure A.3   Installer dialog box. Click Continue and follow the steps from there.

Click Continue (Accept and so on) on the various screens that appear; the default install configuration is typically sufficient. Once you click Install, you'll be asked for your password; enter it and then click Install Software. After that, the installation will take a few minutes to complete. If all goes well, you'll see the screen shown in figure A.4, indicating success.

miniAudicle is now available in your Applications folder. You can now return to chapter 1 and begin using miniAudicle!

Figure A.4   Success! You can now click Close and return to chapter 1 to learn ChucK.

Installing on Windows

To install ChucK and miniAudicle on Windows, from the main ChucK : Release download page click the Executable link under the Windows downloads section, as shown in figure A.5.

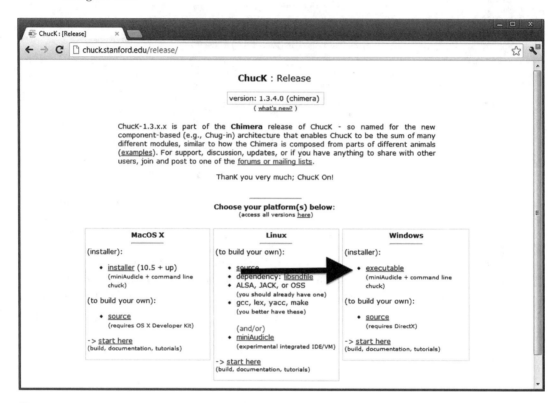

Figure A.5   Download link for Windows installer

Clicking this link will download a file called chuck-W.X.Y.Z.msi (where W, X, Y, and Z correspond to the current version numbers). Open this file when it finishes downloading, and you'll see a standard setup dialog, as shown in figure A.6.

Figure A.6 Installer dialog box. Click Next and then Accept, and do what it asks from there on.

Click through the various screens of this dialog, being sure to agree to ChucK's license. After you click the Install button, Windows will ask if you want to allow changes to your computer; click Yes. The installer will take a few minutes to proceed at this point; after it finishes, you'll see the screen shown in figure A.7. You can now return to chapter 1 and begin to use miniAudicle to learn ChucK programming, as shown in figure A.8.

Figure A.7 Success! You can now click Finish and return to chapter 1 to learn ChucK.

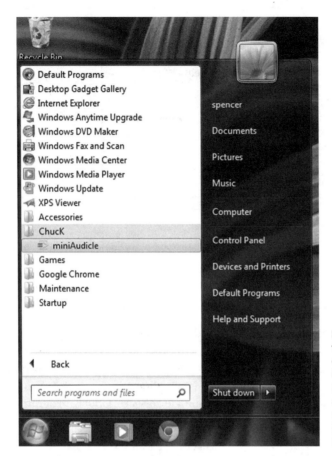

Figure A.8   ChucK is now listed in the Start menu. In Windows 7 and earlier, miniAudicle is now available in the Start menu under All Programs > ChucK. In Windows 8 and 8.1, there should now be a miniAudicle icon on the desktop (navigate there from the Windows home screen).

Installing on Ubuntu Linux

Installing ChucK and miniAudicle on Linux requires a little more work, but with a few Terminal commands you can be on your way to ChucKian bliss. Given the variety of Linux systems available, we've geared these instructions toward Ubuntu Linux, a popular choice for novices and experts alike. For other Linux systems, the installation procedure is conceptually similar, although the exact commands will vary.

To start, open the Terminal app. On Linux, ChucK and miniAudicle are compiled from source code, and a number of additional programs and libraries must be installed to enable this. In the Terminal window, enter the following command (on a single line) and then hit Return:

```
$ sudo apt-get install make gcc g++ bison flex libasound2-dev libsndfile1-dev
    libqt4-dev libqscintilla2-dev libpulse-dev
```

(The $ character indicates the shell prompt and should not be typed.) If asked for your password, enter it and hit Return again. This command will automatically install make, gcc, g++, bison, and flex, which are tools for building software from source code, whereas the rest are support libraries used by ChucK and miniAudicle. This command can take some time to finish, because it downloads and installs each component and its dependencies individually.

Once the command finishes, head to the ChucK website (http://chuck.stanford .edu/), click the Download link, and then click Source under the Linux category. This links to a tar-zip file (with a .tgz extension), which is an archive containing the source code. You should save the source archive to a location on your hard disk, such as the Downloads folder. While that's downloading, click the miniAudicle link under the Linux section of the webpage. This will take you to the miniAudicle web page, where a link to the miniAudicle source code can be found. Click that link, and it will also begin a .tgz file download.

After both downloads have completed, hop back to Terminal. Enter the command

```
$ cd Downloads
```

where `Downloads` is whatever folder you downloaded the .tgz files into. This will navigate your terminal session to that directory. Now unpack the archives with these commands:

```
$ tar xzf chuck-W.X.Y.Z.tgz
$ tar xzf miniAudicle-A.B.C.tgz
```

When you enter the commands, ensure that `W.X.Y.Z` and `A.B.C` match the actual version numbers of ChucK and miniAudicle you downloaded. Now navigate to the ChucK source directory, freshly unpacked, and enter the command to start the build procedure:

```
$ cd chuck-W.X.Y.Z/src
$ make linux-pulse
```

This will take some time, because all of the source code files are compiled into a single program. When the `make` command completes, the last step is to install the newly compiled program:

```
$ sudo make install
```

You'll need to enter your password. You can test that it works by entering this command:

```
$ chuck --version
```

This will print the following:

```
chuck version: W.X.Y.Z (chimera)
    linux (pulse) : 64-bit
    http://chuck.cs.princeton.edu/
    http://chuck.stanford.edu/
```

Compiling miniAudicle, the graphical editor for ChucK, is a similar procedure: navigate to the miniAudicle source directory, compile the program, and then install.

```
$ cd ../../miniAudicle-A.B.C/src
```

```
$ make linux-pulse
lots of stuff printed here …
$ sudo make install
```

If all went well, you can now start miniAudicle by typing the following in the command line:

```
$ miniAudicle
```

The miniAudicle editor and associated windows should pop up on your screen. Now you're ready to start ChucKing!

ChucK on Raspberry Pi

Running ChucK on the Raspberry Pi is also very straightforward. If your Raspberry Pi is running Ubuntu Linux or a related variant, you can just follow the previous instructions for Linux. Alternatively, we recommend installing Satellite CCRMA on your Raspberry Pi. Satellite CCRMA is an entire customized version of Linux that includes a number of applications for computer music and physical computing, including ChucK. For more information, visit https://ccrma.stanford.edu/~eberdahl/satellite/.

appendix B
Library functions:
Std, Math, other

In chapter 2 you first learned about the Standard library (Std) and some of the tools (functions) available in that collection. You also learned about the Math library and have since been using many functions from both Std and Math. In later chapters you encountered some of the Machine VM functions. You've used `me.dir()` and some other built-in ChucK library and class methods.

There are many other useful tools related to shreds, objects, and other classes built into ChucK. The tables in this appendix list and briefly describe them. Because the appendix is basically only a list, we won't show you how you might use each function. Nor will we introduce each table. Consider joining one of the ChucK forums or mailing lists (at http://chuck.stanford.edu/community/) for more information on using the full power of ChucK.

B.1   The ChucK Standard Library

You use these in this way: `Std.functionName(args)`.

Example: `Std.abs(x) => float myAbs;`

Table B.1   Std functions for converting and dealing with basic data types

Function name and arguments	What the function does
`int abs(int value);`	Returns absolute value of integer.
`float fabs(float value);`	Returns absolute value of floating point number.
`float sgn(float value);`	Computes sign of input as -1.0 (neg), 0, or 1.0 (pos).
`int atoi(string value);`	Converts ASCII (`string`) to integer (`int`).

Table B.1   Std functions for converting and dealing with basic data types *(continued)*

Function name and arguments	What the function does
`string itoa(int value);`	Converts integer to ASCII (`string` character).
`int ftoi(float value);`	Converts floating-point number to integer (by truncation).
`float atof(string value);`	Converts ASCII (`string`) to floating-point value (`float`).
`string ftoa(float value, int precision);`	Converts `float` to ASCII (`string` character) (precision = # decimal points).

Table B.2   Std functions for dealing with music and sound quantities

Function name and arguments	What it does
`float mtof(float value);`	Converts a MIDI note number to frequency (Hz). Note the input value is of type `float` (supports fractional note number).
`float ftom(float value);`	Converts frequency (Hz) to MIDI note number space.
`float powtodb(float value);`	Converts signal power ratio to decibels (dB).
`float rmstodb(float value);`	Converts linear amplitude to decibels.
`float dbtopow(float value);`	Converts decibels to signal power ratio.
`float dbtorms(float value);`	Converts decibels to linear amplitude.

Table B.3   More Std functions (system power tools); be wary!

Function name and arguments	What it does
`string getenv(string key);`	Returns the value of an environment variable (such as PATH).
`int setenv(string key, string value);`	Sets environment variable key to value.
`int system(string cmd);`	Passes cmd to be executed by the system shell.

NOTE   To use the system command function, you must run ChucK with the flag

`--caution-to-the-wind`

This tells ChucK that you're going to be responsible with your code, because it's possible to delete files or wreak other mayhem using system calls. In command-line ChucK, you specify the --caution-to-the-wind flag. You can't currently use this in the miniAudicle, which is largely for your protection.

Consult appendix G, "ChucK on the command line," to learn how to use ChucK in this way.

B.2   The ChucK Math library

You call all of these functions using `Math.functionName(args)`.

Example: `Math.sin(x) => float mySine;`

Table B.4   Math library: trigonometric and transcendental functions

Function name and arguments	What it does
`float sin(float x);`	Computes the sine of x.
`float cos(float x);`	Computes the cosine of x.
`float tan(float x);`	Computes the tangent of x.
`float asin(float x);`	Computes the arc sine of x.
`float acos(float x);`	Computes the arc cosine of x.
`float atan(float x);`	Computes the arc tangent of x.
`float atan2(float y, float x);`	Computes the principal value of arc tangent of y/x using the signs of both arguments to determine the quadrant of the return value.
`float sinh(float x);`	Computes the hyperbolic sine of x.
`float cosh(float x);`	Computes the hyperbolic cosine of x.
`float tanh(float x);`	Computes the hyperbolic tangent of x.
`float hypot(float x, float y);`	Computes the square root of $(x^2 + y^2)$; can be seen as computing the hypotenuse of a right triangle with sides x and y or the magnitude of a two-dimensional vector (x,y).
`float pow(float x, float y);`	Computes x taken to the y-th power.
`float sqrt(float x);`	Computes the positive square root of x $(x >= 0)$.
`float exp(float x);`	Computes e^x, the base-e exponential of x.
`float log(float x);`	Computes the natural logarithm of x.
`float log2(float x);`	Computes the logarithm of x to base 2.
`float log10(float x);`	Computes the logarithm of x to base 10.

Table B.5   Math library: random number functions

Function name and arguments	What it does
`int random();`	Generates random integer between 0 and `Math.RANDOM_MAX`.

Table B.5   Math library: random number functions (*continued*)

Function name and arguments	What it does
`int random2(int min, int max);`	Generates random integer in the range [min, max].
`float randomf();`	Generates random floating-point number in the range [0, 1].
`float random2f(float min, float max);`	Generates random floating point number in the range [min, max].

Table B.6   Math library: operations and calculations on numbers

Function name and arguments	What it does
`float floor(float x);`	Rounds to largest integral value (returns `float`) not greater than x.
`float ceil(float x);`	Rounds to smallest integral value (returns `float`) not less than x.
`float round(float x);`	Rounds to nearest integral value (returns `float`) .
`float trunc(float x);`	Rounds to largest integral value (returns `float`) no greater in magnitude than x.
`float fmod(float x, float y);`	Computes the floating point remainder of x / y.
`float remainder(float x, float y);`	Computes the value r such that r = x − n * y, where n is the integer nearest the exact value of x / y. If there are two integers closest to x / y, n shall be the even one. If r is zero, it is given the same sign as x.
`float min(float x, float y);`	Chooses lesser of two values.
`float max(float x, float y);`	Chooses greater of two values.
`int nextpow2(int x);`	Computes the integral (returned as `int`) smallest power of 2 greater than the value of x.
`float isinf(float x);`	Tests if x is infinity.
`float isnan(float x);`	Tests if x is not a number.

You access the constants in table B.7 using `Math.constantName`.

Example: `0.75* Math.PI => float threeFourthsPI;`

Table B.7   Math library: constants

Function name and arguments	What it is
`float PI;`	Constant PI; use as `Math.PI`.
`float TWO_PI;`	Constant PI*2; example usage: `Math.TWO_PI`.

Table B.7 Math library: constants *(continued)*

Function name and arguments	What it is
`float e; // also E`	Euler's constant, base of natural logarithm; same as `Math.exp(1);` use as: `Math.e` or `Math.E`.
`complex i; // also j, I, or J`	Square root of -1, the imaginary number *i* as a complex value; use as `Math.i` or `Math.j` or `Math.I` or `Math.J`.
`int RANDOM_MAX;`	Max value returned by `Math.random()`.

B.3 Virtual machine commands and functions

You access these using `Machine.functionName(args)`.

Example: `Machine.add ("foo.ck");`.

Table B.8 VM commands and functions

Function name and arguments	What it does
`int add(string path);`	Compiles and sporks a new shred from file at `path` into the VM now and returns the shred ID.
`int spork(string path);`	Same as `add`.
`int remove(int id);`	Removes shred from the VM by shred ID (returned by `add/spork`).
`int replace(int id, string path);`	Replaces shred with new shred from file.
`int status();`	Displays current status of the VM.
`void crash();`	Literally causes the VM to crash, a last resort; use with care.

B.4 Shred object functions

Using an instance of the `Shred` class `shredObj`, you can access these with `shredObj.functionName(args)`. Example: `shredObj.dir(-2) @=> string aPath2Up;`. The most commonly used instance of `Shred` is `me`, which corresponds to the currently running shred, for example: `me.dir() @=> string path`. Additionally, the spork operator (introduced in chapter 8) returns an instance of `Shred`, with which you can also use these methods. Lastly, a static member function, `Shred.fromid()`, returns a `Shred` object corresponding to a given shred ID.

Table B.9 Shred object functions

Function name and arguments	What it does
`Shred.fromId(int id)`	Returns shred object corresponding to `id`.
`int id();`	Returns the ID number of the shred.

Table B.9   Shred object functions *(continued)*

Function name and arguments	What it does
`void yield();`	Causes the shred to temporarily discontinue processing and allows other active shreds to run.
`void exit();`	Schedules the shred for immediate termination.
`int running();`	Returns 1 if shred is still running, 0 otherwise.
`int done();`	Returns 1 if shred has finished, 0 otherwise; except in rare cases, this is the opposite of `done()`.
`int args();`	Returns the number of command-line arguments.
`string arg(int num);`	Returns command-line argument at position num.
`string me.dir();`	Returns the directory from whence this shred came.
`string me.dir(int numUp);`	Returns numUp directories from whence this shred came; numUp can be positive or negative, with the same result.

B.5   *String object functions*

ChucK allows for many different manipulations of strings using these functions. In addition to these functions, strings can be combined using the + operator.

Example: `"foo"` + `"bar"` `@=> string val;` `// val == "foobar"`

Table B.10   String object functions

Function name and arguments	What it does
`int length();`	Returns number of characters in the string.
`int charAt(int i);`	Returns ASCII value of character at position i.
`int setCharAt(int i, int c);`	Sets character at position i to ASCII value c.
`int find(int c);`	Returns position of first character matching c in the string. Returns −1 if no matching character is found.
`int find(int c, int p);`	Returns position of first character matching c in the string, at or after position p. Returns −1 if no matching character is found.
`int find(string s);`	Returns position of first substring matching s in the string. Returns −1 if no matching substring is found.
`int find(string s, int p);`	Returns position of first substring matching s in the string, at or after position p. Returns −1 if no matching substring is found.
`int rfind(int c);`	Returns position of last character matching s in the string. Returns −1 if no matching character is found.

Table B.10   String object functions *(continued)*

Function name and arguments	What it does
`int rfind(int c, int p);`	Returns position of last character matching c in the string, at or before position p. Returns –1 if no matching character is found.
`int rfind(string s);`	Returns position of last substring matching s in the string. Returns –1 if no matching substring is found.
`int rfind(string s, int p);`	Returns position of last substring matching s in the string, at or before position p. Returns –1 if no matching substring is found.
`string substring(int i);`	Returns a new string with the substring from position i to the end of the string.
`string substring(int i, int len);`	Return a new string with the substring from position i of length len, or to the end of the string.
`void insert(int i, string str);`	Inserts str at position i in the string, shifting existing string at i to after str.
`void replace(int i, string str);`	Replaces characters from position i to end of string with str.
`void replace(int i, int len, string str);`	Replaces len characters starting from position i with str.
`void erase(int i, int len);`	Removes len characters from string, starting at position i.
`string ltrim();`	Returns new string with leading spaces removed.
`string rtrim();`	Returns new string with trailing spaces removed.
`string trim();`	Returns new string with leading and trailing spaces removed.
`string upper();`	Returns new string with all letters in uppercase.
`string lower();`	Returns new string with all letters in lowercase.

B.6   *Array object functions*

Arrays in ChucK are easy to manipulate, adding and removing elements as needed. For example, you can append items to an array using the << operator:

```
[64, 65, 60, 59] @=> int notes[];
notes << 58 << 60; // notes is now [64, 65, 60, 59, 58, 60]
```

Table B.11   Array-supported functions

Function name and arguments	What it does
`int size();`	Number of elements in the array.
`int size(int n);`	Sets number of elements in the array to n. Fills any new elements with default values (0 for `int` and `float`, `0::second` for dur and `time`, `null` for strings and objects).
`void popBack();`	Removes last element in array.
`void clear();`	Removes all elements in array.

appendix C
Unit generators

You've used many unit generators throughout this book, but we didn't touch on all of them or on all of the things that UGens can do. This appendix lists all current ChucK UGens and the methods and variables available for you to access in using them.

In general, UGens deal with audio on a per-sample basis. This means that in a UGen connection such as

```
adc => Gain myGain => dac;
```

at each point, `dac` asks `myGain` for a sample, which in turn asks `adc` for a sample. The `adc` passes the most recent sample to `myGain`, which then scales it according to the set gain; then passes it to `dac` for output. Audio samples in ChucK have a nominal range of -1.0 to 1.0. They're `floats` and can be any value, but before they reach the `dac` or `WvOut` for sound file writing, they should get back down to approximately the +/- 1.0 range.

For each UGen in this appendix, we list the methods that it implements. Most of these can be accessed by ChucKing a value to them, as in `0.3 => myGain.gain`, or by using them in their function call form, like `myGain.gain(0.3);`. In most cases, using the function form with an empty argument causes the UGen to return that value, so `<<< myGain.gain() >>>` would print out the current gain of that UGen.

C.1 Audio input and output UGens

These special ChucK system UGens (`dac`, `adc`, and `blackhole`) are different from all others, in that they're persistent (always exist as long as the VM is running), so you don't have to make an instance of them. In fact, trying to execute `SinOsc s => dac myDac;` generates warnings. `SinOsc s => dac` is the proper way to use `dac`.

- dac—Digital-to-analog converter, abstraction for underlying audio output device.
  - `.left`—Input to left channel output.
  - `.right`—Input to right channel output.

- ○ `.chan(int n)`—nth channel; all UGens obey this function.
- adc—Analog/digital converter, abstraction for underlying audio input device.
  - ○ `.left`—Input from left channel.
  - ○ `.right`—Input from right channel.
  - ○ `.chan(int n)`—Returns nth channel; all UGens obey this function.
- blackhole—Sample rate sample sucker (like dac, blackhole ticks UGens, but the samples aren't heard; see section 6.1 for more details on using blackhole).

Because these UGens are always in existence, it's a bad idea to modify their gain because that gain will persist as long as the VM runs, and other shreds might not be expecting that. Neither should you connect them directly (don't do adc => dac), because they're stuck there forever, as long as the VM runs. There are some other things you should likely not do with adc/dac, such as changing .op as described in the next section.

C.2   *Methods common to all unit generators*

Unit generators are designed to be connected together, so they all obey the ChucK operator, like this:

```
adc => Gain myGain => blackhole;
```

Once connected, UGens can be un-ChucKed like this:

```
myGain =< blackhole;
```

Some unit generators only yield samples of audio, so ChucKing to their input does nothing. Because Noise only generates noise, ChucKing something to its input isn't necessary and doesn't do anything if you do it anyway.

Other methods that all unit generators, where applicable, obey are these:

- `.gain(float)`—Sets gain; all UGens have this, can be any float value.
- `.gain()` (with no argument)—Returns current value of gain.
- `.last()`—Returns last sample output as a float.
- `.channels()`—Returns an integer, the number of channels output by the UGen, usually 1.
- `.chan(int)`—Returns a reference to the int-th channel of the UGen.
  Example: `Noise n => dac.chan(0); // connect to left or 0-th channel`
- `.op(int)`—Changes relationship of inputs; the following are the available options:
  - ○ 0: Silence, stop, output 0.0 forever.
  - ○ 1: Add inputs (default).
  - ○ 2: Subtract all subsequent inputs from the first connected.
  - ○ 3: Multiply all inputs.
  - ○ 4: Divide all subsequent inputs into the first connected.
  - ○ –1: Passthrough, sum all inputs, output sum, don't apply gain.
- `.isConnectedTo(UGen otherUG)`—Returns 1 if this UGen is connected to otherUG.

C.3 Gain and stereo/mono UGens

Even though every UGen obeys the .gain method, there is a Gain UGen dedicated to gain and other functions. As you learned early on in the book, making one or more common patches or mixing points out of Gain UGens is a useful thing.

- Gain—Gains control. Note: all unit generators can change their own gain. A Gain UGen provides a way to add *N* outputs together and scale them.
  - .gain(float)—Sets gain. All UGens have this ability.
  - .op(int)—Changes relationship of inputs: 1=add, 3=multiply.

Because by default everything ChucKed to a Gain sums together, it acts as a mixer, unless you use the .op method to change how Gain treats its inputs, as described previously. So if you wanted a make a patch that squares a signal (multiplies it by itself), you could do this:

```
adc => Gain mySquarer => blackhole;    // so far so good
adc => mySquarer;     // connect again
3 => mySquarer.op;    // and set to multiply
```

These unit generators help in converting between stereo and mono UGen inputs/outputs:

- Pan2—Spreads mono signal to stereo.
  - .left(UGen)—Left (mono) channel out.
  - .right(UGen)—Right (mono) channel out.
  - .pan(float)—Pan location value (-1 to 1).

- Mix2—Mixes stereo input down to mono channel.
  - .left(UGen)—Left (mono) channel in.
  - .right(UGen)—Right (mono) channel in.
  - .pan(float)—Mix parameter value (0 to 1).

C.4 Basic sound waves and function generator UGens

- Impulse—Pulse generator; default output is 0.0, unless you set the .next value.
  - .next(float v)—Sets value of next sample to be generated. After one sample time has passed, the Impulse UGen outputs 0.0 again until .next is set.

- Step—Step generator; like Impulse, but once the .next value is set, it's held for all following samples, until the value is set again.
  - .next(float v)—Sets the step value to v.

- Noise—White noise generator, uncorrelated random samples (in range -1.0 to 1.0).

- SubNoise—STK subsampled noise generator. Generates a new random number with every integer-rate sample using the C rand() function. The quality of the rand() function varies from one OS to another.
  - .rate(int)—subsampling rate

C.5   *Oscillator unit generators*

All Oscillator UGens obey the following methods:

- `.freq(float)`—Oscillator frequency (Hz), phase-matched.
- `.sfreq(float)`—Oscillator frequency (Hz).
- `.phase(float)`—Current phase.
- `.sync(int)`—(0) frequency sync, (1) phase sync, (2) fm synth.
- `SinOsc`—Sine wave oscillator.
    - Obeys `.freq`, `.sfreq`, `.phase`, and `.sync` as described previously.
- `TriOsc`—Triangle wave oscillator.
    - Obeys `.freq`, `.sfreq`, `.phase`, and `.sync` as described previously.
    - `.width(float)`—Controls midpoint of triangle, 0 to 1 (0.5 default).
- `SawOsc`—Sawtooth wave oscillator.
    - Obeys `.freq`, `.sfreq`, `.phase`, and `.sync` as described previously.
    - `.width(float)`—Increasing (w > 0.5) or decreasing (w < 0.5).
- `SqrOsc`—Square wave oscillator (pulse with fixed width of 0.5).
    - Obeys `.freq`, `.sfreq`, `.phase`, and `.sync` as described previously.
- `PulseOsc`—Pulse wave oscillator with variable width.
    - Obeys `.freq`, `.sfreq`, `.phase`, and `.sync` as described previously.
    - `.width(float)`—Length of duty cycle (0.0–1.0)
- `Phasor`—Simple ramp generator (range 0.0–1.0), can be used as a phase control for other oscillators/table UGens.
    - Obeys `.freq`, `.sfreq`, `.phase`, and `.sync` as described previously.
    - `.width(float)`—Sets duration of ramp in each cycle (default 1.0).
- `Modulate`—STK periodic/random modulator. This class combines random and periodic (sine) modulations to give a natural modulation function.
    - `.vibratoRate(float)`—Sets rate of vibrato.
    - `.vibratoGain(float)`—Gain for vibrato.
    - `.randomGain(float)`—Gain for random contribution.

C.6   *Lookup table unit generators*

These UGens were all ported from RTcmix, by Brad Garton, Dave Topper, and others (after CMIX by Paul Lansky): www.music.columbia.edu/cmix/makegens.html.

The ChucK/RTcmix Lookup Table UGens are commonly used in one of two ways. The first is to drive them with a `Phasor` UGen, which ramps from 0.0 to 1.0 and repeats, essentially reading out the values in the table from beginning to end as a waveform, synchronous with the `phasor` cycle. The other way to use these is as a table lookup, using a `Step` UGen as input, or by using the `.lookup()` method. Input should range from 0.0 (beginning of the table) to 1.0 (end of table). Absolute value is used for inputs between -1.0 and 0.0. Note: currently coefficients past the 100th are ignored.

- GenX—Base class for classic MusicN lookup table unit generators.
  - .lookup(float i) (float)—Returns lookup table value at index i [-1, 1]; absolute value is used in the range [-1, 0).
  - .coefs(float[])—Sets lookup table coefficients; meaning is dependent on subclass.
- Gen5 extends GenX—Exponential line segment lookup table generator. Constructs a lookup table composed of sequential exponential curves. For a table with N curves, starting value of y', and value y_n for lookup index x_n, set the coefficients to [y', y_0, x_0, ..., y_{N-1}, x_{N-1}]. Note that there must be an odd number of coefficients. If an even number of coefficients is specified, the behavior is undefined. The sum of x_n for $0 \leq n < N$ must be 1. $y_n = 0$ is approximated as 0.000001 to avoid strange results arising from the nature of exponential curves.
- Gen7 extends GenX—Line segment lookup table generator. Constructs a lookup table composed of sequential line segments. For a table with N lines, starting value of y', and value y_n for lookup index x_n, set the coefficients to [y', y_0, x_0, ..., y_{N-1}, x_{N-1}]. Note that there must be an odd number of coefficients. If an even number of coefficients is specified, behavior is undefined. The sum of x_n for $0 \leq n < N$ must be 1.
- Gen9 extends GenX—Additive sinusoidal lookup table with harmonic ratio, amplitude, and phase control. Constructs a lookup table of partials with specified amplitudes, phases, and harmonic ratios to the fundamental. Coefficients are specified in triplets of [ratio, amplitude, phase] arranged in a single linear array.
- Gen10 extends GenX—Sinusoidal lookup table with partial amplitude control and constructs a lookup table of harmonic partials with specified amplitudes. The amplitude of partial n is specified by the *n*th element of the coefficients. For example, setting coefs to [1] produces a sine wave.
- Gen17 extends GenX—Chebyshev polynomial lookup table. Constructs a Chebyshev polynomial wavetable with harmonic partials of specified weights. The weight of partial n is specified by the *n*th element of the coefficients. Primarily used for waveshaping, driven by a SinOsc instead of a Phasor.
- CurveTable extends GenX—Flexible curve/line segment table generator. Constructs a wavetable composed of segments of variable times, values, and curvatures. Coefficients are specified as a single linear array of triplets of [time, value, curvature] followed by a final duple of [time, value] to specify the final value of the table. Time values are expressed in unitless, ascending values. For curvature equal to 0, the segment is a line; for curvature less than 0, the segment is a convex curve; for curvature greater than 0, the segment is a concave curve.

C.7   LiSa: a live sampling unit generator

Dan Trueman really wanted to do live sampling, recording data from adc into a UGen on the fly, for immediate manipulation and playback. His creation of LiSa began in 2007, and this is the result. An internal buffer stores samples ChucKed to LiSa's input. Segments of this buffer can be played back, with ramping and speed/direction control. Multiple voice facility is built in, allowing for a single LiSa object to serve as a source for sample layering and granular textures. See http://wiki.cs.princeton.edu/ index.php/LiSa_examples for examples and http://dtrueman.mycpanel.prince-ton.edu/LiSa/LiSa_tutorial.html for a tutorial.

- LiSa—Live sampling utility.
  - .duration(dur)—Sets buffer size; required to allocate memory; also resets all parameter values to default.
  - .record(int)—Turns recording on and off.
  - .getVoice()—Returns the voice number of the next available voice.
  - .maxVoices(int)—Sets the maximum number of voices allowable, 10 by default; 200 is the current hardwired internal limit.
  - .play(int, WRITE)—Turns on/off sample playback (voice 0).
  - .play(int voice, int, WRITE)—For a particular voice (arg 1), turns on/off sample playback.
  - .rampUp(dur, WRITE)—Turns on sample playback, with ramp (voice 0).
  - .rampUp(int voice, dur, WRITE)—For a particular voice (arg 1), turns on sample playback, with ramp.
  - .rampDown(dur, WRITE)—Turns off sample playback, with ramp (voice 0).
  - .rampDown(int voice, dur, WRITE)—For a particular voice (arg 1), turns off sample playback, with ramp.
  - .rate(float, WRITE)—Sets playback rate (voice 0). Note that the int/float type for this method will determine whether the rate is being set (float, for voice 0) or read (int, for voice number).
  - .rate(int voice, float, WRITE)—For a particular voice (arg 1), sets playback rate.
  - .rate()—Gets playback rate (voice 0).
  - .rate(int voice, READ)—For a particular voice (arg 1), gets playback rate. Note that the int/float type for this method will determine whether the rate is being set (float, for voice 0) or read (int, for voice#).
  - .playPos()—Gets playback position (voice 0).
  - .playPos(int voice, READ)—For a particular voice (arg 1), gets playback position.
  - .playPos(dur, WRITE)—Sets playback position (voice 0).
  - .playPos(int voice, dur, WRITE)—For a particular voice (arg 1), sets playback position.

- ○ .recPos(dur)—Gets/sets record position.
- ○ .recRamp(dur)—Sets ramping when recording (from 0 to loopEndRec).
- ○ .loopRec(int)—Turns on/off loop recording.
- ○ .loopEndRec(dur)—Sets end point in buffer for loop recording.
- ○ .loopStart(dur)—Sets loop starting point for playback (voice 0). Applicable only when 1 => loop.
- ○ .loopStart(int voice, dur, WRITE)—For a particular voice (arg 1), sets loop starting point for playback. Applicable only when .loop(voice, 1).
- ○ .loopEnd (dur)—Sets loop ending point for playback (voice 0). Applicable only when 1 => loop.
- ○ .loopEnd(int voice, dur, WRITE)—For a particular voice (arg 1), sets loop ending point for playback. Applicable only when .loop(voice, 1).
- ○ .loop(int)—Turns on/off looping (voice 0).
- ○ .loop(int voice, int)—For a particular voice (arg 1), turns on/off looping.
- ○ .bi(int)—Turns on/off bidirectional playback (voice 0).
- ○ .bi(int voice, int, WRITE)—For a particular voice (arg 1), turns on/off bidirectional playback.
- ○ .voiceGain(float)—Sets playback gain (voice 0).
- ○ .voiceGain(int voice, float, WRITE)—For a particular voice (arg 1), sets gain.
- ○ .feedback(float)—Gets/sets feedback amount when overdubbing (loop recording, how much to retain).
- ○ .valueAt(dur, READ)—Gets value directly from record buffer.
- ○ .valueAt(float, dur, WRITE)—Sets value directly in record buffer.
- ○ .sync(int, READ/WRITE)—Sets input mode; (0) input is recorded to internal buffer:
    - – Input sets playback position [0,1] (phase value between loopStart and loopEnd for all active voices).
    - – Input sets playback position, interpreted as a time value in samples (works only with voice 0).
- ○ .track(int, READ/WRITE)—Identical to sync.
- ○ .clear—Clears recording buffer.

C.8 STK Envelope generators

- ■ Envelope—STK envelope base class. Simple envelope generator that's capable of ramping to .target value by a specified .time or duration or at a specified rate. Also responds to simple .keyOn (ramps to 1.0) and .keyOff (ramps to 0.0) messages.
    - ○ .keyOn(int, WRITE only)—Ramps to 1.0.
    - ○ .keyOff(int, WRITE only)—Ramps to 0.0.

- ○ .target(float)—Ramps to arbitrary value.
- ○ .time(float)—Sets time to reach target (in seconds).
- ○ .duration(dur)—Sets duration to reach target.
- ○ .rate(float)—Sets rate of change.
- ○ .value(float)—Sets immediate value.

- ADSR extends Envelope—STK Attack Decay Sustain Release envelope class.
  - ○ Responds to simple .keyOn and .keyOff messages, keeping track of its state. The state = ADSR.DONE after the envelope value reaches 0.0 in the ADSR .RELEASE state.
  - ○ .keyOn(int, WRITE only)—Starts the attack for non-zero values.
  - ○ .keyOff(int, WRITE only)—Starts release for non-zero values.
  - ○ .attackTime(dur)—Sets attack time.
  - ○ .attackRate(float)—Sets attack rate.
  - ○ .decayTime(dur)—Sets decay time.
  - ○ .decayRate(float)—Sets decay rate.
  - ○ .sustainLevel(float)—Sets sustain level.
  - ○ .releaseTime(dur)—Sets release time.
  - ○ .releaseRate(float)—Sets release rate.
  - ○ .state(int, READ only)—Attack: 0, Decay: 1, Sustain: 2, Release: 3, Done: 4.
  - ○ .set(dur, dur, float, dur)—Set A, D, S, and R all at once.

C.9   *STK delays, reverberators, and delay-based effects*

- Delay—STK non-interpolating delay line class.
  - ○ .delay(dur)—Length of delay (default is 0).
  - ○ .max(dur)—Max delay (buffer size, default is 4095).

- DelayA—STK allpass interpolating delay line class.
  - ○ .delay(dur)—Length of delay (default is 0.5 samples).
  - ○ .max(dur)—Max delay (buffer size, default is 4095).

- DelayL—STK linear interpolating delay line class.
  - ○ .delay(dur)—Length of delay (default is 0).
  - ○ .max(dur)—Max delay (buffer size, default is 4095).

- Echo—STK echo effect class.
  - ○ .delay(dur)—Length of echo.
  - ○ .max(dur)—Max delay.
  - ○ .mix(float)—Mix level (wet/dry).

- PRCRev—Perry's way-simple reverberator class. This class is based on some of the famous Stanford/CCRMA reverbs (NRev, JCRev, KipRev), which were based on the

Chowning/Moorer/Schroeder reverberators using networks of simple allpass and comb delay filters. This class implements two series allpass units and two parallel comb filters.

- ○ .mix(float)—Mix level.

- JCRev—John Chowning's reverberator class. This reverb is implemented using three allpass filters in series, followed by four parallel comb filters, and two decorrelation delay lines in parallel at the output.

  - ○ .mix(float)—Mix level.

- NRev—CCRMA's NRev (we think this means New) reverberator class. This reverb consists of six comb filters in parallel, followed by three allpass filters, a low-pass filter, and another allpass in series, followed by two allpass filters in parallel with corresponding right and left outputs.

  - ○ .mix(float)—Mix level.

- Chorus—STK chorus effect class. Implements a chorus effect using time-varying delay lines.

  - ○ .modFreq(float)—Modulation frequency.
  - ○ .modDepth(float)—Modulation depth.
  - ○ .mix(float)—Effect mix.

- PitShift—STK simple pitch shifter effect class. This class implements a simple pitch shifter using time-varying, overlapping, cross-fading, delay lines.

  - ○ .mix(float)—Effect dry/web mix level.
  - ○ .shift(float)—Amount of pitch shift (1.0: normal, .5: octave down, 2: octave up, ...).

C.10 *Sound file unit generators*

- SndBuf—Sound buffer (interpolating). Reads a variety of uncompressed audio file formats.

  - ○ .read(string, WRITE only)—Loads file for reading.
  - ○ .chunks(int)—Size of chunk (# of frames) to read on demand; 0 implies entire file, default; must be set before reading to take effect.
  - ○ .samples(int, READ only)—Gets total file size in samples.
  - ○ .length(dur, READ only)—Gets length as duration.
  - ○ .channels(int, READ only)—Gets number of channels.
  - ○ .pos(int)—Sets position (0 < p < .samples).
  - ○ .rate(float)—Sets/gets playback rate (relative to file's natural speed).
  - ○ .interp(int)—Sets/gets interpolation (0=drop, 1=linear, 2=sinc).
  - ○ .loop(int)—Toggles looping.
  - ○ .freq(float)—Sets/gets loop rate (file loops/second).
  - ○ .phase(float)—Sets/gets phase position (0–1).

- ○ `.channel(int)`—Sets/gets channel ($0 < p < $ `.channels`).
- ○ `.phaseOffset(float)`—Sets/gets a phase offset.

- SndBuf2—Stereo sound buffer (interpolating). Reads a variety of uncompressed audio file formats. If loaded with a stereo file, connecting to `dac` connects left to left, right to right. All previous methods, plus:
  - ○ `.chan(int)`—Returns mono UGen for the channel specified by `int`.

- WvIn—STK audio data input base class. Provides (different from `SndBuf`, primarily for legacy compatibility) input support for various audio file formats.
  - ○ `.rate(float)`—Playback rate.
  - ○ `.path(string)`—Specifies file to be played.

- WaveLoop extends WvIn—STK waveform oscillator class. Provides audio file looping functionality.
  - ○ `.freq(float)`—Sets frequency of playback (loops/second, not necessarily pitch!).
  - ○ `.addPhase(float)`—Offset by phase.
  - ○ `.addPhaseOffset(float)`—Sets phase offset.

- WvOut—STK audio data output base class. Allows for sound file writing.
  - ○ `.matFilename(string, WRITE only)`—Opens MATLAB file for writing.
  - ○ `.sndFilename(string, WRITE only)`—Opens snd file for writing.
  - ○ `.wavFilename(string, WRITE only)`—Opens WAVE file for writing.
  - ○ `.rawFilename(string, WRITE only)`—Opens raw file for writing.
  - ○ `.aifFilename(string, WRITE only)`—Opens AIFF file for writing.
  - ○ `.fileGain(float)`—Gain applied to samples before writing to file (different from `.gain`).
  - ○ `.closeFile()`—Closes file properly.

- WvOut2—Stereo version of STK audio data output base class. For sound file writing.

C.11   *Synthesis ToolKit filters*

- OnePole—STK one-pole filter class, implements `y(n) = b0*x(n) + a1*y(n-1)`. A method is provided for setting the pole position along the real axis of the z-plane while maintaining a constant peak filter gain.
  - ○ `.a1(float)`—Filter coefficient.
  - ○ `.b0(float)`—Filter coefficient.
  - ○ `.pole(float)`—Sets pole position along real axis of z-plane; maintains constant maximum gain.

- TwoPole—STK two-pole filter class, implements `y(n) = b0*x(n) + a1*y(n-1) + a2*y(n-2)`.
  - ○ `.a1(float)`—Filter coefficient.

- ○ `.a2(float)`—Filter coefficient.
- ○ `.b0(float)`—Filter coefficient.
- ○ `.freq(float)`—Filter resonance frequency.
- ○ `.radius(float)`—Filter resonance radius.
- ○ `.norm(int)`—Toggles filter auto-normalization.

- `OneZero`—STK one-zero filter class. A method is provided for setting the zero position along the real axis of the z-plane while maintaining a constant max filter gain.
  - ○ `.zero(float)`—Sets zero position.
  - ○ `.b0(float)`—Filter coefficient.
  - ○ `.b1(float)`—Filter coefficient.

- `TwoZero`—STK two-zero filter class, implements `y(n) = b0*x(n)+b1*y(n-1)+b2*y(n-1)`.
  - ○ `.b0(float)`—Filter coefficient.
  - ○ `.b1(float)`—Filter coefficient.
  - ○ `.b2(float)`—Filter coefficient.
  - ○ `.freq(float)`—Filter notch frequency.
  - ○ `.radius(float)`—Filter notch radius.

- `PoleZero`—STK one-pole, one-zero filter class, implements `y(n) = b0*x(n)+b1*y(n-1)-a1*x(n-1)`.
  - ○ `.a1(float)`—Filter coefficient.
  - ○ `.b0(float)`—Filter coefficient.
  - ○ `.b1(float)`—Filter coefficient.
  - ○ `.blockZero(float)`—DC blocking filter with given pole position.
  - ○ `.allpass(float)`—Allpass filter with given coefficient.

- `BiQuad`—STK biquad (two-pole, two-zero) filter class. Implements `a0*y[n] = b0*x[n] + b1*x[n-1] + b2*x[n-2]- a1*y[n-1] - a2*y[n-2]`. Can access raw coefficients or freq/radius for poles and zeroes. A method is provided (`.eqzs`) for creating a resonance in the frequency response while maintaining a (roughly) constant filter gain.
  - ○ `.b2(float)`—b2 coefficient.
  - ○ `.b1(float)`—b1 coefficient.
  - ○ `.b0(float)`—b0 coefficient.
  - ○ `.a2(float)`—a2 coefficient.
  - ○ `.a1(float)`—a1 coefficient.
  - ○ `.a0(float, READ only)`—a0 coefficient (used for normalization).
  - ○ `.pfreq(float, READ/WRITE)`—Sets resonance frequency (poles).
  - ○ `.prad(float)`—Pole radius (less than 1 to be stable).
  - ○ `.zfreq(float)`—Notch frequency.
  - ○ `.zrad(float)`—Zero radius.

- ○ `.norm(float)`—Normalization.
- ○ `.eqzs(float)`—Equal gain zeroes.

- ▪ `FilterBasic`—Base/parent class for the next few filters, which are all special BiQuads. You don't use one of these by itself, only subclasses.
  - ○ `.freq(float)`—Cutoff/center frequency.
  - ○ `.Q(float)`—Resonance (default is 1).
  - ○ `.set(float,float)`—Sets freq and Q at once.

- ▪ `LPF extends FilterBasic`—Resonant low-pass filter. 2nd order Butterworth.
  - ○ `.freq`, `.Q`, and `.set` as described previously.

- ▪ `HPF extends FilterBasic`—Resonant high-pass filter. 2nd order Butterworth.
  - ○ `.freq`, `.Q`, and `.set` as described previously.

- ▪ `BPF extends FilterBasic`—Band-pass filter. 2nd order Butterworth.
  - ○ `.freq`, `.Q`, and `.set` as described previously.

- ▪ `BRF extends FilterBasic`—Band-reject filter. 2nd order Butterworth.
  - ○ `.freq`, `.Q`, and `.set` as described previously.

- ▪ `ResonZ extends FilterBasic`—Resonance filter. BiQuad with equal-gain zeroes.
  - ○ `.freq`, `.Q`, and `.set` as described previously.

C.12 *Non-linear signal-processing UGens*

- ▪ `HalfRect`—Half-wave rectifier (only allows samples >= 0.0 through, blocks negative).
- ▪ `FullRect`—Full-wave rectifier (passes absolute value of all samples).
- ▪ `ZeroX`—Zero crossing detector. Emits a single pulse at zero crossings, in the direction of the zero crossing. Outputs +1.0 when signal crosses from negative to positive, and -1 for xing in other direction.
- ▪ `Dyno`—Dynamics processor. Includes presets for limiter, compressor, expander, noise gate, and ducker. Default is a hard-limiter (limiter with zero attack/release times).
  - ○ `.limit()`—Sets parameters to default limiter values:
    - – slopeAbove = 0.1   slopeBelow = 1.0   thresh = 0.5
    - – attackTime = 5 ms   releaseTime = 300 ms
      externalSideInput = false
  - ○ `.compress()`—Sets parameters to default compressor values:
    - – slopeAbove = 0.5   slopeBelow = 1.0   thresh = 0.5
    - – attackTime = 5 ms   releaseTime = 300 ms
      externalSideInput = false
  - ○ `.expand()`—Sets parameters to default expander values:
    - – slopeAbove = 2.0   slopeBelow = 1.0   thresh = 0.5

     – attackTime = 20 ms   releaseTime = 400 ms
       externalSideInput = false

- o .gate()—Sets parameters to default noise gate values:
  - – slopeAbove = 1.0   slopeBelow = 10000000   thresh = 0.1
  - – attackTime = 11 ms   releaseTime = 100 ms
    externalSideInput = false
- o .duck()—Sets parameters to default ducker values:
  - – slopeAbove = 0.5   slopeBelow = 1.0   thresh = 0.1
  - – attackTime = 100 ms   releaseTime = 1000 ms
    externalSideInput = true
- o Note that the input to sideInput determines the level of gain, not the direct signal input to Dyno.
- o .thresh(float)—The point above which to stop using slopeBelow and start using slopeAbove to determine output gain versus input gain.
- o .attackTime(dur)—Duration for the envelope to move linearly from current value to the absolute value of the signal's amplitude.
- o .releaseTime(dur)—Duration for the envelope to decay down to around 1/10 of its current amplitude, if not brought back up by the signal.
- o .ratio(float)—Alternate way of setting slopeAbove and slopeBelow; sets slopeBelow to 1.0 and slopeAbove to 1.0/ratio.
- o .slopeBelow(float)—Determines the slope of the output gain versus the input envelope's level in dB when the envelope is below thresh. In general, setting slopeBelow to be lower than slopeAbove results in expansion of dynamic range.
- o .slopeAbove(float)—Determines the slope of the output gain versus the input envelope's level in dB when the envelope is above thresh. In general, setting slopeAbove to be lower than slopeBelow results in compression of dynamic range.
- o .sideInput(float)—If externalSideInput is set to true, replaces the signal being processed as the input to the amplitude envelope. See dynoduck.ck for an example of using an external side chain.
- o .externalSideInput(int)—Set to true to cue the amplitude envelope off of sideInput instead of the input signal. Note that this means you'll need to manually set sideInput every so often. If false, the amplitude envelope represents the amplitude of the input signal whose dynamics are being processed. See dynoduck.ck for an example of using an external side chain.

C.13   STK instruments

- StkInstrument (imported from Instrmnt)—Superclass for STK instruments.
  - o .noteOn(float velocity)—Triggers note on.
  - o .noteOff(float velocity)—Triggers note off.

- ○ `.freq(float frequency)`—Sets/gets frequency (Hz).
- ○ `.controlChange(int number, float value)`—Instrument specific, range: [0.0–128.0].

- **`Clarinet extends StkInstrument`**—STK clarinet physical model class. Implements a simple clarinet physical model, as discussed by Smith (1986), McIntyre, Schumacher, Woodhouse (1983), and others.
  - ○ `.reed(float)`—Reed stiffness [0.0–1.0].
  - ○ `.noiseGain(float)`—Noise component gain [0.0–1.0].
  - ○ `.clear()`—Clears instrument.
  - ○ `.vibratoFreq(float)`—Vibrato frequency (Hz).
  - ○ `.vibratoGain(float)`—Vibrato gain [0.0–1.0].
  - ○ `.pressure(float)`—Pressure/volume [0.0–1.0].
  - ○ `.startBlowing(float, WRITE only)`—Starts blowing [0.0–1.0].
  - ○ `.stopBlowing(float, WRITE only)`—Stops blowing [0.0–1.0].
  - ○ `.rate(float)`—Rate of attack (sec).
  - ○ Inherited from `StkInstrument`: `.noteOn`, `.noteOff`, `.freq`, `.controlChange`
  - ○ Control change numbers:
    - – Reed Stiffness = 2   Noise Gain = 4   Vibrato Frequency = 11
    - – Vibrato Gain = 1   Breath Pressure = 128

- **`BlowBotl extends StkInstrument`**—STK blown pop-bottle instrument class. This class implements a Helmholtz resonator (biquad filter) with a polynomial jet excitation (see Cook, *Real Sound Synthesis for Interactive Applications* [A K Peters/CRC Press, 2002]).
  - ○ `.noiseGain(float)`—Noise component gain [0.0–1.0].
  - ○ `.vibratoFreq(float)`—Vibrato frequency (Hz).
  - ○ `.vibratoGain(float)`—Vibrato gain [0.0–1.0].
  - ○ `.volume(float)`—Yet another volume knob [0.0–1.0].
  - ○ `.rate(float)`—Rate of attack (sec).
  - ○ `.startBlowing(float, WRITE only)`—Starts blowing [0.0–1.0].
  - ○ `.stopBlowing(float, WRITE only)`—Stops blowing [0.0–1.0].
  - ○ Inherited from `StkInstrument`: `.noteOn`, `.noteOff`, `.freq`, `.controlChange`.
  - ○ Control change numbers:
    - – Noise Gain = 4   Vibrato Frequency = 11   Vibrato Gain = 1
    - – Volume = 128

- **`Flute extends StkInstrument`**—STK flute physical model class. Implements a simple flute physical model, as discussed by Karjalainen, Smith, Waryznyk, etc. The jet model uses a polynomial jet, a la Cook.
  - ○ `.jetDelay(float)`—Jet delay [...].
  - ○ `.jetReflection(float)`—Jet reflection [...].

- ○ `.endReflection(float)`—End delay [...].
- ○ `.noiseGain(float)`—Noise component gain [0.0–1.0].
- ○ `.vibratoFreq(float)`—Vibrato frequency (Hz).
- ○ `.vibratoGain(float)`—Vibrato gain [0.0–1.0].
- ○ `.pressure(float)`—Pressure/volume [0.0–1.0].
- ○ `.clear()`—Clear instrument.
- ○ `.startBlowing(float, WRITE only)`—Start blowing [0.0–1.0].
- ○ `.stopBlowing(float, WRITE only)`—Stop blowing [0.0–1.0].
- ○ `.rate(float)`—Rate of attack (sec).
- ○ Inherited from `StkInstrument`: `.noteOn`, `.noteOff`, `.freq`, `.controlChange`
- ○ Control change numbers:
  - – Jet Delay = 2   Noise Gain = 4   Vibrato Frequency = 11
  - – Vibrato Gain = 1   Breath Pressure = 128

- ■ `BlowHole` extends `StkInstrument`—STK clarinet physical model with a two-port register hole and a three-port dynamic tonehole implementation, as discussed by Scavone and Cook (1998).
  - ○ `.reed(float)`—Reed stiffness [0.0–1.0].
  - ○ `.noiseGain(float)`—Noise component gain [0.0–1.0].
  - ○ `.tonehole(float)`—Tonehole size [0.0–1.0].
  - ○ `.vent(float)`—Vent frequency [0.0–1.0].
  - ○ `.pressure(float)`—Pressure [0.0–1.0].
  - ○ `.startBlowing(float, WRITE only)`—Start blowing [0.0–1.0].
  - ○ `.stopBlowing(float, WRITE only)`—Stop blowing [0.0–1.0].
  - ○ `.rate(float)`—Rate of attack (sec).
  - ○ Inherited from `StkInstrument`: `.noteOn`, `.noteOff`, `.freq`, `.controlChange`.
  - ○ Control change numbers:
    - – Reed Stiffness = 2   Noise Gain = 4   Tonehole State = 11
    - – Register State = 1   Breath Pressure = 128

- ■ `Saxofony` extends `StkInstrument`—STK faux conical bore reed instrument class. Hybrid digital waveguide instrument that can generate a variety of wind-like sounds. Also called the blowed string. Essentially a string with one rigid end and one lossy (filter) end. The non-linear function is a reed table, but the string can be blown at any point between the terminations. If the excitation is placed at the string midpoint, the sound is that of a clarinet. Closer to the bridge, the sound is closer to that of a saxophone.
  - ○ `.stiffness(float)`—Reed stiffness [0.0–1.0].
  - ○ `.aperture(float)`—Reed aperture [0.0–1.0].
  - ○ `.pressure(float)`—Pressure/volume [0.0–1.0].
  - ○ `.vibratoFreq(float)`—Vibrato frequency (Hz).
  - ○ `.vibratoGain(float)`—Vibrato gain [0.0–1.0].

- ○ .noiseGain(float)—Noise component gain [0.0–1.0].
- ○ .blowPosition(float)—Lip stiffness [0.0–1.0].
- ○ .clear()—Clear instrument.
- ○ .startBlowing(float, WRITE only)—Start blowing [0.0–1.0].
- ○ .stopBlowing(float, WRITE only)—Stop blowing [0.0–1.0].
- ○ .rate(float)—Rate of attack (sec).
- ○ Inherited from StkInstrument: .noteOn, .noteOff, .freq, .controlChange.
- ○ Control change numbers:
  - – Reed Stiffness = 2   Reed Aperture = 26   Noise Gain = 4
  - – Blow Position = 11   Vibrato Frequency = 29   Vibrato Gain = 1
  - – Breath Pressure = 128

- **Brass extends StkInstrument**—STK simple brass instrument class. Implements a simple brass instrument waveguide model (a la Cook, TBone ICMC 1991 and HosePlayer, ICMC 1992).
  - ○ .lip(float)—Lip tension [0.0–1.0].
  - ○ .slide(float)—Slide length [0.0–1.0].
  - ○ .vibratoFreq(float)—Vibrato frequency (Hz).
  - ○ .vibratoGain(float)—Vibrato gain [0.0–1.0].
  - ○ .volume(float)—Volume [0.0–1.0].
  - ○ .clear(float, WRITE only)—Clear instrument.
  - ○ .startBlowing(float, WRITE only)—Start blowing [0.0–1.0].
  - ○ .stopBlowing(float, WRITE only)—Stop blowing [0.0–1.0].
  - ○ .rate(float)—Rate of attack (sec).
  - ○ Inherited from StkInstrument: .noteOn, .noteOff, .freq, .controlChange.
  - ○ Control change numbers:
    - – Lip Tension = 2   Slide Length = 4   Vibrato Frequency = 11
    - – Vibrato Gain = 1   Volume = 128

- **Bowed extends StkInstrument**—STK bowed string instrument class. Implements a bowed string model, a la Smith (1986), after McIntyre, Schumacher, Woodhouse (1983).
  - ○ .bowPressure(float)—Bow pressure [0.0–1.0].
  - ○ .bowPosition(float)—Bow position [0.0–1.0].
  - ○ .vibratoFreq(float)—Vibrato frequency (Hz).
  - ○ .vibratoGain(float)—Vibrato gain [0.0–1.0].
  - ○ .volume(float)—Volume [0.0–1.0].
  - ○ .startBowing(float, WRITE only)—Start bowing [0.0–1.0].
  - ○ .stopBowing(float, WRITE only)—Stop bowing [0.0–1.0].
  - ○ .rate(float)—Rate of attack (sec).
  - ○ Inherited from StkInstrument: .noteOn, .noteOff, .freq, .controlChange.

- ○ Control change numbers:
  - – Bow Pressure = 2   Bow Position = 4   Vibrato Frequency = 11
  - – Vibrato Gain = 1   Volume = 128

- `StifKarp` extends `StkInstrument`—STK plucked stiff string instrument. Implements a simple plucked string algorithm (Karplus-Strong) with enhancements (Jaffe-Smith, Smith, and others), including string stiffness (allpass filters) and pluck position controls.
  - ○ `.pickupPosition(float)`—Pickup position [0.0–1.0].
  - ○ `.sustain(float)`—String sustain [0.0–1.0].
  - ○ `.stretch(float)`—String stretch [0.0–1.0].
  - ○ `.pluck(float, WRITE only)`—Pluck string [0.0–1.0].
  - ○ `.baseLoopGain(float)`—Frequency-independent gain of the feedback loop [0.0–1.0].
  - ○ `.clear()`—Reset instrument.
  - ○ Inherited from `StkInstrument`: `.noteOn`, `.noteOff`, `.freq`, `.controlChange`. Control change numbers:
    - – Pickup Position = 4   String Sustain = 11   String Stretch = 1

- `Sitar` extends `StkInstrument`—STK sitar string model class. Implements a sitar plucked string physical model based on the Karplus-Strong algorithm.
  - ○ `.pluck(float, WRITE only)`—Pluck string [0.0–1.0].
  - ○ `.clear()`—Reset.
  - ○ Inherited from `StkInstrument`: `.noteOn`, `.noteOff`, `.freq`.
  - ○ No available control changes.

- `Mandolin` extends `StkInstrument`—STK mandolin instrument model class. Uses commuted synthesis techniques to model a mandolin.
  - ○ `.bodySize(float)`—Body size (percentage).
  - ○ `.pluckPos(float)`—Pluck position [0.0–1.0].
  - ○ `.stringDamping(float)`—String damping [0.0–1.0].
  - ○ `.stringDetune(float)`—Detuning of string pair [0.0–1.0].
  - ○ `.afterTouch(float, WRITE only)`—Aftertouch (currently unsupported).
  - ○ `.pluck(float, WRITE only)`—Pluck instrument [0.0–1.0].
  - ○ Inherited from `StkInstrument`: `.noteOn`, `.noteOff`, `.freq`, `.controlChange`.
  - ○ Control change numbers:
    - – Body Size = 2   Pluck Position = 4   String Sustain = 11
    - – String Detuning = 1 Microphone Position = 128

- `ModalBar` extends `StkInstrument`—STK resonant bar instrument class.
  - ○ `.stickHardness(float)`—Stick hardness [0.0–1.0].
  - ○ `.strikePosition(float)`—Strike position [0.0–1.0].

- ○ `.vibratoFreq(float)`—Vibrato frequency (Hz).
- ○ `.vibratoGain(float)`—Vibrato gain [0.0–1.0].
- ○ `.directGain(float)`—Direct gain [0.0–1.0].
- ○ `.masterGain(float)`—Master gain [0.0–1.0].
- ○ `.volume(float)`—Volume [0.0–1.0].
- ○ `.preset(int)`—Choose preset (see below).
- ○ `.strike(float, WRITE only)`—Strike bar [0.0–1.0].
- ○ `.damp(float, WRITE only)`—Damp bar [0.0–1.0].
- ○ `.clear()`—Reset [none].
- ○ `.mode(int)`—Select mode [0.0–1.0].
- ○ `.modeRatio(float)`—Edit selected mode ratio [...].
- ○ `.modeRadius(float)`—Edit selected mode radius [0.0–1.0].
- ○ `.modeGain(float)`—Edit selected mode gain [0.0–1.0].
- ○ Inherited from `StkInstrument`: `.noteOn`, `.noteOff`, `.freq`, `.controlChange`.
- ○ Control change numbers:
  - – Stick Hardness = 2   Tick Position = 4   Vibrato Gain = 11
  - – Vibrato Frequency = 7   Direct Stick Mix = 1   Volume = 128
- ○ Modal presets = 1 (`.preset` arguments)
  - – Marimba = 0   Vibraphone = 1   Agogo = 2
    Wood1 = 3   Reso = 4
  - – Wood2 = 5   Beats = 6   Two Fixed = 7   Clump = 8

- **`BandedWG` extends `StkInstrument`**—Banded waveguide modeling class. For more information, see Essl and Cook, ICMC 1999.
  - ○ `.bowPressure(float)`—Bow pressure [0.0–1.0].
  - ○ `.bowMotion(float)`—Bow motion [0.0–1.0].
  - ○ `.bowRate(float)`—Bow attack rate (sec).
  - ○ `.strikePosition(float)`—Strike position [0.0–1.0].
  - ○ `.integrationConstant(float)`—A cool non-physical parameter [0.0–1.0].
  - ○ `.modesGain(float)`—Amplitude for modes [0.0–1.0].
  - ○ `.preset(int)`—Instrument presets (0–3, see Control change below).
  - ○ `.pluck(float, WRITE only)`—Pluck instrument [0.0–1.0].
  - ○ `.startBowing(float, WRITE only)`—Start bowing [0.0–1.0].
  - ○ `.stopBowing(float, WRITE only)`—Stop bowing [0.0–1.0].
  - ○ Inherited from `StkInstrument`: `.noteOn`, `.noteOff`, `.freq`, `.controlChange`.
  - ○ Control change numbers:
    - – Bow Pressure = 2   Bow Motion = 4   Strike Position = 8
      (not implemented)
    - – Vibrato Frequency = 11   Gain = 1   Bow Velocity = 128
    - – Set Striking = 64

- Instrument Presets = 16
  - Uniform Bar = 0   Tuned Bar = 1   Glass Harmonica = 2
  - Tibetan Bowl = 3

- `Moog` extends `StkInstrument`—STK analog swept filter synthesis class. Uses one attack wave, one looped wave, and an `ADSR` envelope and adds two sweepable formant (`FormSwep`) filters.
  - `.filterQ(float)`—Filter Q value [0.0–1.0].
  - `.filterSweepRate(float)`—Filter sweep rate [0.0–1.0].
  - `.vibratoFreq(float)`—Vibrato frequency (Hz).
  - `.vibratoGain(float)`—Vibrato gain [0.0–1.0].
  - `.afterTouch(float, WRITE only)`—Aftertouch [0.0–1.0].
  - Inherited from `StkInstrument`: `.noteOn`, `.noteOff`, `.freq`, `.controlChange`.
  - Control change numbers:
    - Filter Q = 2   Filter Sweep Rate = 4   Vibrato Frequency = 11
    - Vibrato Gain = 1   Gain = 128

- `Shakers` extends `StkInstrument`—PhISEM and PhOLIES (particle models) class. PhISEM (Physically Informed Stochastic Event Modeling) is a statistical algorithmic approach for simulating collisions of multiple independent sound producing objects. This class is a meta-model that can simulate a maraca, sekere, cabasa, bamboo wind chimes, water drops, tambourine, sleigh bells, and a guiro. PhOLIES (Physically-Oriented Library of Imitated Environmental Sounds) is a similar approach for the synthesis of environmental sounds. This class implements simulations of breaking sticks, crunchy snow (or not), a wrench, sandpaper, and more.
  - `.preset(int)`—Select instrument (0–22; see below).
  - `.energy(float)`—Shake energy [0.0–1.0].
  - `.decay(float)`—System decay [0.0–1.0].
  - `.objects(float)`—Number of objects [0.0–128.0].
  - Inherited from `StkInstrument`: `.noteOn`, `.noteOff`, `.freq`, `.controlChange`.
  - Control change numbers:
    - Shake Energy = 2   System Decay = 4   Number Of Objects = 11
    - Resonance Frequency = 1 Shake Energy = 128
  - Instrument selection = 1071
    - Maraca = 0   Cabasa = 1   Sekere = 2
    - Guiro = 3   Water Drops = 4   Bamboo Chimes = 5
    - Tambourine = 6   Sleigh Bells = 7   Sticks = 8
    - Crunch = 9   Wrench = 10   Sand Paper = 11
    - Coke Can = 12   Next Mug = 13   Penny + Mug = 14
    - Nickle + Mug = 15   Dime + Mug = 16   Quarter + Mug = 17

- Franc + Mug = 18   Peso + Mug = 19   Big Rocks = 20
- Little Rocks = 21   Tuned Bamboo Chimes = 22

- FM extends `StkInstrument`—STK abstract FM synthesis base class. This class controls an arbitrary number (usually four) of waves and envelopes, determined via a constructor argument.
    - `.lfoSpeed(float)`—Modulation Speed (Hz).
    - `.lfoDepth(float)`—Modulation Depth [0.0–1.0].
    - `.afterTouch(float)`—Aftertouch [0.0–1.0].
    - `.controlOne(float)`—Control one [instrument specific].
    - `.controlTwo(float)`—Control two [instrument specific].
    - Inherited from `StkInstrument`—`.noteOn`, `.noteOff`, `.freq`, `.controlChange`
    - Control change numbers:
        - Control One = 2   Control Two = 4   LFO Speed = 11
        - LFO Depth = 1   ADSR 2 & 4 Target = 128

- BeeThree extends `FM`—STK Hammond-oid organ FM synthesis instrument. This class implements a simple four-operator topology, also referred to as algorithm 8 (simple additive) of the TX81Z.
    - Control parameters: See super classes
    - Control change numbers:
        - Operator 4 (feedback) Gain = 2 (`.controlOne`)
        - Operator 3 Gain = 4 (`.controlTwo`)
        - LFO Speed = 11   LFO Depth = 1   ADSR 2 & 4 Target = 128

- HevyMetl extends `FM`—STK heavy metal FM synthesis instrument. This class implements three cascade operators with feedback modulation, also referred to as algorithm 3 of the TX81Z.
    - Control parameters: See super classes
    - Control change numbers:
        - Total Modulator Index = 2 (`.controlOne`)
        - Modulator Crossfade = 4 (`.controlTwo`)
        - LFO Speed = 11   LFO Depth = 1   ADSR 2 & 4 Target = 128

- PercFlut extends `FM`—STK percussive flute FM synthesis instrument. This class implements algorithm 4 of the TX81Z.
    - Control parameters: See super classes
    - Control change numbers:
        - Total Modulator Index = 2 (`.controlOne`)
        - Modulator Crossfade = 4 (`.controlTwo`)
        - LFO Speed = 11   LFO Depth = 1   ADSR 2 & 4 Target = 128

- Rhodey extends FM—STK Fender Rhodes-like FM electric piano. This class implements two simple FM pairs summed together, also referred to as algorithm 5 of the TX81Z.
  - Control parameters: See super classes
  - Control change numbers:
    - Modulator Index One = 2 (.controlOne)
    - Crossfade of Outputs = 4 (.controlTwo)
    - LFO Speed = 11   LFO Depth = 1   ADSR 2 & 4 Target = 128

- TubeBell extends FM—STK FM synthesis tubular bell (orchestral chime) FM. This class implements two simple FM pairs summed together, also referred to as algorithm 5 of the TX81Z.
  - Control parameters: See super classes
  - Control change numbers:
    - Modulator Index One = 2 (.controlOne)
    - Crossfade of Outputs = 4 (.controlTwo)
    - LFO Speed = 11   LFO Depth = 1   ADSR 2 & 4 Target = 128

- Wurley extends FM—STK FM Wurlitzer electric piano synthesis. This class implements two simple FM pairs summed together, also referred to as algorithm 5 of the TX81Z.
  - Control parameters: See super classes
  - Control change numbers:
    - Modulator Index One = 2 (.controlOne)
    - Crossfade of Outputs = 4 (.controlTwo)
    - LFO Speed = 11   LFO Depth = 1   ADSR 2 & 4 Target = 128

- FMVoices extends FM—STK singing FM synthesis instrument. This class implements three carriers sharing a common modulator, also referred to as algorithm 6 of the TX81Z.
  - Control parameters: See super classes, plus
  - .vowel(float, WRITE only)—Select vowel [0.0–1.0].
  - .spectralTilt(float, WRITE only)—Spectral tilt [0.0–1.0].
  - .adsrTarget(float, WRITE only)—ADSR targets [0.0–1.0].
  - Control change numbers:
    - Vowel = 2 (.controlOne)Spectral Tilt = 4 (.controlTwo)
    - LFO Speed = 11   LFO Depth = 1   ADSR 2 & 4 Target = 128

- VoicForm extends StkInstrument—Four formant filter voice synthesis instrument. This instrument contains an excitation singing wavetable (looping wave with random and periodic vibrato, smoothing on frequency, etc.), excitation noise, and four sweepable resonances. Measured formant data presets are included.
  - Control parameters:
    - .phoneme(string)—Select phoneme (see previous).

○ Phoneme names:
- "eee" "ihh" "ehh" "aaa" "ahh" "aww" "ohh" "uhh"
- "uuu" "ooo" "rrr" "lll" "mmm" "nnn" "nng" "ngg"
- "fff" "sss" "thh" "shh" "xxx" "hee" "hoo" "hah"
- "bbb" "ddd" "jjj" "ggg" "vvv" "zzz" "thz" "zhh"
○ .phonemeNum(int)—Select phoneme by number [0.0 - 128.0].
○ .speak(float, WRITE only)—Start singing [0.0–1.0].
○ .quiet(float, WRITE only)—Stop singing [0.0–1.0].
○ .voiced(float)—Set mix for voiced component [0.0–1.0].
○ .unVoiced(float)—Set mix for unvoiced component [0.0–1.0].
○ .pitchSweepRate(float)—Pitch sweep [0.0–1.0].
○ .voiceMix(float)—Voiced/unvoiced mix [0.0–1.0].
○ .vibratoFreq(float)—Vibrato frequency (Hz).
○ .vibratoGain(float)—Vibrato gain [0.0–1.0].
○ .loudness(float)—Loudness of voice [0.0–1.0].
○ Inherited from StkInstrument—.noteOn, .noteOff, .freq, .controlChange
○ Control change numbers:
- Voiced/Unvoiced Mix = 2   Vowel/Phoneme Selection = 4
- Vibrato Frequency = 11   Vibrato Gain = 1
- Loudness (Spectral Tilt) = 128

C.14   *Blit: band-limited oscillator family*

This class generates band-limited waveforms (impulse Train, sawtooth, etc.) using a closed-form algorithm reported by Stilson and Smith in "Alias-Free Digital Synthesis of Classic Analog Waveforms," 1996. The user can specify both the fundamental frequency of the impulse train and the number of harmonics contained in the resulting signal. If .harmonics is 0, then the signal will contain all harmonics up to half the sample rate. Note that this setting may produce aliasing in the signal when the frequency is changing (no automatic modification of the number of harmonics is performed by freq()).

All Blit family oscillators support the following methods:

- .freq(float)—Base frequency (Hz).
- .harmonics(int)—Number of harmonics in pass band.
- .phase(float)—Phase of the signal.

The Blit family of oscillators consists of the following UGens:

- Blit—STK band-limited impulse train.
- BlitSaw—STK band-limited sawtooth wave.
- BlitSquare—STK band-limited square wave.

appendix D
Network communication with Open Sound Control

Open Sound Control (OSC) is a popular network protocol for interconnecting digital media software systems. In ChucK, OSC is used to connect instances of ChucK software running on different computers. This is an easy way to link up different ChucK programs (or multiple copies of the same ChucK program) for collaborative music programming, such as in a laptop orchestra. OSC can also be used to connect ChucK to other audiovisual programming environments, like Processing (processing.org), Max/MSP (cycling74.com), or others.

From a practical level, OSC consists of messages passed from a *client* application to a *server* application. These messages consist of an *address* and zero or more *arguments*, for example:

```
/bass/play 58 1.0
/texture/alpha/amp 0.8
/jam/message "davetronic" "slow tempo to 90 bpm!"
```

Resembling a file path, a valid OSC address is any sequence of alphanumeric components separated by forward slashes and beginning with an initial forward slash. Each argument can be a floating-point number, integer, or string. (There are a few additional argument types, but these three are the most common.) Every message also has a *typetag*, which is a string indicating what the type of each argument is: the character at index n indicates the nth argument's type, where i corresponds to an int, f is float, and s is string. For example, a typetag of siff means the OSC message's arguments are a string, int, float, and float, in that order. Usually, the typetag can be inferred from the arguments, but there are times when you must work with it explicitly.

An OSC server must specify a *port* to listen to, which is simply an integer between 1024 and 65535 (ports below 1024 are possible but are usually reserved for system services and only accessible with administrator privileges on a system). A given port can be listened to by only one server at a time. An OSC client connects to a server by its hostname and port.

You can send messages via the OscOut class. The following code sends the message /bass/play 58 1.0:

```
OscOut oout;
("localhost", 6449) => oout.dest;
oout.start("/bass/play").add(58).add(1.0).send();
```

After declaring an instance of OscOut, you set the hostname and port of the server you wish to connect to. "localhost" corresponds to "this computer;" that is, the machine that the program is running on, and 6449 is a port chosen arbitrarily—whatever it is, this must match the port used by the server you wish to connect with.

.start() begins a message by providing the OSC address, and .add() can be called multiple times to add arguments as desired. .add() accepts any of the aforementioned OSC argument types: float, int, or string. .send() takes the supplied address and any arguments and sends the message to the set destination. .start() and .add() both return the same OscOut object, allowing calls to be chained. Thus, the following code snippets accomplish the same thing:

```
oout.start("/bass/play").add(58).add(1.0).send();
// same as:
oout.start("/bass/play");
oout.add(58);
oout.add(1.0);
oout.send();
```

Some more examples of sending:

```
// send: /texture/alpha/amp 0.8
oout.start("/texture/alpha/amp").add(0.8).send();
// send: /jam/message "davetronic" "slow tempo to 90 bpm!"
oout.start("/jam/message").add("davetronic").add("slow tempo to 90
    bpm!").send();
```

Receiving messages takes a bit more work but is still relatively straightforward. The OscIn class manages starting a server and handling incoming OSC messages. For example, to receive the /bass/play message you sent earlier, you would use the following program:

```
OscIn oin;
6449 => oin.port;
"/bass/play" => oin.addAddress;

OscMsg msg;

while(true)
{
    oin => now;

    while(oin.recv(msg))
    {
```

```
        <<< msg.address, ",", msg.typetag >>>;
        <<< msg.getInt(0), msg.getFloat(1) >>>;
    }
}
```

That's a lot of new code, so let's look at it bit by bit. First, you declare your OscIn object, set the port to listen to (of course, this should match the port used by whatever is sending the message), and set the address of the message you want to listen for by ChucKing it to .addAddress(). You also declare an OscMsg object, which you'll need later.

In the while(true) loop, ChucKing the OscIn to now will wait until a message matching the specified pattern is received. The inner while loop—while (oin.recv(msg))—pulls off any incoming messages, one by one, processing them in the loop's body. The address of the message can be retrieved by getting the .address member of OscMsg, and similarly the typetag is available from .typetag (note that these are member variables rather than functions). You can retrieve the arguments themselves using OscMsg's .getInt(), .getFloat(), and .getString() functions. If the *n*th argument of the OscMsg is an int, then .getInt(n) will contain that value; likewise for float arguments and .getFloat(n), as well as for string arguments and .getString(n). Because you happen to know that /bass/play has two arguments, an int followed by a float, you can easily pull out these values with .getInt(0) and .getFloat(1). From here, you could map the arguments to whichever musical parameters you like.

This is all fine when you know what arguments to expect from the OSC messages, but you must be cleverer when a message might have a variable number of arguments or no arguments:

```
OscIn oin;
6449 => oin.port;
"/bass/play" => oin.addAddress;

OscMsg msg;

while(true)
{
    oin => now;

    while(oin.recv(msg))
    {
        <<< msg.address, ",", msg.typetag >>>;
        for(int n; n < msg.numArgs(); n++)
        {
            if(msg.typetag.charAt(n) == 'i') // integer
                <<< "arg", n, ":", msg.getInt(n) >>>;
            else if(msg.typetag.charAt(n) == 'f') // float
                <<< "arg", n, ":", msg.getFloat(n) >>>;
            else if(msg.typetag.charAt(n) == 's') // string
                <<< "arg", n, ":", msg.getString(n) >>>;
        }
    }
}
```

Here, you iterate through each argument, determining the type of argument *n* from the *n*th character of the typetag; msg.numArgs() returns the number of arguments in the message. Usually you don't want a given message to have arguments of arbitrary number and type, but this technique can be useful for some types of interactions. For example, an additive synthesizer might accept a variable number of amplitudes for the sinusoids it generates, which could be sent over OSC by a sequence of float arguments.

OscIn can also handle messages with different addresses—you might have guessed this, because the function for setting an address is called .addAddress() instead of just "address." Calling .addAddress() multiple times will cause OscIn to listen for messages that have any of the supplied addresses. These messages will come in through .recv() as before, but you need to check the value of each OscMsg's .address member to see the address of an individual message, for example:

```
OscIn oin;
6449 => oin.port;
"/bass/play" => oin.addAddress;
"/texture/alpha/amp" => oin.addAddress;
"/jam/message" => oin.addAddress;

OscMsg msg;

while(true)
{
    oin => now;

    while(oin.recv(msg))
    {
        if(msg.address == "/bass/play")
            { <<< "got bass" >>>; } // do one or more things
        else if(msg.address == "/texture/alpha/amp")
            { <<< "got texture" >>>; } // do another thing
        else if(msg.address == "/jam/message")
            { <<< "got jam" >>>; } // do something else
    }
}
```

Finally, what if you want to receive *all* OSC messages coming in, even if you don't know what address they'll have beforehand? OscIn has you covered with the .listenAll() method. Calling this will cause any incoming message to trigger the OscIn object:

```
OscIn oin;
6449 => oin.port;
oin.listenAll();

OscMsg msg;

while(true)
{
    oin => now;

    while(oin.recv(msg))
    {
```

```
        <<< "got message:", msg.address, msg.typetag >>>;
    }
}
```

In this way, you could process the addresses using ChucK's `string` object utility functions (see appendix B) to route messages with any level of intricacy you can think of.

Using ChucK's `OscOut` and `OscIn` classes, digital artists can create a variety of network interactions, from simple on/off messages to complex OSC server/routers. Armed with these mechanisms, ChucK programs are able to communicate with other media arts software programs, interaction devices, and combinations of these running on multiple networked computers.

appendix E
File I/O

Like all software, ChucK programs often need a way to save data for when they stop running and to reload that data when they resume running. They also need a way to read data generated by other programs or written manually by a human and to output data that can be used by another program or examined by a human. If you think this sounds like a good use for files, then you're correct. Files are the backbone of any complex software ecosystem, and naturally ChucK provides several easy-to-use mechanisms to work with them.

E.1   File basics

The FileIO class is ChucK's primary mechanism for interacting with files, providing a number of standard mechanisms for file input and output. Each instance of FileIO corresponds to a single file on disk that you can read and/or write to. Again, the venerable ChucK operator is overloaded to provide the main functionality for reading and writing to files, though we also need to introduce a new variant, the *backchuck* operator, which looks like this: <=. In the next sections, we'll cover opening and writing files and then opening and reading files. We'll then cover options for opening files (data types, restrictions, and so on), and then we'll investigate nonsequential (jumping around) file access.

E.1.1   Opening and writing files

To read from or write to a file, you must first open it. Start by creating a FileIO object and then calling the .open() function on it, supplying a file path and some options:

```
FileIO file;
file.open("thefile.txt", FileIO.WRITE);
```

The first argument to the .open() function is the path of the file you want to open. This can be simply a single filename or a file path encompassing one or more directories, for example, path/to/directory/file.txt. In the miniAudicle, the default path can be found or changed under Preferences > Miscellaneous > Current Directory. In command-line ChucK, the current path is the location where ChucK is run. You can also create file paths relative to your ChucK script by using me.dir, as in me.dir() + "thefile.txt" (see chapter 4 and appendix B for more on me.dir).

The second argument provides options for opening the file, such as whether you want to read from or write to the file and whether to treat the file as ASCII text or binary data (more on that later). For now you only need to worry about FileIO.WRITE, which will open an ASCII-text file for writing, creating the file if necessary.

Opening a file with FileIO.WRITE will create the file if it doesn't already exist and will also *truncate* the file, which means if the file already exists, any data in it will be erased. If any errors occur in opening the file, .open() will return false; otherwise it will return true. It's usually a good idea to check the return value of .open(), printing an error message if the operation fails.

You can write data to the file using the backchuck operator, <=. A value or variable of any basic type can be backchucked to an open file, and it will be written to that file.

```
file <= 60; // write number '60' as ASCII characters to file
file <= " is a number"; // write string
file <= IO.newline(); // write newline
file <= "so is " <= 33.47 <= IO.nl(); // backchuck chain
```

The resulting text file will have the following contents:

```
60 is a number
so is 261.63
```

As shown here, backchuck operations can be chained in sequence to write multiple items in the same line; this is functionally the same as backchucking each item individually but can provide logical and aesthetic structure to your code. The previous code also backchucks IO.newline() to the file, which adds the character or character sequence representing a new line, typically \n on Mac OS X and Linux and \r\n on Windows. ChucK programs theoretically may be run on any of these OSes, so using IO.newline() or its abbreviated variant, IO.nl(), saves the programmer from having to be concerned as to which newline convention the underlying system actually uses.

Once you've finished writing to the file, you need to close it. This is achieved by the aptly named .close() function. Attempts to write to the file after calling .close() will fail:

```
file.close();
```

E.1.2 Reading files

Reading from a file is similarly straightforward. First, you open the file, indicating that you'd like to read it:

```
file.open("readfile.txt", FileIO.READ);
```

This function will fail (and return false) if the specified file doesn't exist. Once the file is open, reading can proceed via the standard ChucK operator.

```
file => int i; // read an int
file => string s; // read a string
file => float f; // read a float
```

ChucKing the file object to a variable reads a value of that type from the file and stores the value in the variable. Values are read in linear order from the file, from first to last, until the end of the file is reached. Each read operation takes the next value, keeping track of which values have already been read. Within the file itself, values must be separated from each other, or delimited, by one or more whitespace characters: a single space, a new line, or a tab.

For example, consider the following file, fib.txt:

```
0 1 1 2
3 5 8 13
```

And consider the following program, reading this file:

```
FileIO file;
file.open("fib.txt", FileIO.READ);
while(true)
{
    file => int val;
    if(file.eof()) break;
    <<< "next val:", val >>>;
}
```

This program will produce the following output:

```
next val: 0
next val: 1
next val: 1
next val: 2
next val: 3
next val: 5
next val: 8
next val: 13
```

This program also introduces another file function, .eof(). This function, whose name is an abbreviation of *end of file*, returns true if you've reached the end of the file and there's no more data to read and returns false if more data is available. There is one catch: .eof() only returns true *after* you try to read from the file and there's no more data left. That's why the previous program calls .eof() after each read from file; the last read operation before the eof condition returns an invalid value, having reached the end of the file.

A companion function to .eof() is .more(), which returns the answer to the question, is there more data left? .more() always returns the negation of .eof(), so you can use either in your programs. Here you assume a successfully opened file of integers:

```
while(!file.eof()) file => int val; // read file until end
```

```
while(file.more()) file => int val; // same thing
```

And this structure works as well:

```
while(file => int val)
{
    <<< "next val:", val >>>;
}
```

Often you'd like to read files one line at a time, because many file formats use new-lines as a delimiter for individual data items. You can't use the ChucK operator to do this, but there is a function to help you out, .readLine(). This program prints out each individual line from a file; if you wanted to, you could do further processing on each line:

```
FileIO file;
file.open("lines.txt", FileIO.READ);
while(true)
{
    file.readLine() => string line;
    if(file.eof()) break;
    <<< "next line:", line >>>;
}
```

E.1.3   *Options for opening files*

A few additional functions round out ChucK's file I/O system. First, let's take a closer look at the .open() function. As mentioned previously, this function takes two arguments: a file path and a set of options for opening the file. Besides FileIO.READ and FileIO.WRITE, there are a few additional options you can supply here. You can open a file for both reading and writing by combining these two options:

```
file.open("rwFile.txt", FileIO.READ | FileIO.WRITE); // read + write
```

The binary OR operator, |, can be used to combine different options, though not every combination of options will be valid (you'll see which ones are invalid shortly). There's an option, FileIO.READ_WRITE, that achieves the same thing as the previous code; using either a combination of FileIO.READ | FileIO.WRITE or FileIO .READ_WRITE will produce the same results:

```
file.open("rwFile.txt", FileIO.READ | FileIO.WRITE); // read + write
file.open("rwFile.txt", FileIO.READ_WRITE); // same thing
```

Unlike FileIO.WRITE, opening a file for both reading and writing will *not* truncate the file, so you can safely read existing data while writing new data. Writing to that opened file will overwrite data already in that file, however, starting at the beginning (or other location, if .seek is used; see section E.1.4).

With FileIO.APPEND you can open a file for *appending*, which means write operations will be added at the end of the file. This can be used, for example, to log data to a single file over several runs of a program, while preserving the history of data over these runs:

```
file.open("log.txt", FileIO.APPEND); // open for appending
file <= "appending: " <= Math.randomf() <= IO.nl();
file.close();
```

`FileIO.APPEND` can't be combined with `FileIO.READ`, `FileIO.WRITE`, or `FileIO` `.READ_WRITE`; attempting to do so will cause `.open()` to return an error. As with `FileIO` `.WRITE`, if the file doesn't already exist, it will be created.

Two more options for opening a file are `FileIO.ASCII` and `FileIO.BINARY`, corresponding to ASCII-mode files and binary-mode files, respectively. The default is ASCII, which basically means you're reading or writing plain text to a file; all of the I/O we've examined so far in this appendix has been ASCII mode. In binary mode, values are written exactly as they're encoded in memory, which uses your hard disk more efficiently but is usually harder to work with. It's often better to use text files for the relatively small quantities of data dealt with in ChucK, and for this reason we won't spend much time looking at binary files. Suffice it to say that you can combine `FileIO.ASCII` and `FileIO.BINARY` with any of the previous options, but they can't be combined with each other, being mutually exclusive:

```
file.open("ascii.txt", FileIO.WRITE); // default (ASCII-mode)
file.open("ascii2.txt", FileIO.WRITE | FileIO.ASCII); // ASCII-mode
file.open("binary.txt", FileIO.WRITE | FileIO.BINARY); // binary-mode
file.open("binasc.txt", FileIO.WRITE | FileIO.ASCII | FileIO.BINARY); // error!
```

E.1.4   *Non-sequential file access*

So far we've looked at reading to and writing from files sequentially. You can reposition where you read/write in a file using `.seek()`. You can also determine the current position in the file with `.tell()`. Finally, you can determine the total size of the file with `.size()`. Each of these functions deals with byte position in the file, so `.seek(4)` moves the read/write pointer to just after the fourth byte in the file, and `.size()` returns the size in bytes:

```
file.seek(12); // read/write after 12th byte of file
file.seek(0); // go to beginning of file
file <= Math.randomf(); // write to file
<<< file.tell() >>>; // print current file position
file.seek(file.size()); // move to end of file
```

One last function that comes in handy when working with files is `.good()`. This function tells you whether the file is ready for the operation specified when you opened it (reading, writing, and the like). If it returns `true`, the file is ready; if `false`, the open operation failed, and attempting to read or write it will also fail:

```
file.open("aFile.txt", FileIO.WRITE);
if(!file.good()) { <<< "opening file failed" >>>; me.exit(); }
// otherwise, continue using file
```

E.2   *Standard output and error*

ChucK also has two built-in objects that represent special-purpose files. chout provides a way to write to the *ChucK standard output* file, and cherr similarly provides access to the *ChucK standard error* file. Usually, writing to either of these files simply causes the written data to appear on the Console Monitor, though advanced users may be interested to know that chout corresponds to console stdout and cherr corresponds to console stderr.

You can write to these the same way as with any file open for writing:

```
60 => int note;
chout <= "the note is " <= note <= " = " <= Std.mtof(note) <= " Hz" <= IO.nl();
cherr <= "there was no error!" <= IO.nl();
```

This prints

```
the note is 60 = 261.626 Hz
there was no error!
```

You can attempt to read from chout or cherr, but your program will just wait forever, because these files never produce any input. You also can't close or reopen chout or cherr, and seeking doesn't work either, because unlike standard FileIO objects, these files don't normally correspond to actual files on disk. Instead they're like ephemeral, endless streams of data; once you write to chout or cherr, you can't unwrite or change it.

You might ask why we bother with chout and cherr when we already have the <<< >>> operator for printing to the console. chout and cherr behave a lot like regular FileIO objects, so any code that already uses FileIO can easily switch to chout and cherr. Additionally, chout / cherr provide more control over formatting and spacing of console output, such as when to jump to a new line or where spaces are placed. Command line users will appreciate that chout, by virtue of mapping to stdout, can be piped to other command line programs and utilities (see appendix G for more information about using ChucK on the command line).

appendix F
Serial I/O

In times past, serial port communication (the colloquial term for the RS-232 computer interface) enjoyed a wide-ranging prevalence not unlike USB in today's computing world. Formerly used for devices such as mice, dial-up modems, PC–PC networking, and many others, serial I/O is now largely obsolete in the presence of USB. But the basic mechanism of serial I/O, a bidirectional stream of data between two connected computers, has found new life in the realm of physical computing, such as the Arduino platform. In this appendix we'll discuss functions and methods ChucK provides for interacting with serial devices. When necessary, we'll refer to Arduino programs as an example of a serial device that ChucK might be interacting with, although ChucK's serial capabilities extend to any serial hardware.

F.1 Serial I/O reading

To start, we'll assume that you've connected and set up a serial device and are generally familiar with how to connect to it and program for it. If this isn't the case, we recommend checking out the Arduino platform at http://arduino.cc/.

The first step to programming with serial devices in ChucK is to verify that ChucK can find your device. The following code retrieves a list of all serial devices ChucK can communicate with on your system and then prints each item in the list.

```
SerialIO.list() @=> string list[];
for(int i; i < list.size(); i++)
{
    <<< i, ":", list[i] >>>;
}
```

First, you see that there's a new class, SerialIO, whose static .list() function returns a list of available serial devices. The SerialIO class will mediate all of your interactions with serial hardware.

Now, let's open a serial device and read from it. First, let's load up your device with code, which will give you some serial data to read. Assuming you're using

Arduino, open the Graph example (File > Examples > 04.Communication > Graph) and upload it to your device. If you're using a different hardware platform, no problem—this example simply reads an analog pin, writes its value as an ASCII integer, and then writes a newline. Once the program has finished uploading to the Arduino, you can continue.

On the ChucK side, the code should look familiar at this point, with a few new twists:

```
SerialIO cereal;
cereal.open(0, SerialIO.B9600, SerialIO.ASCII);
while(true)
{
    cereal.onLine() => now;
    cereal.getLine() => string line;
    chout <= "line: " <= line;
}
```

Once you run this code, you should see a printout like the following, continuing indefinitely (feel free to remove the shred after a few seconds). Note that the exact number values will vary depending on how your Arduino is configured.

```
line:  276
line:  277
line:  276
```

Take a closer look at this ChucK code. On the first line you create an instance of serial I/O, which you'll use to communicate with a specific serial device. You initiate a connection to this device by calling .open(). The first argument of .open() selects which device to connect with—this refers to the list of devices SerialIO.list() gave you, so it can be any integer between 0 and SerialIO.list().size()-1. Thus, you may need to change it from 0 in the previous code depending on where your Arduino appears in the list. The next argument specifies the baud, which should match the baud used by the serial device, for example, the parameter given to Serial.begin() on the Arduino. The last argument indicates whether to use ASCII (text) mode (SerialIO.ASCII) or binary mode (SerialIO.BINARY). The code proceeds with the venerable while(true) loop, followed by something being chucked to now. Just what is chucked to now is different here. cereal.onLine() => now can be interpreted as "wait until a line of text has been received," where a line is formally a string of text, with any number of characters, ending in a newline character (\n). Once the line has been received, cereal.getLine() will retrieve it. So, your while loop continuously reads lines from the serial device, printing them as they're received.

F.1.1 *Bytes, ints, floats, strings*

The SerialIO class isn't limited to reading lines of text. In ASCII-mode, SerialIO can read ints, floats, and full lines of text. In binary mode, 8-bit bytes, 32-bit ints, and 32-bit floats can be read. Each read type has corresponding .on() and .get() functions, as summarized by the following table.

Table F.1   Functions for reading from SerialIO

.on() function	.get() function	ASCII-mode description	Binary-mode description
.onByte()	.getByte() Returns int in range 0–255	Not available	Single byte
.onBytes(int n)	.getBytes() Returns int[] of length n, each in range 0–255	Not available	Series of n bytes
.onInts(int n)	.getInts() Returns int[] of length n	Series of n ASCII- formatted ints	Series of n 32-bit ints
.onFloats(int n)	.getFloats() Returns float[] of length n	Series of n ASCII- formatted floats	Series of n 32-bit floats
.onLine()	.getLine() Returns string	Series of ASCII charac- ters terminated by newline	Not available

As an example, you could modify the previous code to read bytes instead of lines, like this:

```
SerialIO cereal;
cereal.open(0, SerialIO.B9600, SerialIO.BINARY);
while(true)
{
    cereal.onByte() => now;
    cereal.getByte() => int bite;
    chout <= "byte: " <= bite <= IO.nl();
}
```

Note the change to SerialIO.BINARY on the second line; the program won't work without this, because .onByte() is available only in binary mode. If you still have the Graph program running on your Arduino, the output should look something like the following (as before, the exact values may vary):

```
byte:   50
byte:   50
byte:   54
byte:   13
byte:   10
byte:   50
byte:   50
byte:   54
byte:   13
byte:   10
```

Each byte in this case corresponds to an ASCII character; for example, 50 = '2', 54 = '6', 13 = '\r', the carriage return character, and 10 = '\n', the newline character.

Furthermore, reads from a serial device can be chained, in case you want to read more than one item at a time. This is accomplished by adding more .on() function calls to the end of the initial .on() function call and ensuring there are a matching number of .get()s. You can even mix and match different types, as long as you stick to purely ASCII types or purely binary types.

```
SerialIO cereal;
cereal.open(0, SerialIO.B9600, SerialIO.BINARY);
while(true)
{
    // read 1 byte, 1 int, and then 2 more bytes
    cereal.onByte().onInts(1).onBytes(2) => now;
    cereal.getByte() => int firstByte;
    cereal.getInts() @=> int theInts[];
    cereal.getBytes() @=> int moreBytes[];
    <<< "first byte:", firstByte, "int:", theInts[0], "more bytes:",
      moreBytes[0], moreBytes[1] >>>;
}
```

F.2   *Serial I/O writing*

Writing to a serial device in ChucK is almost the same as writing to a file, which is no coincidence. Most OSes treat serial devices just like normal files, and similarly SerialIO is a subclass of IO, as is FileIO. Thus, SerialIO supports most of the same operations that FileIO provides.

Let's look at an example. First, you should load up a different Arduino program. Although you we can write to the serial port freely, the Graph program won't respond to it in any way. Instead, load PhysicalPixel (File > Example > 04.Communication > PhysicalPixel) to your Arduino. This program reads one character of input, turning on the built-in LED if the character is H (HIGH) and turning it off if the character is L (LOW).

The ChucK side of this interaction looks like the following code, which should cause the built-in LED to toggle on or off every second:

```
SerialIO cereal;
cereal.open(0, SerialIO.B9600, SerialIO.ASCII);
// loop forever
while(true)
{
    cereal <= "H"; // turn LED on
    1::second => now; // wait
    cereal <= "L"; // turn LED off
    1::second => now; // wait
}
```

Declaring and opening the SerialIO object proceeds the same as before. This time, in your while loop, you backchuck the string "H" to the SerialIO instance (turning the Arduino's LED on), let that persist for 1 second, and then backchuck "L" to the device (turning the LED off), letting that continue for a second. This is repeated ad infinitum, or until you stop the shred.

Anything you can backchuck to a file can also be backchucked to a `SerialIO` instance. This includes `ints`, `floats`, and `strings`, in either ASCII or binary mode. As with `FileIO`, you can chain sequences of backchucks:

```
cereal <= "the value at position " <= 1 <= " is " <= 0.62 <= IO.nl();
```

Unlike `FileIO`, `SerialIO` has no notion of read-only or write-only modes. You can both read from and write to any `SerialIO` object.

appendix G
ChucK on the
command line

The command line is one of the oldest and most venerated computer UIs. With decades of continued development, the presence of a command-line interface within every major commercial OS is a testament to its power and versatility. ChucK's roots are in the command line; its original release was as a command-line application. In this chapter we'll review command-line usage of ChucK, through the chuck command.

The command line on Mac OS and Windows share enough similarities that we cover them both in this appendix. But we must first cover a few foundational aspects of command-line usage that are unique to either OS, so Windows users should feel free to skip the Mac OS–specific section (G.1), and likewise Mac OS users can pass over the Windows-specific section (G.2). Users of the miniAudicle (appendix A) can ignore all of this.

G.1   Mac OS command-line basics

The command line in Mac OS is accessed by opening the Terminal application. This can be found in the Utilities folder, which is within the Applications folder. When you first open Terminal, a window will open and display the initial *shell prompt*, which might look something like this:

```
My-Computer-Name:~ my-user-name$
```

My-Computer-Name and my-user-name will be whatever your respective computer name and username are. The $ indicates Terminal is ready to accept commands. Command-line prompts vary greatly, and yours might have been customized or inherited from some other user. But some form of prompt appears in Terminal, and you can enter commands followed by pressing the Return key.

Commands are usually run serially, one after another, which means once you run a command, you have to wait until it finishes before running another one. Every time a command finishes and the shell is ready for a new command, it will print the shell prompt again, indicating that it's ready.

Try entering the chuck command. This command is installed by default by the ChucK installer, so assuming you've run that already, you should be ready to go. Type the word chuck (all lowercase) into the Terminal window and then hit Return. It should look something like this:

```
My-Computer-Name:~ my-user-name$ chuck
[chuck]: no input files... (try --help)
My-Computer-Name:~ my-user-name$
```

That's not super exciting; let's give it a program to run. We'll use miniAudicle to create it. Open miniAudicle, and then select File > Open Example. Select otf_06.ck, and then select File > Save As and save the file to your Documents directory. This is important: make sure you save it to precisely the Documents folder and not any subfolder, because you'll have to type in the full name later.

Now, back in Terminal, enter the chuck command again, this time telling it the file you want to run. After typing chuck, type a space and then the filename (Documents/otf_06.ck), and then press Return:

```
My-Computer-Name:~ my-user-name$ chuck Documents/otf_06.ck
```

At this point, you should hear sound coming out—you've successfully run ChucK from the command line! If you don't hear sound, then you might have saved the program to a different folder than Documents, or your Documents directory may have a different name. In either case be sure you're entering the correct filename for the command to work!

Let's go ahead and stop the running program with Ctrl-C: hold the Control key and then hit the C key. This is the universal shell keybinding to terminate the active command, if there is one. Once you start it, chuck will usually continue making sound for as long as you let it, so you need to kill it with Ctrl-C (don't worry, ChucK doesn't mind; it's used to it). After you type Ctrl-C, the sound should stop, and you'll see something like this in the Terminal:

```
^C[chuck]: cleaning up...
My-Computer-Name:~ my-user-name$
```

For those who are completely new to the command line, we'll take a minute to break down what has happened. You entered the chuck command, followed by a space, followed by the name of the file you want to run. This second part, the filename, is an *argument* to the chuck command. Similar to how functions in ChucK code have arguments, shell commands can also have arguments. But unlike ChucK code, you can usually have as many or as few shell arguments as you want, in any order, and the command can figure it out. The only requirement is that each argument has to have a space in between it and the next one. Finally, when you've finished listening to the results of your chuck command, you shut it down with Ctrl-C.

With all of that in mind, let's try an experiment. By the way, the shell prompt hereafter will be abbreviated to just $, for clarity.

```
$ chuck Documents/otf_06.ck Documents/otf_06.ck
```

Here you run the same program twice, at the same time, by giving chuck two arguments, each of which is the same file. You could run otf_06.ck six times in parallel the same way, by simply repeating the filename six times, or as many times as you want. Ctrl-C the command when you've finished listening. From now on, you should implicitly do this with every program you run, and we won't explicitly tell you to for brevity's sake.

Running the same program in parallel is fun, but you can do better. Let's run two different example programs at the same time. Open the otf_05.ck example in mini-Audicle and save it to your Documents directory as before. But before running both programs at once, you can make your life slightly easier by entering this command:

```
$ cd Documents
```

Remember, you only type the part that comes after the shell prompt $, and then hit Return. The cd command stands for *change directory*, which means it puts you in the directory specified in its (single) argument. Here you're putting your shell session into the Documents directory. We'll talk more on that later. For now, run your next chuck command:

```
$ chuck otf_05.ck otf_06.ck
```

This should play both programs simultaneously: bass plops and high-pitched plops. Cool!

So far you've learned the basics of ChucK on the command line. Before we move on, let's return to that cd command. Every shell session has a notion of a *current working directory*, and the cd command allows you to change it. Typically if you are dealing with files in a particular directory, you'll want to make that the current directory so you don't have to type long path names every time, as you did with the Documents directory. If you want to go with a directory within another directory, you can use cd multiple times to jump there, or you can type out the full path in one go, for example:

```
$ cd "Documents/My ChucK Programs/project1"
```

This will take you to the project1 directory, which is contained in the My ChucK Programs directory, which is within Documents. cd will fail if any of these directories don't exist.

Also note that the entire path is surrounded by double quotes. On the command line, a space is almost always used to separate individual arguments. So if there are spaces within a single argument, you need a way to indicate that the space is part of the argument and not a separator between arguments. Surrounding the entire argument in double quotes is just the way. You can also use single quotes, for example, `'Documents/My ChucK Programs/project1'`, which accomplishes the same thing. The minor differences in how the shell interprets double quotes compared to single quotes aren't important for our purposes.

There are two special incantations of cd that are frequently useful. cd with no arguments changes the working directory to your home directory, and cd .. (with two periods as the argument) takes you up one directory, to whatever folder encloses your current directory.

Two more commands will come in handy as you hop around the command line. ls lists the contents of the current directory, and pwd prints the full path of your current directory in case you're unsure. For example, assuming you're still in the Documents directory from the previous section, you'll see this:

```
$ ls
otf_05.ck otf_06.ck
$ pwd
/Users/your-user-name/Documents
```

There are thousands more common commands available in the command line, and entire books have been written about just those. Fortunately, knowing these basic Terminal commands is enough to make your command-line ChucK sessions a lot easier to work with.

G.2   *The command line on Windows*

To start, open the command prompt. On Windows 7 and earlier, click the Start button > All Programs > Accessories > Command Prompt. On Windows 8, you can open a command prompt by moving the mouse to the upper-right corner, selecting Search, ensuring that Apps is the selected category, typing Command into the search box, and selecting Command Prompt from the search results.

When the command prompt opens, you should see a black window open with text that looks similar to (but probably not exactly like) this:

```
Microsoft Windows [Version 6.1.7601]
Copyright (c) 2009 Microsoft Corporation. All rights reserved.

C:\Users\Username>
```

The first two lines are system information. On the last line, the current directory is printed, followed by the > character, which is called the shell prompt. The current directory is the directory from which relative path names are interpreted, so if you type myChuckProgram.ck, it will refer to the file C:\Documents and Settings\Username \myChuckProgram.ck in this case. The shell prompt indicates that the command line is ready for you to enter commands. When we show text from the command prompt, you should enter only the part that comes *after* the > prompt (sometimes we may only show the command prompt, for brevity).

Start by running the chuck command, which should have been installed when you ran the ChucK installer. Type the word chuck (all lowercase) and then hit Enter. You should see the following:

```
C:\Users\Username>chuck
[chuck]: no input files... (try --help)

C:\Users\Username>
```

This isn't very interesting—let's try running some actual code. Open miniAudicle, select Open Example, and then choose otf_06.ck from the examples browser. Then select Save As and save the file to the current directory in the command prompt (in our case, C:\Documents and Settings\Username). Now that you have a source code file in your current directory, you can run it like so:

```
>chuck otf_06.ck
```

Here, you supply the chuck command with an *argument*. Similar to function arguments, command-line arguments are parameters or input data that are given to the command for processing. Here you're passing only a single filename, but you could specify any number of filenames to run, or a command-line *flag*, which tells chuck how to run rather than what to run (you'll see some concrete examples of this later).

When you run this command, you should hear the sound of reverberating sine plops; if not, you should make sure your computer volume is high enough and that there aren't any other issues with sound output. Also, if you didn't save the file to the correct directory, or the file's name is something other than otf_06.ck (all lowercase), then this command probably won't work.

The chuck command will keep running until the program finishes or until you stop it manually. otf_06.ck runs indefinitely, but you can terminate it by entering Ctrl-C into the command prompt. If you're not familiar with this key sequence, just hold the Control key on your keyboard, then press C, and then release both keys. Ctrl-C kills whichever program is currently running on the command prompt. This may sound mean to constantly do to chuck, but starting, stopping, and restarting chuck, while editing your code in between, is the essence of command-line ChucKing.

After you terminate chuck, it should print a brief exit message and then return you to the shell prompt, indicating that the shell is ready for another command:

```
C:\Users\Username>chuck otf_06.ck
[chuck]: cleaning up...

C:\Users\Username>
```

Now enter your next command. This one runs otf_06.ck two times, in parallel:

```
>chuck otf_06.ck otf_06.ck
```

You should hear two sets of sine plops running. You could run otf_06.ck any number of times, in parallel, simply by specifying that many times to the chuck command. Ctrl-C out of chuck when finished listening. You can run two or more different programs simultaneously, simply by specifying whichever programs you want to run as arguments to chuck.

Now, let's run two different programs. In miniAudicle, open the otf_05.ck example and save it to the same directory as you did otf_06.ck. To run them both in parallel, you need to enter only

```
>chuck otf_05.ck otf_06.ck
```

You should now hear two different programs running, one with low-pitched sine plops and the other with higher-pitched plops.

There are a few additional commands that are useful when working on the Windows command prompt. We previously discussed the notion of a *current directory*; this is a directory by which all relative paths are interpreted, allowing you to enter otf_06.ck instead of the full path (for example, C:\Documents and Settings\Administrator\ otf_06.ck). You can see what files are in the current directory using the dir command; dir will print out the name of every file in the current directory.

You can also change the current directory using cd. You need to provide an argument to tell cd which directory you want to change to:

```
C:\Users\Username>cd "My Documents"

C:\Users\Username\My Documents>cd C:\

C:\>
```

Your prompt moves first to the My Documents directory and then the C:\ (root) directory, and the text leading up to the shell changes to match at each step. Notice that we enclosed the entire My Documents argument in double quotes. In the command line, spaces are normally used to separate distinct arguments, but My Documents is a single argument that happens to have a space within it. To distinguish spaces within an argument and spaces separating two arguments, you must enclose any arguments with spaces in them between double-quote characters. C:\ has no spaces in it, so you don't have to use double quotes when you pass it as an argument.

There's one special version of cd that comes in handy often. cd .. will change to whichever directory encloses the current directory, for example:

```
C:\Users\Username>cd ..

C:\Users>
```

There are many more cool commands and functions you can use on the command line, but these should be enough to get you to the interesting stuff—on-the-fly (OTF) programming in ChucK!

G.3   *On-the-fly programming*

On-the-fly programming is one of the most powerful features of ChucK, and command-line chuck has all of the OTF features of miniAudicle and even a few more. All of these features existed in chuck before miniAudicle was ever created. To begin, start chuck with the --loop argument. Windows users: here we use $ to represent the shell prompt. Which character specifically isn't important; you can just pretend it's a >.

```
$ chuck --loop
```

--loop is a command-line *option* or *flag*. It's a special argument that, instead of telling chuck what program to run, tells it how it should run, what mode of operation it should use, or some other parameter. In this case, --loop tells chuck to keep operating continuously, even if it has no files to run. This is step 1 to on-the-fly programming on the command line.

Next, open a new Terminal or command-prompt window. You need a new window because chuck --loop is going to monopolize the entire first window as it continuously processes the OTF commands you send to it. In the new Terminal window, cd to the directory where you previously saved the otf_05 and otf_06 examples. Now execute this command:

```
$ chuck + otf_05.ck otf_06.ck
```

Note the + argument that comes before the filenames; this tells chuck to add the files to the local VM, which is the chuck --loop instance you ran in the other window. This is more or less the same as clicking the Add Shred button in miniAudicle. You should also see in the other window a status message indicating that the shreds were added:

```
[chuck](VM): sporking incoming shred: 1 (otf_05.ck)...
[chuck](VM): sporking incoming shred: 2 (otf_06.ck)...
```

To stop these from running, instead of using Ctrl-C, go back to the second Terminal window and enter this command:

```
$ chuck --clear.vm
```

This OTF command removes all of the shreds from the local VM and clears public classes, the exact analogue of Clear VM in miniAudicle. Suppose now that you add just otf_06.ck:

```
$ chuck + otf_06.ck
```

Check the text that gets printed out in the --loop window, specifically the shred number, which is the number right before the filename (it will probably be 1 in this case, but it could be anything). This shred number will become important for later commands.

```
[chuck](VM): sporking incoming shred: 1 (otf_06.ck)...
```

Now, make some changes to otf_06.ck. For example, you could change the SinOsc to a SawOsc or change the root note (the number 69 on line 35 of the program) to a different pitch. Once you've finished, you can use the replace command from the command line:

```
$ chuck = 1 otf_06.ck
```

The = removes the shred with the specified ID and replaces it with the file you provide. The 1 corresponds to the shred number from earlier; if the shred number is different, you'll want to put whatever it is instead of 1.

Finally, if you want to stop the shred entirely without replacing, the – (remove) command is available:

```
$ chuck - 1
```

Again, you'll want to substitute 1 with whatever shred ID was printed by the VM instance when the program was first added.

There are a few more OTF programming directives that come in handy on the command line. -- invokes remove-last, removing whichever shred was most recently sporked:

```
$ chuck --
```

```
[chuck](VM): removing recent shred: 2 (otf_06.ck)...
```

The --status command causes the local VM to print out status information about running time and currently active shreds. The ^ (caret character) can also be used as shorthand for --status:

```
$ chuck --status
$ chuck ^
```

The status information is printed out in whichever window the VM is running in, looking something like this:

```
[chuck](VM): status (now == 0h3m40s, 9729280.0 samps) ...
    [shred id]: 1 [source]: otf_05.ck [spork time]: 11.46s ago
    [shred id]: 2 [source]: otf_06.ck [spork time]: 11.46s ago
```

As you can see, this is the command line's version of miniAudicle's Virtual Machine monitor. --time is similar but just prints out the running time of the VM:

```
$ chuck --time
```

```
[chuck](VM): the values of now:
  now = 18350080.000000 (samp)
      = 416.101587 (second)
      = 6.935026 (minute)
      = 0.115584 (hour)
      = 0.004816 (day)
      = 0.000688 (week)
```

Lastly, --kill stops the VM remotely when you want to shut the entire VM down:

```
$ chuck --kill
```

```
[chuck](VM): KILL received....
```

Ctrl-C also works to shut the VM down—just make sure you enter Ctrl-C into the window the chuck --loop command is running in.

G.4   ChucK command-line reference

This section covers options that you can use when invoking chuck from the command line. Typing and entering

```
$   chuck -h
```

will list all of the command-line options available:

```
chuck --[options|commands] [+-=^] [file1 [file2 [file3 [...]]]]
[options] = version|halt|loop|audio|silent|dump|nodump|server|about|probe|
      channels:|out:|in:|dac:|adc:|srate:|bufsize:|bufnum:|
      shell|empty|remote:|port:|verbose:|level:|blocking|callback| adaptive:|
      deprecate:{stop|warn|ignore}|chugin-load:{auto|off}|chugin-
      path:|chugin:|--caution-to-the-wind
[commands] = add|remove|replace|remove.all|status|time|kill|clear.vm
[+-=^] = shortcuts for add, remove, replace, status
```

G.4.1 Source ChucK files

ChucK can run one or more processes in parallel and interactively. The programmer only needs to specify them all on the command line, and they'll be compiled and run in the VM. Each input source file (.ck suffix by convention) will be run as a separate shred (user-level ChucK threads) in the VM. Shreds can spork additional shreds and interact with existing shreds. Thanks to the ChucK timing mechanism, shreds don't necessarily need to know about each other in order to be precisely shreduled in time; they only need to keep track of their own time, so to speak. Additionally, more shreds can be added/removed/replaced manually at runtime, using OTF programming.

G.4.2 Basic command-line ChucK options

- --version—Prints version information and then exits.
- --probe—Probes the system for all audio devices and MIDI devices and prints them.
- --about/--help—Prints the usage message, with the ChucK URL.
- --verbose:(N)/-v(N)—Sets the reporting level to (N), from 0–10; 0 is none, 10 is all, default is 1. Sets higher levels to see more information and warnings regarding ChucK's internal operation.
- --halt/-t (Default)—Tells the VM to halt and exit if there are no more shreds in the VM.
- --loop/-l—Tells the ChucK VM to continue executing even if there are no shreds currently in the VM. This is useful because shreds can be added later on the fly. It's legal to specify this option without any input files, for example: $ chuck --loop will infinite time-loop the VM, waiting for incoming shreds.

G.4.3 Audio options

- --audio/-a (Enabled by default)—Uses real-time audio output.
- --silent/-s—Disables real-time audio output. Computations in the VM aren't changed, except that the actual timing is no longer clocked in real time and there's no live sound output. Timing manipulations (such as operations on now) still function fully. This is useful for synthesizing audio to disk or network. Also, it's handy for running a non-audio program.
- --srate:(N)—Sets the internal sample rate to (N) Hz. By default, ChucK runs at 44100 Hz on OS X and Windows and 48000 Hz on Linux. Even if the VM is

running in --silent mode, the sample rate is still used by some unit generators to compute audio, which is important for computing samples and writing to a file. Not all sample rates are supported by all devices!

- --bufsize:(N)—Sets the internal audio buffer size to (N) sample frames. Larger buffer size often reduces audio artifacts due to system/program timing. Smaller buffers reduce audio latency. The default is 512. If (N) is not a power of 2, the next power of 2 larger than (N) is used. For example, $ chuck --bufsize:950 sets the buffer size to 1024.

- --adaptive:(N) (For power users. Default: 0)—Enables adaptive block processing with a block size of (N). This option can greatly speed up your ChucK programs, but feedback loops in your UGen graph won't work unless they're delayed by (N) or more samples. As with --bufsize, (N) must be a power of 2 or is rounded to the next larger power of 2. The adaptive block size should generally not be larger than the bufsize.

- --dac:(N)—Opens audio output device #(N) for real-time audio. By default, (N) is 0.

- --adc:(N)—Opens audio input device #(N) for real-time audio input. By default, (N) is 0.

- --channels:(N)/-c(N)—Opens (N) number of input and output channels on the audio device. By default, (N) is 2.

- --in:(N)/-i(N)—Opens (N) number of input channels on the audio device. By default (N) is 2.

- --out:(N)/-o(N)—Opens (N) number of output channels on the audio device. By default (N) is 2.

G.4.4   *Network options*

- --remote:(hostname)/-@hostname)—Sets the hostname to connect to if accompanied by the OTF programming commands. (hostname) can be the name or IP address of the host. The default value is 127.0.0.1 (localhost).

- --port:(N)/-p(N)—Sets the port to use for sending or receiving OTF programming commands.

G.4.5   *ChuGin options*

- --chugin-load:{auto|off} (Default: auto)—Indicates whether to automatically load ChuGins (auto) or disable ChuGin loading entirely (off).

- --chugin-path:(path)/-G(path)—Adds (path) to the list of paths searched for ChuGin to load. Any .ck files in the ChuGin path are also loaded and executed when chuck is run. By default, on Mac OS X the paths consist of /usr/lib/chuck and /Library/Application Support/ChucK/ChuGins. On Windows the only default path is C:\Program Files\ChucK\chugins. On Linux, the only path in the default list is /usr/lib/chuck.

- `--chugin:(path)/-g(path)`—Loads the ChuGin at file (path). This may be used to specify additional ChuGins to load that are not in the ChuGin path discussed previously.

G.4.6   *Advanced options*

- `--deprecate:{stop|warn|ignore}` (Default: `warn`)—Indicates how to handle deprecated classes, UGens, and functions. `Stop` will cause a program to not compile if it uses any deprecated features. `Warn` will issue a warning. `Ignore` will cause the program to compile normally without complaint. For example, $ `chuck --deprecate:stop file.ck` will cause `chuck` to stop compilation if file.ck uses any deprecated features.

- `--dump/+d`—Dumps the virtual instructions emitted to `stderr`, for all the files after this flag on the command line, until a `nodump` is encountered (see next option). For example, $ `chuck foo.ck +d bar.ck` will dump the virtual ChucK instructions for bar.ck (only), with argument values, to `stderr`. `--dump` can be used in conjunction with `--nodump` to selectively dump files.

- `--nodump/-d` (Default state)—Ceases the dumping of virtual instructions for files that come after this flag on the command line, until a dump is encountered (see previous option). For example, $ `chuck +d foo.ck -d bar.ck +d doo.ck` will dump foo.ck, then doo.ck, but not bar.ck.

These options are useful for debugging ChucK itself and for other entertainment purposes:

- `--callback`—Utilizes a callback for buffering (default).
- `--blocking`—Utilizes blocking audio I/O (advanced usage, necessary for some audio interfaces).
- `--caution-to-the-wind`—Warning: do not use unless you absolutely positively know what you're doing! Enables the `Std.system` function in the ChucK standard library. An attacker can potentially use this function to run arbitrary malicious software on your computer.
- `--shell` (Advanced usage)—Enables ChucK shell mode. ChucK shell is a shell environment for live coding and OTF programming in ChucK. For more information, see Salazar et al., "miniAudicle and ChucK Shell: New Interfaces for ChucK Development and Performance," in *Proceedings of the International Computer Music Conference*, 2006. http://soundlab.cs.princeton.edu/publications/ miniAudicle_icmc2006.pdf.
- `--empty`—Used in conjunction with `--shell`. Disables creation of a VM environment in the ChucK shell instance to allow for connecting to a remote VM.

appendix H
Extending ChucK

ChucK contains multiple levels of extensibility, each essential and appropriate to specific tasks and levels of user expertise. ChucK's ethos of on-the-fly development creates a desire to design and implement new audio processors in ChucK itself in real-time, working down to the per-sample level if necessary. Implementing these components in ChucK allows their use on any OS ChucK supports with no additional effort from the developer. For these cases we have Chugens and Chubgraphs. On the other hand, real-time performance requirements often mandate the use of compiled native machine code for complex audio-rate processing. There also exists a wealth of C/C++-based software libraries for audio synthesis and effects, such as FluidSynth and Faust. These situations can be handled straightforwardly given portable bindings between ChucK and native compiled code, which is the intent of ChuGins.

> **NOTE** Portions of this appendix have been adapted from S. Salazar, and G. Wang (2012), "Chugens, Chubgraphs, ChuGins: 3 Tiers for Extending ChucK," in *Proceedings of the International Computer Music Conference*, Ljubljana, Slovenia, with permission of the authors.

Chugens

Chugens (pronounced "chyoo-jens") facilitate rapid prototyping of audio synthesis and processing algorithms. Chugens also provide a basic framework for extending ChucK's built-in audio processing functionality. Using the Chugen system, a programmer can implement sample-rate audio algorithms within the ChucK development environment, utilizing the full array of programming facilities provided by ChucK. These processing units can be naturally integrated into standard ChucK programs, even in the same script file, providing seamless control of audio-rate processing, control-rate manipulation, and higher-level compositional organization.

A Chugen is created first by subclassing the built-in Chugen class. This subclass is required to implement a tick function, which accepts a single float argument (the input sample) and returns a single float (the output sample). The tick function is fundamental to a ChucK's audio architecture; to produce a continuous audio stream, ChucK produces 44100 or 48000 samples per second, and each UGen in your program has its own tick function which generates its contribution to the current sample.

The following code uses a Chugen to synthesize a sinusoid using the cosine function, Math.cos.

```
class MyCosine extends Chugen
{
    0 => int p;
    440 => float f;
    second/samp => float SRATE;

    fun float tick(float in)
    {
        return Math.cos(p++*2*pi*f/SRATE);
    }
}
```

Note that a cosine wave is a sine wave that is 90° "behind" (out of phase with) a sine wave—in most cases it will sound exactly like a sine wave.

A Chugen, once defined, may then be integrated into audio graphs like any standard ChucK UGen.

```
MyCosine cos => NRev reverb => dac;
```

Since the tick function is a standard ChucK class member function, it can be as simple or as elaborate as required. Standard library calls, file I/O, multiprocessing (using spork), and other general ChucK programming structures can be integrated into the tick function and supporting code. In the case of an audio synthesizer that does not process an existing signal, the input sample may be ignored. For performance reasons, it's important to consider that the tick function will be called for every sample of audio, so simple tick functions will typically perform better. Moreover, the intrinsic overhead of ChucK's VM architecture will cause Chugens to underperform compared to a native C/C++ implementation.

Since Chugens are only a type of ChucK class, they may define functions to provide structured access to whichever parameters they wish to expose to the programmer.

```
class MyCosine extends Chugen
{
    0 => int p;
    440 => float freq;
    second/samp => float SRATE;

    fun void setFreq(float theFreq)
    {
        theFreq => freq;
    }
```

```
    fun float tick(float in)
    {
        return Math.cos(p++*2*pi*freq/SRATE);
    }
}
```

Here, we have added a `setFreq` function, which allows us to set the frequency of the cosine wave. As a general rule, you should always provide a function to set or get parameters from your Chugens, instead of allowing direct manipulation of member variables within the class. Providing a function to get and set a Chugen parameter indicates which parameters make sense to manipulate, and which ones are only important internally; messing with internal properties of any class is almost always a bad idea.

Lastly, we can make a public Chugen, just like normal classes, using the `public` keyword.

```
public class MyCosine extends Chugen
```

By making a Chugen public, we can use it in other ChucK scripts running in the same virtual machine.

Chubgraphs

Chubgraphs (pronounced "chub-graphs") provide a way to construct new unit generators by composition, arranging multiple existing UGens into a single unit. In this way, common arrangements of existing UGens can be defined and instantiated. Chubgraph parameters can be exposed in a structured manner via class member functions.

A Chubgraph is defined by extending the `Chubgraph` class, which has built-in member variables named `inlet` and `outlet`. `inlet` is a UGen that represents the input signal to the Chubgraph, and `outlet` is the output signal. The Chubgraph's internal audio processing graph is created by spanning a sequence of UGens between `inlet` and `outlet`. The following Chubgraph implements a basic feedback echo processor:

```
class Feedback extends Chubgraph
{
    inlet => Gain dry => outlet;
    dry => Delay delay => outlet;

    delay => Gain feedback => delay;

    0.8 => feedback.gain;
    1::second => delay.delay;
}
```

(Chubgraphs that don't need to process an input signal, such as audio synthesis algorithms, may omit the connection from `inlet`.)

Compared to Chugens, Chubgraphs have significant performance advantages, as audio-rate processing still occurs in the native machine code underlying its component UGens. However Chubgraphs are limited to audio algorithms that can be expressed as combinations of existing UGens. Implementing, for example, intricate mathematical formulae or conditional logic in the form of a UGen graph is possible but fraught with hazard.

Chubgraphs can be included in your audio patch like any other UGen. Like with Chugens, Chubgraphs can be declared as public to be used in other ChucK scripts, and can define member functions to provide control over any parameters that are available.

ChuGins

ChuGins (pronounced "chug-ins") allow near limitless possibilities for expansion of ChucK's capabilities. A ChuGin is a distributable dynamic library, typically written in C or C++ compiled to native machine code, which ChucK can load at runtime. When loaded, the ChuGin defines one or more classes that are then made available to ChucK programs. These classes may define new UGens or provide general programming functionality beyond that built into ChucK. Since these classes are normal ChucK classes implemented with native code, member functions and variables can be used to provide an interface to control parameters.

ChuGins are best suited for audio algorithms that are reasonably well understood and stand to gain from the performance of compiled machine code. The write-compile-run development cycle and C/C++-based programming mandated by ChuGins make implementation of audio processors require more effort than the Chubgraph or Chugen approaches. For UGens you intend to use over an extended period of time, the effort to implement a ChuGin will quickly pay off in the form of lower CPU usage.

An additional advantage of ChuGins is that they may provide functionality far outside the intrinsic capabilities of ChucK. Complex C/C++-based synthesis packages can be imported wholesale into ChucK, opening up an abundance of sonic possibilities. ChuGins have been implemented to bring audio processing programs from the Faust programming language into ChucK, for example. Similarly, the SoundFont renderer FluidSynth has been packaged as a ChuGin. This functionality is not limited to audio processing, as they may also be used to create general purpose programming libraries.

All of this power comes at the cost of ease of use, and as such we do not have enough pages to fully cover the ChuGin development process. We encourage programmers interested in making ChuGins to head to the ChucK extensions website for an online tutorial on ChuGin development: http://chuck.stanford.edu/extend/. The source code for many existing ChuGins can be found at https://github.com/ccrma/chugins.

index

Symbols

; semicolon 67
:: (double colon) 20
&& operator 40
% modulo operator 86–88
++ operator 41
== operator 38
=> (ChucK operator) 19
|| operator 40

A

–about option 295
abs method 241
acos method 243
acoustics, room 132–135
–adaptive option 296
ADC (analog-to-digital
        converter) 71–72
–adc option 296
adc UGen 118, 250
add function 169
add method 245, 272
Add Shred button 23
addAddress method 273
ADSR (attack, decay, sustain,
        release) 123, 256
ADSR Envelope 123–125
.aif files 70, 75
amplitude 14
analog-to-digital converter.
        See ADC
Anvil Studio 221
appending to files 279
Arduino platform 282
args method 246

arpeggiation 200
arrays
    declaring 62–63
    defined 62
    functions for 247
    playing melody from array
        data 64
    reading 63–64
    storing durations in 65–66
    storing strings in 67
asin method 243
atan method 243
atan2 method 243
atof method 242
atoi method 241
attack, decay, sustain, release.
        See ADSR
–audio option 295

B

backchuck operator 276, 286
Bahn, Curtis 6
band pass filter. *See* BPF
band reject filter. *See* BRF
BandedWG 149, 266
beats per minute. *See* BPM
BeeThree 152, 268
begin method 283
BiQuad 259
blackhole UGen 118–119, 250
Blit oscillators 270
–blocking option 297
BlowBotl 143, 262
BlowHole 143, 263
bodySize method 145
BoSSA 6

Bowed 145–147, 264
BPF (band pass filter) 260
BPM (beats per minute) 32
Brass 141–142, 264
BRF (band reject filter) 260
Bristow-Johnson, Robert 91
broadcast function 213
–bufsize option 296

C

Cakewalk 221, 225
–callback option 297
cap method 64
carrier 125
–caution-to-the-wind option
        297
cd command 289
ceil method 244
chan function 250
chan method 57
channels function 250
–channels option 296
charAt method 246
cherr 281
child shreds 163–164
chords 112
Chorus 135, 257
chout 281
Chowning, John 125–126,
        134, 147, 155, 257
Chubgraphs 232, 300–301
ChucK
    advantages of using 4–5
    creating new instruments
        and 5–9
    downloading 233

ChucK *(continued)*
    installing
        on Mac OS X 234–235
        on Ubuntu Linux 238
        on Windows 236–238
    need for programming 2–3
    overview 3–4, 21
ChucK operator (=>) 19
Chugens 232, 298–300
ChuGin 232, 296–297, 301
Clarinet 141, 262
clarinet sound 122–123
classes
    creating custom 181–183
    inheritance
        defined 195
        modeling parents 195–197
        polymorphism 197–198
    initialize.ck file and 188–190
    objects and 178–179
    overloading functions
        183–185
    overview 179–181
    public
        applications for 186–187
        Clear VM button and 187
        private vs. 185–186
        static variables 187–188
clear method 248
Clear VM button 187
command-line usage
    audio options 295–296
    ChuGin options 296–297
    general options 295, 297
    on Mac OS 287–290
    network options 296
    on-the-fly programming
        292–294
    source ChucK files 295
    on Windows 290–292
comments 23
compositional forms
    changing scale pitches
        104–106
    drum machine 107–108
    playing scale 102–104
concurrency
    controlling shared objects
        167–168
    defined 160
    drum machine example
        165–167
    jazz band example
        architecture for running
            concurrent code
            175–176

creating individual players
    171–174
file structure 171
overview 170–171
machine commands
    adding and running files
        169
    controlling composition
        169–170
    overview 161–163
    shreds and 163–165
Console Monitor 17
constants 244
controllerists 1
Cook, Perry xxviii, 4, 6, 91, 134,
        140, 159
Cook/Morrill Trumpet 5
cos method 243
cosh method 243
crash method 245
Csound 4
CurveTable 253
cutoff frequency 131

D

DAC (digital-to-analog
        converter) 71–72
–dac option 296
dac UGen 118, 249
data types
    converting float to int 51–52
    converting string to number
        52–53
    overview 24–29
DAWs (digital audio
        workstations) 3, 219
day keyword 31
dbtopow method 242
dbtorms method 242
debugging 23
Delay 129, 133, 256
delay line 127
DelayA 129, 256
DelayL 129, 256
delays 256–257
–deprecate option 297
digital audio workstations.
        See DAWs
digital signal processing.
        See DSP
DigitalDoo 6
digital-to-analog converter.
        See DAC

dir method 74, 246
DJs 1
done method 246
double colon (::) 20
drum machine
    controlling when drums
        play 85–86
    logic for different drums on
        different beats 83–85
    overview 83, 88
    using classes 190–195
    using concurrency 165–167
    using functions 107–108
DSP (digital signal processing)
        145
–dump option 297
dur type 30–32, 35
duration 65–66
Dyno 136, 260

E

e constant 245
Echo 256
EDholak 6
–empty option 297
encapsulation 178
Envelope 255
    making clarinet sound
        122–123
    making violin sound
        123–125
    overview 121–122
environments 2
eof method 278
erase method 247
ETabla 6
event.signal function 209
events
    gamelan orchestra example
        213
    keyboard input 205–208
    overview 204–205
    shred communication using
        event.signal function 209
    overview 208–209
    synchronizing multiple
        shreds 210–211
    triggering multiple shreds
        using events 212–213
exit method 246
exp method 243
extending chucK
    Chubgraphs 300–301

extending chucK *(continued)*
  Chugens 298–300
  ChuGins 301

F

fabs method 241
factorial, computing 109–110
Fiebrink, Rebecca xx
FileIO class
  non-sequential file access 280
  opening files 276–277, 279–280
  overview 276
  reading files 277–279
  standard error file 281
  standard output file 281
  writing files 276–277
Fillup Glass 6
FilterBasic 260
find method 246
flags, command-line 293
float type 28, 35
  converting string to 52–53
  converting to int 51–52
  random methods 54
  rounding 55–56
floor method 244
Flute 142–143, 262
FM (frequency modulation) 125–126, 268
fmod method 244
FMVoices 155, 269
fractional delay 129–130
FreePiano 224
frequency
  computations using functions
    gradually changing volume 100–101
    granular synthesis 101–102
    overview 97–99
  octaves and 27
frequency modulation. *See* FM
frequency-dependent decay 129
frequency-dependent gain 130–132
fromId method 245
FruityLoops 21
ftoa method 242
ftoi method 242

ftom method 51, 242
FullRect 260
functions
  for arrays 247
  compositional forms
    changing scale pitches 104–106
    drum machine 107–108
    playing scale 102–104
  creating 93–96
  gain and frequency computations
    gradually changing volume 100–101
    granular synthesis 101–102
    overview 97–99
  Math library 53–56, 243–245
  naming 94
  overloading 183–185
  overview 92–93
  playing chords 112
  recursive
    computing factorial 109–110
    making rhythmic structures 111
    overview 108–109
  for shredObj 245–246
  Standard library 48–53, 241–243
  for strings 246–247
  variable scope and 96–97
  virtual machine 245

G

gain
  computations using functions
    gradually changing volume 100–101
    granular synthesis 101–102
    overview 97–99
  frequency-dependent 130–132
  unit generators 251
gain function 250
gain method 19, 75
gamelan orchestra example 213
GarageBand 21
GenX class and extensions 253
get method 283

getBytes method 284
getenv method 242
getFloat method 273
getFloats method 284
getInt method 273
getInts method 284
getLine method 283–284
getString method 273
global scope 96
good method 280
granular synthesis 101–102
granularizing 97

H

Hahn, Tomie 6
half notes 65
HalfRect 260
–halt option 295
harmonic, defined 16
–help option 295
Hendrix, Jimi 152
Hertz, Heinrich 15
HevyMetl 152, 268
Hid object 205
hour keyword 31
HPF (high pass filter) 260
hypot method 243
Hz (Hertz, cycles per second) 15

I

i constant 245
I/O (input/output)
  non-sequential file access 280
  opening files 276–277, 279–280
  overview 276
  reading files 277–279
  serial reading 282–285
  serial writing 285
  standard error file 281
  standard output file 281
  unit generators 249–250
  writing files 276–277
id method 245
IDE (integrated development environment) 233
if statements
  nesting 85
  overview 37–40
Impulse 127, 251

–in option 296
index, array 62
Indian music example 156
infinite loop 77
inheritance
    defined 195
    modeling parents 195–197
    polymorphism 197–198
initialize.ck file 188–190
input/output. *See* I/O
insert method 247
installing
    on Mac OS X 234–235
    on Ubuntu Linux 238
    on Windows 236–238
instantiation 179
instruments, creating new 5–9
int type 24, 35
    converting string to 52–53
    converting to float 51–52
    random methods 54
integrated development envi-
        ronment. *See* IDE
isConnectedTo() function 250
isinf method 244
isnan method 244
itoa method 242

J

Jaffe, David 127, 144, 147, 265
JavaMug 6
jazz band example
    architecture for running con-
        current code 175–176
    creating individual players
        171–174
    file structure 171
    overview 170–171
JCRev 134, 257
jetDelay method 142
JSyn 4

K

Kapur, Ajay xviii, xxviii, 5
Kapur, Raakhi 6
KarmetiK Machine Orchestra 7
Karplus, Kevin 127, 129, 144,
        265
Karplus-Strong algorithm 127
keyboard input 205–208
keywords 30

L

laptop artists 1
Laptop Orchestra. *See* LOrk
last function 250
left method 56
Leider, Colby 6
length method 81, 246
libraries
    Math 243–245
        random functions 53–55
        rounding numbers 55–56
    panning 56–58
    random music generator
        example 58–60
    Standard 241–243
        converting float to int
            51–52
        converting string to
            number 52–53
        MIDI note-to-frequency
            converter 48–51
        overview 48
LiSa (live sampler) 254–255
list method 282
listenAll method 274
live coders 1
LMMS 221
local scope 96
locality 96
log method 243
log10 method 243
log2 method 243
Logic 221, 223
logic statements 37–40
–loop option 295
looping samples 75–77
loopMIDI 225
loops
    for 40–41
    nesting 85
    while
        example using 35–37
        overview 42
LOrk (Laptop Orchestra) 230
LPF (low pass filter) 260
ltrim method 247

M

Mac OS X
    command-line usage
        on 287–290
    installing ChucK on 234–235

Mandolin 145, 172, 265
mandolin player example 199
Math library
    functions 243–245
    random functions 53–55
    rounding numbers 55–56
Mathews, Max 118
max method 244
Max/MSP 4, 6, 271
melody 64
MIDI (Musical Instrument Digi-
        tal Interface)
    controlling robots via
        226–227
    defined 48
    external controllers for
        ChucK 223–225
    messages 220–223
    note-to-frequency converter
        48–51
    overview 218–220
    using virtual port 225
MidiPiano 221, 224
min method 244
miniAudicle
    on Mac OS X 234–235
    on Ubuntu Linux 238
    on Windows 236–238
minute keyword 31
Mix2 251
ModalBar 147–149, 167, 265
Modulate 252
modulator 125
modulo operator (%) 86–88
Moog 151, 267
Moog, Robert (Bob) 151
Morrill, Dexter 5
.mp3 files 75
ms keyword 31
mtof method 48, 242
multithreading
    controlling shared objects
        167–168
    defined 161
    drum machine example
        165–167
    jazz band example
        architecture for running
            concurrent code
            175–176
        creating individual
            players 171–174
        file structure 171
        overview 170–171
    machine commands 169–170

multithreading *(continued)*
  overview 161–163
  shreds and 163–165
Musical Instrument Digital
      Interface. *See* MIDI

N

nesting loops 85
network communication
      271–275
nextpow2 method 244
–nodump option 297
Noise 58, 128–129, 250–251
noiseGain parameter 141
non-linear signal-processing
      260–261
noteOff message 220
noteOn message 220
now keyword 30, 33–35
NRev 134, 257
numArgs method 274

O

object-oriented programming.
      See OOP
objects 178–179
Ocarina 6
octaves 27
on method 283
onBytes method 284
OnePole filter 258
OneZero filter 130–132, 259
onFloats method 284
onInts method 284
onLine method 283–284
on-the-fly programming
      292–294
OOP (object-oriented pro-
      gramming)
  classes
    creating custom 181–183
    overview 179–181
    public vs. private 185–188
  drum pattern example
      190–195
  inheritance
    defined 195
    modeling parents 195–197
    polymorphism 197–198
  initialize.ck file and 188–190
  mandolin player example
      199

objects 178–179
overloading functions
      183–185
overview 178
op function 250
open method 276, 283
openKeyboard function 205
operators 38
OSC (Open Sound
      Control) 227–230,
      271–275
oscillation 15
oscillators
  unit generators 252
  using multiple 43
–out option 296
overloading functions 183–185

P

Pan2 57, 251
panning 56–58
parent shreds 163–164
particle models 150
passing by value 105
patches 19
PD (Pure Data) 4
PercFlut 152, 268
periodic oscillation 14–15
Phasor 125, 252
physical modeling. *See* PM
PI constant 244
piano keyboard 49
PikaPika 6
pitch 15
PitShift 135, 257
PLOrk (Princeton Laptop
      Orchestra) 7
plucked string sound
  with noise 128–129
  simple 127–128
PM (physical modeling)
  modeling fractional
      delay 129–130
  modeling frequency-
      dependent decay 129
  overview 126–127
  plucked string with
      noise 128–129
  plucked string, simple
      127–128
Pohlmann, Ken 91
PoleZero 259
polymorphism 197–198

popBack method 248
–port option 296
pos method 75
pow method 243
powtodb method 242
PRCRev 134, 256
Princeton Laptop Orchestra.
      See PLOrk
private classes 185–186
Pro Tools 223, 225
–probe option 295
Processing 271
programs
  creating 18–20
  data types 24–29
  debugging 23
  playing notes 20–22
  testing 23
  time in
    dur variables 30–31
    importance of 31–32
    now 33–35
    time variables 32–33
  using different waveforms
      22–24
  using multiple oscillators 43
  variables 24–29
public classes
  applications for 186–187
  Clear VM button and 187
  static variables 187–188
PulseOsc 120–121, 252
Pure Data. *See* PD

Q

Qtractor 221
quarter notes 65

R

ragajam 156
RAM (random access memory)
      80
random functions 53–55
random method 54, 243
random music generator
      example 58–60
random walk 59
random2 method 54, 244
random2f method 54, 244
randomf method 54, 244
RANDOM_MAX constant 245
Raspberry Pi 240

readLine method 279
real time 3
recursive functions
    computing factorial 109–110
    making rhythmic structures
        111
    overview 108–109
recv method 274
reed parameter 141
relational operators 38
remainder method 244
–remote option 296
remove method 245
replace function 169
replace method 245, 247
reserved words 38
resonance 148
ResonZ 130, 260
reverberation 132–135
rfind method 246
Rhodey 171, 269
rhythmic structures 111
right method 56
rmstodb method 242
robots 226–227
round method 244
rounding numbers 55–56
rtrim method 247
running method 246

S

Salazar, Spencer xviii, xxix, 298
samp keyword 31
samples method 78
samples, defined 72
sampling
    looping samples 75–77
    overview 71–72
    playing samples backward
        77–78
SawOsc 123–125, 252
Saxofony 143, 263
SBass 6
scale
    changing pitches using
        function 104–106
    playing using function
        102–104
Schism Tracker 221
scope, variable 96–97
second keyword 31
seek method 280
semicolon (;) 67

send method 272
serial input/output 230–231
SerialIO class 282–285
setCharAt method 246
setenv method 242
sgn method 241
Shakers 150, 267
–shell option 297
shell prompt 287
shredObj 245–246
shreds
    communicating using events
        event.signal function 209
        overview 208–209
        synchronizing multiple
            shreds 210–211
        triggering multiple shreds
            using events 212–213
    concurrency and 163–165
signal function 209
–silent option 295
SimpleSynth 221
sin function 48
sin method 58, 243
sinh method 243
SinOsc 125, 252
Sitar 144, 265
size method 248, 280
SLOrk (Stanford Laptop
        Orchestra) 8
Smith, Julius O. 127, 144, 147,
        159, 265
SndBuf 257
    looping samples 75–77
    organizing sound files 73–75
    playing multiple sounds
        78–80
    playing samples backward
        77–78
SndBuf2 80–82, 258
sonification 86, 110
sound files
    drum machine example
        controlling when drums
            play 85–86
        logic for different drums
            on different beats
            83–85
        overview 83, 88
    modulo operator and 86–88
    sampling and 71–72
SndBuf
    looping samples 75–77
    organizing sound files
        73–75

playing multiple sounds
    78–80
playing samples backward
    77–78
stereo 80–82
sound waves
    overview 14–17
    unit generators 251
speaking threshold 141
speech formants 153
spork method 245
sporking 163–164
SqrOsc 120, 122–123, 252
sqrt method 243
square brackets 62
SqueezeVox 6
srandom method 55, 60
–srate option 295
SSPeaPer 6
Standard library
    converting float to int 51–52
    converting string to number
        52–53
    functions 241–243
    MIDI note-to-frequency
        converter 48–51
    overview 48
Stanford Laptop Orchestra. See
        SLOrk
start method 272
static variables 187–188
status method 245
Steiglitz, Ken 91
Step 251
stereo
    panning 56–58
    playing sound files 80–82
    unit generators 251
StifKarp 144, 265
STK (Synthesis ToolKit) 5–6
    envelope unit generators
        255–256
    filters 258–260
    Indian music example 156
    instruments 261–270
    ModalBar 147–149
    overview 139–140
    particle models 150
    stringed instruments
        Bowed 145–147
        Mandolin 145
        overview 143–144
        Sitar 144
    synthesizer sounds 151–153
    voices 153–156

STK (Synthesis ToolKit)
  (continued)
  wind instruments
    Brass 141–142
    Flute 142–143
    overview 140–141
stopband 131
stringed instruments
  Bowed 145–147
  Mandolin 145
  overview 143–144
  Sitar 144
strings 35
  converting to numbers
    52–53
  functions for 246–247
  storing in arrays 67
Strong, Alan 127, 144, 265
SubNoise 251
substring method 247
SuperCollider 4
Synthesis ToolKit. *See* STK
synthesizer sounds 151–153
system method 242

T

tan method 243
tanh method 243
tell method 280
testing 23
this keyword 183
time
  dur variables 30–31
  importance of 31–32
  now 33–35
  time variables 32–33
  units of 20, 31
time type 32–33, 35
transposition 28
Triangle Wave oscillator 50
triggering events 208
trim method 247
TriOsc 252
Trueman, Dan 6
trumpet
  coffee mug as 7
  MIDI 5
trunc method 244
TubeBell 269
TWO_PI constant 244
TwoPole filter 258
TwoZero filter 259
typetag 271

U

Ubuntu Linux 238
unit generators
  acoustics of room 132–135
  basic sound waves 251
  Blit oscillators 270
  delay-based audio effects
    135–136
  delays 256–257
  Envelope
    making clarinet sound
      using SqrOsc and
      Envelope 122–123
    making violin sound with
      SawOsc and ADSR
      Envelope UG
      123–125
    overview 121–122
  example using 136–138
  frequency modulation
    125–126
  frequency-dependent gain
    130–132
  gain 251
  input 249–250
  LiSa 254–255
  lookup table 252–253
  methods for 250
  non-linear signal-processing
    260–261
  OneZero 130–132
  oscillator 252
  output 249–250
  overview 117–120
  physical modeling
    modeling fractional delay
      129–130
    modeling frequency-
      dependent decay 129
    overview 126–127
    plucked string with noise
      128–129
    plucked string, simple
      127–128
  PulseOsc 120–121
  reverberation 132–135
  sound file 257–258
  stereo 251
  STK envelope 255–256
  STK filters 258–260
  STK instruments 261–270
upper method 247

V

variables
  naming 25
  overview 24–29
  scope 96–97
–verbose option 295
–version option 295
vibratoFreq parameter 141
vibratoGain parameter 141
violin sound 123–125
virtual MIDI port 225
VirtualMIDISynth 221
VM (virtual machine) 17, 245
VMPK (Virtual MIDI Piano
    Keyboard) 223
voices 153–156
VoicForm 154, 269
void return type 100
void type 35
volume 75, 100–101
von Helmholtz, Herman 17

W

Wang, Ge xxix, 4, 6, 298
.wav files 70, 75
waveforms 14–17, 72
WaveLoop 258
wavetable 72
week keyword 31
while loops
  example using 35–37
  overview 42
wind instruments
  Brass 141–142
  Flute 142–143
  overview 140–141
Windows
  command-line usage
    on 290–292
  installing ChucK on 236–238
Wittstruck, Anna xx
Wurley 269
WvIn 258
WvOut 258
WvOut2 258

Y

yield method 246

Z

ZeroX 260

MORE TITLES FROM MANNING

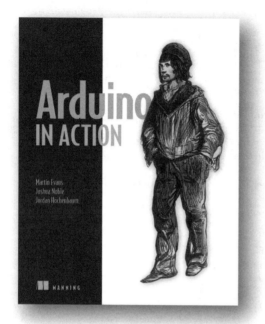

Arduino in Action

by Martin Evans, Joshua Noble, and Jordan
  Hochenbaum

ISBN: 9781617290244
368 pages
$39.99
May 2013

Generative Art
A practical guide using Processing

by Matt Pearson

ISBN: 9781935182627
240 pages
$39.99
June 2011

For ordering information go to www.manning.com

Hello World! Second Edition
Computer Programming for Kids
and Other Beginners

by Warren Sande and Carter Sande

ISBN: 9781617290923
464 pages
$39.99
December 2013

Hello App Inventor!
Android programming for kids and
the rest of us

by Paula Beer and Carl Simmons

ISBN: 9781617291432
360 pages
$39.99
October 2014

For ordering information go to www.manning.com

MORE TITLES FROM MANNING

Hello! Python
by Anthony Briggs

   ISBN: 9781935182085
   424 pages
   $34.99
   February 2012

HTML5 in Action
by Rob Crowther, Joe Lennon, Ash Blue
  and Greg Wanish

   ISBN: 9781617290497
   466 pages
   $39.99
   February 2014

MORE TITLES FROM MANNING

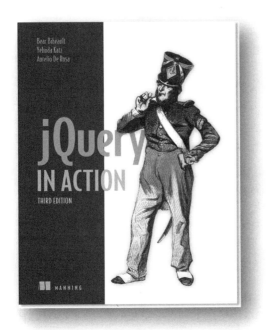

jQuery in Action, Third Edition
by Bear Bibeault, Yehuda Katz,
    and Aurelio De Rosa

ISBN: 9781617292071
475 pages
$44.99
April 2015

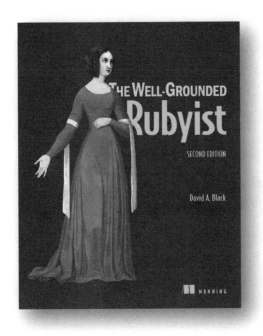

The Well-Grounded Rubyist,
Second Edition
by David A. Black

ISBN: 9781617291692
536 pages
$44.99
June 2014

For ordering information go to www.manning.com

MORE TITLES FROM MANNING

The Responsive Web
by Matthew Carver

   ISBN: 9781617291241
   200 pages
   $39.99
   October 2014

Soft Skills
The software developer's life manual
by John Z. Sonmez

   ISBN: 9781617292392
   504 pages
   $34.99
   December 2014

For ordering information go to www.manning.com